If Men Were Angels

American Political Thought
edited by
Wilson Carey McWilliams and Lance Banning

If Men Were Angels

James Madison and the Heartless Empire of Reason

RICHARD K. MATTHEWS

UNIVERSITY PRESS OF KANSAS

"The Gift Outright," from *The Poetry of Robert Frost*, edited by Edward Connery Lathem. ©1942 by Robert Frost. ©1970 by Lesley Frost Ballantine. ©1969 by Henry Holt and Company, Inc.

Reprinted by permission of Henry Holt and Company, Inc.

Published by the University Press of Kansas (Lawrence, Kansas 66049), which was organized by the Kansas Board of Regents and is operated and funded by Emporia State University, Fort Hays State University, Kansas State University, Pittsburg State University, the University of Kansas, and Wichita State University

Library of Congress Cataloging-in-Publication Data

Matthews, Richard K., 1952–
    If men were angels : James Madison and the heartless empire of
reason / Richard K. Matthews.
        p.   cm. — (American political thought)
    Includes bibliographical references (p.   ) and index.
    ISBN 0-7006-0643-2 (alk. paper)
    1. Madison, James, 1751-1836—Contributions in political science.
    I. Title.   II. Series.
    JC211.M35M38   1995
973.5′1′092—dc20   94-36168

British Library Cataloguing in Publication Data is available.

Printed in the United States of America

10 9 8 7 6 5 4 3 2 1

To Zack . . .
the rest cannot be spoken

The value of a society is the value it places upon man's relation to man. It is not just a question of knowing what the liberals have in mind but what in reality is done by the liberal state within and beyond its frontiers. . . . To understand and judge a society, one has to penetrate its basic structure to the human bond upon which it is built; this undoubtedly depends upon legal relations, but also upon forms of labor, ways of loving, living, and dying.

—*Maurice Merleau-Ponty*

Contents

Acknowledgments

Madison's observation on the genesis of the Constitution as not the product of one individual but rather the "work of many heads & minds" certainly applies as well to this book. The generous efforts of many people went into the writing, shaping, and publishing of *If Men Were Angels*.

The preparation of the manuscript for publication was made possible by the skillful efforts of Matilda DiDonato and Dorothy Windish. Jane Hahn proved to be a most talented and resourceful research assistant and historian.

This project would not have been possible without a fellowship from the National Endowment for the Humanities. In light of this book's critical appraisal of Madison's machine, something positive must be said of a political system that not only encourages but financially supports dissent. I would like to believe that Madison would appreciate the spirit of this project. Lehigh University and in particular the Lawrence Henry Gipson Institute for Eighteenth-Century Studies provided release time and further financial assistance. Bill Shade, director of the Gipson Institute, not only read the entire manuscript but sustained the wonderful illusion of never tiring of talking about the Virginians. I also learned much from the critical conversations at three Liberty Fund Conferences on Madison, Jefferson, and Hamilton. The University Press of America gave permission to use an article I wrote, "The Presidency and the Public Philosophy: Jefferson's Permanent Revolution," for *The Virginia Papers on the Presidency*, vol. xxvi, ed. Kenneth W. Thompson. Finally, I benefited enormously from students at Lehigh University who, in the "Empire of Reason" seminar, provided an ongoing and ruthless criticism of most of the arguments in this book.

Many gracious colleagues read portions of the text. John Murrin, Alkis Kontos, J. G. A. Pocock, Laura Olson, Howard Whitcomb, Ted

Morgan, Frank Davis, Frank Kalinowski, Bob Jones, and Robert Duffy provided valuable insights. Lance Banning, Carey McWilliams, David Ingersoll, Michael Lienesch, Isaac Kramnick, and Forrest McDonald each read the entire manuscript, helping to mold the final project, which I hope they see as reflecting their insightful and sound advice. Surely one of the real joys of writing is the opportunity to participate in the life of the community of scholars that surrounds the founding era.

Other individuals provided the spiritual support without which no author can continue to face the uncertainty and challenge of empty space on sheets of paper. Jeff Burtaine, Jim Gunton, Asher Horowitz, Leon Skweir, Jim Lennertz, Ed Kerns, Meredith Margolis, and especially Katherine Restuccia helped supply the energy, encouragement, and escape needed to sustain this project. Last, a note of gratitude to my parents, David and June Matthews. In countless ways, they have made it possible to write this book.

Introduction: In Search of the "Great Little Madison"

The principles & Modes of Government are too important to be disregarded by an Inquisitive mind and I think are well worthy [of] a critical examination by all students that have health & Leisure.[1]

—*Madison*

Descending from atop Monticello, heading north to Montpelier at the foot of the Blue Ridge Mountains, even in the final decade of the twentieth century a traveler can imagine what this thirty-mile journey might have been like for Thomas Jefferson, James Madison, their friends, their allies, and their acquaintances. While much of the landscape alongside the highway from Charlottesville is blemished by the modern markings of progress, the countryside beyond the commercial shoulder stands as quiet testimony to the beauty of unspoiled Virginia. As one approaches Montpelier, a road sign indicates a railroad station across the street from the entrance to the Madison estate. This sign presents a reminder and an omen. It warns visitors that they are no longer at Monticello, surrounded by the mystique of Thomas Jefferson; and it reminds them that what once was James Madison's estate has undergone profound alterations since his charming and dutiful wife, Dolley, was forced to sell it off to satisfy the gambling debts of her wastrel son.

Shortly after beginning the official tour, the visitor learns that William du Pont, head of the chemical conglomerate as well as the Delaware Trust Company, constructed the rail depot when he purchased Montpelier thereby meeting the official requirements for having the train stop at his front door. Literally the machine in the

---

1. James Madison (hereafter cited as JM) to William Bradford, 1 Dec. 1773, *The Papers of James Madison*, ed. William T. Hutchinson et al., 17 vols. (Chicago and Charlottesville: University of Chicago Press and University of Virginia Press, 1962–), I:101.

garden, the train symbolizes the enormous and nearly devastating impact of modernity on Madison's former home. After viewing a brief slide presentation visitors, waiting to board the minibuses that will transport them to the house, browse through the souvenir shop that used to be a company store established for the convenience of the du Ponts' servants and staff. The short bus trip around the grounds of what *was* Madison's estate but *is* now the du Ponts'—covering 2,780 acres, more than four square miles of Orange County—terminates in front of the cold, rectangular, white manor, which currently contains fifty-five rooms, more than half of which had been constructed after Madison's tenure.

The journey reveals much. What first strikes the eye and assaults the mind are the horse tracks—a flat track and a steeplechase course—that suddenly pop up out of the earth in spite of the builder's efforts to have them blend into the environment. As the bus moves along its course dozens of other structures, from Sears, Roebuck & Co. barns to an indoor training ring for horses, litter the landscape. Later in the tour, visitors learn that during Madison's lifetime alfalfa and corn grew where the tracks now lie and that slave cabins once stood on the land.

When the bus finally arrives at the front of the house, visitors walk up the steps, stand on the du Ponts' front porch and listen politely to a knowledgeable guide explain the house's legal history. In 1723 grandfather Ambrose Madison secured a patent on the land and three years later built a small house; between 1755 and 1765, James Madison Sr. constructed a two-story dwelling in which he raised his family; in 1797, his son, James Madison Jr., and new wife Dolley began a thirty-foot addition to the northeast section of the house and renovated the inside so that a significant portion of the house could be reserved for the senior Madisons; borrowing Thomas Jefferson's craftsmen, Madison further expanded and remodeled the house from 1809 to 1813; it descended to his widow upon his death in 1836; and within half a dozen years she sold the estate to meet pressing financial needs. From 1842 until 1902, the estate passed through several hands, undergoing no major alterations until purchased by William du Pont in 1902. Du Pont added approximately twenty-five rooms and supervised major structural changes to the interior of the house. Meanwhile, his wife, Anne R. du Pont, altered the exterior by replacing the Madison gardens, attributed by legend to the Marquis de La-fayette, with designs of her own fancy. Their child, Marion du Pont Scott, inherited the property from her father in 1936, the same year she married the silver screen cowboy actor Randolph Scott. Shortly after her death in 1983, the National Trust for Historic Preservation acquired the estate.

Once permitted inside the house, visitors realize why so many minutes were spent on the front porch listening to an embellished ti-tle search: the interior of the structure displays virtually no sign that Madison slept—let alone once lived—there. Most of the walls inside the house show stains and watermarks, signs that the building has not been properly maintained for some time. Paper cutouts and marker lines indicate where doorways stood when Madison owned the property. The guide encourages visitors to imagine "servants" walking through the portals or Madison's mother coming from her portion of the house through a passageway to visit her son and daughter-in-law in their section of the manor. But not every room in the mansion requires renovation due to the ravages of time and the building's neglect. In fact, all the preceding tremors to the visitor's historic consciousness are but minor ripples compared to the shock wave upon entering Marion du Pont Scott's Red Room.

The guide again suggests that visitors imagine Mr. Madison seated in the room, discussing with family and friends American history, world events, or the coming planting season. This is hard: the one-time parlor has been recreated into a testimonial to Marion's most beloved horse, Battleship, his ancestry, his legacy, and his notable ac-complishments. The Red Room's glass and wrought iron, art deco decor—with photograph upon photograph of horse after horse—makes it difficult to picture "little Jimmy Madison" in this *mo-derne* salon, unless it is as a jockey. The tour concludes. Pilgrims are invited to walk on the grounds and through the vast gardens planted by Anne du Pont. Outdoors, back in the pastoral Virginia country-side, the cool spring air cleanses the mind and soothes the soul, making it again possible to pretend that maybe, once upon a time, Madison actually lived here.

When the National Trust secured the estate in 1984 the terms of the lengthy will required that the property be preserved as "an his-toric shrine . . . to James Madison and his times." It further directed that two rooms of the main house memorialize the du Pont years and, naturally, that "horses must continue to race on the course below the great front lawn." Early each November, consequently, the house closes for Montpelier race day. These few legal qualifications give the impression that the issue of renovation should be straightforward. It continues to be, however, anything but. Only after forty million dollars have been raised, and serious as well as contentious issues of the most appropriate approach to renovation been settled, can major restoration of Montpelier begin. Even then, the search for Madison's Montpelier inside the structure of the du Ponts' Montpelier, will be a Herculean task while finding Madison the individual at Montpelier will be Sisyphean.

Ironically, there may be a tragic—if poetically just—quality to the Montpelier saga. Madison, perhaps more than any other individual, worked tirelessly to help construct a political system where politics would be secondary to economics and created a social system that ultimately developed into what has aptly been called "the Economic Polity."[2] To be sure, Madison could never have envisioned the extreme concentrations of power and capital that developed in the robber baron age of monopolies, conglomerates, and trusts, let alone the limitless power of the contemporary bureaucratic-administrative state. Nevertheless, that an opulent family of extraordinary wealth and influence, possessing no feeling of shame, should have been able to erase all vestiges of "the father of the Constitution" from their property constitutes an appropriate memorial for this American political theorist: he valued the stability of society and the security of property rights on a plane above democratic politics and the rights of individuals to exercise their uniquely human, all too human, powers and capacities.[3]

2. Sheldon S. Wolin, *The Presence of the Past* (Baltimore: Johns Hopkins University Press, 1989), pp. 174, 29: "The twentieth century is the century of totalizing power, of the concerted attempt to unify state and civil society. . . . We live in an Economic Polity in which the state is merely the symbol of the legitimate public authority, not the autonomous power suggested by early modern political theory."

3. J. R. Pole, "Review of Jennifer Nedelsky *Private Property and the Limits of American Constitutionalism*," *William and Mary Quarterly* 49:1 (Jan. 1992): 173, wonders: "What would the Founding Fathers have thought of the republic they wrought if they could have viewed it, a century or so later, dominated by Standard Oil, United States Steel, and a network of railroads and Wall Street Banks? . . . Classical republicanism, while it did protect certain inequalities, had never lent theoretical support to the kind of baronial power that dominated the state or became a cause of political stability."

Discovering James Madison's Montpelier is not unlike trying to locate Madison the political theorist inside his countless and unsystematic writings or among the contentious debates and conflicting interpretations of scholars. To try to make Madison's political theory intelligible requires that attention be given to specific political and economic themes—such as property, rights, civil society, individuality, and government—rather than to a strict chronological account of his public life. Given the diffuse nature of Madison's political writings, and the heated intellectual discussions they have sparked largely among historians but also among political scientists, anyone interested in searching for Madison the political thinker must be a combination of historian, political theorist, archeologist, detective, and masochist. Finding the "great little Madison," as his wife lovingly referred to him, remains no easy task. And yet, if Madison's sound advice that calls for a "critical examination" of "Government" is to be followed, understanding Madison's own political theory becomes indispensable.[4]

If Men Were Angels attempts to follow Madison's suggestion through three separate endeavors. First, it tries to construct the complete political theory of James Madison, wherever applicable analytically separating his ideas from the Constitution of 1787 and the early development of the present American state. Indeed, his theory will be constructed based on his writings throughout his adult life. This necessitates an interpretative posture where his writings surrounding the Constitution hold no privileged position in terms of his overall political theory. Second, the book provides a critical analysis of Madisonian politics. Political theory, after all, remains a normative enterprise; it is, as Sheldon Wolin explains, "primarily a civic and secondarily an academic activity."[5] It would be insufficient, therefore, simply to describe Madison; it becomes essential to question and challenge his understanding of politics as well as his vision of "the good." Given this stance, it will be particularly important to remember that it is quite possible to admire the efforts, energy, de-

---

4. Judith N. Shklar, "Redeeming American Political Theory," *American Political Science Review* 85:1 (Mar. 1991): 3. Madison's advice can be coupled with Shklar's appeal to political scientists to "redeem American political theory" since its study "has long been neglected" by political science to its own detriment.

5. Wolin, *Presence of the Past*, p. 1.

sign, and intellect that went into Madison's creation while disagreeing with many, if not all, of the assumptions and values upon which his theory rests. A critic can respect the artistry and the technique without admiring the ultimate artifice.

Finally, Madison's politics must be understood in comparison to what America has failed to become. To appreciate this negative dimension, Madison's political theory will be placed alongside that of his friend Thomas Jefferson. While the United States embraced much of Madisonian politics when it adopted the Constitution of 1787, the gravity of this choice can be judged not merely when we appreciate what America has become but also when we perceive what it simultaneously rejected. As J. G. A. Pocock reminds us: "What America might have been remains a standing instrument of criticism of what it is."[6] The middle passage of a three-part voyage into history that began with *The Radical Politics of Thomas Jefferson* and will conclude with *Alexander Hamilton and the Creation of the Heroic State, If Men Were Angels* is but one part of a larger project that seeks to reopen a public debate on the meanings of America's pasts and thereby initiate a dialogue on the possibilities for alternative, democratic futures.

6. J. G. A. Pocock, "Cambridge Paradigms and Scotch Philosophers: A Study of the Relations between the Civic Humanist and the Civil Jurisprudential Interpretation of Eighteenth-century Social Thought," in *Wealth and Virtue*, ed. Istvan Hont and Michael Ignatieff (Cambridge: Cambridge University Press, 1985), p. 244.

1 / James Madison:
Constant Liberal Prince

To erect over the whole, one paramount Empire of reason, benevolence and brotherly affection.[1]

—*Madison*

It is curious. While it is now commonplace to refer reverentially to James Madison in any one of his "father" roles—"father of the Constitution," "father of the Bill of Rights," "father of political parties," "father of democracy," "father of American pluralism," "father of preferred freedoms"—his preeminence in the creation of the modern American state has not always been so widely acknowledged. At the turn of this century, when the promoters of a newly created American Hall of Fame determined, on the basis of an opinion poll, who should be enshrined in the hall Madison failed to make the list.[2] Not until Charles Beard's 1913 landmark study, *An Economic Interpretation of*

1. *National Gazette*, 3 Dec. 1791, *The Papers of James Madison*, ed. William T. Hutchinson et al., 17 vols. (Chicago and Charlottesville: University of Chicago Press and University of Virginia Press, 1962–), 14:139 [hereafter cited as *PJM*].

2. The legitimacy of the title "father of the Constitution," first bestowed on Madison by Charles Jared Ingersoll in 1825 then echoed by John Quincy Adams in a speech in Boston on 27 September 1836, has been challenged of late by two eminent historians. See Forrest McDonald, *Novus Ordo Seclorum: The Intellectual Origins of the Constitution* (Lawrence: University Press of Kansas, 1985), p. 209; and Richard Morris, *Witnesses at the Creation* (New York: Holt, Rinehart and Winston, 1985), pp. 19, 94. Madison himself appears to have rejected this mantle. To William Cogswell (10 Mar. 1834) he wrote: "You give me a credit to which I have no claim, in calling me '*the* writer of the Constitution of the U. S.' This was not, like the fabled Goddess of Wisdom, the offspring of a single brain. It ought to be regarded as the work of many heads & many hands" (in Gaillard Hunt, ed., *The Writings of James Madison*, 9 vols. [New York: G. P. Putnam's Sons, 1900–1910], 9:533 [hereafter cited as *WJM*]). See Douglass Adair, *Fame and the Founding Fathers: Essays by Douglass Adair*, ed. Trevor Colbourn (New York: W. W. Norton, 1974), pp. 75–80; and John Q. Adams, "Eulogy on James Madison," in *The Lives of James Madison and James Monroe* (Boston: Phillips, Sampson & Company, 1850); and Drew McCoy, *The Last of the Fathers* (New York: Cambridge University Press, 1989), p. 73.

the Constitution of the United States, did Madison begin to receive much scholarly attention. Increasing numbers of political scientists joined the efforts of historians after Robert Dahl's extended critique of "the 'Madisonian' theory of democracy" appeared in his 1964 *A Preface to Democratic Theory*.[3]

In spite of the intimate and critical association of Madison with the drafting, ratifying, and establishing of the Constitution, relatively less has been published about him than about other founders such as Benjamin Franklin, George Washington, and especially Thomas Jefferson.[4] What has been written about Madison, furthermore, tends to concentrate on one or two of the many roles he played throughout an unparalleled political career that spanned five decades. Ignoring his many minor offices, the following list enumerates most of his major political positions: He was in the forefront of the movement for a new constitution to replace the Articles of Confederation; architect of the Virginia Plan, champion of a strong central government, and unofficial but dedicated note-taker of the proceedings at the Philadelphia convention; a persuasive rhetorician both at the Virginia ratifying convention and as the political propagandist Publius—one of the two principal authors of *The Federalist*; leader of the inaugural House of Representatives where he proved to be a reluctant, but ultimately forceful champion of the Bill of Rights, helped organize the new central government, and served as "ghostwriter" and adviser to President Washington; cofounder of the Republican party; Jefferson's trusted confidant as well as his secretary of state; president during America's second war of independence; and elder statesman, nationalist, and protector of the Constitution.[5]

Where the personal letters of Thomas Jefferson profess his longing to exit the public arena and retire to private life with his family,

3. Charles A. Beard, *An Economic Interpretation of the Constitution of the United States* (New York: Macmillan, 1913); Robert A. Dahl, *A Preface to Democratic Theory* (Chicago: University of Chicago Press, 1956), p. 4.

4. Cf. Ralph Ketcham, *James Madison: A Biography* (New York: Macmillan, 1971), p. ix, who laments the "oppressively abundant" weight of scholarship already available on Madison. Ketcham's 1971 observation is accurate; and since the publication of his excellent study the amount of published material has significantly increased. Nevertheless, the Madison scholarship remains less voluminous relative to that on other founders and framers.

5. *PJM* 12:xvii–xix, 120–121; Marvin Meyers, ed., *The Mind of the Founder*, rev. ed. (Hanover, Mass.: Brandeis University Press, 1981), p. xviii.

friends, books, ideas, and projects, comparable desires did not appear to stir in Madison. He chose public life and never abandoned it, even in retirement. All of his political roles can be combined in a helpful heuristic metaphor of Madison as an ideal Machiavellian Prince: first, he comprehends the problems of a weak, divided sovereign; conceives of the modern, protective state atop a commercial republic as the solution; drafts the government's fundamental charter and sees to it that the necessary precedents are established and enabling laws adopted; runs the infant regime as adviser to two presidents then as the chief executive; and, in retirement, strives to control how the future will interpret the past so that he can, in a very real sense, rule from the grave. From "The Legislator," to chief executive, to keeper of the past and controller of the future, Madison adjusted his political posture as time and opportunity required, just as Machiavelli's virtuous Prince would do.[6]

It would seem logical, then, given Madison's now universally acknowledged importance in the founding of the American republic, that significantly more scholarship would be available that, as in the case of other framers and founders, examines virtually every facet of his private and public existence.[7] But this body of literature has just begun to develop.[8] As Irving Brant, Madison's most thorough biographer, put it in the 1940s: "Among all the men who shaped the present government of the United States of America, the one who did the most is known the least." Neal Riemer, some forty years later, echoes these sentiments, stating that Madison "remains the

6. See David Ingersoll, "The Constant Prince: Private Interests and Public Goals in Machiavelli," *Western Political Quarterly* 21 (Dec. 1968): 588–596; and "Machiavelli and Madison: Perspectives on Political Stability," *Political Science Quarterly* 85:2 (June 1970): 259–280.

7. Jack N. Rakove, *James Madison and the Creation of the American Republic* (Glenview, Ill.: Scott, Foresman, 1990), p. ix: "In his own life time he took care to preserve his political papers as well as to insure that the details of his private life should remain hidden from posterity. . . . It is the public man alone whom we can know with any confidence."

8. Rakove's *James Madison;* Rutland's *James Madison: The Founding Father* (New York: Macmillan, 1987); McCoy's *Last of the Fathers;* Neal Riemer's *James Madison: Creating the American Constitution* (Washington, D.C.: Congressional Quarterly, 1986); Robert Morgan's *James Madison on the Constitution and the Bill of Rights* (New York: Greenwood Press, 1988); and the reprinting of Ralph Ketcham's *Madison* have all contributed enormously to the understanding of Madison.

least popular and the least understood of the towering founders."[9] Questions arise. Why do we know so little about Madison? Why the comparative lack of scholarship? Why does he remain so obscure if not quite unpopular? Several possible reasons offer a plausible explanation for these observations.

To begin, the physical James Madison was hardly the material of which myths are made: barely five-and-a-half feet tall, pale complexioned, a secret (and apparently hysterical) epileptic, this perpetual hypochondriac spent much of his adult life believing that his death was imminent; and legend has it that, as if in preparation for this event, he usually dressed in black. As early as 1772 Madison confided to his friend William Bradford, "I am too dull and infirm now to look out for any extraordinary things in this world for I think my sensations for many months past have intimated to me not to expect a long or healthy life."[10] About this, Madison could not have been more wrong. In spite of his lifelong anxieties and fear of death, he lived to be eighty-five. Robert Rutland, an editor of *The Papers of James Madison* and one of his admiring biographers, states that Madison "had taken pills and purges for most of his adult life, and his small frame surprised most observers because it was in such contrast to the intellectual strength of its possessor." Madison, writes Rutland, was "the kind of man who jumped when a gun went off"; he "was far better fitted for an armchair than a saddle." Rutland claims that for more than "sixty years, hardly a month passed when Madison did not complain of high fevers, diarrhea, or seizures similar to those suffered by epileptics." "One looks in vain through thousands of scraps of paper," writes Rutland, "for a single expression of good health and vigor."[11]

After graduating from Princeton, Madison postponed returning to Virginia in order to rest, regain his health, and further his studies.

9. Irving Brant, *James Madison*, 6 vols. (Indianapolis: Bobbs-Merrill, 1941–1961), 1:preface; Riemer, *James Madison*, p. 4; Riemer also points out (p. 6) that there exists a Washington monument and a Jefferson and Lincoln memorial in the capital, but no comparable Madison monument. Belatedly, a building of the Library of Congress was named after him, but even here Madison stands in the shadow of Jefferson.

10. JM to William Bradford, 9 Nov. 1772, *PJM* 1:75.

11. Robert A. Rutland, *The Presidency of James Madison* (Lawrence: University Press of Kansas, 1990), pp. 20, 105–106; Robert A. Rutland, *James Madison: The Founding Father* (New York: Macmillan, 1987), pp. 8, 10; see also Ketcham, *Madison*, pp. 51–52.

Upon settling back in at Montpelier, Madison's spiritual isolation and loneliness eventually combined with his physical ailments to produce what Douglass Adair describes as "the unhappiest period of his life." This may also be the earliest instance of Madison believing he had epilepsy.[12] While skeptical of the epilepsy claim, Ralph Ketcham acknowledges that "Madison himself described the disease as 'a constitutional liability to sudden attacks, somewhat resembling Epilepsy, and suspending the intellectual functions. They continued thro' [my] life, with prolonged intervals.'" Ketcham concludes that "whatever the diagnosis . . . it caused him moments of serious anxiety . . . and all his life deterred him from sea voyages and other physically arduous undertakings."[13] In the most exhaustive biography of Madison to date, Brant argues that "it is evident that he was not suffering from epilepsy, but from epileptoid hysteria, a purely functional ailment which was not until recently distinguished from the organic disease." Consequently, "it is manifestly impossible to determine the cause of the illness, which lies buried in the obscurity of psychic trauma, but the common connection of hysteria with overstudy, day-dreaming, hypochondria, and a sense of physical inferiority suggests how many avenues of approach there were."[14] Madison's preoccupation with health issues can readily be seen when reading his papers, including his celebrated public essays, where the use of medical language and metaphors to describe the sick and fatal republic is manifest.

Building on the insights of Brant, Forrest McDonald boldly explores the implications of Madison's confrontation with epilepsy. Madison's contemporaries, McDonald persuasively argues, "were almost unanimous in regarding him as remarkably learned, candid, open, and of a sweet and amiable disposition. On all counts but the first they were entirely mistaken: he was, in actuality, so carefully contrived and controlled that in comparison to him Hamilton, Jef-

---

12. Adair, *Fame and the Founding Fathers*, p. 130.
13. Ketcham, *Madison*, pp. 51–52. JM to Thomas Jefferson, 27 Apr. 1785, *PJM* 8:270; Madison declined Jefferson's invitation to visit him in Paris on the grounds that "I have some reason also to suspect that crossing the Sea would be unfriendly to a singular disease of my constitution."
14. Brant, *Madison* 1:106–107; see also Ketcham, *Madison*, pp. 14–16, where he notes two additional sources of trauma: "the terror and anxiety caused by Indian attacks" during Madison's childhood as well as "the severest trauma of his boyhood, an epidemic of the dreaded small pox."

ferson, and even Burr were open books." He further hypothesizes that "the key to his character is that he was either an epileptic or a victim of epileptiform hysteria and that he devoutly guarded the secret of his infirmity, lest he be regarded (in keeping with the superstitious science of the time) as being insane."[15] Perhaps Madison may simply have been suffering from panic attacks of an unknown etiology. Whatever the nature of the ailment, early in life Madison must have discovered that by constant vigilance he could detect the most subtle changes in his psychic and somatic states and thereby prevent the seizures.[16] Madison strove always to remain the most controlled of men. Even during the bleakest days of the War of 1812, his secretary Edward Coles recalled that he never heard Madison "utter one petulant expression, or give way for one moment to passion or despondency." Throughout the ordeal Madison lived by his maxim that "public functionaries should never display, much less act, under the influence of passion." He remained consistently "collected" and "self-possessed."[17]

As if in anticipation of Max Weber's insights on modern bureaucratic government, Madison internalized *"sine ira et studio"* as his behavioral norm throughout his years of public service.[18] This approach can be seen clearly in Madison's private correspondence with Jefferson during the height of their dissatisfaction with John Adams's presidency. In mid-February 1798 Madison lamented that "the public opinion alone can now save us from the rash measures of our hot-heated [*sic*] Executive," whom he perceived as "a perfect Quixotte as a Statesman." Weeks later he charged that "the President's message is only a further developement to the public, of the violent passions, & heretical politics, which have been long privately known to govern him." Again calling Adams a "hot head," Madison further believed that Adams's actions were "not well rel-

15. Forrest McDonald, *The Presidency of George Washington* (Lawrence: University Press of Kansas, 1974), p. 31.
16. Ibid., p. 80, suggests that the "fear of being found out, Madison's inner force, was far more potent than the relatively uncomplicated ambition and avarice that Hamilton believed to motivate men."
17. Quoted in McCoy, *Last of the Fathers*, p. 21.
18. See Max Weber, *Economy and Society*, ed. Guenther Roth and Claus Wittich, 2 vols. (Berkeley: University of California Press, 1978), 1:225, where Weber describes the classic bureaucrat as one who acts in "a spirit of formalistic impersonality, '*Sine ira et studio*,' without hatred or passion, and hence without affection or enthusiasm."

ished in the cool climate of Mount Vernon.'' And his final blast during Adams's presidency came less than a week later: Adams ''is verifying compleatly the last feature in the character drawn of him by Dr. F[ranklin] however his title may stand to the two first. 'Always an honest man, often a wise one, but sometimes wholly out of his senses.' ''[19] Madison's disgust with Adams centered on his apparent inability to control his passion through his reason, a prominent theme repeated throughout Madison's public writings as well as demonstrated in his personal actions.

Richard Morris takes a slightly different view of Madison's rigid character. He argues that Madison ''lacked human warmth'' and, consequently, most people outside his close circle of friends considered him a ''cold fish.'' Still, Morris hypothesized that Madison's youthful indiscretion while at Princeton of penning a few ''ribald verses'' about a ''lecherous rascal'' who

> May whore and pimp and drink and swear
> Nor more the garb of Christian wear
> And free Nassau from such a pest
> A dunce, a fool, an ass at best

might suggest ''depths hidden beneath a sedate, prim, and humorless exterior. Smiles always came hard with Madison, and these off-color literary outpourings may have been a way of sublimating sexual urges.''[20] Madison's diminutive physical presence becomes even more apparent when he is forced by history and geography to stand, dwarflike, in contrast to his fellow Virginians, most notably the statuesque Washington and Jefferson. This remains, however, the physical Madison, the realm of appearances.

In the metaphysical domain Madison may perhaps be considered even less attractive: where Thomas Jefferson and Alexander Hamilton each had their diametrically opposed dreams about what America should aspire to be—Jefferson his democratic pastoral republic, Hamilton his liberal-elite, heroic empire—Madison lacked an analo-

19. JM to Thomas Jefferson, 18 Feb. 1798, *PJM* 17:82; 2 Apr. 1798, *PJM* 17:104; 3 June 1798, *PJM* 17:142; and 10 June 1798, *PJM* 17:150.
20. Richard Morris, *Witnesses at the Creation* (New York: Holt, Rinehart and Winston, 1985), pp. 96–97, 100–101; Morris also notes that ''for fifty years [he] signed his name 'James Madison Junr.,' long after his father's death.''

gous dream.[21] Rather, Madison appears to have been driven by a nightmare. Like Aristotle, Machiavelli, and Calvin, Madison believed that throughout history all governments were subject to temporal forces that guaranteed they would eventually crumble and decay. Drew McCoy best captures the essence of Madison's historic perspective. "If the republican revolution had initially been defined as an escape from time, Madison had always acknowledged that, in the long run, such a revolution was doomed. Eventually the New World would come to resemble the Old."[22]

Madison's exhaustive study of the past had convinced him of the existence of certain laws of economic and political development and decay. Even though the United States was subject to these laws, its constitutional framers had discovered, through the study of the past and the use of reason, certain revolutionary advances in the science of politics that suggested to some the possibility of America escaping the ravages of time. As Michael Lienesch explains, although Madison studied history he also warned against a "blind veneration for antiquity," preferring instead that reasonable men base their decisions on "the lesson of their own experience."[23] Because of his internalized Malthusian disposition, Madison believed that political science could never provide the mechanisms to sustain equilibrium in the face of the inevitable and unrelenting forces of social destruction. While "the New World would come to resemble the Old," if America learned from history (and the social sciences), perhaps it did not have to repeat it, exactly. Ambivalence and anxiety about tomorrow, based on the experiences of the past and the promises of a scientific future, created internalized tensions and uncertainties for Madison.

The maintenance of political stability in the face of the dislocating forces of social and economic change makes up "the good" for Madison. He did not see—indeed how could he—that his worship of reason as the instrument and equilibrium as the goal simultaneously laid the foundation for the creation over time of a society

21. Richard K. Matthews, *The Radical Politics of Thomas Jefferson* (Lawrence: University Press of Kansas, 1986), p. 117.

22. Drew McCoy, *The Elusive Republic: Political Economy in Jeffersonian America* (Chapel Hill: University of North Carolina Press, 1980), p. 259.

23. Michael Lienesch, *New Order of the Ages: Time, the Constitution, and the Making of Modern American Political Thought* (Princeton, N.J.: Princeton University Press, 1988), p. 129.

where the public arena would become dominated by the positive, bureaucratic-administrative state—where citizenship would have even
less meaning than in Madison's own political theory, and where humans would search for meaning inside the iron cages of the private
domain. Madison's "Empire of reason," erected upon his passion-
less notion of reasonable liberal politics, ultimately precludes the
possibilities of the "benevolence and brotherly affection" that his
rhetoric sometimes suggests he also wanted.[24] Madison forgot, as
Harold Laski eloquently stated, that "order is good for what it implies and not for its own sake."[25] Madison's political theory too,
then, is not the stuff of which either dreams or myths are made. And
insofar as scholars remain interested in the interpretation of dreams,
Madison provides neither a rich nor beautiful source of material.

While some of the significant factors that have led to the relative
poverty of scholarship on Madison are related to what can loosely be
called aesthetic considerations, additional causes are due to the difficulties of his political theory itself—both its form and content—and
the confusion associated with his roles in the founding and operating of the new republic. Each of these considerations will be dealt
with in turn.

Madison should be associated almost exclusively with the Constitution of 1787 and not the Revolution of 1776. However, beginning
with the original supporters of the new Constitution, the Federalists
(of whom Madison originally was one), American mythmakers have
tried hard to link, if not blend, these two distinct historic events in
the hearts and minds of the citizens.[26] Madison had a minimal in-

---

24. See opening chapter quote from *National Gazette*, 3 Dec. 1791, *PJM* 14:139.
25. Harold Laski, *Introduction to Politics* (New York: Barnes and Noble, 1963),
p. 26.
26. For example, see McCoy, *Last of the Fathers*, p. xii: "Madison's work as
Revolutionary and as Founder," he writes, "rescued the Revolution and the Constitution from a renewed threat of monarchy in a second revolution." Cf.
Sheldon S. Wolin, *The Presence of the Past: Essays on the State and the Constitution* (Baltimore: Johns Hopkins University Press, 1989), pp. 2–3, where he
warns that "bicentennials are by nature civic rather than scholarly events. They
are rituals organized to promote a mythic history. They appear to be celebrating
the past, but their most important function is to fix the collective identity of
the past. A bicentennial might be thought of as an official story that narrates a
past to support an image of collective identity that confirms a certain conception of the present. The narrative is designed to privilege a certain past in order
to legitimate a particular present."

volvement with the events that led to the break with England. He verbally supported the early activities in favor of independence and served as a member of the Orange County Committee of Safety, but his "involvement in revolutionary activities," reports Jack Rakove, "lagged behind his opinions."[27] In his autobiography Madison explained that "he was restrained from entering into the military service by the unsettled state of his health and the discouraging feebleness of his constitution of which he was fully admonished by his experience during the exercises and movements of a minute Company which he had joined."[28] The military glory that Hamilton longed for and Washington achieved was beyond the reach of Madison's constitution. He did, nevertheless, make a few minor contributions to some of the local politics that led up to the Revolutionary War. His entanglement with the Constitution of 1787, however, remains another matter altogether. Indeed, the importance of his efforts to construct, ratify, and secure the Constitution of 1787 can scarcely be overrated.[29]

Further complicating the conflation of these specific events of the American founding is the celebrated "great collaboration" of Madison and Jefferson.[30] To be sure, for most of their adult lives Madison and Jefferson were exceptionally close friends and quite often formidable political allies. Nevertheless, on issues of political theory—on the nature of humanity, the best political order, the course of history, the promise of democracy—they differed, and their differences were significant. Jefferson was a democrat. Madison was not. The principal author of the Declaration of Independence held markedly

27. Rakove, *Madison*, p. 10.

28. Douglass Adair, "James Madison's 'Autobiography'," *William and Mary Quarterly* 3d ser., 2 (Apr. 1945): 199; Ketcham, *Madison*, pp. 64–67.

29. This is not to suggest that Madison was among the first to push for a constitutional convention. As an editorial note to *PJM* 9:116, describes this issue: "The record shows that in the preceding years JM was opposed in principle to the idea of a regional convention that would concern itself with revising the faltering Articles of Confederation." The editors also cite a 12 Aug. 1786 letter to Jefferson in which JM wrote, "Gentlemen both within & without Congs. wish to make this Meeting subservient to a Plenipotentiary Convention for amending the Confederation. Tho' my wishes are in favor of such an event, yet I despair so much of its accomplishment at the present crisis that I do not extend my views beyond a Commercial Reform. To speak the truth I almost despair even of this" (partly in code; ibid., 119).

30. Adrienne Koch, *Jefferson and Madison: The Great Collaboration* (New York: Oxford University Press, 1976).

different views of government, society, humanity, and the good than did the chief architect of the Constitution. Their historic association, however, has helped construct a potent mythology in which Jefferson's democratic rhetoric provides the smoke and mirrors behind which Madison's machine of reason hides. While the tendency to blur the distinctions between Jefferson and Madison has been all too successful, the ability to conflate the events of 1776 with those of 1787 has been less so.[31]

On some level Americans seem to be aware of the divergent realities and contradictory natures of the two events, shown by their refusal to be swept away by the most recent bicentennial festivities.[32] The "problem" with the Constitution may be that it—like all constitutions—represents a fundamentally conservative political phenomenon. Establishing basic rules of the political and economic game, it forever constricts and limits human behavior to stabilize society; the Revolution, in contrast, symbolizes an activity of breaking away, of freeing ourselves, from a tyrannical past. As one pro-Constitution newspaper in September 1787 described the events: "The year 1776 is celebrated for a revolution in favor of liberty. The year 1787 it is expected will be celebrated with equal joy, for a revolution in favor of government."[33] Nations, like individuals, deceive themselves. While fancying ourselves a revolutionary people, we are part of, as Alexis de Tocqueville observed, a conservative society committed to keeping the status quo. As the prolific historian John Diggins eloquently states it, since *Democracy in America* "we have understood why Americans are a conservative people and why America is a liberal society, a society of free political institutions inhabited by individuals who love property and hate revolutions. That America itself

31. Among the historians who appreciate the differences between Madison and Jefferson are J. R. Pole, *Political Representation in England and the Origins of the American Republic* (New York: St. Martin's Press, 1966), pp. 296–304; and Merrill Peterson, *Jefferson and Madison and the Making of Constitutions* (Charlottesville: University Press of Virginia, 1987).

32. Recall the different public reactions to the centennial and bicentennial celebrations surrounding the Statue of Liberty and the Declaration of Independence compared to that of the Constitution of 1787. For a painstakingly detailed history of the failure of virtually every past public celebration of the Constitution, see Michael Kammen, *A Machine That Would Go of Itself: The Constitution in American Culture* (New York: A. A. Knopf, 1986).

33. Quoted in the "Editor's Introduction" to Isaac Kramnick, ed., *The Federalist Papers* (New York: Viking Penguin, 1987), p. 16 (hereafter cited as *Federalist*).

was born of violent revolution only highlights the irony of liberalism peculiar to us, a liberalism that embraces radical means to achieve conservative ends."[34] Put more succinctly, Americans quote the Declaration of Independence but live *The Federalist*.

Examining the American Revolution from the viewpoint of the rise of modernity, the political theorist Sheldon Wolin explains that "the American Revolution, unlike the French Revolution, was in its political theories importantly a revolution for, not against feudalism; that the Revolution in 1776 was, in a Weberian sense, a counterrevolution against the slowly evolving pressures toward 'rationalization' . . . and that the revolution that actually overthrew the premise of feudalism, or suppressed it, occurred when the Constitution was ratified in 1787." For Wolin, feudalism "signifies primal chaos and political polytheism," while republicanism represents unity, order, and rationality.[35] Given his frame of reference, Wolin is surely accurate. When he views the Revolution of 1776 as a counterrevolution and the Constitution of 1787 as the genuinely revolutionary moment, he reminds readers of the larger movement of history of which the United States remains but a part. Wolin also understands these events as analytically distinct moments that must be kept as such if scholars are to understand the American founding in the context of world history.

Almost twenty-five years earlier, another political theorist, Norman Jacobson, published an inspiring essay, "Political Science and Political Education," in which he argued that at the time of the adoption of the Constitution of 1787 America's elite confronted a

34. John Patrick Diggins, *The Lost Soul of American Politics* (New York: Basic Books, 1984), p. 4.
35. Wolin, *Presence of the Past*, pp. 128–129; see also Gordon Wood, *The Creation of the American Republic, 1776–1787* (Chapel Hill: University of North Carolina Press, 1969), p. 564: "Only as the debates over the Constitution unfolded and the pieces gradually fell into place did the Federalists themselves become conscious of just how revolutionary and how unique the new system they had created was"; and his "The Political Ideology of the Founders," in *Toward a More Perfect Union: Six Essays on the Constitution*, ed. Neil L. York (Provo, Utah: Brigham Young University Press, 1988), p. 9: "There is little doubt that on its face the Constitution violated much of the conventional popular thinking of late eighteenth-century America. It was a very radical proposal, more radical than we today can properly appreciate. . . . No one in 1776 had predicted or had wanted such a strong government. Such national power was then beyond anyone's wildest dreams."

critical choice between two divergent forms of political thought—
that of Thomas Paine or that of James Madison and Alexander Hamilton. Paine's theory "was notable for its expression of friendship
and brotherhood, for its insistence upon individual spontaneity and
uniqueness, and for its disdain for material concerns; it was intuitive
and unsystematic in temper." The alternate option of Madison and
Hamilton, he writes, "displayed a preoccupation with social order,
procedural rationality, and the material bases of political association
and division; it was abstract and systematic in temper."[36] The framers opted for the latter and, by the narrowest of margins, so did the
citizens who voted for the *novus ordo seclorum.*

More recently, Isaac Kramnick has differentiated between politics
under the Articles of Confederation—America's first Constitution—
and life under the second Constitution of 1787. The latter constituted a victory of the center over the periphery, reversing the order of
victory in the Revolutionary War. Both the Revolution and the Articles of Confederation represented "a leveling and more democratic
ideal." The Constitution of 1787, in contrast, represented a centralized, rational form of rule, a victory for "government," "authority"
and "power" over "liberty."[37] Wolin, Jacobson, and Kramnick remind us, then, of the importance of not two but three distinguish-
able events: the Declaration of Independence and the break with England; life in the First Republic under the Articles of Confederation;
and, the reaction to both of these events, in the name of reason, with
the creation of the modern state under the guidelines provided in the
Constitution of 1787. Only when viewed from a rather narrow, isolationist frame of reference does the final event of establishing a new
social contract in 1787 appear to be counterrevolutionary to the spirit
of 1776. When observed through the lens of Hegel and Weber, however, the Constitution defines America's revolutionary moment: it
supplies radical and rational measures to avoid the chaos, anarchy,
disorder, and democracy that flowed from the local politics and self-

---

36. Norman Jacobson, "Political Science and Political Education," *American
Political Science Review* 57:3 (Sept. 1963): 561. Jacobson further maintained that
these early Americans picked unwisely and that twentieth-century Americans
not only continue to legitimize this choice but are persuaded that it is their
moral duty to export this error to the rest of the world.

37. *Federalist,* pp. 15–16.

government encouraged by the Articles of Confederation.[38] Madison, therefore, should be seen as a radical theorist who marched in the forefront of his time.

Nevertheless, the very concept of *a* founding distorts as well as misleads. It collapses significantly different events: the War for Independence (chaos and the periphery); the republic under the Articles of Confederation (democracy and feudalism); and the radical solution of the Constitution of 1787 (rationality, order, the center)—helping create the modern state, which eventually, albeit inevitably, evolved into the modern bureaucratic-administrative state. Although Madison should be associated with the destruction of the first American republic under the Articles of Confederation and the construction of the Second Republic and the creation of the modern state, he should be linked only tangentially to the Revolutionary War.

Finally, there exists the cluster of problems associated with the notion of a single Madisonian political theory. Did he have one? Did he embrace more than one during the course of his extraordinary and lengthy political life? "It is a little unfair," claims Robert Dahl, "to treat Madison as a political theorist. He was writing and speaking for his time, not for the ages. . . . As an admirer of Madison the man and statesman, I would be content to let . . . the theorist lie in peace—if it were not for the fact that he so profoundly shaped and shapes American thinking about democracy."[39] Given Madison's virtually countless and unsystematic political writings, how can any

38. JM appreciated the need for a radical change in the Articles of Confederation. To Edmund Randolph, 25 Feb. 1987, *PJM* 9:299, he wrote: "Our situation is becoming every day more & more critical. No money comes into the federal Treasury. No respect is paid to the federal authority; and people of reflection unanimously agree that the existing Confederacy is tottering to its foundation. Many individuals of weight particularly in the Eastern district are suspected of leaning towards Monarchy. Other individuals predict a partition of the States into two or more Confederacies. It is pretty certain that if some radical amendment of the single one can not be devised and introduced that one or other of these revolutions, the latter no doubt, will take place. I hope you are bending your thoughts seriously to the great work of guarding agst. both." And at the Virginia ratifying convention he rose on 11 June to state that "it was my purpose to resume . . . what I had left unfinished concerning the necessity of a radical change of our system"; Jonathan Elliot, ed., *The Debates of the Several State Conventions on the Adoption of the Federal Constitution*, 5 vols. (Philadelphia: J. B. Lippincott, 1830–1836), 3:247.

39. Dahl, *Preface to Democratic Theory*, p. 5. Dahl is incorrect in believing Madison did not think he was "speaking . . . for the ages." See JM's speech of 26 June 1787, *The Records of the Federal Convention of 1787*, ed. Max Farrand, 4

scholar expect to uncover a coherent, albeit implicit, theory that links his ideas together? This difficulty, however, is not peculiar to Madison.[40]

Like most of our founders, Madison did not write a book or a single major essay, including *Federalist* 10, that provides the outline of his political theory; there is neither a Lockean *Second Treatise* nor a Rousseauian "Discourse on the Origin of Inequality." If a major written treatise establishes the *sine qua non* for being considered a political theorist, then neither Socrates nor Madison should be counted as one.[41] Those scholars interested in finding Madison's political theory, therefore, must sift through his voluminous writings in the form of public addresses, private and public letters, newspaper essays, official correspondences, and personal notes and memorandums.

His brilliant contributions to *The Federalist* do provide a bountiful source of information concerning his understanding of the meaning of the Constitution, a rationale for its adoption, and a chronicle of the anticipated strengths and benefits of the new government; they do not, however, provide more than hints of his initial reservations and serious disappointments with the final product. If anything, Madison's Publius appears more optimistic and "democratic" than the private James Madison, at least at the time of the ratification debates. Given the weight twentieth-century scholars, particularly political scientists, have placed on *Federalist* 10, in some cases treating it as the "Cliff Notes" to Madisonian politics, Madison scholars sometimes wish Hamilton had claimed authorship of the paper. *Federalist* 10 (and *Federalist* 51) surely are important political documents, but reducing Madison's political theory to these two "letters to the editor" is a gross, reductionist distortion of the richness of

---

vols. (New Haven, Conn.: Yale University Press, 1937), 1:422, "In framing a system which we wish to last for the ages, we shd. not lose sight of the changes which age will produce." Dahl (p. 4) also incorrectly viewed Madison as democratic.

40. J. G. A. Pocock, "Cambridge Paradigms and Scotch Philosophers," in *Wealth and Virtue*, ed. Istvan Hont and Michael Ignatieff (Cambridge: Cambridge University Press, 1985), p. 24, writes: "Not all the great intelligences who have engaged in political discourse have engaged, directly or indirectly, in systematic political theorizing."

41. See Donald S. Lutz, *A Preface to American Political Theory* (Lawrence: University Press of Kansas, 1992), pp. 1–42.

Madison's political genius. His theory was developed and articulated over the span of several decades, not constructed in a few weeks. Naturally, *The Federalist* will be consulted here to construct Madison's political theory, but as far as possible it will not be considered the essential Madison nor will it be given a privileged position in terms of uncovering Madison's political thought.

Last, there remains the difficult issue of the consistency, or lack of it, in Madison.[42] For instance, there exists the public versus private dimensions of Madison. Rarely provided the luxury of being an armchair philosopher, Madison spent more than four decades in public service, which required that he deal with specific issues and concrete solutions rather than intellectual musings over the construction in speech of an ideal republic. In light of his public service, it seems unavoidable that he would have had changes of opinion on matters of public policy; indeed, he altered his position on several significant political questions—the necessity of a national veto over all state legislation, the desirability of a bill of rights, the constitutionality of a national bank, and the extent suffrage could safely be extended.

One noted scholar, Marvin Meyers, summarizes Madison's shifting position on the appropriate balance of power between the central government and the state governments by maintaining that Madison "threw his considerable weight to the side of the national authority in the beginning, swung back to the opposite extreme in his role of opposition leader, moved back toward the nationalist position during the years of power, and came to rest, just a little uncertainly, where he had started." These alterations lead Meyers to ask an additional question: "How many Madisons shall we find?"[43] Perhaps it is not so much an issue of there being a single Madisonian political theory as several Madisonian theories. Scholarly responses vary. Meyers himself equivocates: "only by straining words," he writes, can Madison's alterations be reconciled; Madison must have been "embarrassed" by his theoretical shifts when "the analysis in *Federalist* 10 disappeared for a season," to be replaced by a "modified version of Anti-federalism." And yet, Meyers concludes that Madison

42. Rutland, *Presidency,* p. 106; Rakove, *Madison,* p. 93.
43. Meyers, *The Mind,* pp. xxxviii, xxxiii–xxxiv. Adrienne Koch holds a similar position; see *Madison's "Advice to my Country"* (Princeton, N.J.: Princeton University Press, 1966), pp. 117–119.

can be counted "among the finest and firmest American voices of the eighteenth-century liberal tradition."[44]

Meyers's Madison, an "inconsistent eighteenth century liberal," represents one of the four interpretative models of James Madison that can be readily located in the literature. The other three interpretations can be called "the liberal democrat," "the civic humanist," and the "ideologue in search of an ideology." John Zvesper, as many other political scientists, concurs with the liberal characterization. He finds a Madison who "was more consistently attached to the principles of liberalism and prudence than to the devices of pluralism and party government." But Zvesper goes a step further and believes that Madison should be counted as a legitimate patron saint for "participatory democrats."[45]

Following the lead of J. G. A. Pocock, Lance Banning and Drew McCoy discover a consistent Madison who was more than Zvesper's liberal democratic pragmatist; they argue that he must be understood as both a civic humanist and an advocate of representative democracy.[46] This particular interpretation develops out of the recent historiographic debates over the relative influence of liberalism, civic humanism, and other modes of discourse on the founders. Banning and McCoy argue that while liberal values were certainly present during the founding, the significance of liberalism has been

44. Meyers, *The Mind*, pp. xlii–xliii, xix; Cf. Ketcham, *Madison*, p. 50: "Elements of his thought were, of course, not wholly compatible. . . . His thought was eclectic, sensible, and reasonable, if not always wholly consistent." And, see Douglas W. Jaenicke, "Madison v. Madison: The Party Essays v. The Federalist Papers," in Richard Maidment and John Zvesper, eds., *Reflections on the Constitution: The American Constitution after Two Hundred Years* (New York: Manchester University Press, 1989), pp. 116–147.

45. John Zvesper, "The Madisonian Systems," *Western Political Quarterly* 37 (June 1984): 254, 236; and, Dahl, *Preface to Democratic Theory*, pp. 4–33. Most political scientists, trained to focus on power and self-interest, point to *Federalist* 10 and 51 to establish their forceful position that Madison's political theory is grounded in the careful channeling of competitive self-interest. The critics of this view argue, quite appropriately, that these two essays reflect the complete Madison but dimly. Rather, he can be discovered only by examining his private letters and public pronouncements throughout his entire career, including his essays in the *National Gazette* where he helps establish the intellectual and political opposition to the Federalists.

46. Lance Banning, *The Jeffersonian Persuasion* (Ithaca, N.Y.: Cornell University Press, 1978); McCoy, *Elusive Republic*; and Neal Riemer, "James Madison's Theory of the Self-Destructive Features of Republican Government," *Ethics* 65 (Oct. 1954): 34–43, *The Democratic Experiment* (Princeton, N.J.: Van Nostrand, 1967), passim.

over determined; in addition to liberalism, and exercising significant influence on the founders' thinking, existed at least one additional value system, which can be termed republicanism, classical republicanism, or civic humanism. Furthermore, Banning and McCoy believe Madison did his theorizing under the spell of the civic humanist tradition.[47]

Forrest McDonald holds the fourth, and unique, view of Madison. He maintains that Madison was an individual of "doctrinaire temperament, marked by what Jean-Paul Sartre called 'a nostalgia for the absolute.' " While Madison had a "preference for the untried but theoretically appealing," he painfully understood "the inefficaciousness of his theories . . . abundantly demonstrated by the triumph of Hamiltonianism"; when this realization occurred, McDonald writes, "Madison had to begin theorizing anew." Given this perspective, it is understandable why McDonald believes Madison was "an ideologue in search of an ideology," since his Madison shifted both political position and theory as circumstances required.[48]

These four theoretic constructs—inconsistent liberal, liberal-democrat, civic humanist, and "ideologue in search of an ideology"—capture the current spectrum of interpretative views of Madison's politics. While the view of Madison that this book will develop was informed and enriched by the work of these four approaches, I think each interpretation, in one way or another, errs.

The most seriously flawed model is that of Madison as civic humanist. To be sure, a different rhetorical flavor surfaces in Madison's *National Gazette* essays, and at critical political junctures Madison did employ "virtue language" to help establish public support for his position; however, those who discover a civic humanist Madison, either throughout or at different moments in his political career, misunderstand not only the essence of civic humanism but also

47. David Epstein, *The Political Theory of The Federalist* (Chicago: University of Chicago Press, 1984), pp. 3–5, where he implicitly endorses the positions of Zvesper, Banning, and McCoy. Without explanation he asserts that a recent and more "sophisticated" interpretation of *The Federalist* "reveals the liberal beginnings of American liberal democracy," which is linked to civic humanism through its "very emphatic insistence on a 'strictly republican' . . . form of government."

48. McDonald, *Novus Ordo Seclorum*, p. 203; cf. Rakove, *Madison*, p. 93, where he argues that "while Madison valued intellectual consistency he was never a rigid ideologue."

Madison's intellectual and emotional commitment to liberalism. Similar criticisms can be applied to those who read democratic values back into Madison.[49] Those scholars who wish to revive Madison to save the republic by virtue of either his democratic theory or his civic humanism will have to look elsewhere in the pluralistic tradition of American political thought to find the appropriate champion.

Inconsistency links the interpretations offered by McDonald, Meyers, Ketcham, and others who endorse the first and last of the four interpretations. McDonald's insights into Madison's character—his fear of epilepsy and his "nostalgia for the absolute"—are ingenious and persuasive. Nevertheless, McDonald specifically fails to see how it is instrumental reason and equilibrium that make up "the absolute" for which Madison was nostalgic. Indeed, it is Madison's doctrinaire commitment to reason that builds a path of consistency throughout his change of position on public policy throughout his life. He can be viewed as the constant liberal Prince who shifts rhetorical posture and political influence as circumstances require to maintain political stability and protect individual rights—principally property rights to things and, secondarily, freedom of the press and of conscience—from the encroachments of others. Still, the weightiest evidence on the question of consistency comes from Madison himself.

While finally enjoying the luxury of retirement from public service, Madison elected to spend some of his remaining time answering the various charges of what he thought of as "discrediting inconsistencies."[50] In February of 1825, Madison wrote to C. E. Haynes to correct an "injustice" Madison noted in the remarks contained in Judge Clayton's "Report of the Committee of Ways and Means." Madison felt that Clayton charged him with "surrender[ing] all my

---

49. I am in disagreement with both Lance Banning and Martin Diamond on this point. Both argue that Madison is a democrat, or a representative democrat. See Martin Diamond, *"The Federalist,"* in *The History of Political Philosophy,* ed. Leo Strauss and Joseph Cropsey, 2d ed. (Chicago: Rand McNally, 1972), p. 637; and Lance Banning, "The Practicable Sphere of a Republic," in *Beyond Confederation,* ed. Richard Beeman et al. (Chapel Hill: University of North Carolina Press, 1987), pp. 164, 179, 186.

50. JM to N. P. Trist, Dec. 1831, *WJM* 9:471. See Meyers, *The Mind,* xxxiv, where he notes: "Madison was peculiarly vulnerable to accusations of political infidelity or at best slippery equivocation. He did shift alignments and tactics; he did so knowingly; and he carefully provided contemporaries and posterity with a defense of his course."

early opinions at discretion." Not wanting to appear either defensive or opinionated, Madison began by stating, "I am far from regarding a change of opinions, under the lights of experience and the results of improved reflection, as exposed to censure; and still farther from the vanity of supposing myself less in need of that privilege than others." Still, Madison insisted he "had indulged the belief that there were few, if any, of my contemporaries, through the long period and varied scenes of my political life, to whom a mutability of opinion was less applicable."

Moving from the general to the particular, Madison focused on the bank issue, his one change of opinion that most often resulted in the charge of inconsistency. "But even here," wrote Madison, "the inconsistency is apparent only, not real."[51] Madison often used the tactic of juxtaposing appearance to reality to counterattack those who argued he was too mutable. That same year, Madison went to considerable lengths to discredit some not very candid attempts to stamp his political career with "discrediting inconsistencies." While this particular defense dealt with Madison's painful and undoubtedly regrettable connection to the Virginia Resolutions, Madison closed his letter to N. P. Trist returning to the bank issue and the theme of appearance versus reality: "On the subject of the Bank alone is there a color for the charge of mutability on a Constitutional question. But here the inconsistency is apparent, not real, since the change, was in conformity to an early & unchanged opinion, that in the case of a Constitution as of a law, a course of authoritative, deliberate, and continued decisions, such as the Bank could plead was an evidence of the Public Judgement, necessarily superseding individual opinion."[52]

By the following year, Madison must have concluded that his defense was falling on deaf ears. "I had flattered myself, in vain," he

51. JM to C. E. Haynes, 25 Feb. 1831, *WJM* 9:442.
52. JM to N. P. Trist, Dec. 1831, *WJM* 9:476–477; see also JM to Thomas Jefferson, 8 Feb. 1825, *WJM* 9:219–220. When Jefferson suggested to JM that the Virginia Resolutions should be incorporated as part of "a text book for the Law School," JM responded coolly: "With respect to the Virginia Document of 1799, there may be more room for hesitation. Tho' corresponding with the predominate sense of the Nation; being of local origin & having reference to a state of Parties not yet extinct, an absolute prescription of it, might excite prejudices against the University. . . . It may be added that the Document is not on every point satisfactory to all who belong to the same Party." Indeed, JM himself may have had serious regrets about his participation in the document's history.

wrote, "that whatever my political errors may have been, I was little chargeable with inconsistencies, as any of my fellow laborers thro' so long a period of political life."[53] And by 1833, he was alarmed that future generations, reading Robert Yates's notes of the Constitutional Convention, would draw "inferences from votes in the journal of the Convention" that "may often have a meaning quite uncertain, and sometimes contrary to the apparent one." He closed this letter by once again returning to the plaguing issue of the constitutionality of the bank. Referring to himself, Madison justified his shift in favor of the bank "on the ground of the authoritative and multiplied sanctions given it, amounting, he conceived, to an evidence of the judgment and will of the nation; and on the ground of a consistency of this change of opinion with his unchanged opinion, that such a sanction ought to overrule the abstract and private opinions of individuals."[54] However pained the effort to explain his behavior, what matters was that Madison fervently believed that his theory and actions were logical, coherent, and consistent. Given his character, temperament, and commitment to reason it is understandable why he was so troubled by the charges of inconsistency and why he went to such lengths to refute them.

How then, should Madison be understood? If each of the current interpretative frames of reference is found wanting, with what are they to be replaced? To begin with, he is not only a quintessential liberal, he is also a consistent one. During its early genesis, "liberalism was a philosophy of sobriety, born in fear, nourished by disenchantment, and prone to believe that the human condition was and was likely to remain one of pain and anxiety."[55] While liberalism provides the general outline to understanding Madison, it is necessary—given the richness and variety of the intellectual construct called liberalism, a body of thought that has claimed such diverse political advocates as Hobbes, Locke, Rousseau, Bentham, both Mills, Green, Hayek, and Friedman, to list but a few—to describe in detail Madison's *sui generis* blend of liberalism. Then again, perhaps

53. JM to Joseph C. Cabell, 27 Dec. 1832, *WJM* 9:494.
54. JM to W. C. Rives, Oct. 1833, *Letters and Other Writings of James Madison*, ed. William C. Rives and Philip R. Fendall, 4 vols. (Philadelphia: J. B. Lippincott, 1884), 4:310, 321.
55. Sheldon Wolin, *Politics and Vision: Continuity and Innovation in Western Political Thought* (Boston: Little, Brown & Company, 1960), p. 293.

it would be preferable to discard the liberal label altogether and simply describe Madison's political theory as follows.

Six interrelated postulates frame Madison's political theory. (1) Neither a democrat nor a civic humanist, Madison had little faith in either the *demos* or virtue. Mechanical government regulations and automatic social counterpressures established political and social stability; as Galileo and Newton had discovered certain laws of the universe that maintained its balance and equilibrium, political theorists (from Hobbes and Locke to Hamilton and Madison) had discovered analogous social laws that could be implemented to create balance and stability out of the disorder and anarchy of human behavior.[56] Individual human beings, however, could not be counted on to rule themselves, let alone others, justly. (2) The protection of individuals—especially their property and other rights—was one of the cardinal values in Madison's politics. Early in his career he championed religious liberty; later on—as political circumstances required—he briefly emphasized freedom of the press. But he remained always a constant, ever vigilant, protector of the property rights of the minority. It was property rights, above all others, that must be secured. (3) Although the unmolested individual was a goal of Madison's politics, the individual as political actor should be of minor import if the Madisonian system functioned as designed. Individuals, while timid and reasonable when alone, join other individuals and form factions. Madison's primary political concern centered on the maintenance of social stability by the political and social control of factions; control of the government itself was an important, albeit secondary, consideration. (4) If Madison worshipped a deity, it would be reason—not the substantive Reason of philosophers as diverse as Plato, Hegel, and Marcuse, but the instrumental reason of the modern age.[57] Reason provides the theoretical possibility of transcending the experience of the past. If the new sci-

56. See Paul N. Goldstene, *The Collapse of Liberal Empire* (Novato, Calif.: Chandler & Sharp, 1977), p. 11, where he notes that "in its implicit political idea, liberalism is less the child of Locke than of Newton. It is the third law of the physical universe which provides the crucial inspiration to the men of the seventeenth century seeking a new foundation for civil order."

57. See Max Horkheimer, *Eclipse of Reason* (New York: Continuum, 1974), p. 3: "This type of reason may be called subjective reason. It is essentially concerned with means and ends, with the adequacy of procedures for purposes more or less taken for granted and supposedly self-explanatory. It attaches little im-

ences of politics, of economics, of sociology could be developed and their insights followed, they might hold the key to the construction of Madison's "Empire of reason."[58]

The individual and collective tendencies toward the irrational were so multifaceted and powerful that (5) all segments of the political system needed an appropriate degree of defensive power for self-protection. Power, in Madison's view, is negative; it is necessary for individuals to have some power to protect oneself and one's property by stopping others. Rarely does Madison view the exercise of power in an enabling, positive light. Finally, (6) to place Madison in the political spectrum, it is appropriate to view him standing within the predemocratic portion of the liberal tradition, somewhere between Thomas Hobbes and John Locke. While there are Lockean (as well as Jeffersonian) moments to Madison, his worship of reason, his mechanical view of politics, his concept of humanity, and his fear of political life being "poor, nasty, brutish, and short" under a weak government, all combine to make him at least as much a disciple of Hobbes as of Locke.[59] A strong, centralized, rational state was one of Madison's primary solutions to the human condition.

While Madison can be conceived of as the constant liberal Prince, two additional metaphors may be helpful in capturing the essence of his political theory. The first is that of a child's seesaw: government (with its power) sits on one side, individuals (with their rights) on the other; and reason provides the fulcrum that keeps both sides in the air.[60] Since equilibrium, balance, and stability (rather than play) are the goals of Madison's seesaw, he must shift his political weight from side to side, back and forth, as changes in the sociopolitical en-

---

portance to the question whether the purposes as such are reasonable." Horkheimer also notes that this concept of reason "resembles to a certain degree the difference between functional and substantial rationality as these words are used in the Max Weber school" (p. 6). See also James T. Kloppenberg, "The Virtues of Liberalism: Christianity, Republicanism, and Ethics in Early American Political Discourse," *Journal of American History* 74 (June 1987): 19.

58. On a subjective level, reason's ability to control passion spelled freedom for the individual as it did for Madison himself; if reason could construct a political system that channels the irresponsible actions of factions, it might provide stability for the polity as well.

59. Cf. Ketcham, *Madison*, p. 49.

60. Goldstene, *Collapse*, p. 12: "If power is the *bete noire* of liberalism, balance becomes the *raison d'etre* of its order. Reason must prevail, and what reason dictates is balance."

vironment require. He must do so to keep either side from gaining sufficient gravity to crash to the earth, toss the other off the seesaw, and thereby create either tyranny or anarchy and ruin that delicate balance he strove to create and maintain.[61]

The second image, described in detail in chapter 3, comes directly from two passages in Madison's writings. The specific problem with Madison is not his belief that men were not angels; indeed, no political theorist of repute ever has argued that men were angels. The insurmountable difficulty is that Madison believed that "had every Athenian Citizen been a Socrates, every Athenian assembly would still have been a mob."[62] Madison accepted the incredible notion that even a room full of Socrateses could not deal justly with each other without a Leviathan, leaving little hope for politics or humanity. And most importantly, this linchpin to his entire edifice constitutes an unchallenged philosophic assumption on his part.

On the American political landscape, it remains particularly appropriate to view Madison alongside Alexander Hamilton and Thomas Jefferson. It would be difficult to decide who is to the right of whom and, on the basis of what criteria, when the pairing places Madison next to Hamilton. While their political break during the Washington regime has been well noted, Madison and Hamilton's "great collaboration" on the initial construction of the Constitution of 1787 remains conveniently glossed over in American mythology. Whatever the relative position of Madison and Hamilton vis à vis each other, in terms of their political theories both are qualitatively different from Jefferson. Jefferson was a radical democrat. Madison (and Hamilton) were not. Jefferson embraced the chaos, disorder, and uncertainty that comes with his democratic vision of politics. Madison did not. This is not to imply that Madison was not a radical: he surely was. Believing in reason, meritocracy, rights, possessive individualism, order, and stability, Madison must be seen as a radical liberal. But "a meritocracy with a human face," as Wolin ex-

61. Therefore, during the drafting of the Articles of Confederation Madison emphasized the power of government. Once the Constitution of 1787 had been ratified and was operating, he moved to the middle and worked on behalf of a bill of rights. When government became too powerful under the Federalists' guidance he shifted to the individual rights side to rebalance the system. And when the system corrected itself through the election of Jefferson, Madison returned to the middle, waiting to see where he would have to move next.

62. *Federalist* 55:336.

plains, cannot be considered "synonymous with democracy."[63] In the larger movement of history, moreover, Madison represented the man of the times. He stood on the horizon of history. Jefferson tried to stand against it, even while believing in the promise of the future. Nevertheless, in terms of the American future, Madison may have outlived his usefulness, while Jefferson's political theory remains dormant, precariously existing in the realm of ideas as a remote possibility for reawakening America's all too brief democratic past. But these are larger topics to be dealt with later in the book.

63. Wolin, *Presence of the Past*, p. 4.

2 / Madison's Worldview: Indolent Humanity, Malthusian Reality, and "the Economy of Nature"

> The bent of human nature may be traced on the chart of our country. The manufacturer readily exchanges the loom for the plough, in opposition often to his own interest, as well as to that of his country. The cultivator, in situations presenting an option, to the labors of the field, the more easy employment of rearing a herd. And as the game of the forest is approached, the hunting life displays the force of its attractions. Where do we behold a march to the opposite direction? the hunter, becoming the herdsman; the latter a follower of the plough; and the last repairing to the manufactory or workshop.[1]
>
> —*Madison*

Retirement from public office in 1816 left Madison with abundant time to attend to his farm, recall the events that led to the creation of the American state, and contemplate the future of his country. This leisure permitted him to return to his scholarly pursuits and use his considerable talents to ponder the issue of agricultural modernization as the theme for his presidential "Address to the Agriculture Society of Albermarle Virginia." With Madison's permission, his address was published in the *Enquirer* and reproduced in a pamphlet for distribution to the society's membership. Although problems of local agriculture constitute the focus of the speech, Madison introduced his topic with a discussion of the human condition, its inevitable tendency toward overpopulation, and the equally inevitable "economy of nature"; he had thought and written about these interrelated issues since as early as 1786, when he had confided to Jefferson that "a certain degree of misery seems inseparable from a high degree of populousness." He emphasized the gravity of this sit-

---

1. "Address to the Agriculture Society of Albermarle Virginia," 12 May 1818, William C. Rives and Philip R. Fendall, eds., *Letters and Other Writings of James Madison*, 4 vols. (Philadelphia: J. B. Lippincott, 1884), 3:66.

uation to Jefferson, and in the process demonstrated his own anxiety about the future, by claiming that "no problem in political Oeconomy has appeared to me more puzzling than that which relates to the most proper distribution of the inhabitants of a Country fully peopled."[2] Indeed, the tensions created by increasing population, the appropriate distribution of citizens among classes, and the "economy of nature" created enduring and fundamental political problems, which Madison attempted to conquer but knew he could only hold at bay.

When contemplating this address Madison found himself liberated from the pressing concerns of ratifying the Constitution or reigning in the power of the Federalist-controlled executive branch, apprehensions that clearly lurk in the background of Madison's contributions to *The Federalist* and the *National Gazette* essays. He now could enjoy freedom from what he called "the labors and anxieties of public life."[3] Madison's "Address to the Agriculture Society," therefore, offers scholars a rather non–politically motivated essay. It shows, in a rudimentary form, his calm and mature views on certain critical dimensions of human nature and several candid insights into his general philosophic orientation toward life. The purpose of this extended discussion of his address is to gain access to Madison's view of the world and thereby begin to establish the parameters of his politics. From the discussion emerge five initial characteristics of Madison's concept of humanity and his general philosophic understanding of reality.

To begin, (1) humans were both rational and lazy. If free to choose between the two, they would prefer a life of ease without civilization. Although this disposition toward indolence and degeneracy constituted the "bent" of human nature, (2) the inevitability of surplus population and the finiteness of nature's bounty required humans to plan for the future in order to provide for themselves as rationally as possible; if they failed to do so, (3) the automatic checks and balances of nature, her beautiful "economy," would reinstitute

2. JM to Thomas Jefferson, 19 June 1786, *The Papers of James Madison*, ed. William T. Hutchinson et al., 17 vols. (Chicago and Charlottesville: University of Chicago Press and University of Virginia Press, 1962–), 9:76 (hereafter cited as *PJM*); see also JM speech, 26 June 1787, *The Records of the Federal Convention of 1787*, ed. Max Farrand, 4 vols. (New Haven, Conn.: Yale University Press, 1937), 1:422–423.
3. JM to Mr. Gallatin, Mar. 1817, *Letters and Other Writings* 3:38.

the order and sense of proportion in her system. In spite of nature's order, (4) humanity's tendency toward degeneration, whether in terms of economic evolution or urban decay, never disappears and always threatens our best efforts. Consequently, (5) tension and conflict characterized Madison's ambivalent *weltanschauung:* order versus disorder, rationality versus laziness and "redundant" people, civilization versus degeneration, the Enlightenment's promise versus Calvinism's curse.[4] In some ways, this too establishes Madison as the ideal liberal Prince: he achieved *virtu* by the success of his multidimensional political actions, creating social stability in the face of the relatively sure knowledge that, as in the past, all human constructs were doomed.[5]

After thanking his audience for the honor of being selected as their presiding officer, he informed them that his topic would be "improving the agriculture of our country." Madison began by noting that "the faculty of cultivating the earth, and of rearing animals, by which food is increased beyond the spontaneous supplies of nature, belongs to man alone." Planning for the future, beyond immediate physical need, was a capacity humans alone possessed. The ability to produce more than what was needed for the short run, or what was supplied spontaneously from nature, established humanity's "pre-eminence over irrational animals."

It seemed as if Madison elected to respond directly to the concerns raised by Thomas Malthus in his influential 1798 *An Essay on the Principles of Population*, in which he presented his theory of the inevitability of overpopulation and the equally inevitable checks upon this condition provided by war, famine, and disease.[6] Madison's wife, Dolley, proudly claimed that her husband had drawn the same conclusions a full decade before publication of Malthus's controversial *Essay*. Whatever the exact sequence of discovery, Madison took considerable time to explore the relationships between human faculties,

4. See Adrienne Koch, *Madison's "Advice to My Country"* (Princeton, N.J.: Princeton University Press, 1966), p. 7, where she correctly, in my view, uses the "apt but unlovely word" *weltanschauung* to describe Madison's political theory.

5. Although these five features begin to frame Madison's philosophic orientation, a polished portrait of his concept of humanity and of reality will not be completed until the end of subsequent chapters, in which the discussion of these themes continues but centers instead on Madison's politically motivated writings in *The Federalist* and *National Gazette* essays.

6. Cf. Drew McCoy, "Jefferson and Madison," *Virginia Magazine of History and Biography* 88 (July 1980): 259–276.

agriculture, and science and the prospects for posterity.[7] Humans possessed reason; animals did not. While he never explicitly denied that all individuals have this faculty, he observed that not all societies fully develop or employ reason and planning.

> As this peculiar faculty gives to man a pre-eminence over irrational animals, so it is the use made of it by some, and the neglect of it by other communities, that distinguish them from each other, in the most important features of the human character.

> The contrast between the enlightened and the refined nations on some parts of the earth, and the rude and wretched tribes on others, has its foundation in this distinction.

Some human communities are more rational than others; furthermore, Madison comes close to equating less rational humans with irrational animals.

The employment or nonemployment of agriculture distinguished "enlightened and refined nations" from "rude and wretched tribes." Moreover, Madison believed agriculture established the necessary prerequisite to civilization: "Civilization is never seen without agriculture; nor has agriculture ever prevailed where the civilized arts did not make their appearance."[8] Although agriculture was a precondition for, and remained linked to, civilization, advancements in civ-

---

7. See editor's note no. 1 to "Notes on Emigration," 19 Nov. 1791, *PJM* 14:116; for JM's view on Malthus's originality, see JM to Edward Everett, 26 Nov. 1823, in Gaillard Hunt, ed., *The Writings of James Madison*, 9 vols. (New York: G. P. Putnam's Sons, 1900–1910), 9:170 (hereafter cited as *WJM*), where he wrote: "But he [Malthus] has not all the merit of originality which has been allowed him. The principle was adverted to & reasoned upon, long before him, tho' with views & applications not the same with his. The principle is indeed inherent in all the organized beings on the Globe, as well of the animal as the vegetable classes; all & each of which when left to themselves, multiply till checked by the limited fund of their pabulum, or by the mortality generated by an excess of their number." JM himself "averted to & reasoned upon" these notions as early as his "Preliminary Draft of an Essay on Natural Order," Nov. 1791, *PJM* 14:100–104; portions of that draft were published in the *National Gazette* essay "Population and Emigration," 19 Nov. 1791, *PJM* 14:117–122.

8. *Letters and Other Writings* 3:63–64; cf. Richard K. Matthews, *The Radical Politics of Thomas Jefferson* (Lawrence: University Press of Kansas, 1986), pp. 53–75, for Jefferson's contrasting views on Native Americans and civilization.

ilization did not always keep pace with those in agriculture, as the historic examples of China and Japan indicated to Madison.

Having established the importance of an abundant food supply for the progress of humanity, Madison next argued that the very process of moving to the stage of economic evolution, where agricultural development could begin, required nearly heroic acts of will and reason since it appeared to be, from Madison's perspective, counterinstinctive. Throughout his address, Madison demonstrated his indebtedness to the ideas of the Scottish Enlightenment's Adam Smith, although on the point of humanity's reluctance to improve its lot they differed. Nevertheless, Madison echoed the logic of Smith's four stages of human progress, which were based on the mode of subsistence employed—from hunting, to pastoral, to agricultural, to commercial—to sustain society. The last of these stages, described interchangeably as "commercial society" or "civil society," corresponded to America's present condition as a "commercial republic."[9] "It must not be inferred," Madison asserted, "that the transition from the hunter, or even the herds-man's state, to the agricultural, is a matter of course." Noting the reluctance of humans to leave their precivilized condition, he observed that "the first steps in this transition are attended with difficulty; and what is more, with disinclination."[10] Even though agriculture promised a greater probability for a stable and abundant food supply as well as affording the opportunity to support an expanding population, human nature— Madison insisted—always preferred the less civilized social condition: "And that there is a disinclination in human nature to exchange the savage for the civilized life, cannot be questioned."

Madison believed Virginia's recent experience with Indian neighbors supplied ample proof of this generalization:

> The Indian tribes have ever shown an aversion to the change. Neither the persuasive examples of plenty and comfort derived from the culture of the earth by their white brethren, nor the lessons and

9. It should be noted, however briefly, that although Smith and Madison helped establish the preconditions for it, neither theorist ever explicitly endorsed the unmoderated possessive individualism that became associated with moral behavior in market society during the nineteenth and twentieth centuries. See C. B. Macpherson, *The Political Theory of Possessive Individualism: Hobbes to Locke* (Oxford: Clarendon Press, 1962), passim.

10. *Letters and Other Writings* 3:64.

specimens of tillage placed in the midst of them, and seconded by actual sufferings from a deficient and precarious subsistence, have converted them from their strong propensities and habitual pursuits. In the same spirit, they always betray an anxious disposition to return to their pristine life, after being weaned from it by time, and apparently molded by intellectual and moral instruction, into the habits and tastes of an agricultural people.[11]

Not wanting to establish universal principles about humanity on the basis of observations derived from a single society, Madison also acknowledged, and in the process betrayed his own prejudice, that "a still more conclusive evidence of the bias of human nature is seen in the familiar fact, that our own people, nursed and reared in these habits and tastes, easily slide into that of the savage, and are rarely reclaimed to civilized society with their own consent." Madison drove home his implied point about the slothful nature of humanity, one of the seven deadly sins, and further disclosed his own assumptions about the human condition when he hypothesized on the probable development of the United States if the original pilgrims had not been forced by fear of death, and an ongoing contact with Europe, to duplicate their past. "They might have spread themselves into the forests where game and fruits would have abounded," he speculated, "and gradually forgetting the arts, no longer necessary to their immediate wants, have degenerated into savage tribes."[12]

"Liberalism, at its origins, is an ideology of work," Isaac Kramnick reminds us. And from this perspective, "the essence of humanity is the obligation to work."[13] This simple characterization of liberalism's genesis is helpful to keep in mind. Before John Stuart Mill and T. H. Green expanded and ennobled liberalism's concept of the individual, liberalism appeared particularly Protestant in its conception of humanity and hu-

---

11. Ibid., 3:64–65.
12. Ibid., 3:65.
13. Isaac Kramnick, *Republicanism and Bourgeois Radicalism* (Ithaca, N.Y.: Cornell University Press, 1990), p. 1. See also C. B. Macpherson, *The Real World of Democracy* (Toronto: CBC Learning Systems, 1965), p. 38, who notes a particular irony to the vision of the individual in the theory behind the free enterprise system: "It is almost incredible, until you come to think of it, that a society whose keyword is *enterprise*, which certainly sounds active, is in fact based on the assumption that human beings are so inert, so adverse to activity, that is, to expenditure of energy, that every expenditure of energy is considered to be painful, to be, in the economists' term, a disutility."

manity's relationship to labor. And for Madison, it was John Calvin who initially helped shape his Protestant perspective. "So pervasive was Christian influence, especially in rearing students, that an education under other than Christian auspices was virtually unknown" throughout colonial America, Ralph Ketcham explains.

In this, Madison proved no exception: every one of his teachers was "either a clergyman or a devoutly orthodox Christian layman."[14] This included his years at Princeton. While Madison was a student there, Princeton was under the influence of John Witherspoon, who had earned his reputation abroad by defending orthodox Calvinism, albeit on the basis of a rather modern epistemology. Based on a letter from Samuel Stanhope Smith, John Murrin argues persuasively that as late as 1778 Madison "defended Calvinist predestination," even though "as an adult he never joined a church."[15] In the letter, Smith reminded Madison that Madison had "attacked" him "on that knotty question of *liberty & necessity* that has so much embarrassed philosophers, & has raised such furious war among divines."[16] Their disagreement was simply this: Smith believed in free will; and, at least in 1778, Madison did not. Given Madison's success in keeping his religious views private, Murrin suggests that it is difficult "to know what he still believed by the 1780's, but he was no longer an orthodox Calvinist."[17] While Madison seems to have consciously abandoned orthodox Calvinism relatively early in his adulthood, given its pervasiveness throughout his earlier life there should be little doubt of its influence on his view of reality.[18]

Since humans, from Calvin's perspective, could do nothing to

14. Ralph L. Ketcham, *James Madison: A Biography* (New York: Macmillan, 1971), p. 47.

15. John M. Murrin, "Fundamental Values, The Founding Fathers, and the Constitution," in *To Form a More Perfect Union: The Critical Ideas of the Constitution*, ed. Herman Belz, Ronald Hoffman, and Peter J. Albert (Charlottesville: University of Virginia Press, 1992), p. 29; see n. 42, where Murrin states that "Madison's explicit defense of Calvinism is no longer extant, but much of its contents can be inferred," from a letter from Samuel Stanhope Smith to JM, Nov. 1777–Aug. 1778, *PJM* 1:194–212.

16. Samuel Stanhope Smith to JM, Nov. 1777–Aug. 1778, *PJM* 1:194.

17. Murrin, "Fundamental Values," p. 29.

18. Madison was hardly unique in this regard. In fact, Richard Hofstadter begins his classic (1948) *The American Political Tradition and the Men Who Made It* (New York: Vintage Books, 1974), p. 3, boldly claiming that "the men who drew up the Constitution in Philadelphia during the summer of 1787 had a vivid Calvinistic sense of human evil and damnation and believed with Hobbes that men are selfish and contentious." See also Ralph C. Hancock, *Calvin and the Foundations of Modern Politics* (Ithaca, N.Y.: Cornell University Press, 1989).

change their situation relative to being one of God's "elect"—indeed, even "their best deeds stink in the nostrils of the Lord" as Murrin colorfully described it—a deterministic fatalism surrounds this theology.[19] But this fatalism does not lead to passive acceptance of fate. "Where Lutheranism had been socially conservative, deferential to established political authorities, the exponent of a personal, almost quietistic piety," writes R. H. Tawney, "Calvinism was an active and radical force." The significant factor was that Luther's background had been "the traditional stratification of rural society. It is natural, rather than a money, economy." Calvin, on the other hand, "assumed an economic organization which was relatively advanced and expounded his social ethics on the basis of it."[20] Calvin, in short, represented the future, modern commercial world; Luther stood for the past. Although Calvin believed that it was man's duty to maintain political order, stability was not a self-sustaining condition as it existed in the cosmos; once established, order had to be maintained through continuous exercises of political power.[21] These central tenets of Calvinism were part of Madison. In fact, it may be appropriate to conceive of Madison as a Calvinist liberal. John Diggins soberly captures the profound dilemma this contains: "Religion compels us to doubt what politics asks us to believe—that virtue can triumph over sin."[22] And it will be no surprise to find Calvinism's judgmental language of sin and corruption spread across the pages of Madison's public writings.

An 1825 letter to Frederick Beasley, on the *a priori* "proofs of the Being & Attributes of God," presents Madison at his metaphysical

19. Murrin, "Fundamental Values," p. 12; Murrin also challenges Hofstadter's sweeping assertion on Calvinism and the Constitutional Convention by maintaining that Anglicanism was the largest religious affiliation of convention delegates.

20. R. H. Tawney, *Religion and the Rise of Capitalism* (New York: Harcourt, Brace & World, 1926), p. 91. See also Michael Lienesch, *New Order of the Ages* (Princeton, N.J.: Princeton University Press, 1988), p. 88, who notes, "In the agrarian vocabulary, terms like 'industry,' 'enterprise,' and 'investment,' were personal attributes. Similarly 'labor' was a moral concept, implying dedication or diligence. Even 'property' was understood in terms of personal character, a sign, in Calvinist terms of inner grace, or a manifestation, in Lockean fashion, of self-control."

21. Sheldon Wolin, *Politics and Vision: Continuity and Innovation in Western Political Thought* (Boston: Little, Brown & Company, 1960), pp. 165–194.

22. John Patrick Diggins, *The Lost Soul of American Politics* (New York: Basic Books, 1984), pp. 18, 7; cf. Jack N. Rakove, *James Madison and the Creation of the American Republic* (Glenview, Ill.: Scott, Foresman, 1990), p. 3, where he writes that JM "never lost . . . his faith, typical of the Enlightenment, in the capacity of reason to deal with human affairs."

peak. "The belief in a God All Powerful wise & good, is so essential to the moral order of the World & to the happiness of man," wrote Madison, "that arguments which enforce it cannot be drawn from too many sources." After pointing out the political utility of this type of God, Madison then addressed the philosophic difficulties associated with rationally proving first causes. Tactfully, he suggested to Beasley that "whatever effect may be produced on some minds by the more abstract train of ideas which you so strongly support, it will probably always be found that the course of human reasoning from the effect to the cause, 'from Nature to Nature's God,' Will be the more universal & more persuasive application."

Madison knew that this shift from effect to cause ultimately could not help from an empiricist's standpoint. More importantly, his own predilections ran against such abstract thinking: "The finiteness of the human understanding betrays itself on all subjects, but more especially when it contemplates such as involve infinity." Presented with the uncertainties of similar abstractions, the mind conceives of what pleases it, and refutes what displeases it, all to make sense of reality. For Madison, what pleased the mind was "an invisible cause possessing infinite power, wisdom & goodness": the alternative, a "universe, visibly destitute of those attributes," was unacceptable to his belief in a rational universe. He explained it thus:

> What may safely be said seems to be, that the infinity of time & space forces itself on our conception, a limitation of either being inconceivable; that the mind prefers at once the idea of a self-existing cause to that of an infinite series of cause & effect, which augments, instead of avoiding the difficulty; and that it finds more facility in assenting to the self-existence of an invisible cause possessing infinite power, wisdom & goodness, than to the self-existence of the universe, visibly destitute of those attributes, and which may be the effect of them.

Given Madison's commitment to reason and desire not to "get farther beyond my depth," he diplomatically closed his letter by acknowledging the limits of reason: "In this comparative facility of conception & belief, all philosophical Reasoning on the subject must perhaps terminate."[23] While questions in religion and theology interested Madison at different moments of his life, he preferred the security of the empirical world, where reason's utility appeared more evident.

The introduction to Madison's agriculture address establishes clearly his commitment to his particular Calvinistic-Lockean liberal frame of reference.[24] Humans are usually lazy and often unreasonable. Fortunately, reality has been constructed in such a manner that humans must labor if they are to survive. Nevertheless, if humans use their reason and exercise their will, they can extend the bounds of nature and thereby sustain and increase the population. To Madison, the lessons of human nature were self-evident. Although given the faculty of reason, humans—if offered the choice—preferred the short-term path of least resistance to their goals of immediate and easy gratification. If fear of the "savage tribes," or of an inadequate food supply, had not forced American settlers to employ agriculture, their natural inclinations would have led them back to a primitive existence where the knowledge of progress would eventually have disappeared. While this tendency always remained part of the human condition, Madison also viewed it as unreasonable: humans are rational, animals irrational. It may be significant that when Madison thought about the Indians in isolation from Europeans, he wrote of their living in "tribes"; and yet, when he compared them to Europeans and considered the threat their example presented to civilization, he worried about European "degeneration" and, at this point, described the tribes as "savage."

Although his fundamental point about human nature had been established, it was so central to his worldview that he took even more time to elaborate upon it. "The bent of human nature" prefers the earlier stages of human development. "The manufacturer readily exchanges the loom for the plough in opposition often to his own interest, as well as that of his country. The cultivator, in situations presenting an option, to the labors of the field, the more easy employment of rearing the herd. And as the game of the forest is ap-

23. JM to Frederick Beasley, 25 Nov. 1825, *WJM* 9:229–231. See Perry Miller, *Errand into the Wilderness* (Cambridge, Mass.: Belknap Press of Harvard University Press, 1956), pp. 53–56.
24. See Quentin Skinner, *The Foundations of Modern Political Thought* (Cambridge: Cambridge University Press, 1978), 2:239.

proached, the hunting life displays the force of its attractions."[25] So universal was this tendency to retreat that Madison rhetorically asked: "Where do we behold a march to the opposite direction? the hunter, becoming the herdsman; the latter a follower of the plough; and the last repairing to the manufactory or workshop." While reasoning about this selection pattern in human priorities, in a rare Rousseauian moment that perhaps expressed Madison's own enjoyment of leisure after decades of public service, he candidly acknowledged that there was much to be said "for the fascination of that personal independence which belongs to the uncivilized state, and such the disrelish and contempt of the monotonous labor of tillage, compared with the exciting occupations of the chase, or with the indolence enjoyed by those who subsist chiefly on the mere bounties of nature."[26]

Given Madison's view of human nature and social development, why humans ever created civilization becomes a question he cannot easily resolve. On the side of the simple past stood "personal independence," "exciting occupations," and "indolence enjoyed"; on the side of a rational future existed social stability, "monotonous labor," and the prospects of increased population. Unable to explain rationally why humans left the excitement, independence, and joys of the garden, Madison simply leaped to conjecture that "the first introduction of agriculture among a savage people appears, accordingly, never to have taken place without some extraordinary interposition." Agriculture, its use and abuse, is a useful yardstick by which to measure human progress and rationality.[27] So important for the progress of humanity was the revolution produced by agriculture that Madison claimed that agriculture must have been introduced into different societies by "some individual, whose singular endowments, and supernatural pretensions, had given him an ascendancy for the purpose. All these great reformers, in ancient times," Madison wrote, "were regarded as more than men, and ultimately worshipped as gods." Once knowledge of agriculture had been estab-

25. *Letters and Other Writings* 3:66.
26. Ibid.; to Richard Rush, 21 Apr. 1821, *WJM* 9:54, he wrote about "the natural love of indolence [being] overcome by avarice & vanity."
27. *Letters and Other Writings* 3:37; cf. Jean-Jacques Rousseau, "Origins of Inequality among Men," in *The First and Second Discourses*, ed. Roger Masters (New York: St. Martin's Press, 1964).

lished, in spite of human disinclination toward regimented work, social dynamics were initiated that made turning back too painful for too many. With agriculture securely in place, "the mouths fed by it increasing, and the supplies of nature decreasing, necessity becomes a spur to industry; which finds another spur in the advantages incident to the acquisition of property, in the civilized state." A Malthusian reality linked with a conception of property taken directly out of the pages of John Locke were additional "spurs" to human history.[28]

Madison's Calvinist assumption of a natural human antipathy to labor and preference for indolence combined with a Malthusian reality can be seen as well in his sometimes vehement critiques of the socialist Robert Owen and the "utopian" anarchist William Godwin. Writing to Nicholas Trist about Owen's experimental community at New Harmony, Madison ultimately had to rely on his Malthusian assumptions to dismiss Owen. He began his assault by discussing how the problems then plaguing Owen's Great Britain should have instructed him that "such diseases are, however, too deeply rooted in human society to admit of more than great palliatives." After explaining the reason why "every populous country is liable to contingencies that must distress a portion of its inhabitants," Madison criticized Owen directly: "Mr. Owen's remedy for these vicissitudes implies that labor will be relished without the ordinary impulses to it; that the love of equality will supersede the desire for distinction; and that the increasing leisure, from the improvements of machinery, will promote intellectual cultivation, moral enjoyment, and innocent amusements, without any of the vicious resorts, for the ennui of idleness."[29]

Clearly, Madison did not think most humans could enjoy labor. And even if they were inclined to desire leisure, the "ennui of idleness" presented social problems to be avoided. Indeed, Madison had previously shown his concern for the social consequences of the necessity of labor and the love of idleness when he offered the following comment to Thomas Hertell in 1809 on his "laudable," but ulti-

---

28. *Letters and Other Writings* 3:67; see John Locke, "On Property," *Second Treatise of Government*, ed. C. B. Macpherson (Indianapolis: Hackett, 1980), pp. 18–30.

29. JM to N. P. Trist, Apr. 1827, *Letters and Other Writings* 3:576.

mately doomed, project of "abolishing altogether the use of intoxicating, and even exhilarating drinks."

> A *compleat* suppression of every species of stimulating indulgence, if attainable at all, must be the work of peculiar difficulty, since it has to encounter not only the force of habit, but propensities in human nature. In every age and nation some exhilarating or exciting substance seems to have been sought for as a relief from the languor of idleness, or the fatigues of labor. In the rudest state of Society, whether in hot or cold climates, a passion for ardent spirits is in a manner universal. . . . And where all these sources of excitement have been unknown, or been totally prohibited by a religious faith, substitutes have been found in opium, in the nut of the betel, the root of the ginseng, or the leaf of the tobacco plant.[30]

When Solomon Southwick sent Madison a copy of an 1821 address announcing the opening of an "Apprentice's Library," Madison commented most favorably about the occasion. He noted that "this class of our youth is a valuable one, and its proportionate numbers must increase as our population thickens." He also observed that given their age, lack of parental guardianship, and urban residence, "where groups are readily formed, in which the example of a few may taint many, create snares into which their relaxations from labor too often betray them," the creation of libraries to occupy their idle minds was indeed a blessing.[31]

Madison's criticisms of William Godwin were even more strident

---

30. JM to Thomas Hertell, 20 Dec. 1809, *Letters and Other Writings* 2:461–462; see Douglass Adair, "James Madison's 'Autobiography'," *William and Mary Quarterly* 3d ser., 2 (Apr. 1945): 199–200, where JM recounts his unsuccessful 1777 candidacy for the Virginia legislature: "It was as there [England] the usage for the candidates to recommend themselves to the voters, not only by personal solicitation, but by the corrupting influence of spirituous liquors, and other treats, having a like tendency. Regarding these as equally inconsistent with the purity of moral and of republican principles; and anxious to promote, by his example, the proper reform, he trusted the new views of the subject which he hoped would prevail with the people." In subsequent elections, JM allowed his supporters to purchase the campaign liquor without his consent.

31. JM to Solomon Southwick, 21 Apr. 1821, *Letters and Other Writings* 3:216; see also JM to Dr. Jesse Terry, 30 Jan. 1822, *Letters and Other Writings* 3:258–259, where JM again endorsed a plan for free local libraries: "A tree of useful knowledge planted in every neighborhood would help to make a paradise, as that of forbidden use occasioned the loss of one."

than his criticisms of Owen. This might be explained because he had met Owen; or, perhaps it was because Godwin's 1820 *On Population; an Enquiry Concerning the Power of Increase in the Numbers of Mankind, being an Answer to Mr. Malthus's Essay on the Subject* constituted a direct challenge to Malthus, and therein, to Madison's worldview. To Edward Everett he wrote that "the theory of Mr. Godwin, if it deserves the name, is answered by the barefaced errors both of fact and of inference which meet the eye on every page."[32] Two years earlier, in an 1821 letter to Richard Rush, Madison had compiled a detailed list of errors the "dogmatic" Godwin committed. While Madison suspected that "in this country the fallacies of the Author will be smiled at," he concluded his letter by telling Rush that "if the heretical Work should attract conversations in which you may be involved, some of the facts, which you are saved the trouble of hunting up [thanks to Madison's letter], may rebut misstatements from misinformed friends or illiberal opponents of our Country."[33] Both Owen and Godwin endorsed philosophic notions that directly contradicted Madison's. And insofar as their efforts might influence Americans, Madison tried to refute the more threatening propositions of their philosophies, especially those concerning human nature.

Madison briefly interrupted the presentation of his concept of humans and paused to explore nature and its capacity to support life. He began this portion of the address by noting a certain "economy of nature," what today might be called an eco-logic, in the relationships among animals, humans, plants, and the environment that requires a long run notion of order and balance if any are to live.[34] In a draft essay on "Natural Order," which Madison drew upon for his 1791 "Population and Emigration" article in the *National Gazette*, he wrote:

> The planetary system, the greatest portion of the Universe, as yet brought under human observation, is regulated by fixed

32. JM to Edward Everett, 26 Nov. 1823, *WJM* 9:170.

33. JM to Richard Rush, 21 Apr. 1821, *WJM* 9:45–55; in a 1 May 1822, *Letters and Other Writings* 3:264, letter to the same person, Madison referred to "the hollow theory of Mr. Godwin, and that the late census here must give the *coup de grace* to his Book, if it should not have previously died a natural death." See Jefferson's more favorable view of Godwin in his letter to Bishop James Madison, 31 Jan. 1800, *The Works of Thomas Jefferson*, ed. Paul Leicester Ford, 12 vols. (New York: Knickerbocker Press, 1904), 9:108.

34. *Letters and Other Writings* 3:70–72.

laws, and presents most demonstrably, a scene of order and proportion.

From analogy we conclude that the whole universe, if it were equally understood, would exhibit equal proofs of a like arrangement.

The general aspect of the earth leads us to remark the same plan of nature. Order and symmetry equally appear in the great outlines and in the most minute features of it.[35]

In his 1821 agriculture address, he explained that "we can scarcely be warranted in supposing that all the productive powers of the surface can be made subservient to the use of man." He drew this conclusion from observation as well as common sense.

On comparing the vast profusion and multiplicity of beings with the few grains and grasses, the few herbs and roots, and the few fowls and quadrupeds, which make up the short list adapted to the wants of man, it is difficult to believe that it lies with him so to remodel the work of nature as it would be remodelled, by a destruction not only of individuals, but of entire species; and not only of a few species, but of every species, with the very few exceptions which he might spare for his own accommodation.[36]

If this argument against excessive "remodelling" did not persuade his audience, Madison offered the more pragmatic one that if all the earth was employed for the consumption of humans alone, "so great an innovation might be found, in this respect, not to accord with the order and economy of nature." His point—and it is interesting to think about why, as a Protestant liberal, he might be concerned about this—was that even if humans wanted, and had the capacity, to exploit the entire earth, nature would not permit it.[37] Perhaps on

35. "Preliminary Draft of an Essay on Natural Order," ca. 10 Nov. 1791, *PJM* 14:100; Madison continues his logic and notes that he believes even where there appears to be "less regularity" in nature, "it may reasonably be ascribed to the imperfect insight to which her work is subjected."

36. *Letters and Other Writings* 3:68.

37. See "Natural Order," *PJM* 14:101-102: "Such being the prerogatives of man, at once capable of breaking in on the law of proportion established among the other inhabitants of the globe, and not himself confined like them, to such a law; what is to restrain him from multiplying his race to any given number whatever? At least he must be able by extirpating every useless production of na-

some level Madison believed that the human propensities toward excessive appropriation were so strong that, as he implied, such automatic checks of this extreme, hypothetical situation were both necessary and good: "May it not be concluded from the admirable arrangement and beautiful feature in the economy of nature, that if the whole class of animals were extinguished, the use of the atmosphere by the vegetable class alone would exhaust it of its life-supporting power? that, in like manner, if the whole class of vegetables were extinguished, the use of it by the animal class alone would deprive it of its fitness for their support?"

Madison viewed the ecological system as a "compound body." While there was a hierarchical structure to this body, with "animals, including man" as "the most important part of the terrestrial creation"—and the reason for which the lesser parts had been created—both "the visible and invisible" parts of nature contributed to the entire system. If, by implication, some apparently insignificant portion of the system would be destroyed, "the order and economy of nature" would be altered at considerable human costs.[38] A quarter century earlier, he had stated it thus: "It is not probable that nature, after covering the earth with so great a variety of animal & vegitable inhabitants, and establishing among them so systematic a proportion, could permit one favorite offspring, by destroy[in]g every other, to render vain all her wise arrangements and contrivances."[39]

Nevertheless, surplus population always seemed to concern Madison, and it was a subject to which he returned. He acknowledged the "known tendency in all organized beings to multiply beyond the degree necessary to keep up their actual numbers." He recognized the wisdom of nature in providing automatic checks against this phenomenon: "Nature has been equally provident in guarding against an excessive multiplication of any one species which might too far encroach on others, by subjecting each, when duly multiplying itself, to be arrested in its progress by the effect of the multiplication—1, in producing a deficiency of food; and where that may not happen, 2, in producing a state of the atmo-

---

ture to convert the whole productive power of the earth into a supply of those particular plants & animals which serve his own purpose; and to increase his race as far as these will administer subsistence to it. Plausible as this inference may appear, it may be opposed by the following considerations."
38. *Letters and Other Writings* 3:70-71.
39. "Natural Order," *PJM* 14:102.

sphere unfavorable to life and health." In light of Madison's own tendencies toward hypochondria, his claim about overcrowding seems understandable. He argued that "all animals as well as plants sicken and die in a state too much crowded." More to his point, he wrote that "to the same laws mankind are equally subject."

Madison presented historic evidence to support his position. "It was the vitiated air alone," he claimed, "which put out human life in the crowded hole of calcutta." Nor was Calcutta an isolated incident: the effects of overcrowding appeared universal. "In all confined situations, from the dungeon to the crowded workhouses, and from these to the compact population of overgrown cities, the atmosphere becomes, in corresponding degrees, unfitted by reiterated use, for sustaining human life and health." Nature, therefore, has not only the need for balance and moderation but also contains limits beyond which it cannot sustain human life: "And were the whole habitable earth covered with a dense population, wasteful maladies might be looked for, that would thin the numbers into a healthy proportion."[40] While definite upper limits to growth existed in Madison's view, the earth remained a long way from reaching such an unsustainable position. Madison even hazarded a guess that if scientific agricultural methods were employed, in combination with certain environmental policies he clearly refused to endorse—such as banishing from existence all animals that consumed food humans could use—then "the maximum of population on earth . . . would be more than a hundred individuals for every one now upon it."[41] But given the "beautiful . . . economy of nature," he had few doubts that this situation would correct itself.

Having presented his audience with his thoughts on human progress and the parameters of nature, Madison returned once more to conclude his discussion of human nature and build his case for scientific agriculture and rational planning. While animals other than Homo sapiens can be called "organized," man was "essentially distinguished" from other creatures not by physical differences but "by the intellectual and moral powers with which he is endowed." What Madison initially called "intellectual and moral powers" he further refined to the fact that humans "possess a reason and a will" that en-

40. *Letters and Other Writings* 3:72–73; he also implied that *all* life could perish under certain conditions of imbalance.
41. Ibid., 3:73.

abled them to develop "beyond the spontaneous supplies of nature" through the rational use of the other parts of the "terrestrial system." Although he explicitly listed morality as a species-specific characteristic of humanity, it was a word and a topic that completely vanished from Madison's subsequent discussion: it seemed to play no role in humanity's relationship to the environment or in the issues confronting agriculture and a sustainable growth in population.[42]

History, in the form of increasing numbers of plants and animals, supported Madison's contention that species other than humans had the tendency "to multiply beyond the degree necessary to keep up their actual numbers."[43] Madison therefore concluded that

> these views of the subject seem to authorize the conclusion that although there is a proportion between the animal and vegetable classes of beings on our globe, and between the species in each class, with respect to which nature does not permit such a change as would result from a destruction of the animals and vegetables not used by man; and a multiplication of the human race, and of the several species of animals and vegetables used by it, sufficient to fill up the void; yet that there is a degree of change which the peculiar faculties of man enable him to make, and by making which his fund of subsistence and his number may be augmented; there being at the same time, whenever his numbers, and the exchange, exceed the admitted degree, a tendency in that excess to correct itself.

While humans could expand their numbers through rational agricultural and economic measures, should they overstep the natural limits, nature had "a tendency in that excess to correct itself."[44]

42. Ibid., 3:74; see "Population and Emigration," *PJM* 14:117; and "Natural Order," *PJM* 14:101, where he is silent on human morality and claims that "man . . . is distinguished from all [other species] by two remarkable characters: *First,* he is a prey to no other animals. *Second,* he is not limited to the spontaneous supplies of food administered by nature, but can by his reason and his hands multiply them as he pleases."

43. *Letters and Other Writings* 3:72; see "Population and Emigration," *PJM* 14:117, where he wrote: "Both in the vegetable and animal kingdoms, every species derives from nature, a reproductive faculty beyond the demand for merely keeping up its stock: the seed of a single plant is sufficient to multiply it one hundred or a thousand fold. The animal offspring is never limited to the number of its parents."

44. *Letters and Other Writings* 3:75–76.

Although the issue of emigration as a partial solution to overpopulation was not raised in Madison's address to Virginia farmers, it was the central concern of his 1791 *National Gazette* article "Population and Emigration." Even then, a Malthusian frame of reference supplied the background logic for Madison's discussion of solutions to the "redundancy of population" problem. "What becomes of the surplus of human life?" Madison asked. He responded: "It is either, 1st. destroyed by infanticide, as among the Chinese and Lacedemonians; or 2d. it is stifled or starved, as among other nations whose population is commensurate to its food; or 3d. it is consumed by wars and endemic diseases; or 4th. it overflows, by emigration, to places where a surplus of food is attainable."[45] The first three solutions were unacceptable so long as the fourth option remained available. As a result, Madison set out to establish how emigration benefited all parties involved, both the home country and the colony. He began to construct his argument on the candid observation that "every country, whose population is full, may annually spare a portion of its inhabitants, like a hive of bees its swarm, without any diminution of its number: nay, a certain portion must, necessarily, be either spared, or destroyed, or kept out of existence."[46]

Madison demonstrated that experience taught how colonization could "spare" a portion of the population, to the benefit of all, and that if this method was not taken advantage of, the "internal resources of life" would "restore" the overpopulated nation to an appropriate level.[47] In light of Madison's view of the human tendency to prefer ease, it seemed natural for him to observe further that "the course of emigrations [was] always, from places where living is more difficult, to places where it is less difficult." It may be interesting to note that, on this occasion, Madison observed a connection between population and morality, with emigration proving to be a positive influence:

> It may not be superfluous to add, that freedom of emigration is favorable to morals. A great proportion of the vices which distinguish crouded from thin settlements, are known to have their rise in the facility of illicit intercourse between the sexes, on

45. *PJM* 14:117.
46. Ibid., 14:118.
47. Ibid.

one hand, and the difficulty of maintaining a family, on the other. Provide an outlet for the surplus of population, and marriages will increase in proportion. Every four or five emigrants will be the fruit of a legitimate union which would not otherwise have taken place.[48]

Before making his six suggestions to improve agriculture in Virginia, Madison discussed one additional factor that benefited humanity in its attempts at development—the invention of "political and social institutions" that allowed the free flowering of human potential. Although the richness of the Virginia environment certainly contributed to its progressive state of development, Madison attributed a measure of credit to "the fertile activity of a free people, and the benign influence of a responsible Government." And yet, Virginia would be better off if it devoted more energy to "the study and practice of [agriculture's] true principles." The appropriate mechanisms to initiate these studies, Madison suggested, were "patriotic societies," like the one he was currently addressing.[49]

Madison finished his talk by briefly discussing "some of the most prevalent errors in our husbandry." From crop rotation, ploughing techniques, and manure usage, to irrigation, rearing of cattle, and excessive destruction of timber and firewood, Madison conveyed his sense of the state of agriculture in Virginia. Even when discussing specifically agricultural themes, Madison's method of analysis remained consistent: Reason (and empirical evidence) was the best guide to behavior, often requiring that habit, custom, and past practice be abandoned. Historical study, furthermore, may supply supportive evidence for what would, or would not, work under identical conditions, but reason—not tradition—should guide the future.[50] A "more rational management" of Virginia farms, using the latest scientific knowledge and technological innovations in fertilizer, ploughing techniques, and crop rotation, would increase the productivity of the land; and, to Madison's mind, "every acre made by an improved management to produce as much as two acres, is, in effect, the addition of a new acre."[51]

48. Ibid., 14:121.
49. *Letters and Other Writings* 3:76–77.
50. Ibid., 3:77–94.
51. Ibid., 3:79, 86.

Of all the errors then being made in Virginia, Madison's presentation of ''the injudicious and excessive destruction of timber and firewood'' was the most instructive. Noting the fundamental economic irrationality of the farmers' exploitation of trees, ''It seems never to have occurred that the fund was not inexhaustible, and that a crop of trees could not be raised as quickly as one of wheat or corn.'' His use of the phrases ''crop of trees'' and ''crop of wood'' revealed the economic reality behind his concerns; aesthetic considerations were, at most, of secondary importance, and he gave no hint that either trees or forests had meaning or utility in and of themselves.[52]

Nevertheless, Madison deftly employed this case study as another example of reason demanding an end to tradition. ''Here again,'' he concluded, ''we are presented with a proof of the continuance of a practice for which the reasons have ceased.'' The original ''reason'' for deforestation had been that the trees presented ''the great obstacle to . . . settlement and cultivation.'' The simple solution ''was, of course, to destroy the trees.'' Madison then offered an interesting psychological insight into this behavior: ''It would seem that they contracted and transmitted an antipathy to them; for the trees were not even spared around the dwellings, where the shade would have been a comfort, and their beauty an ornament; and it is of late years only that these advantages have been attended to.'' The original ancestors allowed their ''antipathy,'' their passion, to cloud their judgment (reason) and this ''injudicious'' practice became ever more costly over time. ''In fact,'' explained Madison, ''such has been the inconsiderate and indiscriminate use of the axe, that this country is beginning to feel the calamity as much as some of the old countries of Europe; and it will soon be forced to understand the difficulty of curing it.''[53]

Interesting as his agricultural advice may have been to Virginians, in terms of political theory it was his cool and sober evaluation of the human condition that is of most interest here. Even though humans possess rationality and free will, at least in the world of politi-

52. Ibid., 3:93–94.
53. Ibid. For a contemporaneous but contrasting view of the value of forests and trees, see Alexis de Tocqueville's ''Fortnight in the Wilderness'' in *Tocqueville and Beaumont in America*, ed. George Wilson Pierson (New York: Oxford University Press, 1938). If Tocqueville's sketch of the frontier is accurate, Madison marched right in step with the pioneer spirit of the time.

cal œconomy, their inclination toward boredom and sloth led them to prefer the least amount of civilization still consistent with appropriate levels of happiness. Fortunately, nature had so arranged things that once agriculture had been introduced into society, an irreversible dynamic forced humanity to develop itself almost in spite of its inclination to the contrary. Nevertheless, this wish to retreat remained part of human desires, even after it had been (temporarily) conquered. Surplus population and the parsimony of nature provide additional difficulties that wise political thinkers could not ignore. And finally, the order and proportion that Madison (through Newton) discovered in nature, maintained by fixed laws and automatic checks, curiously mirrored the insights he had gained from his study of the science of politics.[54] It now seems appropriate, therefore, to turn to an examination of Madison's more politically conscious public writings to fill out our understanding of his views of humanity and political reality.

54. For example, see JM's speech of 8 June 1787, Farrand, *Records* 1:165: "In a word, to recur to the illustrations borrowed from the planetary System, This prerogative of the General Govt. is the great pervading principle that must control the centrifugal tendency of the States; which, without it, will continually fly out of their proper orbits and destroy the order & harmony of the political system."

3 / Madisonian Humanity: The Timid Individual and Passionate Groups

> Place three individuals in a situation wherein the interest of each depends on the voice of the others, and give to two of them an interest opposed to the rights of the third? Will the latter be secure? The prudence of every man would shun the danger. The rules & forms of justice suppose & guard against it. Will two thousand in a like situation be less likely to encroach on the rights of one thousand?[1]
>
> —Madison

What remains to complete Madison's concept of humanity can be gleaned from an extended discussion of his public political writings. While many issues central to political theory can be found in his private letters, the answer to the question—what is the nature of man?—seems to be taken for granted in his correspondence. Before proceeding to his plentiful comments on human nature in *The Federalist,* and to a lesser extent in the *National Gazette* essays, it is important to remember that both sets of newspaper expositions were politically motivated and designed to have a direct impact on public opinion.

The issue of immediate concern in the former writings was the successful ratification of the Constitution; Madison feared anarchy,

---

1. "Vices of the Political System of the United States," Apr. 1787, *The Papers of James Madison,* ed. William T. Hutchinson et al., 17 vols. (Chicago and Charlottesville: University of Chicago Press and University of Virginia Press, 1962–), 9:356 (hereafter cited as *PJM*). Cf. Jefferson's sharply contrasting position: "I know but one code of morality for men whether acting singly or collectively. He who says I will be a rogue when I act in company with a hundred others but an honest man when I act alone, will be believed in the former assertion but not in the latter. . . . If the morality of one man produces a just line of conduct in him, acting individually, why should not the morality of one hundred men produce a just line of conduct in them acting together?" Thomas Jefferson to JM, 28 Aug. 1789, *The Works of Thomas Jefferson,* ed. Paul Leicester Ford, 12 vols. (New York: Knickerbocker Press, 1904), 5:492.

actual and potential, in some of the states because of their weak, overly democratic governments.[2] In the latter essays, his fear shifted and concerned an executive branch and a Federalist party that seemed out of control; he moved to marshal those "auxiliary precautions" he had helped build into the political system to check an overly energetic government that, from his perspective, was teetering on the edge of tyranny. In spite of these legitimate political concerns, at least from Madison's perspective, many of his blunt remarks on human nature in *The Federalist* may strike twentieth-century readers, conditioned to receive their political thought through a television camera lens darkly, as neither diplomatic nor politically astute. Be that as it may, Madison's private writings disclose an even more pessimistic and unflattering analysis of human nature and government than his public works.[3] This divergence should be expected in all modern political rhetoric because, as Douglass Adair points out in reference to *The Federalist*, "there is a certain disadvantage in making derogatory remarks to a majority that must be persuaded to adopt your arguments."[4]

The political essays, then, provide a rich, if slightly less forthright, source of information on Madison's view of people. Even though a concept of humanity underpins every political theory, Madison

2. See Forrest McDonald, *Novus Ordo Seclorum: The Intellectual Origins of the Constitution* (Lawrence: University Press of Kansas, 1985), pp. 143–144, who suggests that there was little cause for alarm: "Objectively, the first decade of the history of the United States was a whopping success. The greatest achievement, of course, was the winning of independence, but there was more. Despite certain postwar economic dislocations, most Americans were prospering. . . . The vast majority of people would probably have agreed that they had no need for a stronger union. . . . But none of that mattered to many Americans who were concerned about the nation's honor, or were concerned that the nation be great, or were concerned lest the experiment in republicanism should fail. From those perspectives, by the winter of 1786–1787, the American republic was in peril, and the institutional safeguards for liberty and property that had been erected had proved inadequate."

3. See Gordon Wood, *The Creation of the American Republic, 1776–1787* (Chapel Hill: University of North Carolina Press, 1969), p. 562, where he argues: "Considering the Federalist [of whom Publius was one] desire for high-toned government filled with better sorts of people, there is something decidedly disingenuous about the democratic radicalism of their arguments. . . . In effect they appropriated and exploited the language that most rightfully belonged to their opponents. The result was the beginning of a hiatus in American politics between ideology and motives that was never again closed."

4. Douglass Adair, *Fame and the Founding Fathers: Essays by Douglass Adair,* ed. H. Trevor Colbourn (New York: W. W. Norton, 1974), p. 102.

never addressed the issue in a sustained and systematic manner. Once again, scholars have to piece together his numerous and separate sentences, paragraphs, and thoughts on this topic to create a theoretically complete conception. To comprehend humans through Madison's mind's eye, it may be helpful to make a few analytic distinctions: This chapter will begin by looking at his sparse comments on the individual *qua* individual, the human agent in isolation, in a nonpolitical context. From there, it discusses how Madison believed the individual relates to other individuals in a political context. Last, it moves to examine his abundant thoughts on group behavior: how factions, interests, sects, classes, and parties fit into his conception of humanity. The analytic distinction between an individual, individuals, and groups is but one of the distinguishing categories of people Madison appears to have drawn. It seems essential, furthermore, to follow Madison's lead and differentiate between groups based on passion and groups based on reason. And, in light of the recent and influential scholarship of the civic humanist historians, it becomes necessary to examine, briefly at this point, Madison's thoughts on virtue, self-interest, and citizenship, with a fuller discussion of these issues reserved for chapter 6, on Madisonian government.

Madison maintained three fundamental divisions in his concept of humanity. First, there exists an essential division between the people and their rulers—which is not to suggest that the individual's place in society was determined by birth or that either the rulers or the ruled could be trusted. Second, when joining in the actions of a faction, the individual undergoes a profound alteration where the more antisocial tendencies come to the surface and find group support for unreasonable behavior. And finally, these factions can be separated into two broad categories, one based on reason and one on passion: the former, in spite of its intentions, allows republican government to exist; the latter creates unpredictable but potentially fatal difficulties that the wise state builder must systematically temper and control since they cannot be eliminated.

This last division reflects the basic and ultimately unresolvable conflict Madison perceived in the individual: though endowed with the capacity to reason, the individual was no less—indeed, perhaps more (or, more so when in the company of like-minded individuals)—a creature of passion.[5] Where David Hume drew a distinction between the "calm" and the "violent" passions, Madison did not. While reason remained humanity's best hope for the future, its influence was limited by language, perception, and comprehension; it was, moreover, continually threatened and thwarted by passion.[6] Madison's concept of humanity, therefore, fits squarely into the liberal tradition of Thomas Hobbes and John Locke, two theorists who viewed man as a product of civil society, as an infinitely self-interested and power-acquisitive creature. Reason, experience, and political science must be employed to develop appropriate social and political structures to create social stability, but individuals will not develop beyond what they already are—competitive actors in civil society. Put differently, Madisonian man remains a static creature who could not be trusted beyond his capacity to look out for his own self-interest. And yet, the fact that the individual can be relied upon to do precisely this permits stability to be maintained and self-government to work.[7] From Madison's view of the individual, democracy was a fool's illusion; in the long run, little could be done, beyond playing for time, to forestall the decline or to improve the human condition.

Madison's writings, public as well as private, usually have a practical air about them. It should not be surprising to find but a handful of references to the individual in complete isolation: most of Madison's insights are about man in a political context, an individual

5. See Sheldon Wolin, *Politics and Vision: Continuity and Innovation in Western Political Thought* (Boston: Little, Brown & Company, 1960), p. 332: "It is necessary to rid our thinking of the caricature of liberal man as a reasoning machine. Rather, liberal writers . . . emphasized repeatedly that man was a creature of strong passions."

6. David Hume, *A Treatise of Human Nature*, in Henry Aiken, ed., *Hume's Moral and Political Philosophy* (New York: Hafner Publishing Company, 1972), p. 27; and on p. 25: "We speak not strictly philosophically when we talk of the combat of passion and reason. Reason is, and ought only to be, the slave of the passions, and can never pretend to any other office than to serve and obey them."

7. Rousseau and Jefferson, on the other hand, conceived of the individual as an inherently social being. Humans have the possibility of ontological development and, under the appropriate social and political conditions, might knowingly participate in that process. Given their contrasting model of humanity, both believed that mass participatory democracy was the sole form of government consistent with human dignity and virtue. These ideas will be discussed in chapter 7.

dealing with other individuals. An unusual instance where Madison wrote about the individual outside a political context occurred briefly in his seminal (1787) "Vices of the Political System of the United States."[8]

Months before the commercial convention at Annapolis, Madison concluded that the Articles of Confederation were worthless and had to be, at the very least, substantially altered. Consequently, he spent considerable time studying political history with an eye to what would be useful to the American situation; in the spring of 1786 he compiled his "Notes on Ancient and Modern Confederacies" and a year later, in the spring of 1787, outlined his "Vices of the Political System." His studies and notes help to substantiate the claim that of all the delegates at the Constitutional Convention, Madison came to the event the best prepared. These two collections of personal notes, originally intended for his eyes only, were deftly employed by Madison in his speeches at Philadelphia and Richmond as well as in his contributions to *The Federalist*. The two documents are, however, quite different in style and tone: the former, fragmentary and incomplete, presents nearly insurmountable interpretative problems; the latter, a more polished albeit uncompleted essay, reveals Madison's early insights and dismal diagnosis of the political problems overwhelming the Confederation.

In his thoughts on the penultimate vice, "Injustice of the laws of States," Madison cut to the heart of his serious and growing reservations toward republicanism: "If the multiplicity and mutability of laws prove a want of wisdom, their injustice betrays a defect still more alarming: more alarming not merely because it is a greater evil in itself, but because it brings more into question the fundamental principle of republican Government, that the majority who rule in such Governments, are the safest Guardians both of public Good and of private rights." To resolve this question he proceeded to inquire into the causes of this "evil" by looking for possible human defects; he examines, therefore, the "Representative bodies" and "the people themselves."[9]

Madison asked himself what, under a republican government, could possibly restrain a majority "from unjust violations of the

8. Chapter 6, on Madison's theory of an "ideal" government, will present a more detailed discussion of his "Vices" essay.

9. *PJM* 9:354.

rights and interests of the minority, or of individuals?'' This constituted perhaps the fundamental political question for Madison, at
least in the late 1780s and throughout much of the 1790s. With regard
to self-restraints on the people themselves, Madison could conceive
of ''three motives only'': (1) ''a prudent regard to their own good as
involved in the general and permanent good of the Community''; (2)
''respect for character''; and (3) ''Religion.''[10] About the first of these
motives, he remarked that it ''is found by experience to be too often
unheeded.'' Moreover, ''It is too often forgotten, by nations as well
as individuals that honesty is the best policy.'' While ''respect for
character,'' the second motive, ''may be in individuals, it is considered as very insufficient to restrain them from injustice. In a multitude its efficacy is diminished in proportion to the number which is
to share the praise or the blame.''[11] Here we see an early formulation
of Madison's foundational belief, repeated throughout *The Federalist*, that groups tend to magnify and encourage the worst aspects of
individual behavior.[12]

By ''respect for character,'' Madison may be interpreted in two different ways, neither of which will restrain individuals from doing
harm. The first meaning would be that of individual self-respect, or
regard for one's personal reputation. Given the context of the phrase,
however, Madison may have meant the respect for another, in some
meaningful sense, superior individual(s). In late twentieth-century
America, where the myth of liberal equality often clouds the public
mind, respect for character, or following the example of one's bet-

10. Ibid., 9:355–356. Notice that Madison's reasoning with regard to the first
motive is that of liberal prudence, not a classical sense that an individual ought
to do good, or behave justly, because justice is its own reward.

11. Ibid., 9:355. While Jefferson was president and JM was secretary of state, in
response to some ''venal suggestions emanating from the French functionaries,'' JM wrote: ''It is impossible that the destinies of any Nation, more than
of an individual, can be injured by an adherence to the maxims of virtue. To suppose it would be to arraign the justice of Heaven, and the order of nature''; JM to
John Armstrong, 6 June 1805, in Gaillard Hunt, ed., *The Writings of James Madison*, 9 vols. (New York: G. P. Putnam's Sons, 1900–1910), 7:183 (hereafter cited as
WJM).

12. See Isaac Kramnick, ed., *The Federalist Papers* (New York: Viking Penguin, 1987), 10:126: ''If the impulse and the opportunity be suffered to coincide,
we well know that neither moral nor religious motives can be relied on as an adequate control. They are not found to be such on the injustice and violence of
individuals, and lose their efficacy in proportion to the number combined together, that is, in proportion as their efficacy becomes needful.'' See also *Federalist* 49:314; 51:322; and 55:336.

ter(s), sounds like an odd notion; and yet, in Madison's day, this idea constituted the norm. Gordon Wood explains that "despite the fact that most of colonial society was vertically organized, there was one great horizontal division that cut through it . . . between extraordinary and ordinary people, gentlemen and commoners."[13] Madison certainly accepted this natural division (based on merit rather than birth), felt no need whatsoever to justify this perspective, and assumed that respect for character, or deference, could not be counted on by itself to stop a majority composed of "ordinary people."[14] His notion of representation as a filtering device, however, clearly indicates his acceptance of this idea as part of his overall plan to restrain majorities. After all, an electoral district of no fewer than thirty thousand voters ensured an elite ruling body preferably made up of gentlemen. This class bias can be seen throughout his writings. Its occurrence was usually implicit—which is how it should be—since Madison assumed the bias to be true and universally accepted. In "Vices" he simply wrote: "Individuals of extended views, and of national pride . . . will never be followed by the multitude," as recent efforts of "an ordinary citizen or even an assembly-man of R. Island" had taught him.[15]

Finally, concerning the third motive of religion, he asked: "Will Religion the only remaining motive be a sufficient restraint? It is not pretended to be such on men individually considered. Will its effect be greater on them considered in an aggregate view? quite the reverse." Finding religion to produce anything but a restraining or calming effect on groups of humans, Madison then presented the

13. Gordon Wood, *The Radicalism of the American Revolution* (New York: Alfred A. Knopf, 1992), p. 24; on p. 27 he writes that "gentlemen and commoners had different psyches, different makeups. . . . [The commoners] had, said Gouverneur Morris, 'no morals but their interests.' "

14. Richard R. Beeman, "Deference, Republicanism, and the Emergence of Popular Politics in Eighteenth-Century America," *William and Mary Quarterly* 49:3 (July 1992): 401–430.

15. *PJM* 9:355; see for example JM to Thomas Jefferson, 19 Feb. 1788, *PJM* 10:519, where, commenting on the small majority that voted for ratification in Massachusetts, JM wrote: "The prevailing party comprised however all the men of abilities, of property, and of influence. In the opposite multitude there was not a single character capable of uniting their wills or directing their measures. It was made up partly of deputies from . . . Maine . . . partly of men who had espoused the disaffection of Shay's; and partly of ignorant and jealous men, who had been taught or had fancied that the Convention at Philada. had entered into a conspiracy against the liberties of the people at large, in order to erect an aristocracy for the rich the *well-born*, and the men of Education" (JM's emphasis).

first of five examples of individual behavior when the person acted alone, in the "closet." In "Vices," as well as in a subsequent 1787 letter to Jefferson, he wrote: "The conduct of every popular assembly acting on oath, the strongest of religious Ties, proves that individuals join without remorse in acts, against which their consciences would revolt if proposed to them under the like sanction, separately in their closets."[16] It appears, then, that a person's conscience would indeed operate correctly as long as the individual stood alone. But in the "closet," would his conscience merely "revolt?" Or would it restrain his behavior as well? As long as the individual remained in isolation, from whom would he have to be restrained? Madison never raised these questions. And yet, he assumed that as soon as the individual left isolation, the presence of other like-minded souls would stir the person's passion, and the group would probably try to override reason and justice.[17] He noted, in addition, that "when indeed Religion is kindled into enthusiasm, its force like that of other passions, is increased by the sympathy of a multitude."

Religion kindled into enthusiasm spelled political trouble to Madison; hence, it too must be controlled. Even where religion existed "in its coolest state," it "is not infallible, [and] it may become a motive to oppression as well as a restraint from injustice."[18] Founded on faith and not subject to reason, religion is unpredictable—even when "cool" it has only a coin-toss chance of being right. Its unpredictability requires that the wise legislator effectively deal with its passionate tendencies: first, by banishing it from the political arena; second, by endorsing religious freedom for all citizens, thereby encouraging religion to flourish in civil society where multiple sects

16. *PJM* 9:356; JM to Thomas Jefferson, 24 Oct. 1787, *PJM* 10:213; in the letter JM shares his insights from "Vices" with Jefferson and repeated verbatim this passage.

17. This example maybe even more telling than it appears at first blush. The first sentence, on religious restraint, applied to humans in general and stated: "It is not pretended to be such on men individually considered." In the second instance discussed above and in seeming contradiction, JM then argued that an individual from a "popular assembly" might find the suggestion of some inappropriate action "revolting" if he was in his closet. Given Madison's view of ordinary humans, and his reliance on elections as filtering devices of the popular will, this passage suggests that JM thought only those "superior" individuals elected to some office might be constrained by conscience when in their closet.

18. *PJM* 9:356.

can counteract one another, diminishing the negative effects of each and securing the social peace. The ultimate politics of this artful orchestration are predestined: a nation of religious freedom and toleration (for believers) in the private arena combined with a governmental system where religion (and other passionate concerns) plays no direct political role at all.[19] This strategy will be covered in greater detail in a later chapter. For now, it seems helpful to look at three other instances of Madison's use of the closet metaphor taken from *The Federalist*.

The collection of celebrated essays known as *The Federalist* is one of the most remarkable accomplishments in the history of political thought. Published between 17 October 1787 and 28 May 1787, these eighty-five papers, according to Madison, "were first meant for the important and doubtful state of New York and signed a 'Citizen of New York'—afterwards meant for all the States under 'Publius'." The essays were the brainchild of Alexander Hamilton, who conceived of them as a way to secure adoption of the proposed constitution, even though he, like Madison, was less than enthusiastic about the final document.[20] The original plan for the papers appears to have called for John Jay, William Duer, and Gouverneur Morris to join Hamilton in writing them. Morris refused; Duer's essays were rejected; and due to illness, Jay contributed a mere five. Hamilton did not approach Madison until the middle of November, immediately upon Madison's return from Philadelphia. Wasting no time, Madison sent the first seven papers to George Washington. After characterizing them as an "antidote" to "the views of a party in Virginia" about which he had heard rumors, Madison asked Washington if he would place the papers "into the hand of some of your confidential correspondents at Richmond who would have them reprinted there." Madison confided, "I will not conceal *from you* that I am likely to have such *a degree* of connection with the publication here, as to afford a restraint of delicacy from interesting myself directly in

19. See Daniel Boorstin, *The Genius of American Politics* (Chicago: University of Chicago Press, 1953), passim; and Louis Hartz, *The Liberal Tradition in America* (New York: Harcourt, Brace, & Company, 1955), chapter 1.

20. Douglass Adair, "James Madison's 'Autobiography,'" *William and Mary Quarterly* 3d ser., 2 (Apr. 1945): 202; see JM to Thomas Jefferson, 8 Feb. 1825, *WJM* 9:219.

the republication elsewhere."[21] Although Madison professed his concern of "delicacy" to Washington, the incident demonstrated that his primary consideration was the appearance, rather than the reality, of ethics. Given the ends at stake, Madison easily rationalized his actions to secure ratification.

At the beginning of the collaboration, "the papers were shown by the writers to each other before going to press." This practice proved "inconvenient" and had to be discontinued.[22] Jay was incapacitated, Hamilton was busy with his law practice, but Madison was relatively free; he proved to be an indispensable partner to Hamilton. Armed with his "Notes on Ancient and Modern Confederacies" and his "Vices of the Political System," Madison wrote twenty-nine of the essays, including some of the most significant ones.[23] The bulk of his contributions, *Federalist* 37 to 58, 62, and 63, consisted of a defense of the Constitution as being in conformity with the principles of republican government; they were published between 11 January and 1 March 1788. Given the cogency of the arguments and the comprehensiveness of the presentation—all generated under the pressures of conditions where there was "seldom time for even a perusal of the pieces by any but the writer before they were wanted at the press"—Madison's (and Hamilton's) contributions to *The Federalist*

21. JM to George Washington, 18 Nov. 1787, *PJM* 10:254; JM's emphasis. It is noteworthy that JM did not inform Jefferson about his collaboration with Hamilton until 10 Aug. 1788; by then, Jefferson already knew about it from other sources. When JM informed Jefferson, ratification had been secured and the entire series of papers had been published. Furthermore, JM's letter indicates he had little choice but to tell Jefferson of his involvement. "Col. Carrington tells me he has sent you the first volume of the federalist, and adds the 2d. by this conveyance," wrote JM. Then, using the cipher he and Jefferson employed to ensure secrecy, he awkwardly confessed: "I believe I never have yet mentioned to you that publication. It was undertaken last fall by Jay[,] Hamilton and myself. The proposal came from the two former." Almost apologetically, he ended on the note that "though carried in concert the writers are not mutually answerable for all the ideas of each other there being seldom time for even a perusal of the pieces by any but the writer before they were wanted at the press and sometimes hardly by the writer himself." JM to Thomas Jefferson, 10 Aug. 1788, *PJM* 11:226–227.

22. Adair, "Autobiography," p. 202.

23. For a brief but thorough discussion of both the disputes about who wrote which papers and the background to them, see the "Editorial Note" in *PJM* 10:259–263.

constitute a genuinely remarkable achievement in the history of political thought.[24]

In *Federalist* 37, 53, and 56 Madison presented further examples of individual behavior in a sequestered, closet setting. This time, the common theme was not conscience, but rather what political ideas the human mind, aided by imagination and unencumbered by political experience, can concoct.[25] In at least two of the examples, Madison criticized these abstract constructs because they appeared divorced from the lessons of political reality.

Although contemporary political scientists rarely devote much attention to *Federalist* 37, it remains one of the most intriguing and significant contributions Madison made to the series. Its primary purpose, beyond establishing the appropriately sympathetic context for the essays that were to follow, was to give the public some idea of the many difficulties the convention overcame in creating the Constitution: these included internal tensions among the delegates themselves and the task of discovering political solutions to human inadequacies. Madison raised the closet metaphor after a prolonged discussion of the limits of the human mind to express itself through language as well as the limited ability of humans to understand either the natural or political worlds. Madison pointed out the enor-

---

24. JM to Thomas Jefferson, 10 Aug. 1788, *PJM* 11:227. Because *The Federalist* was ultimately published under the single pen name Publius—taken from *Plutarch's Lives* in reference to Publius Publicola, the "people pleaser"—it is appropriate for some scholarly purposes to consider it as the work of one, rather than three separate authors. Indeed, as I argued in *The Radical Politics of Thomas Jefferson* (Lawrence: University Press of Kansas, 1986), pp. 97-100, I consider Hamilton and Madison to be "*the* great collaboration" in American history. At the time of the original publication of *The Federalist* there was much that united Hamilton and Madison and little that separated them. In this present work, however, I am treating Madison's contributions as separate from those of his collaborator(s). For an enlightening discussion of *The Federalist* and how to read it, see Martin Diamond's "*The Federalist,*" in *The History of Political Philosophy,* ed. Leo Strauss and Joseph Cropsey (Chicago: Rand McNally, 1974), pp. 631-651, and his "Democracy and the Federalist: A Reconsideration of the Framers' Intent," *American Political Science Review* 53 (Mar. 1959): 52-68; see also Albert Furtwangler, *The Authority of Publius: A Reading of The Federalist Papers* (Ithaca, N.Y.: Cornell University Press, 1984). For a contrasting approach to *The Federalist* delineating some of the differences between Madison and Hamilton, see Forrest McDonald, *Alexander Hamilton: A Biography* (New York: W. W. Norton & Comapny, 1979), pp. 108-113.

25. See JM's attack on Rousseau in his "Universal Peace," *National Gazette,* 31 Jan. 1792, *PJM* 14:207; "A universal and perpetual peace, it is to be feared, is in the catalogue of events, which will never exist but in the imaginations of visionary philosophers, or in the breasts of benevolent enthusiasts."

mous difficulties the framers faced due to the variety of districts, classes, and interests they reflected—the presence of which made the running of the new political system possible but should have had a "contrary influence . . . in the task of forming it." He then rhetorically asked: "Would it be wonderful if, under the pressure of all these difficulties, the convention should have been forced into some deviations from that artificial structure and regular symmetry which an abstract view of the subject might lead an ingenious theorist to bestow on a Constitution planned in his closet or in his imagination?"

Madison's intent seems to have been to allow his audience to appreciate fully the enormous achievement of the delegates in confronting, on the convention floor rather than in isolation, these divisive difficulties through rational debate and compromise. Given the power of his analysis in *Federalist* 10, perhaps he did not go too far in his assertion that

> the real wonder is that so many difficulties should have been surmounted, and surmounted with a unanimity almost as unprecedented as it must have been unexpected. It is impossible for any man of candor to reflect on this circumstance without partaking of the astonishment. It is impossible for the man of pious reflection not to perceive in it a finger of that Almighty hand which has been so frequently and signally extended to our relief in the critical stages of the revolution.[26]

In addition to analyzing the internal political challenges of the convention, Madison presented his thoughts concerning broader epistemological issues: How does the individual come to understand the world? How does he or she communicate that comprehension to others?[27] Since these questions are germane to a philosophic understanding of the human essence, Madison's thoughts on each will be explored.

26. *Federalist* 37:246. Of course, a more logical explanation consistent with Madison's analysis would be that the framers themselves represented a single faction since, at least on the issue of the institution of property, they were of one mind.

27. David Epstein, *The Political Theory of The Federalist* (Chicago: University of Chicago Press, 1984), p. 114, suggests that this portion of *Federalist* 37 "must be ranked as the most astonishing passage in *The Federalist*."

"It is misfortune, inseparable from human affairs," he wrote, "that public measures are rarely investigated with that spirit of moderation which is essential to a just estimate of their real tendency to advance or obstruct the public good." As we know from his other writings, Madison believed that whenever humans act immoderately, or with their passions not fully in check, reason usually cannot operate accurately. When the political innovations recommended at Philadelphia were the focus of inquiry, Madison suggested that

> it could not appear surprising that the act of the convention, which recommends so many important changes and innovations, which may be viewed in so many lights and relations, and which touches the springs of so many passions and interests, should find or excite dispositions unfriendly, both on one side and on the other, to a fair discussion and accurate judgement of its merits. In some, it has been too evident from their own publications that they have scanned the proposed Constitution, not only with a predisposition to censure, but with a predetermination to condemn: as the language held by others betrays an opposite predetermination or bias, which must render their opinion also of little moment in the question.[28]

After making this initial attempt at the appearance of balance, showing how the two sides of the ratification debate were predisposed against "a fair discussion and accurate judgement of its merits," Madison still made it clear, at least in this critical political situation, that some predetermined biases are more palatable than others. Under the pseudonym Publius, he wrote:

> In placing, however, these different characters on a level with respect to the weight of their opinions I wish not to insinuate that there may not be a material difference in the purity of their intentions. It is but just to remark in favor of the latter description that as our situation is universally admitted to be peculiarly critical, and to require indispensably that something should be done for our relief, the predetermined patron of what has been actually done may have taken his bias from the weight of these

28. *Federalist* 37:242.

considerations, as well as from considerations of a sinister nature. The predetermined adversary, on the other hand, can have been governed by no venial motive whatever. The intentions of the first may be upright, as they may on the contrary be culpable. The views of the last cannot be upright, and must be culpable.[29]

Permitting his audience to raise and answer for themselves the question of a just punishment for the "venial" and "culpable," Madison strategically asserted that Publius's real audience consisted of the third side to the debate, the mass of citizens who had yet to make up their minds on the inherently complicated issue of ratification. But even when the human mind focused on scientific questions concerning nature, a topic with fewer immediate political implications than the proposed Constitution, subjective and objective difficulties of knowing inevitably intervene and must be acknowledged.

As evident from the prior discussion of Madison's views of nature in the "Agriculture Address" and his draft essay "Natural Order," he conceived of nature in political terms and politics in "natural" terms. It seemed quite natural for him to begin a section of his argument assessing how "arduous must have been the task of marking the proper line of partition between the authority of the general and that of the State governments"; deftly move his attention to compare this task with philosophers' efforts at mapping the human mind; and then shift once more to comparable problems in categorizing nature itself.

The faculties of the mind itself have never yet been distinguished and defined with satisfactory precision by all the efforts of the most acute and metaphysical philosophers. Sense, perception, judgment, desire, volition, memory, imagination are found to be separated by such delicate shades and minute gradations that their boundaries have eluded the most subtle investigations, and remain a pregnant source of ingenious disquisition

29. Ibid.; cf. JM to Archibald Stuart, 30 Oct. 1787, *PJM* 10:232, "I am truly sorry to find so many respectable names on your list of adversaries to the federal Constitution. The diversity of opinions on so interesting a subject, among men of equal integrity & discernment, is at once a melancholy proof of the fallibility of the human judgment, and of the imperfect progress yet made in the science of Government."

and controversy. The boundaries between the great kingdoms of nature, and, still more, between the various provinces and lesser portions into which they are subdivided, afford another illustration of the same important truth. The most sagacious and laborious naturalists have never yet succeeded in tracing with certainty the line which separates the district of vegetable life from the neighboring region of unorganized matter, or which marks the termination of the former and the commencement of the animal empire.

Constitutionally, philosophically, and historically unable to acknowledge that nature might be better characterized by chaos and uncertainty than by order and harmony, Madison, before returning to scrutinize further the political and epistemological difficulties confronting the convention delegates, asserted that "when we pass from the works of nature, in which all the delineations are perfectly accurate and appear to be otherwise only from the imperfection of the eye which surveys them, to the institutions of man, in which the obscurity arises as well from the object itself as from the organ by which it is contemplated, we must perceive the necessity of moderating still further our expectations and hopes from the efforts of human sagacity."[30] Madison, at least for the sake of appearance, asserted that nature, or "Nature's God," must be "perfectly accurate"; human "imperfection" in perception or understanding had to account for any apparent inaccuracies in nature. Moving on to politics, however, both the human subject and his political constructs constituted even richer sources of obscurity and confusion.

At this juncture in his paper, Madison turned to a critical analysis of humanity's determinate ability to conceptualize politics and to communicate those conceptions, consequences of the imprecise, indiscriminating, and undefinable nature of political science. "Experience has instructed us that no skill in the science of government has yet been able to discriminate and define, with sufficient certainty, its three great provinces," Madison wrote; and, he continued, "labors of the most enlightened legislators and jurists, has been equally unsuccessful in delineating the several objects and limits of different codes of laws and different tribunals of justice."[31] Turning to the

30. *Federalist* 37:244.
31. Ibid., 37:244–245.

matter of language, in words that every student, scholar, and author should keep in mind, he persuasively conveyed a sophisticated and modern analysis of the limits of intersubjective communication.

> Besides the obscurity arising from the complexity of objects and the imperfection of the human faculties, the medium through which the conceptions of men are conveyed to each other adds a fresh embarrassment. The use of words is to express ideas. Perspicuity, therefore, requires not only that the ideas should be distinctly formed, but that they should be expressed by words distinctly and exclusively appropriate to them. But no language is so copious as to supply words or phrases for every complex idea, or so correct as not to include many equivocally denoting different ideas. Hence it must happen that however accurately objects may be discriminated in themselves, and however accurately the discrimination may be considered, the definition of them may be rendered inaccurate by the inaccuracy of the terms in which it is delivered. And this unavoidable inaccuracy must be greater or less, according to the complexity and novelty of the objects defined.

To drive home his point—that no matter how hard humans labor to understand and to communicate their understanding of politics, their efforts will fall far short of the ideal—Madison closed the section with this thought: "When the Almighty himself condescends to address mankind in their own language, his meaning, luminous as it must be, is rendered dim and doubtful by the cloudy medium through which it is communicated."[32] Having examined Madison's rather sophisticated understanding of the philosophic uncertainties associated with human perception and comprehension as well as the ambiguous nature of language—all of which in part made up his concept of man—it appears appropriate now to return to Madison's penchant for thinking about the individual in isolation, or in the "closet."

32. Ibid., 37:245; difficult as it must be for most humans to read the divine handwriting on the wall, just a few paragraphs after this insight into God, Madison (37:246) unabashedly asserted: "It is impossible for the man of pious reflection not to perceive in [the convention] a finger of that Almighty hand which has been so frequently and signally extended to our relief in the critical stages of the revolution."

In *Federalist* 53, the immediate issue centered on term limits for members of the House of Representatives. Although in private, Madison always preferred the longest feasible term for federal legislators to give the legislative body the added stability gained from an increased distance from the people's direct will, in *The Federalist* he nevertheless defended the two-year position of the convention. On the question of the requisite knowledge of foreign affairs members of the House of Representatives needed, he wrote: "Some portion of this knowledge may, no doubt, be acquired in a man's closet; but some of it also can only be derived from the public sources of information; and all of it will be acquired to best effect by a practical attention to the subject during the period of actual service in the legislature."[33]

His final use of the closet image, from *Federalist* 56, does not explicitly deal with the inadequacies of knowledge gained in isolation from the world. Yet it arguably could be the conclusion every "attentive reader" of *The Federalist* would draw. Still describing and legitimizing the House of Representatives, Madison argued that "commerce, taxation, and the militia" are three issues that "seem most to require local knowledge." On taxation, he wrote:

> In every State there have been made, and must continue to be made, regulations on this subject which will, in many cases, leave little more to be done by the federal legislature than to review the different laws and reduce them in one general act. A skilful individual in his closet, with all the local codes before him, might compile a law on some subject of taxation for the whole Union, without any aid from oral information, and it may be expected that whenever internal taxes may be necessary, and particularly in cases requiring uniformity throughout the States, the more simple objects will be preferred.

Of course, Madison told his reader that "oral information" will be available to a "skilful" legislator and that much of this "local knowledge" will come from "the representatives of each State" who "will probably in all cases have been members, and may even at the

---

33. *Federalist* 53:330.

very time be members, of the State legislature, where all the local information and interests of the State are assembled."[34]

These closet images from *The Federalist* demonstrate Madison's reluctance to engage in abstract thinking. His preference ran for real political situations; more important, they show his aversion to visionary ideals that are not backed up with political experience, even though the study of the past remained a necessary but insufficient guide to the future. After his extended historical analysis in *Federalist* 18, 19, and 20, he maintained that "it has been shown that the other confederacies which could be consulted as precedents have been vitiated by the same erroneous principles" as those destroying the Articles of Confederation. The past, consequently, "can therefore furnish no other light than that of beacons, which give warning of the course to be shunned, without pointing out that which ought to be pursued."[35] Here, Madison firmly established his liberal credentials: history can whisper to the wise Prince what will not work, *ceteris paribus*; history cannot, however, reveal what new experiments must be tried and whether they will succeed, since other things, sociopolitically, are rarely equal. That would always remain an issue to be guided by the reason and logic of political science and, like every other human construct, ultimately judged by history and destroyed over time.

Madison's private illustrations from "Vices" and the corresponding Jefferson letter indicate his appreciation of the necessity, on occasion, to shade or omit one's true thoughts when writing for public persuasion. It captured as well his frank position on the volatile political nature of religion and the sharp contrast of its effect on individual compared to group behavior. This significant contradistinc-

34. Ibid., 56:340–341.
35. Ibid., 37:343. See *Federalist* 14:144, "Is it not the glory of the people of America that, whilst they have paid a decent regard to the opinions of former times and other nations, they have not suffered a blind veneration for antiquity, for custom, or for names, to overrule the suggestions of their own good sense, the knowledge of their own situation, and the lessons of their own experience?"; *Federalist* 20:172, "Experience is the oracle of truth; and where its responses are unequivocal, they ought to be conclusive and sacred"; and, *Federalist* 52:324. Cf. Adair, *Fame and the Founding Fathers*, p. 96, who reminds modern readers of the difficult relationship between precedent and political experimentation: "In 1776, however, [Adam] Smith could only theorize from scattered historical precedents as to how a projected free enterprise system might work, because *nowhere in his mercantilist world* was a free enterprise system of the sort he described on paper actually operating."

tion was plainly presented in *Federalist* 49: "The reason of man, like man himself, is timid and cautious when left alone, and acquires firmness and confidence in proportion to the number with which it is associated."[36] Alone, in the closet (or voting booth), man appears "timid and cautious" and perhaps even moral—without the need of external threats or inducements. However, when the individual joins a faction, which Madisonian individuals always do, "passion . . . not the reason . . . would sit in judgement."[37]

That Mr. Hyde would always turn into a convention of Dr. Jekylls found no bolder expression than in *Federalist* 55. Here Madison succinctly captured his theory of humanity with a single sentence, conveying an exceptionally powerful image: "Had every Athenian citizen been a Socrates, every Athenian assembly would still have been a mob."[38] Think about this allusion. Madison selects the epitome of Western civilization's notion of the just and wise individual, Socrates, and claims that a room full of Socrates*es* would inevitably turn into a mob![39] But he never even bothered to address the obvious and logical question—Why? Why did he assume this to be true? The consequences and implications of this assumption are disconcerting, to say the least. If Socrates cannot freely and willfully participate in politics without the presence of a coercive threat, what chance do the *demos* have? Even allowing for the fact that Madison's specific context dealt with "very numerous assemblies," he never explained why in such an assembly made up of Socrateses "passion never fails to wrest the scepter from reason."[40] Given this view of humanity, no wonder in *Federalist* 63, Madison's final contribution to the collection, he boasted that "the true distinction" between the ancient re-

---

36. *Federalist* 49:314.
37. Ibid., 49:315.
38. Ibid., 55:336.
39. See Maynard Smith, "Reason, Passion and Political Freedom in *The Federalist*," *Journal of Politics* 22 (Feb. 1960): 530, where he points out that in *Federalist* 49 (p. 314) JM argued that "in a nation of philosophers, this consideration ought to be disregarded. A reverence for the laws would be sufficiently inculcated by the voice of an enlightened reason. But a nation of philosophers is as little to be expected as the philosophical race of kings wished for by Plato." To be consistent, then, JM must have conceived of his "nation" of "enlightened" philosophers acting in isolation and never assembling.
40. *Federalist* 51:336; compare, once more, Jefferson's alternative view in n. 1.

gimes and the proposed experiment in government, "lies *in the total exclusion of the people in their collective capacity.*"[41]

These passages all too neatly anticipate Madison's conception of citizenship: do not give "the people" any power when they are assembled; allow some of the white males, acting in isolation, the fleeting participation of voting for their representatives and restrict that right for as long as politically possible to one branch of the legislature. Beyond this minimalist approach to politics, ask little else of the people, except under extraordinary conditions. In addition, it may be best for Americans not to ask themselves: What of fraternity? What of community? What of the individual as the *zoon politikon*? These questions encompass ideas and ideals, values and dreams, too fraught with the risks and uncertainties associated with potentially passionate group activity, the last thing Madison wanted to encourage.

While it is certainly true that the fundamental contrast for Madison was the individual in isolation compared to the individual as part of a group, it may prove helpful to note briefly what Madison assumes about hypothetical situations where a few individuals interact as nongroup members. Madison constructed the following pedagogical illustration in his personal notes on "Vices" and in the follow-up letter to Jefferson; it is an example he found useful in several other private contexts, even as late as 1821: "Place three individuals in a situation wherein the interest of each depends on the voice of the others? and give to two of them an interest opposed to the rights of the third? Will the latter be secure? The prudence of every man would shun the danger. The rules & forms of justice suppose & guard against it. Will two thousand in a like situation be less likely to encroach on the rights of one thousand?"[42] Madison responded negatively. Although Madison was usually concerned with the difficulties surrounding majority oppression of minority rights, what he assumed about the behavior of the individuals in this passage remains instructive. Madison cannot envision even as few as three individuals living together peacefully without the presence of "rules

41. Ibid., 63:373; Madison's emphasis.
42. *PJM* 9:356; for other instances see JM to Thomas Jefferson, 24 Oct. 1787, *PJM* 10:213; "Notes for Essays," 19 Dec. 1791–3 Mar. 1792, *PJM* 14:159; and *The Records of the Federal Convention of 1787*, ed. Max Farrand, 4 vols. (New Haven, Conn.: Yale University Press, 1937), 3:451. It should be noted that the last example cited from Farrand would, after JM's death, become public since it derives from an addition JM made to his convention notes.

& forms of justice."[43] This, of course, means some structure of government is necessary to enforce the rules.

Echoing the logic of Hobbes that "Covenants, without the Sword, are but words," Madison stated that "a sanction is essential to the idea of law, as coercion is to that of Government. The federal system being destitute of both, wants the great vital principles of a Political Cons[ti]tution." Madison's reasoning over how "so fatal an omission" could have occurred sheds further light. He argued that it must have been the result of "a mistaken confidence that the justice, the good faith, the honor, the sound policy, of the several legislative assemblies would render superfluous any appeal to the ordinary motives by which the laws secure the obedience of individuals."[44] This hardly reflects the ethos of civic humanism.[45] When Madison repeated this object lesson in other writings, the language usually stayed identical, with the following noteworthy exception. Between December 1791 and March 1792, when he was preparing to write some of his essays for the *National Gazette*, Madison assembled pages of notes for each planned article. In his private notes he reworded his example as follows: "Among 3 men in a Wilderness, two would never obey one—nor perhaps the one escape the oppression of the two should any real or fancied interest unite them agst. him."[46]

From the two versions of his heuristic device, several implicit yet significant dimensions to Madison's concept of man can be inferred. To begin, this seems to be a Hobbesian view of man as inherently quarrelsome, contentious, and power acquisitive. This perspective becomes clearer in the second passage, where he placed the individuals outside civil society and in the "Wilderness." Each of the pas-

43. Cf. Morton White, *Philosophy, The Federalist, and the Constitution* (New York: Oxford University Press, 1987), p. 95: "Madison's denigration of man's motives applies primarily to man *in politics*. . . . Madison did not explicitly attribute evil to the motives of individual men who might not be members of factions. . . . I do not think that Madison held that the hearts or inward parts of all individual men are depraved, corrupt, and filled with evil motives." Cf. John Patrick Diggins, *The Lost Soul of American Politics* (New York: Basic Books, 1984), p. 91: "Madison perceived self-advantage as the basis of all action undertaken by all men whose moral capacity is less than that of an 'angel.'"

44. Thomas Hobbes, *Leviathan*, ed. C. B. Macpherson (New York: Penguin, 1968), p. 223; *PJM* 9:351, 352.

45. See Diggins, *Lost Soul*, p. 24, who writes that during "the Constitutional era . . . a virtuous citizenry was considered, debated, and rejected."

46. "Notes for Essays," 19 Dec. 1791–3 Mar. 1792, *PJM* 14:159.

sages assumes no government to check the behavior of these individuals, thus constituting Hobbes's state of nature. In *Federalist* 51 Madison made the connection explicitly: "In a society under the forms of which the stronger faction can readily unite and oppress the weaker, anarchy may as truly be said to reign as in a state of nature, where the weaker individual is not secured against the violence of the stronger."[47] Like Hobbes, Madison automatically assumed that the individuals involved in these situations were market men from civil society, not some abstract concept of humanity independent of cultural factors.[48] In his 1797 letter to Jefferson, in the same paragraph containing his verbatim account of the original passage, Madison uncharacteristically observed: "We know however that no Society ever did or can consist of so homogeneous a mass of Citizens. In the savage State indeed, an approach is made towards it; but in that State little or no Government is necessary. In all civilized Societies, distinctions are various and unavoidable."[49]

In this passage, it becomes evident that Madison privately acknowledged to Jefferson that the American Indians approached, perhaps even achieved, a legitimate anarchist community. It is also evident that he did not consider this "savage State," lacking agriculture or commerce, to be either a "society" or "civilized." Consequently, Madison spent little energy thinking about the Indians. Perhaps he should have, especially in light of *Federalist* 51, where he penned what may arguably be his most famous statement on humanity: "It may be a reflection on human nature that such devices should be necessary to control the abuses of government. But what is government itself but the greatest of all reflections on human nature? If

47. *Federalist* 51:322; note also how Publius subtly keeps the fearful image of a Hobbesian state of nature in the background throughout his presentation, suggesting to his readers that if the Constitution was not ratified the states would inevitably break down to this intolerable condition.

48. Even when JM discusses man in a nonpolitical context, he assumed political beings. The mistake for which Rousseau derided Hobbes and Locke in his "Second Discourse" (p. 102) could equally be attributed to JM: "All of them, finally, speaking continually of need, avarice, oppression, desires, and pride, have carried over to the state of nature ideas they had acquired in society: they spoke about savage man and they described civil man."

49. *PJM* 10:212–213. Note that JM writes this passage specifically to Jefferson, fully aware of his generally favorable view of Native American life contained in *Notes on the State of Virginia.*

men were angels, no government would be necessary."[50] The rhetoric is brilliant. By presenting the issue with a false dichotomy—angels versus men—Madison created the implied contrast of angelic versus demonic creatures. Because everyone reading *Federalist* 51 knew humans were hardly angelic, Publius's conclusion on the necessity of energetic government obviously would appear to follow.[51] Like Hobbes and Locke who preceded Madison, when these liberal theorists talked about man, they had the commercial model in mind. Even when the first two described life in the state of nature, they read back into human nature characteristics of man in civil society. As a result, the state of nature always appears as a state of war.[52] So too Madison. Although he admitted to Jefferson that he had some appreciation of Indian communities, he either ignored or more likely, given his personal experiences, forgot these memories.[53]

50. *Federalist* 51:319. See White, *Philosophy,* p. 97: "And one can fall short of being an angel without becoming a beast."

51. See Matthews, *Radical Politics,* pp. 61–65. At least one important founder, Jefferson, genuinely believed that government was not always necessary even though men were not angels. Jefferson raises this specific point where he rhetorically asks "whether no law . . . or too much law . . . submits man to the greatest evil?" He answers: "I am convinced that those societies [as the Native Americans] which live without government enjoy in their general mass an infinitely greater degree of happiness than those who live under European government."

52. Hobbes, *Leviathan,* p. 186; John Locke, appreciating the power of a political theory ultimately derived from God compared to one based on secular reason, presented two rather contrasting views of the state of nature. As if desiring to separate himself explicitly from Hobbes, Locke explained "the plain *difference between the state of nature and the state of war,* which were however some men have confounded, are as distant, as a state of peace, good will, mutual assistance and preservation, and a state of enmity, malice, violence and mutual destruction, are one from another. Men living together according to reason, without a common superior on earth, with authority to judge between them, is *properly the state of nature"* (*Second Treatise of Government,* ed. C. B. Macpherson [Indianapolis: Hackett, 1980], p. 15). From this and other passages, Locke seems to think it possible, under certain conditions, for humans to live "according to reason, without a common superior." And yet, a few paragraphs later, Locke confuses the difference when he directly equates the state of war with the state of nature: "To avoid this *state of war* (wherein there is no appeal but to heaven, and wherein every least difference is apt to end, where there is no authority to decide between the contenders) is one great reason of men's putting themselves into society, and quitting the state of nature." (*Second Treatise,* p. 16); see also C. B. Macpherson, *The Political Theory of Possessive Individualism* (Oxford: Clarendon Press, 1962), pp. 194–250.

53. See Irving Brant, *James Madison,* 6 vols. (Indianapolis: Bobbs-Merrill, 1941–1961), 1:45–48, where he notes: "The deepest impressions of Madison's

Even after they have moved out of the state of nature and are placed in a political context, individuals will behave as though they are back in Hobbes' state of nature if provided the opportunity.[54] Given his view of the individual and the magnifying effect groups seem to have on the more antisocial human tendencies, it was no wonder Madison wrote in *Federalist* 10 that "so strong is this propensity of mankind to fall into mutual animosities that where no substantial occasion presents itself the most frivolous and fanciful distinctions have been sufficient to kindle their unfriendly passions and excite their most violent conflicts."[55] Except in total isolation, individual humans needed rational governmental supervision. It was not the association of small groups, however, that concerned Madison: he wanted to solve the problems confronting a nation, which meant dealing with social problems of a much grander magnitude.

Madison began his maiden voyage in *The Federalist* with the promise that he would reveal to his readers how "to break and control the violence of faction"—the "mortal diseases" of all prior republics. As manifested in his notes, he had read, thought, and written about this

---

childhood, however, resulted from the wave of fear that swept over the Virginia frontier in 1755 following Braddock's defeat by the French and Indians near Fort Duquesne. . . . What Madison knew, and remembered vividly all his life, was the terror that gripped the people of the Piedmont as they saw their land, stripped of its frontier defenses, exposed to the creeping approach of the French and Indians. . . . The exaggerated nature of the ensuing fears, as far as the safety of the settlers east of the Blue Ridge was concerned, did not subtract from its reality either to the young or old. . . . The contrast in Madison's childhood between his reliance on Negroes and dread of Indians greatly affected his adult attitude toward these two 'tributary races'. . . . [H]e had seen the tomahawk and the torch too vividly in his mind's eye to permit him to view the Indian as anything but a savage." See also Richard Morris, *Witnesses at the Creation* (New York: Holt, Rinehart and Winston, 1985), p. 98.

54. For instance, see Jonathan Elliot, ed., *The Debates of the Several State Conventions on the Adoption of the Federal Constitution*, 4 vols. (Philadelphia: J. B. Lippincott, 1836), 3:250, where on 11 June 1788 JM argued, "States will be governed by the motives that actuate individuals. When a tax is in operation in a particular state, every citizen, if he knows the energy of the laws to enforce payment, and that every other citizen is performing his duty, will cheerfully discharge his duty; but were it known that the citizens of one district were not performing their duty, and that it was left to the policy of the government to make them come up with it, the other districts would be very supine and careless in making provisions for payment."

55. *Federalist* 10:124.

topic for an extended period. Although *Federalist* 10 is cogent, compelling, and clear, it is, ironically, rather easy to skim through its sophisticated analysis and miss some of its sweeping implications. The discussion that follows, consequently, will be painstakingly detailed.

Confronted by the "vice" and "violence of faction," Madison set out looking for a "cure" to this mortal disease. He preceded his initial formulation of a faction by asserting that

> complaints are everywhere heard from our most considerate and virtuous citizens, equally the friends of public and private faith and of public and personal liberty, that our governments are too unstable, that the public good is disregarded in the conflicts of rival parties, and that measures are too often decided, not according to the rules of justice and the rights of the minor party, but by the superior force of an interested and overbearing majority.[56]

He then defined a faction to be, "a number of citizens, whether amounting to a majority or minority of the whole, who are united and actuated by some common impulse of passion, or of interest, adverse to the rights of other citizens, or to the permanent and aggregate interests of the community."[57]

From a first glance, it appeared that not all organized groups were factions; only those with "passion" or "interest" contrary to those of other citizens or to the community as a whole." In his splendid study of *Federalist* 10, David Epstein argues that a closer textual analysis, emphasizing the "impulse," rather than the actual presence, of passion or interest reveals such "a factious impulse at the heart of even a respectable lobby."[58] Factions, therefore, are ubiquitous, power acquisitive, and dangerous; in *Federalist* 43, Madison called "violent factions, the natural offspring of free government."[59] In a systematic and thorough manner, the hallmark of Madison's style of writing on politics, he explained that there are two methods

56. Ibid., 10:122–123; among JM's earliest usage of the term *faction* can be found in JM to Edmund Pendleton, 7 Nov. 1780, *PJM* 2:165.

57. *Federalist* 10:123.

58. Epstein, *Political Theory,* pp. 64–65. See also White, *Philosophy,* p. 57: "We must bear in mind that 'faction' as used by Madison might well be regarded as a moral epithet."

59. *Federalist* 43:280.

of "curing the mischiefs of faction": "removing its causes" or "controlling its effects." Similarly, there were "two methods of removing the causes of faction," neither of which could be employed: the first, to destroy the liberty essential to the growth of factions (and republican government); the second, to give "to every citizen the same opinions, the same passions, and the same interests." Regarding the first remedy, Madison stated "that it was worse than the disease." The second remedy, however, he called merely "impracticable."[60]

He claimed that "as long as the connection subsists between his reason and his self-love, his opinions and his passions will have a reciprocal influence on each other; and the former will be objects to which the latter will attach themselves." This supposition logically led Madison to the base of the problem: "The diversity in the faculties of men, from which the rights of property originate, is not less an insuperable obstacle to a uniformity of interests." This concern becomes central not only to this paper and the entire *Federalist*, but to Madisonian politics. The reason behind this particular focus is simple. Madison frankly asserted that "the protection of these faculties is the first object of government. From the protection of different and unequal faculties of acquiring property, the possession of different degrees and kinds of property immediately results; and from the influence of these on the sentiments and views of the respective proprietors ensues a division of the society into different interests and parties."[61]

"The first object of government" was to protect these "diverse faculties"; and in *Federalist* 51, again addressing the problem of dominating factions, he claimed: "Justice is the end of government. It is the end of civil society. It ever has been and ever will be pursued un-

---

60. Ibid., 10:123. This subtle difference in evaluations is interesting in at least two respects. First, Madison does not reject the latter remedy for either moral or political reasons; he merely thinks that, given the diversity of human nature, it is an unfeasible solution. Yet less than half a century later Alexis de Tocqueville and John Stuart Mill observed with alarm the increasing ability of society, rather than government, to control and homogenize opinions and interests—through what Tocqueville termed "the tyranny of the majority." Second, the homogeneity of passion and interest for the *institution* of property may help explain why the federal convention—an assembly no less than the Athenian assembly of Socrates that Madison assured his readers would turn into a mob—did not dissolve into uncompromising and violent factions.

61. *Federalist* 10:123–124.

til it be obtained, or until liberty be lost in the pursuit."[62] Diverse but unequal human faculties, different and unequal property holdings, combined with justice as the purpose of government and of civil society, all were linked together in Madison's political theory. Since the latter two topics will be extensively treated later in this book, they will be all but ignored here. Nevertheless, it should be pointed out that Madison had established for himself *the* problem for liberal political theorists who wanted to establish government by consent: how to justify class-divided society to a majority who must learn to accept willingly this state of affairs if social stability was to be maintained. Still, the relations of the diversity of human faculties to factions remains an important topic.

Finding it impossible to remove the causes of faction—since he had traced them to the heart of darkness, "the nature of man" in "civil society"—Madison proceeded to explain how to control their effects through an elaborate social, economic, and political construct. Adopting and adapting David Hume's prescriptions primarily from "Parties" and "Idea of a Perfect Commonwealth," Madison established his own basic dichotomy between factions.[63] Some are based on "passion," such as those established on religious or political beliefs; others are based on "interest," that is, on economic fac-

62. Ibid., 51:322. See Sheldon S. Wolin, *The Presence of the Past* (Baltimore: Johns Hopkins University Press, 1989), pp. 126–129: "The great threat to difference is democracy: it wants men to 'be perfectly equalized and assimilated in their possessions, their opinions and their passions.' Thus, difference becomes praiseworthy when it is associated with inequality of ability and acquisition. Unum's relation to pluris now appears equivocal: it needs to prevent the coalescence of certain differences while protecting those differences of ability which produce inequalities. It would be but a small step from Madison's concept of unequal faculties to a full-blown conception of meritocracy in which a just society is one where social goods are distributed in accordance with one's deserts and the only significant differences will be earned and hence deserved."

63. See Hume, *Human Nature*, p. 4, where he draws the following distinction: "When we take a survey of the passions, there occurs a division of them into *direct* and *indirect*. . . . This distinction I cannot at present justify or explain further. I can only observe in general that under the indirect passions I comprehend pride, humility, ambition, vanity, love, hatred, envy, pity, malice, generosity, with their dependents. And under the direct passions, desire, aversion, grief, joy, hope, fear, despair, and security." See White, *Philosophy*, pp. 69–72, where he establishes that "Hume denies that 'the *landed* and *trading* part of the nation' constituted factions in The England of his day, thereby showing how much Madison diverged from Hume." "Madison did more than 'expand' Hume's views on faction from interest; he added to it significantly." Cf. Franklin Kalinowski, "David Hume on the Philosophic Underpinnings of Interest Group Politics," *Polity* 25 (Spring 1993): 355–374.

tors. The latter are not only more reasonable, their multiplicity becomes the "grand elixir" to social instability.[64] The former, less predictable and more volatile, require a particularly cunning scheme to control them. Here Madison describes the first category:

A zeal for different opinions concerning religion, concerning government, and many other points, as well of speculation as of practice; an attachment to different leaders ambitiously contending for pre-eminence and power; or to persons of other descriptions whose fortunes have been interesting to the human passions, have, in turn, divided mankind into parties, inflamed them with mutual animosity, and rendered them much more disposed to vex and oppress each other than to co-operate for their common good.[65]

The images and words characterizing these types of factions are poignant: "zeal," "ambitiously contending for pre-eminence," "inflamed . . . mutual animosity," "vex and oppress," "unfriendly passions," and "violent conflicts." Fortunately, the hot-blooded amalgam of factions must share the social landscape with the relatively more sedate factions based on rational economic interest.[66]

But the most common and durable source of factions has been the various and unequal distribution of property. Those who hold and those who are without property have ever formed distinct interests in society. Those who are creditors, and those who are debtors, fall under a like discrimination. A landed interest, a manufacturing interest, a mercantile interest, a moneyed interest, with many lesser interests, grow up of necessity in civilized nations, and divide them into different classes, actuated by different sentiments and views.

It becomes "the principal task of modern legislation" to regulate "these various and interfering interests."[67] But notice, Madison did

64. Adair, *Fame and the Founding Fathers*, p. 106.
65. *Federalist* 10:124.
66. Diggins, *Lost Soul*, p. 88: "Passion implied the weakness of the will and the failure of self-control. Thus 'passion' was dangerous because it was 'sudden,' whereas interest could be reasonable when it was not 'private' and 'partial' but instead tied to what might permanently benefit The Republic."
67. *Federalist* 10:124.

not argue that the passion-based factions were to be controlled by modern legislation, just those that made up "interfering interests." Why does he make this distinction?

To begin with, economic factions have a tangible interest that governments can control in a variety of ways, from taxation to confiscation. Furthermore, utility maximization underlies economic activity, which means that humans can logically (even mathematically) understand and predict the behavior of other humans. "Thus liberal man emerges," writes Sheldon Wolin, "as a being supremely sensitive to the specific form of pain produced by the loss of wealth or status."[68] But how could a society deal politically with an intangible belief, be it politically or religiously based? Furthermore, since beliefs do not have a rational or logical foundation, nor do their rewards lend themselves to the calculus of utility maximization, their predictability remained extremely problematic. This is especially true when individuals believe they are divinely authorized in their actions. In addition, how can earthly power genuinely punish an individual motivated by divine sanction? Although somewhat difficult to control through legislative action, these threats to social stability had to be checked. Consequently, Madison would eventually draw a wall of separation around the religious sects and play them off against each other in civil society. This strategy could not be employed quite so directly for political groups. For obvious reasons, he could not a priori ban them from politics; he would, however, permit them free reign to establish any form of government, provided it was republican, as guaranteed in the Constitution.[69] He also used the advantages of geographic space in combination with multiple political hurdles, like federalism, bicameralism, and representative government, to impede the progress of impetuous factions.

Madison repeated this dichotomized view of factions at the end of Federalist 10 after he had explained how the great size of the proposed republic would help neutralize factions: "The influence of factious leaders may kindle a flame within their particular States but will be unable to spread a general conflagration through the other States. A religious sect may degenerate into a political faction in a part of the Confederacy; but the variety of sects dispersed over the

68. Wolin, Politics of Vision, p. 328.
69. Federalist 39:256.

entire face of it must secure the national councils against any danger from that source." Having completed his discussion of factions based on passion, he noted how geographic space would help control factions based on economics as well: "A rage for paper money, for an abolition of debts, for an equal division of property, or any other improper or wicked project, will be less apt to pervade the whole body of the Union than a particular member of it, in the same proportion as such a malady is more likely to taint a particular county or district than an entire State."

He finished this magnificent contribution concluding that "in the extent and proper structure of the Union, therefore, we behold a republican remedy for the diseases most incident to republican government."[70] Ultimately it was the virtue of political space that constituted Madison's illuminating discovery in reading Hume. Like most dimensions of Madison's political plan, its beauty resided in the fact that success occurred independent of human will or virtue, and it fit the immediate, real political situation. To Madison, humans were antisocial creatures who would break into violence over "the most frivolous and fanciful distinctions." It is not that humans are virtuous, but that they are selfish—and government has been appropriately constructed—that permits them the illusion of self-government. Contrary to Montesquieu who argued that a republican form of government could rule a small territory, Hume and Madison claimed the reverse. As will be clearer at a later point, an "extended sphere" became the only appropriate base upon which republican government could be erected. "Extend the sphere and you take in a greater variety of parties and interests; you make it less probable that a majority of the whole will have a common motive to invade the rights of other citizens; or if such a common motive exists, it will be more difficult for all who feel it to discover their own strength and to act in unison with each other."[71]

70. Ibid., 10:128.
71. Ibid., 10:127; see *Federalist* 51:321: "The society itself will be broken into so many parts, interests and classes of citizens, that the rights of individuals, or of the minority, will be in little danger from interested combinations of the majority. In a free government the security for civil rights must be the same as that for religious rights. It consists in the one case in the multiplicity of interests, and in the other in the multiplicity of sects . . . and this may be presumed to depend

In at least three other significant instances in his discussion of factions, Madison employed the passion (opinion)/interest (reason) axis to distinguish among groups. The initial and sketchiest formulation is in "Vices"; by the time he wrote to Jefferson to share his insights, Madison had clarified his position considerably. By this time he included a reason as natural, some passions as artificial slant on the division:

> In all civilized Societies, distinctions are various and unavoidable. A distinction of property results from that very protection which a free Government gives to unequal faculties of acquiring it. There will be rich and poor; creditors and debtors; a landed interest, a monied interest, a mercantile interest, a manufacturing interest. These classes may again be subdivided. . . . In addition to these natural distinctions, artificial ones will be founded, on accidental differences in political, religious or other opinions, or an attachment to the persons of leading individuals.[72]

He repeated the interest/passion dichotomy (*sans* the natural/artificial component), in his convention speeches of 6 and 26 June 1787.[73] Madison acknowledged that property inequality, the result of natural human inequalities, was "the most common and durable source of factions." Government had been instituted not to protect any particular property, but to protect the human faculties of acquiring it

---

on the extent of country and number of people comprehended under the same government." See also *Records of the Federal Convention* 1:136, where on 6 June 1787 JM presented an early version of his extended sphere argument. Hamilton noted, *The Papers of Alexander Hamilton*, ed. Harold C. Syrett et al., 26 vols. (New York: Columbia University Press, 1961–1979), 4:165, that JM's theory contained some truth but did "not conclude strongly as he supposes. The Assembly when chosen will meet in one room if they are drawn from half the globe—& will be liable to all the passions of popular assemblies."

72. "Vices," *PJM* 9:357; JM to Jefferson, 24 Oct. 1787, *PJM* 10:212–213. What JM meant by "artificial" can be located in his notes for the *National Gazette, PJM* 14:160: "Natural divisions exist in all political societies, which should be made mutual checks on each other. But it does not follow that artificial distinctions, as kings & nobles, should be created, and then formed into checks and balances." See "Parties," 23 Jan. 1792, *PJM* 14:198, where he calls "absurd" the idea of creating artificial distinctions to help balance the system. Indeed, given JM's concept of the natural divisiveness among humanity, why would it be necessary to do so?

73. Farrand, *Records* 1:135, 422–423.

now and in the future.[74] One theoretical, closet solution would be to legislate equality. This Madison would not allow: property owner- ship must be respected since protection of "the faculties" of acquir- ing property constituted the "first object of government" while jus- tice was the goal of both politics and civil society. Perhaps more significantly, even if property could be evenly distributed, the Madi- sonian individual would remain quarrelsome and contentious over "the most frivolous and fanciful distinctions."

Of course, it is still crucial to remember that Madison's real fear at this historic moment consisted not of some abstract, unspecified majority faction. Rather, in Martin Diamond's words, Madison feared "*the* majority faction, i.e., the great mass of the little proper- tied and the unpropertied." In fact, to operate successfully Diamond maintains that Madison's political theory assumed a "modern com- mercial republic" where "the commercial life must be made honor- able and universally practiced."[75] In another essay, Diamond appears even bolder. He accurately exposes what Madison was up to: "With- out wrenching Madison's meaning too greatly, the problem may be put crudely this way: Madison gave a before hand answer to Marx." Diamond argues that "an inflamed Marxian proletariat would not indefinitely be deterred by institutional checks or extent of terri- tory." Characteristic of his style, Diamond unabashedly reached the logical and insightful conclusion: "Madison's whole scheme essen- tially comes down to this. The struggle of classes is to be replaced by a struggle of interests. The class struggle is domestic convulsion; the struggle of interests is a safe, even energizing, struggle which is com- patible with, or even promotes, the safety of society."[76]

Diamond's linkage of the language of *The Federalist* to the spe- cific historic context remains essential. Madison rarely wrote about intellectual abstractions. His theory grounded itself in the real world of economics and politics. In particular, he continued to be alarmed at the political conditions in the states, where a significant number of the white males had incurred debts that they had little realistic prospect of repaying. The situation was perhaps most acute in Mas-

74. Epstein, *Political Theory,* p. 74.
75. Diamond, "The Federalist," pp. 647, 648, 650.
76. Martin Diamond, *As Far as Republican Principles Will Admit,* ed. Wil- liam A. Schambra (Washington, D.C.: American Enterprise Institute Press, 1992), pp. 32, 33.

sachusetts. Madison read Henry Knox's imaginative report on Shays's rebellion. Knox maintained that the rebels endorsed the position "that since 'the property of the United States has been protected from the confiscation of Britain by the joint exertions of all, it therefore ought to be the common property of all.' "[77]

Forrest McDonald estimates that throughout the revolutionary years Americans expropriated "without either due process or compensation of any kind . . . more than $20 million" by bill of attainder and another $8 million from holders of large proprietary grants. Much of this activity had abated by the Constitutional Convention, but "large property holders had no reason to be cocksure that it would never be resumed. . . . Most frightening of all was the prospect that the *demos* might rise and . . . redistribute all property by force."[78] Shays's rebellion fed the leveling fears of the framers. In his 26 June 1787 speech at the convention, Madison noted, "There will be particularly the distinction of rich & poor." Foreshadowing Malthus, he argued:

> In framing a system which we wish to last for ages, we shd. not lose sight of the changes which ages will produce. An increase of population will of necessity increase the proportion of those who will labour under all the hardships of life, & secretly sigh for a more equal distribution of its blessings. These may in time outnumber those who are placed above the feelings of indigence. According to the equal laws of suffrage, the power will slide into the hands of the former. No agrarian attempts have yet been made in this Country, but symptoms of a leveling spirit, as we have understood, have sufficiently appeared in a certain quarters to give notice of the future danger.[79]

Madison, along with his propertied colleagues, had to put a lid on the increasing political pressure generated by the small propertied interests if the republic was to survive. And this, we will see, remained a troubling concern for Madison as late as 1821.

It may be helpful to look even more analytically at Madison's

77. Morris, *Witnesses at the Creation*, pp. 171–172. He also points out (p. 114) that Madison was in attendance at Congress when the "mutineers poked their fusils through the State House windows."
78. McDonald, *Novus Ordo Seclorum*, pp. 91–92, 154–157.
79. Farrand, *Records* 1:422–423.

treatment of reason and passion, after having seen how factions pre-occupied him throughout *The Federalist*, especially since he argued that "it is the reason, alone, of the public, that ought to control and regulate the government. The passions ought to be controlled and regulated by the government."[80] In his contributions to *The Federalist* Madison raised the issue of passion(s) in twelve papers, with thirty-one separate usages. The words he associated with passion are usually negative: "adverse" to other citizens, "vex and oppress," "mutual animosity," "schemes of oppression," "selfish," "inflame," and "unruly."[81] In fact, there does not appear to be a single positive reference to passion in Madison's arguments. Hamilton, on the contrary, did write favorably at least about "fame, the ruling passion of the noblest minds," and hence its directly positive impact on individuals and society.[82] When it came to the term *reason*, however, Madison employed it in twenty of his twenty-nine essays. While the context of each usage indicates that he did not view reason as un-problematic—it was "fallible," could be linked to an individual's "self-love" or his "passions" as well as to "an impatient avidity for immediate and immoderate gain"—it nonetheless unlocked the door to the Muse of political science.[83]

Since human passions tend to make it impossible for either the individual or the group to reason clearly, it seemed crucial to postpone action until the passions cooled and reason could be brought to focus on the question. Through space, Madison played for time. He constructed an elaborate political system that required many different actors to take positive steps to institute change; no political action would automatically maintain the political status quo. This state,

80. *Federalist* 49:315; see also JM's 8 Feb. 1791, *PJM* 13:383, speech on the bank bill: "The present is a question which ought to be conducted with moderation and candor—and therefore there is no occasion to have recourse to those tragic representations, which have been adduced—warmth and passion should be excluded from the discussion of a subject, which ought to depend on the cool dictates of reason for its decision."

81. See Diggins, *Lost Soul*, p. 87: "To grasp the motives that activated conduct, the framers tried to identify the prevalent internal causes of action, and these were often not so much political ideas as emotions: fear, desire, aversion, jealousy, envy, avarice, pride, ambition, humility, vanity. . . . Such emotional states were in turn driven by deeper forces, which the framers variously referred to as 'motives,' 'springs,' 'impulses,' 'inducements,' 'inclinations,' 'dispositions,' 'propensities,' or 'humors.'"

82. *Federalist* 72:414.

83. Ibid., 10:123, 124; 42:276; 50:317.

moreover, had been designed to stand atop a competitive civil society spread over an extended territory. All these factors combined to permit reason to function and control humanity. Stability would be assured thanks to specific structures created by human reason, not because humans were virtuous. Madison described this state in 1792: "A government, deriving its energy from the will of the society, and operating by the reason of its measures, on the understanding and interest of the society. Such is the government for which philosophy has been searching, and humanity been sighing, from the most remote ages. Such are the republican governments which it is the glory of America to have invented."[84]

84. "Spirit of Governments," *National Gazette*, 18 Feb. 1792, *PJM* 14:234.

4 / Civil Society: The Politics of Economics and Society

The best provision for a stable and free Govt. is not a balance in the powers of the Govt. tho' that is not to be neglected, but an equilibrium in the interests & passions of the Society itself, which can not be attained in a small Society. Much has been said on the first. The last deserves a thorough investigation.[1]

—*Madison*

In the spring of 1786, Madison complained to Jefferson about the "present anarchy of our commerce" under the Articles of Confederation and how he "almost despair[ed] of success" concerning the upcoming Annapolis convention. He observed, furthermore, the inalienable connection between politics and economics: "In fact most of our political evils may be traced up to our commercial ones, as most of our moral may to our political."[2] What must be kept in mind about Madison's ingenious political construct is that both the public and the private arenas constituted significant components to the creation and maintenance of national stability. His Newtonian strategy of one force counteracting and balancing another, "ambition . . . made to counteract ambition," was to be employed throughout his political system: in society (religious sects), in economics (interests and classes), and in government (representatives, administrators, branches, states).

Now commonly used by the contemporary social sciences to distinguish between government, economics, and society, this triad Madison appreciated as more of a conscious political construct than

1. "Notes for Essays," 19 Dec. 1791–3 Mar. 1792, *The Papers of James Madison*, ed. William T. Hutchinson et al., 17 vols. (Chicago and Charlottesville: University of Chicago Press and University of Virginia Press, 1962–), 14:158–159 (hereafter cited as *PJM*).

2. JM to Thomas Jefferson, 18 Mar. 1786, *PJM* 8:502–503.

a naturally occurring division. Civil society (the socioeconomic realms) and government not only shared justice as their common end, but both were centers of power. Both, therefore, had to be subject to balance.[3] Indeed, the apparent apolitical and natural balancing of social passions and economic interests in a well-constructed commercial republic constituted one of Madison's major contributions to political theory. His system cleverly institutionalized the emerging liberal double standard of freedom for civil society, especially economics, in combination with restraint for the polity.[4]

Madison's system rested on the understanding that social and economic factions always involve power and contain the potential to upset the overall equilibrium. By constructing the appropriate social-economic-political system, itself the supreme political act, "The Legislator" could artfully establish a balanced commercial polity by denying immediate and direct political power to certain groups in exchange for relative freedom from political interference in social and economic dealings. By consciously denying virtually all but a handful of citizens any role in a governmental structure that, by design, was to be run by an elite of superior ability (who nonetheless would have to check and balance each other), Madison left the private arena open as the prime avenue for humanity to search for meaning. The private arena—relatively unencumbered by government interference, so long as individuals continued to obey the political rules silently governing the economic and social spheres—provided the space where individuals and groups could pursue their self-interest however they desired. All of this self-interested activity, moreover, would continue to produce balance and equilibrium.[5] Under this arrangement, most men by necessity and choice would find ownership of property instrumental to their personal pursuits of happiness. Of this, Madison seemed all too aware. Property, then, constituted the specific link between economics and government:

3. Isaac Kramnick, ed., *The Federalist Papers* (New York: Viking Penguin, 1987), 51:322.
4. Henry Kariel, *Beyond Liberalism* (New York: Harper & Row, 1977), p. 25.
5. Drew McCoy, "An Unfinished Revolution: The Quest for Economic Independence in the Early Republic," in *The American Revolution: Its Character and Limits*, ed. Jack P. Greene (New York: New York University Press, 1987), p. 132; see also Edmund Morgan, "The Puritan Ethic and the American Revolution," in his *The Challenge of the American Revolution* (New York: W. W. Norton, 1976), passim.

ownership was the price for suffrage. More significantly, as civil society developed, prosperity became the real cost for individual economic autonomy. Madison clearly appreciated and feared the genuine political and economic dimensions to property; throughout his public life he agonized over the tension that, in the long run, democracy and property would inevitably create.

The twentieth century's concern over whether Madison should be considered a pluralist depends entirely on the definition of pluralism being used. If it is the pluralism of David Truman or Robert Dahl, who argued that out of the fierce competition among interest groups public policy (or the common good) is created, then Madison certainly cannot be considered a pluralist. As Gordon Wood explains Madison: "He hoped that these competing parties and interests in an enlarged republic would neutralize themselves, which in turn would allow rational men to promote the public good."[6] Yet Madison conceived of society, economics, and government as being composed of plural sects, factions, interests, classes, parties, and other groups. Insofar as his empirical theory told him that these self-interested and passionate factions could automatically check and balance each other, creating social and political equilibrium, he most assuredly must be counted as a pluralist. Madison never thought the common good developed out of these struggles; rather, they canceled each other out, so that equilibrium resulted. As a state-builder, all he had to do—given factious human nature—was accept the plural nature of reality and permit the multiple factions to perform collectively and unknowingly their self-balancing act. When this conception of pluralism becomes linked with Madison's governmental system, designed both to balance itself and to permit an elite, limited ruling power, his theory can be seen as an early form of what C. B. Macpherson calls the pluralist-elitist-equilibrium model of political theory.[7]

6. Gordon Wood, "Democracy and the Constitution," in *How Democratic Is the Constitution?* ed. R. A. Goldwin and W. A. Schambra (Washington, D.C.: American Enterprise Institute Press, 1980), p. 11; cf. Russel Hanson, *The Democratic Imagination in America* (Princeton, N.J.: Princeton University Press, 1985), p. 69; and Neal Riemer, *James Madison: Creating the American Constitution* (Washington, D.C.: Congressional Quarterly, 1986), p. 105.

7. C. B. Macpherson, *The Life and Times of Liberal Democracy* (New York:

Civil society, then, constituted a rich political realm. Madison understood it to be crucial to sustaining an overall social equilibrium, where economic activity provided the outlet for human interests and passions. To that end, he read Adam Smith, David Hume, Robert Owen, William Godwin, J. B. Say, among others, hoping to discover "the true principles of political economy [which] are everywhere needed . . . more so in our young country than in some old ones."[8] This chapter, then, will continue the discussion of the socioeconomic base of Madison's political theory. It will focus on his understanding of economic development (and decay), his general support of free trade, and his rather unsophisticated view of public credit. In addition, some time will be spent considering Madison's intriguing, hopelessly nostalgic but heroic quest for economic justice in the repayment of the Revolutionary War debt. Once this segment of Madison's view of civil society has been sketched out, the subsequent chapter will analyze his thoughts on property and rights, including religious-based rights, since religious factions had the potential to disrupt civil society and had to be neutralized.

Madison firmly believed in the idea of economic progress. In this, he followed the path articulated by Adam Smith, where civilization developed from hunting and gathering tribes to civil society. And like Smith, Madison found a natural linkage between reason, philosophy, and commerce. In an 1785 letter to Lafayette on the subject of Spanish control of the Mississippi River, Madison wrote that "Nature has given the use of the Mississippi to those who may settle on its waters, as she gave to the United States their independence." See-

---

Oxford University Press, 1979), p. 77: "Perhaps the only adequately descriptive name would be one which combined all three terms, 'the pluralist elitist equilibrium model', for these three characteristics are equally central to it. It is pluralist in that it starts from the assumption that the society which a modern democratic political system must fit is a plural society, that is, a society consisting of individuals each of whom is pulled in many directions by his many interests, now in company with one group of his fellows, now with another. It is elitist in that it assigns the main role in the political process to self-chosen groups of leaders. It is an equilibrium model in that it presents the democratic process as a system which maintains an equilibrium between the demand and supply of political goods."

8. JM to J. B. Say, 4 May 1816, *Letters and Other Writings of James Madison*, ed. William C. Rives and Philip R. Fendall, 4 vols. (Philadelphia: J. B. Lippincott, 1884), 3:2.

ing the hand of Nature (and God) everywhere he wished, Madison told Lafayette that "Nature seems on all sides to be reasserting those rights which have so long been trampled on by tyranny & bigotry. Philosophy & Commerce are the auxiliaries to whom she is indebted for her triumphs. Will it be presumptuous to say that those nations will shew most wisdom as well as acquire most glory, who, instead of forcing her current into artificial channels, endeavor to ascertain its tendency & to anticipate its effects."[9]

If the United States could follow the laws of political economy, certain substantial benefits would automatically follow. In terms of control of the Mississippi, Madison demonstrated to Lafayette that Spain's interest stood separate and antithetical to that of the rest of Europe, especially those Europeans who supported American independence. "The commerce of the U.S.," wrote Madison, "is advantageous to Europe in two respects, first by the unmanufactured produce which they export; secondly by the manufactured imports which they consume." Madison told Lafayette that if the Mississippi could be "shut up" by Spain, settlements would be discouraged, producing negative consequences for Europe and the United States. For Europeans, the cost of American products would rise while demand for imports would fall. National wealth, however, was rarely Madison's main preoccupation. Rather, he concerned himself with the artificial closure of American territory from future agricultural development. In 1785, he merely stated that "the hands without land at home being discouraged from seeking it where alone it could be found, must be turned in a great degree to manufacturing."[10] In other writings, Madison spelled out the negative—albeit inevitable—dimensions to this specific labor transfer away from agriculture to less desirable forms of employment such as manufacturing.

About a year later, Madison more candidly discussed the issue of the distribution of labor in a letter to Jefferson. After reading Jeffer-

9. JM to Lafayette, 20 Mar. 1785, *PJM* 8:251.

10. Ibid., 8:252–253; see also JM to Thomas Jefferson, 20 Aug. 1784, *PJM* 8:107, where he wrote that "the settlement of the back country, which will be greatly promoted by a free use of the Missipi. will be beneficial to all the nations who either directly or indirectly trade with the U. S. By this expansion of our people, the establish. of internal manufactures will not only be for many years delayed, but the consumption of foreign manufactures will be continually increasing with the increase of our numbers."

son's vivid accounts of the conditions of the "idle poor of Europe," Madison reflected further on the relationship between population and social contentment. He urged Jefferson to conduct a comparative study of the European poor. "I have no doubt," Madison wrote, "that the misery of the lower classes will be found to abate wherever the Government assumes a freer aspect, & the laws favor a subdivision of property." Still he doubted that this could account for the "comparative comfort of the Mass of people in the United States." Their comfort he attributed neither to fair government nor to more egalitarian property laws, as Jefferson believed, but simply to the more "limited population" in the United States: "A certain degree of misery seems inseparable from a high degree of populousness."

To prove his point to Jefferson and simultaneously reveal his Malthusian inclinations, he raised a speculative query: "If the lands in Europe which are now dedicated to the amusement of the idle rich, were parcelled out among the idle poor, I readily conceive the happy revolution which would be experienced by a certain proportion of the latter." As was often Madison's habit, especially when he hoped to challenge if not outright destroy a correspondent's position, he began by appearing to agree with him. He would then continue to articulate his own opinion, which in effect refuted the other's. Again, he raised a rhetorical question with Jefferson and then supplied his own devastating reply.

But still would there not remain a great proportion unrelieved? No problem in political Oeconomy has appeared to me more puzzling than that which relates to the most proper distribution of the inhabitants of a Country fully peopled. Let the lands be shared among them ever so wisely, & let them be supplied with labourers ever so plentifully; as there must be a great surplus of subsistence, there will also remain a great surplus of inhabitants, a greater by far than will be employed in cloathing both themselves & those who feed them, and in administering to both, every other necessary & even comfort of life. What is to be done with this surplus? Hitherto we have seen them distributed into Manufacturers of superfluities, idle proprietors of productive funds, domestics, soldiers, merchants, mariners, and a few other less numerous classes. All these classes notwithstanding have been found insufficient to absorb the redundant members of populous society; and yet a reduction of most of those classes enters into the very reform which appears so necessary & desireable.

Recalling that he was writing to Jefferson, Madison acknowledged some advantages to "a more equal partition of property" and a "juster Government," but the problems he foresaw were inevitable and unrelenting. Rather than push his argument to its logical conclusion, he broke off his attack by apologizing: "I forget that I am writing a letter not a dissertation."[11]

The next year, at the Constitutional Convention, Madison's speech of 26 June 1787 demonstrated that trends in economic development and issues of property distribution still weighed on his mind. He argued that "in framing a system which we wish to last for ages, we shd. not lose sight of the changes which ages will produce. An increase of population will of necessity increase the proportion of those who will labour under all the hardships of life, & secretly sigh for a more equal distribution of its blessings."[12] While Madison viewed surplus population as directly linked to pressures to redistribute property, he simultaneously believed that land, territory, and space could postpone and neutralize the building up of such pressures—at least for a time. This was sound Newtonian physics: enlarge the system that must contain the increasingly powerful forces, and the overall pressure of the system will be diminished; when the system can no longer be expanded, the increasing pressure will cause it to explode. In other words, paraphrasing Drew McCoy in his exceptional study of Madison's political economy, Madison thought in terms of developing across space in a race against time.[13] Furthermore, he perceived land, in its essence, as containing certain inherent characteristics that made it the keystone of a healthy and stable

11. JM to Thomas Jefferson, 19 June 1786, *PJM* 9:76–77.
12. JM speech, 26 June 1787, *The Records of the Federal Convention of 1787*, ed. Max Farrand, 4 vols. (New Haven, Conn.: Yale University Press, 1937), 1:422; cf. Joyce Oldham Appleby, *Capitalism and a New Social Order* (New York and London: New York University Press, 1983), p. 99, where she argues: "In so thoroughly embracing the liberal position on private property and economic freedom, the Jeffersonians seemed unable to envision a day when the free exercise of men's wealth-creating talents would produce its own class-divided society." This observation could not apply to Madison.
13. Drew McCoy, *The Elusive Republic: Political Economy in Jeffersonian America* (Chapel Hill: University of North Carolina Press, 1980), pp. 121, 131.

political system. This view can be seen in his *National Gazette* essay "Republican Distribution of Citizens."

Madison's rather elegant "Republican Distribution of Citizens" almost sounds as if it came from the more gifted hand of Thomas Jefferson, who peppered his writings with poetic passages on the basic goodness of farmers and the virtues associated with a pastoral life.[14] Madison started this brief essay with a list of the appropriate values by which to judge the "best distribution" of citizens: "*health, virtue, intelligence* and *competency* in the *greatest number* of citizens." Unlike Jefferson, who preferred freedom and instability to stability without freedom, *if* a choice between the two conditions had to be made, Madison amended these four values with the following qualification: "It is needless to add to these objects, *liberty* and *safety*. The first is presupposed by them. The last must result from them."[15]

Even at his Jeffersonian best, Madison was concerned primarily with a search for balance and safety. Armed with his criterion, Madison evaluated the life of the husbandman compared to that of the sailor; the former represented the ideal economic lifestyle for a citizen, the latter the worst. While health "is an appurtenance of" the husbandman's "property and employment," virtue—which here Madison defined as "the health of the soul"—was "another part of his patrimony." On the issue of intelligence, Madison admitted that a tradeoff existed: "*Intelligence* may be cultivated in this as well as in any other walk of life. If the mind be less susceptible of polish in retirement than in a croud, it is more capable of profound and comprehensive efforts. Is it more ignorant of some things? It has a compensation in its ignorance of others." The question of "competency" was similarly settled in favor of farmers since "liberty is at the same time their lot." Madison closed this paragraph exhorting his readership: " 'Tis not the country that peoples either the Bridewells or the Bedlams. These mansions of wretchedness are tenanted from the distresses and vices of overgrown cities."

In light of his tendency to conceive of issues in terms of extremes

---

14. For example, see Jefferson's response to Query XIX in his *Notes on the State of Virginia*, ed. William Peden (New York: W. W. Norton, 1972), pp. 164–165.

15. "Republican Distribution of Citizens," *National Gazette, PJM* 14:245; JM's emphasis.

and his own reluctance to travel, it may be interesting that Madison selected the occupation of the sailor as the one where "the blessings of life are most denied." "His health is continually assailed," wrote Madison, and "his virtue, at no time aided, is occasionally exposed to every scene that can poison it." Madison continued his assault and maintained that the sailor's "mind, like his body, is imprisoned within the bark that transports him." Although he said nothing explicitly about the sailor's competency, it would appear he had no need to. He ended this paragraph with a somber observation: "How unfortunate, that in the intercourse, by which nations are enlightened and refined, and their means of safety extended, the immediate agents should be distinguished by the hardest condition of humanity."[16]

Between "the two extremes" of the husbandman and the sailor existed "those who work the materials furnished by the earth in its natural or cultivated state." Madison acknowledged that a whole spectrum of "manufacturing and mechanical industry" existed, which possessed different "merits" that should be "graduated accordingly" when considering the best distribution of citizens. Consistent with his earlier values, he argued: "Whatever is least favorable to vigor of body, to the faculties of the mind, or to the virtues or the utilities of life, instead of being forced or fostered by public authority, ought to be seen with regret *as long as* occupations more friendly to human happiness, lie vacant." Notice the Malthusian note of reality creeping into the last simple words of Madison's advice: "*as long as* occupations more friendly to human happiness, lie vacant."[17] As we know, Madison believed that in time such choices would be closed. He expressed his view to Richard Rush in 1818: "I have looked over Malthus, and I think the world much indebted to him for the views he has given of an interesting subject; and for the instructive application he makes of them to a state of things inseparable from old countries, and awaiting the maturity of young ones."[18]

16. Ibid. Even making allowances for the fact that the essay was about "Citizens," it is amazing how Madison, like Jefferson, could conveniently forget that "the hardest condition of humanity" had to be that of the slave.

17. Ibid., 14:245–246.

18. JM to Richard Rush, 24 July 1818, *Letters and Other Writings* 3:102.

And when equal opportunity expired with the closure of free land, Madison agonized over what would happen next.[19]

In his 1792 essay, however, the perceived Federalist threat to political balance, not the exhaustion of the frontier, produced Madison's immediate fear. Consequently, he noted that in addition to agriculture, sailing, the mechanical and manufacturing arts there existed the alternative of "several professions of more elevated pretensions, the merchant, the lawyer, the physician, the philosopher, the divine." While these professions were clearly preferable to other occupations, Madison never specifically endorsed them as options for the public; indeed, with his view of the inequality of human faculties how could he? He merely observed how these professions "form a certain proportion of every civilized society, and readily adjust their numbers to its demands, and its circumstances."[20]

Madison himself did not really fit into any of the occupational categories he described. In his private notes for this essay, he wrote that "the class of literati is not less necessary than any other. They are the cultivators of the human mind—the manufacturers of useful knowledge—the agents of the commerce of ideas—the censors of public manners—the teachers of the arts of life and the means of happiness."[21] Since "the class of literati" may perhaps be the most appropriate place to put Madison, notice how, in private, he associated only positive attributes with the literati, believing they fulfilled functions analogous to those of farmers, merchants, manufacturers, and others. Yet in the public expression of his thoughts, he failed to mention the literati, preferring to emphasize the Jeffersonian heart of the distribution question: "The class of citizens who provide at once their own food and their own raiment, may be viewed as the most truly independent and happy. They are more: they are the best basis of public liberty, and the strongest bulwark of public safety. It follows, that the greater the proportion of this class to the whole so-

19. See JM to Thomas Jefferson, 20 Aug. 1784, *PJM* 8:107, where Madison suggested that if the Mississippi were free from Spain's control it would have the positive effect of increasing the availability of cheap land and thereby forestalling the development of "internal manufactures . . . for 20 or 25 years."

20. "Republican Distribution of Citizens," *PJM* 14:246.

21. "Notes for Essays," *PJM* 14:168. This passage becomes even more instructive when one recalls that JM held rather sophisticated views on the powerful influence of public opinion in a republic.

ciety, the more free, the more independent, and the more happy must be the society itself."[22]

Although farmers established the healthy base of Madison's civil society, given his Malthusian view of the rise and fall of economic development he remained always on guard to watch out for the labor transfer from agriculture to other pursuits. In *Federalist* 41 he warned that the harmonious interdependence of agriculture and importation of manufactured goods could last only so long. With the inevitable exodus from farming to other occupations, government had to be prepared to deal with these "revolutions."

> As long as agriculture continues the sole field of labor, the importation of manufactures must increase as the consumers multiply. As soon as domestic manufactures are begun by the hands not called for by agriculture, the imported manufactures will decrease as the numbers of people increase. In a more remote stage, the imports may consist in considerable part of raw materials which will be wrought into articles for exportation, and will, therefore, require rather the encouragement of bounties than to be loaded with discouraging duties. A system of government meant for duration ought to contemplate these revolutions and be able to accommodate itself to them.[23]

Madison fully appreciated the advantages inherent in the diversity of economic development found in the infant nation. "Some of the states," he wrote, "are little more than a society of husbandmen. Few of them have made much progress in those branches of industry, which give a variety and complexity to the affairs of a nation." In spite of this lack of progress in preparing for a future tied to manufacturing, Madison predicted that even in these more primitive segments of the nation, "the fruits of a more advanced population" would necessitate an increase in political representation while economically the additional "fruit" would have to find employment somewhere beyond the farm.

Madison's preference for agriculture can be seen as well in his thoughts on immigration and naturalization. In the early 1790s, he argued in Congress in favor of a residency requirement for aliens

22. "Republican Distribution," *PJM* 14:246.
23. *Federalist* 41:271–272.

seeking citizenship. In the course of his remarks, he acknowledged the desirability of America holding "out as many inducements as possible, for the worthy part of mankind to come and settle amongst us, and throw their fortunes into a common lot with ours." He defined "the worthy part" as those who could "encrease the wealth and strength of the community" rather than "merely . . . swell the catalogue of people." Always concerned about surplus population, Madison wanted only productive immigrants who established and maintained a residence in the United States to be granted citizenship; he even speculated on the desirability of establishing a "step by step" procedure by which citizenship would be conferred over time.[24]

More than a quarter of a century later, Madison still advocated that the government "communicate the rights of Citizens by degrees, and in that way, preclude or abridge the abuses committed by naturalized merchants particularly Ship owners." In this private correspondence to Richard Peters, Madison revealed his reasons for concern over immigration and presented a "graduated" scale of occupational desirability. As always, farmers ranked first: "The Cultivators of the soil are of a character and in so minute a proportion to our Agricultural population, that they give no foreign tint whatever to its complexion. When they come among us too, it is with such a deep feeling of its being for good & all, that their adopted Country soon takes the place of a native home."[25] At this time, Madison did not see a significant difference between the cultivators and "the Mechanical class."

The same cannot be said for "the mercantile class." Madison's discussion of the "different features" of this class reveals some of his deeper insights into the attributes of property. "Their proportional number, their capital or their credit, and their intelligence often, give them pretensions, and even an influence among the native class," complained Madison. The root of his reservations with the mercantile class, however, concerned not their pretensions, but their property holdings: "They are also less permanently tied to their new Country by the nature of their property & pursuits than either of the other classes, a translation of them to another being more easy."

24. Naturalization speech, 3 Feb. 1790, *PJM* 13:17.
25. JM to Richard Peters, 22 Feb. 1819, in Gaillard Hunt, ed., *The Writings of James Madison*, 9 vols. (New York: G. P. Putnam's Sons, 1900–1910) 8:425, 424 (hereafter cited as *WJM*).

Given the portability and liquidity of their property, Madison suspected that their condition would "facilitate violations of the duties" to their new nation. "I believe it cannot be doubted," he concluded, "that naturalized Citizens among us have found it more easy than native ones to practice certain frauds."[26]

An 1812 letter to "My Red Children" betrayed additional Madison prejudices concerning agriculture, among other things. Wanting to keep the various tribes out of the war with Great Britain, Madison began his message sounding somewhat like Socrates retelling the myth of metals found in *Plato's Republic*. "The red people who live on this same great Island with the White people of the 18 fires are made by the Great Spirit out of the same earth, from parts of it differing in colour only."[27] With the appearance of abstract equality established, Madison proceeded to lecture on the nature of paternal and filial obligations. "A father ought to give good advice to his children, and it is the duty of his children to hearken to it." On this occasion his "fatherly advice" consisted of warning his "children" not to be fooled: "The British, who are weak, are doing all they can by their bad birds to decoy the red people into the war on their side. I warn all the red people to avoid the ruin this must bring upon them. And I say to you, my children, your father does not ask you to join his warriors. Sit still on your seats, and be witnesses that they are able to beat their enemies and protect their red friends."[28]

Madison further advised them to follow the agricultural example of "the white people." In a passage reminiscent of Locke's natural law justification for unequal property holdings, Madison juxtaposed the living conditions of the two peoples.

You see how the Country of the 18 fires is filled with people. They increase like the corn they put in the ground. They all have good houses to shelter them from all weathers, good clothes, suitable to all seasons, and as for food of all sorts, you see they have enough and to spare. No man, woman, or child of the 18 fires ever perished of hunger. Compare all this with the

26. Ibid., 8:424–425; notice that JM does not suggest that some concept of virtue explained the lack of "fraud" committed by native citizens, but rather that it was not as "easy" to "practice" them.
27. "Talk to Indians," 1812, *Letters and Other Writings* 2:553.
28. Ibid., 2:555.

condition of the red people. They are scattered here and there in handfuls. Their lodges are cold, leaky, and smoky. They have hard fare, and often not enough of it.

When Madison asked "Why this mighty difference?" he responded in pure Lockean terms. "The white people," he wrote, "breed cattle and sheep. They plow the earth, and make it give them every thing they want. They spin and weave. Their heads and their hands make all the elements and productions of nature useful to them." For Locke as well as Madison, the rational employment of the earth explained its bounty. If the tribes would simply follow the correct example, as God intended them to, they too could enjoy "constant peace and friendship." Madison told them, "It is in your power to be like them. The ground that feeds one Lodge by hunting would feed a great band by the plow and the hoe. The Great Spirit has given you, like your white brethren, good heads to contrive, strong arms, and active bodies. Use them."[29] Of course, if they used their heads in the manner Madison urged, they would have lost nothing but their way of life.

In 1828 Madison further conveyed his understanding of the dynamic economic relationship between agriculture and manufacturing in a letter to Nicholas Trist. Under ideal conditions what was good for one would be good for the other; and conversely, under contrary circumstances, the opposite would obtain. In this letter, Madison explained the low price of Virginia real estate as being dependent on several economic factors. While he had no interest in watching the bottom fall out of the land market, Madison appreciated the need for cheap land for both immigrants and the excess domestic population. Moreover, he demonstrated here that crude economic considerations of profitability could not explain the attractiveness of

29. Ibid., 2:555. See John Locke, *Second Treatise of Government*, ed. C. B. Macpherson (Indianapolis: Hackett, 1980), pp. 25–26: "There cannot be a clearer demonstration of any thing, than the several nations of the *Americans* are of this, who are rich in land, and poor in all the comforts of life; whom nature having furnished as liberally as any other people, with the materials of plenty, i. e. a fruitful soil, apt to produce in abundance, what might serve for food, raiment, and delight; yet for *want of improving it by labour*, have not one hundredth part of the conveniences we enjoy: and a king of a large and fruitful territory there, feeds, lodges, and is glad worse than a day-labourer in *England*" (Locke's emphasis).

agriculture compared to other economic endeavors. Among the explanations foremost in Madison's mind was "the pride of ownership when this exists or is expected." If pride seemed significant to humans, then relatively cheap land was critical. It permitted actual possession by the many; and perhaps even more importantly for the future, it provided the hope, the expectation, of possession. Abundant, cheap land supplied Madison with the promise of equal opportunity for humans of unequal talents and abilities.

Ownership, however, constituted only one of agriculture's preferential factors. "The air of freedom, the [loss] of constancy & identity of application, are known to seduce to rural life the drudges in workshops."[30] Madison's assumption that humans preferred the path of least resistance when it came to securing the necessities of life is evident when he asked, "Why do such numbers flee annually from the more populous to less populous parts of the U.S. where land is cheaper? Evidently Because less labour, is more competent to supply the necessaries & comforts of life. Can an instance be produced of emigrants from the soil of the West, to the manufactories of Mass[a-chusetts] or Pen[nsylvania]."

Madison demonstrated his appreciation of the powerful impact of cheap land on the living conditions and wages of urban workers. He speculated: "What w[ould] be the condition of Birmingham or Manchester were 40 or 50 millions of fertile acres placed at an easy distance and offered at the price of our Western lands?" He responded unequivocally: "What a transfer of capital, & difficulty of retaining or procuring operatives w[ould] ensue!" Even more specifically, he noted how this situation would hurt the manufacturers since wages would have to rise significantly to keep labor from moving to agriculture: "And altho' the addition to the products of the earth, by cheapening the necessaries of life, might seem to favor manufactures, the advantage would be vastly overbalanced by the increased price of labour produced by the new demand for it, and by the superior attractiveness of the agricultural demand."[31] Inexpensive land, spread out over a vast territory, could keep economic exploitation to a mini-

---

30. JM to N. P. Trist, 26 Jan. 1828, *WJM* 9:303–304; as published, the letter reads "less" instead of "loss."
31. JM to N. P. Trist, 26 Jan. 1828, *WJM* 9:305.

mum—until the land ran out because of overpopulation and economic development.[32]

Before closing his letter to Trist, Madison explained another significant dimension to the role in social production played by land in contrast to machines and materials. Land he termed "a co-operating *self-agent*, with a surface not extendible by art, as machines & in many cases materials also, may be multiplied by it." Madison's point appears to have been the ultimate scarcity of land in contrast to machines and other materials that could be expanded by reproduction beyond any artificial limit. This does not imply that Madison repudiated his views of the valuable contributions made by scientific agriculture that, in effect, increased the quantity of land by making it more productive. Rather, in comparing the two factors—land to machines and materials—he acknowledged an ultimate limit to the former. As he expressed it: "Were the surface or the fertility of the earth Equally susceptible of increase, artificial & indefinite the cases would be parallel."[33] Since they are not "equal," land's scarcity always made it, in Madison's mind, the central economic factor and an issue of ultimate power.

The uncertainties and travails of commercial life in major cities concerned Madison in his 1792 essay on "Fashion." He seemed appalled and alarmed about what the example of the plight of "BUCKLE MANUFACTURERS of Birmingham, Wassal, Wolverhampton, and their environs" promised for America's future. The immediate result of English consumers following the fashion trend of "SHOESTRINGS & SLIPPERS" rather than buckles meant that more than "TWENTY THOUSAND persons . . . are at present without employ, almost destitute of bread, and exposed to the horrors of want at the most inclement season." In a feeble attempt to change consumer preferences back to shoe buckles, the manufacturers petitioned the prince of Wales to come to their aid.

Madison's specific complaints about fashion could apply equally well to the market itself: "It is to no purpose to address FASHION

---

32. Drew McCoy, *The Last of the Fathers: James Madison and the Republican Legacy* (New York: Cambridge University Press, 1989), p. 185: "Madison did not doubt that with every passing year more and more Americans who might once have expected to own and till their own land would instead find themselves laboring for wages in workshops and factories—if, indeed, they were fortunate enough to find secure employment of any kind."

33. JM to N. P. Trist, 26 Jan. 1828, *WJM* 9:305.

herself, she being void of feeling and deaf to argument.'' The manufacturers incorrectly believed that since royal subjects were ''accus-
tomed to listen[ing] to his voice, and to obey his commands,'' if the
prince would ''give that direction to the *public taste*'' he could be assured of ''the lasting gratitude of the petitioners'' as buckles returned in vogue.[34] The prince of Wales heeded his subjects' pleas. He
ordered his entourage to wear buckles. ''Devoid of feeling and deaf to
argument,'' the market, however, takes its command from no one.
The buckle market collapsed. The economic consequences for many
were devastating. Finally, the arbitrariness of it all seemed too much
for Madison's orderly mind.[35]

While Madison never possessed the economic foresight of Alexander Hamilton, neither did he share Jefferson's naiveté about the human costs of economic progress. If the United States could have remained agricultural and maintained a stable population, political
life would have been more simple. But this, of course, was not possible in Madison's worldview. Consequently, occupations that shared
the desirable characteristics of husbandry—health, virtue, intelligence, competency, liberty, and safety—should be encouraged; those
that resembled the fashion industry should be resorted to only as a
last resort. Madison's critical analysis of the plight of the buckle
manufacturers indicated that he considered the vulnerability, dependency, and arbitrariness of ''mere fashion'' dictating market decisions to be deeply offensive. ''The most precarious of all occupations which give bread to the industrious,'' wrote Madison, ''are
those depending on mere fashion.'' (Then again, from a person who
reputedly always dressed in black, what other response could be expected?)

In a ''free state,'' he continued, the ''least desirable'' occupations
are those that ''produce the most servile dependence of one class of
citizens on another class.'' Dependence always stood subject to
abuse. Madison found ''the evil . . . in its extreme,'' however,
''where the wants on one side are the absolute necessaries; and on

34. ''Fashion,'' *National Gazette*, 20 Mar. 1792, *PJM* 14:257–258; JM's emphasis.
35. Harold Laski, *Introduction to Politics* (New York: Barnes and Noble, 1963),
p. 43, acknowledges ''the desire of the bourgeoisie to protect itself from arbitrary
power.'' Arbitrariness was one of JM's major concerns in matters of political
economy.

the other are neither absolute necessaries, nor result from the habitual oeconomy of life, but are the mere caprices of fancy." This kind of economic dependency produced servility in humans. Madison appealed to the "manly sentiments" of his audience as he further described the buckle incident: "We see a proof of it in the *spirit* of the address. *Twenty thousand* persons are to get or go without their bread, as a wanton youth, may fancy to wear his shoes with or without straps, or to fasten his straps with strings or with buckles. Can any despotism be more cruel than a situation, in which the existence of thousands depends on one will, and that will on the most slight and fickle of all motives, a mere whim of imagination."[36] Still a young nation, the United States benefited from a favorable economic climate. While the country was still in the process of developing beyond an agricultural into a commercial society, even those Americans who did not work the fields were not yet subject to the abuses caused by "a mere whim of the imagination."

The contrast between English city dwellers and Americans appeared stark. Americans either "live on their own soil" or were "occupied in supplying wants, which being founded in, solid utility, in comfortable accommodation, or in settled habits, produce a reciprocity of dependence, at once ensuring subsistence, and inspiring a dignified sense of social rights." From Madison's perspective, "reciprocity of dependence" created the appropriately balanced power relationship; and Americans enjoyed the fruits of this kind of economic activity. A nonreciprocal dependence—where the first party needed the other party but the second party could live without the first—created an unbalanced economic relationship that, if multiplied throughout a nation, would eventually produce civil unrest. Madison concluded his moral instruction by telling his readers that "the condition of those who receive employment and bread from the precarious source of fashion and superfluity, is a lesson to nations, as well as to individuals."[37]

Living at a time when the country remained blessed with abundant free land and therein the promise of equal opportunity, Madison never witnessed this specific problem in the United States. He knew, however, that an American Birmingham was only a matter of

36. "Fashion," *PJM* 14:258; JM's emphasis.
37. Ibid.

time. Haunted by this prospect and the logic of his own critical analysis, Madison published perhaps the most perplexing of his *National Gazette* essays, "Property," less than a week after his "Fashion" essay. His tortured analysis of property and rights remains so central to understanding Madison's perspective on politics, economics, and political economy that an extended discussion of his essay must wait for the next chapter. Prior to that, however, his position on free trade and the free market needs to be explained.

Throughout his life, Madison consistently responded favorably to the theory of free trade: like all abstract intellectual constructions predicting human behavior, it seemed perfect in theory, but in practice it would always fall short of the ideal. In essence, this attitude expressed Madison's position on *laissez-faire* economics. In the summer of 1785, while thinking about the relationship between the power of Congress under the Articles of Confederation and the regulation of trade, Madison characteristically described his position to James Monroe in ideal versus real-world terms. "Viewing in the abstract the question whether the power of regulating trade, to a certain degree at least, ought to be vested in Congress, it appears to me not to admit of a doubt," he told Monroe. Typically, he continued his position with a conditional statement: "If it be necessary to regulate trade at all, it surely is necessary to lodge the power, where trade can be regulated with effect." Still thinking in the speculative "if" mode—as in "if men were angels"—Madison wrote: "Much indeed is it to be wished, as I conceive, that no regulations of trade . . . no restrictions or imposts whatever, were necessary. A perfect freedom is the System which would be my choice." Madison's next words, however, snapped his argument back to the world of humans and politics as he qualified his above observations. "But before such a system will be eligible," he wrote, the United States "must be out of debt" and "all other nations must concur in it."[38] Of course, Madison knew this would never occur. "Perfect freedom" remained not only desirable but perfectly unattainable.

Four decades of political experience solidified this perspective in Madison's mind. In an 1828 letter to Joseph Cabell, Madison took extraordinary care to make sure that his position on the isolationist

38. JM to James Monroe, 7 Aug. 1785, *PJM* 8:333-334.

"Theory of 'Let us alone'" would not be distorted by Cabell, who wanted to publish Madison's views. The problem with "let us alone" centered on its utopian assumption "that all nations concur in a perfect freedom of commercial intercourse." He assured Cabell that "this golden age of free trade has not yet arrived; nor is there a single nation that has set the example. No Nation can, indeed, safely do so, until a reciprocity at least be ensured to it."[39] At this early point in the letter, there appeared to be some slender hope for reaching this "golden age" if all actors would simply behave reasonably. A few paragraphs later, lest he be misunderstood, Madison slammed the door shut on hope: "The Theory supposes moreover a perpetual peace, not less chimerical, it is to be feared, than a universal freedom of commerce."[40]

Appreciating fully the logic behind Madison's view of free trade will demonstrate his commitment to the principles of modern market economics, at least as they were articulated by Adam Smith in its golden age.[41] Always looking for the appropriate balance between extreme positions, Madison, in an 1829 letter to Frederick List, accurately portrayed his position on government support of domestic manufacturing. "The true policy (until all nations make themselves commercially one nation)"—an idea that Madison in other writings dismissed as chimerical—"will be found to lie between the extremes of doing nothing and prescribing everything; between admitting no exceptions to the rule of 'laissez faire,' and converting the exceptions into the rule."[42]

This represented Madison's public position on commercial policy from the first days of the new government. On 8 April 1789, in a speech in the House of Representatives, Madison claimed the issue of import and tonnage duties "to be of the greatest magnitude" and "requires our first attention."[43] The next day, he presented an early expression of the position found in his 1829 letter to List. "If my gen-

39. JM to Joseph C. Cabell, 30 Oct. 1828, WJM 9:317.

40. Ibid., 9:319; JM had already stated the first half of this assessment in "Universal Peace," National Gazette, 31 Jan. 1792, PJM 14:206–208.

41. See Forrest McDonald, Novus Ordo Seclorum: The Intellectual Origins of the Constitution (Lawrence: University Press of Kansas, 1985), p. 128, who states that "Madison was said to have quoted from it [Wealth of Nations] almost unconsciously, without attribution, in his speeches."

42. JM to Frederick List, 3 Feb. 1829, Letters and Other Writings 4:12.

43. JM speech, 8 Apr. 1789, PJM 12:65. The accuracy of the speeches during the

eral principle is a good one, that commerce ought to be free, and labour and industry left at large to find its proper object," he argued,
then "the only thing which remains, will be to discover the exceptions that do not come within the rule I have laid down." The exceptions, however, were inevitable. The ideal of the general principle remained unrealistic. Madison called for "the fostering hand of
government," within sharp limits, to protect infant industries from
the destructive impact of mature, foreign competition.[44] To Joseph
Cabell, nearly forty years later, he made it evident that he had
learned the true spirit behind the developing capitalist world as he
suggested government protection not only from foreign governments, but also from the "great manufacturing capitalists" who
wanted "to strangle in the cradle the infant manufactures of an extensive customer or an anticipated rival."[45]

Among the reasons Madison presented for state involvement was
what he called "national prudence." Since prior governmental encouragement had already developed some industries that otherwise
would not have survived, Madison believed that to abandon them
now would be wrong: "It would be cruel to neglect them and divert
their industry to other channels, for it is not possible for the hand of
man to shift from one employment to another, without being injured by the change." Of course, "national prudence" would be
equally concerned with the autonomy of the nation, which could
only be achieved with a solid and diverse economic base.[46] There can
be no doubt that Madison's fundamental economic concern centered on national independence: power, not profits, drove his calculations. In this speech, he already demonstrated his willingness to employ food as a weapon in international relations. Agriculture must be
encouraged because of the uniqueness of the American situation
where "we may be said to have a monopoly in agriculture." And

---

early days of Congress has been challenged by many people. JM himself condemned the record, yet also acknowledged (*PJM* 12:64) that "the ideas of the
speakers, may for the most part be collected from them" (JM to Edward Everett,
7 Jan. [1832]). For a concise and thorough discussion of this issue, see the editorial note for "Sources for Madison's Speeches of the First Session," *PJM* 12:62–
64.

44. JM speech, 9 Apr. 1789, *PJM* 12:71–72.
45. JM to Joseph Cabell, 30 Oct. 1828, *WJM* 9:321.
46. JM speech, 9 Apr. 1789, *PJM* 12:72.

Madison fully appreciated that food would be a universal necessity, with never-ending power potential, in a Malthusian universe.

What seems particularly revealing in his early speeches, however, was Madison's appreciation and acceptance of the theoretical justification for the division of labor and a free market economy. "I own myself the friend to a very free system of commerce, and hold it as a truth, that commercial shackles are generally unjust, oppressive and impolitic—it is also a truth, that if industry and labour are left to take their own course, they will generally be directed to those objects which are the most productive, and this in a more certain and direct manner than the wisdom of the most enlightened legislature could point out." As if straight out of a primer on the economic virtues of the market, Madison believed that the individual pursuit of self-interest, once filtered through the mechanisms of civil society, would usually produce better social results than activities directed by a central authority. Again emphasizing these themes, as well as endorsing the logic behind the division of labor, Madison continued his oration:

> Nor do I think that the national interest is more promoted by such restrictions, than that the interest of individuals would be promoted by legislative interference directing the particular application of its industry. For example, we should find no advantage in saying, that every man should be obliged to furnish himself by his own labor with those accommodations which depend upon the mechanic arts, instead of employing his neighbour, who could do it for him on better terms. It would be of no advantage to the shoemaker to make his own clothes to save the expence of the taylor's bill, nor of the taylor to make his own shoes to save the expence of procuring them from the shoemaker. It would be better policy to suffer each to employ his talent in his own way.

He pushed his position to its rational conclusion, even though he would momentarily advocate necessary exceptions to this general principle. "The case is the same between the exercise of the arts and agriculture—between the city and the country, and between city and town, each capable of making particular articles in sufficient abundance to supply the other—thus all are benefitted by exchange, and the less this exchange is cramped by government, the greater are the proportions of benefit to each."[47]

More than thirty-five years after this speech, Madison gave Henry Clay a short course in economics and the logic of the invisible hand:

> The Bill, I think loses sight too much of the general principle which leaves to the judgment of individuals the choice of profitable employments for their labor & capital; and the arguments in favor of it, from the aptitudes of our situation for manufacturing Establishments, tend to shew that these would take place without a legislative interference. The law would not say to the Cotton planter you overstock the Market, and ought to plant Tobacco; nor to the Planter of Tobo., you would do better by substituting Wheat. It presumes that profit being the object of each, as the profit of each is the wealth of the whole, each will make whatever change the state of the Markets & prices may require. We see, in fact, changes of this sort frequently produced in Agricultural pursuits, by individual sagacity watching over individual interest. Any why not trust to the same guidance in favor of manufacturing industry, whenever it promises more profit than any of the Agricultural branches, or more than mercantile pursuits, from which we see Capital readily transferred to manufacturing establishments likely to yield a greater income.[48]

Earlier in his retirement, he had expressed this position in an 1819 letter to Clarkson Crolius. Madison wrote that "however true it may be in general that the industrious pursuits of individuals, ought to be regulated by their own sagacity & interest, there are practical exceptions to the Theory, which sufficiently speak for themselves."[49] There existed, moreover, a clear pattern to the "practical exceptions," having to do with creating or sustaining a powerful economy so that the United States would be dependent on no other nation. To that end, Madison willingly shaped a national commercial policy that would employ all the power of the state to establish American

47. Ibid., 12:71. See JM to Joseph Cabell, 30 Oct. 1828, *WJM* 9:317: "I will premise that I concur that, as a *general* rule, individuals ought to be deemed the best judges, of the best application of their industry and resources"; JM's emphasis.

48. JM to Henry Clay, Apr. 1824, *WJM* 9:183–184.

49. JM to Clarkson Crolius, Dec. 1819, *WJM* 9:18.

supremacy.[50] Whether the result of his frustrating experiences throughout the War of Independence and the early years of the Constitution or of his tenure as commander-in-chief throughout the War of 1812, Madison's resentment of America's vulnerability to the power of Great Britain was keen.[51] More importantly, he perceived that the relative strength of each nation could be linked to specific governmental policies that, in the case of Britain, made the most of its economic attributes and, in the case of America, did little to take advantage of its enormous potential.

In 1783 Madison suggested to Edmund Randolph that he watch and learn from England since she "is in the science of commerce particularly worthy of our attention"; Americans could learn much from "the example of old & intelligent nations," and she should not be ignored "or too hastily condemned by an infant & inexperienced one."[52] In fact, Madison learned well the science of commercial policy at the feet of his imperial masters. He knew that a strong, central state replacing the decentralized, powerless government of the Articles of Confederation appeared crucial to correcting the "unhappy effect of a continuance of the present anarchy of our commerce."[53] Once armed with a new Constitution and a central state, Madison eagerly desired "to teach those nations who have declined to enter into commercial treaties with us, that we have the power to extend or withhold advantages as their conduct shall deserve."

Once weak and easily preyed upon, the United States had reversed its situation. "We have now the power to avail ourselves of our natural superiority, and I am for beginning with some manifestation of that ability, that foreign nations may or might be taught to pay us that respect which they have neglected on account of our former imbecility."[54] Madison recalled and employed the lessons of the colonial past:

Let us review the policy of Great Britain toward us; has she ever shewn any disposition to enter into reciprocal regulations? Has

50. McCoy, *Elusive Republic*, p. 125.
51. See *PJM* 14:164, where JM compared the relationship of "Dependent Colonies" to "the superior State, not in the relation of Children and parent . . . but in that of slaves and Master." Small wonder he feared economic dependence so much.
52. JM to Edmund Randolph, 20 May 1783, *PJM* 7:61.
53. JM to Thomas Jefferson, 18 Mar. 1786, *PJM* 8:502.
54. JM speech, 25 Apr. 1789, *PJM* 12:109, 110.

she not by a temporising policy plainly declared, that until we are able and willing to do justice to ourselves, she will shut us out from her ports and make us tributary to her? Have we not seen her taking one legislative step after another, to destroy our commerce? Has not her legislature given discretionary powers to the executive, that so she might be ever on the watch, and ready to seize every advantage the weakness of our situation might expose? Have we not reason to believe she will continue a policy void of regard to us.[55]

Conceiving of this as an issue of justice as well as manhood, Madison warned that "if we are timid and inactive we disappoint the just expectations of our constituents." Demonstrating one of the deeper psychological scars of a slave mentality, he asserted that "I venture to say, we disappoint the very nation against whom the measure is principally directed." Madison concluded his speech by exhorting his colleagues "to teach the nations that are not in alliance with us, that there is an advantage to be gained by the connection: To give some early symptom of the power and will of the new government to redress our national wrongs, must be productive of benefit. We soon shall be in a condition, we now are in a condition, to wage a commercial warfare with that nation." Once again, Madison viewed agriculture as America's trump card: "The produce of this country is more necessary to the rest of the world than that of other countries is to America." This card Madison would willingly play in the interests of "justice" and "reciprocity"; or put differently, he would use it in the national interest of being treated as an equal nation-state.[56]

Relations between nations, like those between individuals, were determined by power, not benevolence. If power had to be balanced, the new nation would have to demand it as well as be able to back up its demand. Failing either, America would continue to be Britain's marionette. In the spring of 1789, while still debating issues of tonnage duties, Madison claimed that at an earlier moment "Britain shewed a disposition to form the treaty we wish for; this resulted from an apprehension, that the United States possessed both the power and inclination to do themselves justice." Perception alone,

55. Ibid., 12:111.
56. JM speech, 25 Apr. 1789, *PJM* 12:112–113. See Richard Rubenstein, *The Cunning of History* (New York: Harper & Row, 1978), passim.

as Madison demonstrated, proved insufficient. For "the moment she discovered we had not the power to perform our contracts, her disposition changed." From his sober, real-world perspective, he argued that "I can discover no motive for that nation to alter its conduct; if now that we have the power we want the inclination."[57] Later that same day he rose to reiterate his warning against the foolhardy reliance on the "gratitude" of England to do the right commercial thing: "I have all along observed her seizing to herself every advantage in commerce that presented to her view by all the ingenuity she could devise." He rhetorically asked his colleagues "if it is not the same thing whether we want the power or the will to compel them to do us commercial justice?" Knowing full well the answer to that, Madison worried about the conclusions England might draw if the United States, out of fear of retaliation, did not stand up and demand justice. "The gentlemens arguments tend to create an opinion that we have not the power? They teach us to be afraid of reprisals. If she [England] really believes us to be afraid on this head, will she not act in the manner she has hitherto done when we really did not possess the power?"[58]

Although the issue would not be resolved until the end of the War of 1812, Madison's position on the universal necessity of one power checking and balancing another—be it domestic or foreign—never wavered. That conflict, in particular, seemed to etch in his mind the significance of economic independence during times of war. In both 1819 and nearly a decade later in 1828, Madison emphasized that "there are certain articles so indispensible that no provident nation would depend for a supply of them on any other nation."[59] With added years of insight and the full knowledge that his ideas on the issue would be made public, Madison wrote:

> It is an opinion in which all must agree, that no nation ought to be unnecessarily dependent on others for the munitions of public defence, or for the materials essential to a naval force, where the nation has a maritime frontier or a foreign commerce to protect. To this class of exceptions to the theory may be added the instruments of agriculture and of mechanic arts, which sup-

57. JM speech, 4 May 1789, *PJM* 12:126–127.
58. Ibid., 12:129–130.
59. JM to Clarkson Crolius, Dec. 1819, *WJM* 9:18.

ply the other primary wants of the community. The time has been when many of these were derived from a foreign source, and some of them might relapse into that dependence were the encouragement to the fabrication of them at home withdrawn. But, as all foreign sources might be liable to interruptions too inconvenient to be hazarded, a provident policy would favor an internal and independent source as a reasonable exception to the general rule of consulting cheapness alone.[60]

The implicit point of his last sentence cannot be forgotten: Madison's world was that of political economy, never economics narrowly conceived. Consequently, power and independence rather than short-run profit maximization constituted his goal.

That Madison never accepted a narrow, abstract view of economics—always thinking of it in terms of political-economy or oeconomics—can be seen most poignantly in his views on the resolution of the national debt incurred during the Revolutionary War. As was typical of the Jeffersonians, Madison never became "a proselyte to the doctrine, that public debts are public benefits." He "consider[ed] them, on the contrary, as evils which ought to be removed as fast as honor and justice will permit." Madison considered this particular debt "so extraordinary" because it involved remarkably complex issues of national integrity, local management, prudence, as well as justice and equity.[61] Indeed, Madison's extended, inspired, and intriguing defense of the original holders of government credit, those who had been coerced into accepting the promissory notes and often had been forced to sell their paper claims against the United States, showed Madison attempting to find a balance between the disinterested judgment of the market and the dictates of his conscience. It demonstrated, moreover, that Madison was searching for economic justice, a plea, like the one for shoe buckles, that would be neither felt nor heard by either the market or his fellow congressmen.

While the ultimate repayment question in Madison's mind cen-

60. JM to Joseph Cabell, 30 Oct. 1828, *WJM* 9:320–321.
61. JM speech, 11 Feb. 1790, *PJM* 13:38; see JM to Henry Lee, 13 Apr. 1790, *PJM* 13:148: "Perhaps it is not possible to shun some of the evils you point out, without abandoning too much the reestablishment of public credit. But as far as this object will permit I go on the principle that a Public Debt is a Public curse and in a Rep. Govt. a greater than in any other."

tered on the choice between economic or political concepts of fairness, the more immediate question was twofold: First, who should be paid what amount to satisfy the debt? Second, to what degree was each state responsible for the fiscal (mis)management of other states during the war? While the latter issue involved questions of fairness, which concerned Madison, it did not appear to trouble him to the same degree as the problem of the original creditors.

In early February 1790, the Committee of the Whole House considered Secretary of the Treasury Alexander Hamilton's report on public credit.[62] Hamilton's comprehensive plan had been designed to meet the nation's obligation to foreign and domestic creditors and to assume the substantial debts accumulated by the individual states during the war; Hamilton believed his plan would present the new state as an environment conducive to secure and stable economic activity. It appears to have taken Madison some time to comprehend fully the financial logic behind Hamilton's report. To Henry Lee, Madison complained that the report "departs particularly from that simplicity which ought to be preserved in finance, more than any thing else."[63]

After another congressman, at Madison's request, moved to provide that "a discrimination be made between the original holders and their assignees, and that a scale of depreciation be prepared accordingly," Madison argued in favor of the idea.[64] Before addressing the complicated issue of exactly who was owed precisely what, Madison first had to refute the notion "that the debt itself does not exist in the extent, and form which is generally supposed" and answer the question of "what amount the public are at present engaged?" To Madison, the only debatable point seemed to be "to whom the payment is really due." While he dismissed the first two questions in a few words, the last he claimed must "lead us to a just and equitable decision"; it required considerable effort on his part to make his position clear.[65]

Since "the debt was contracted by the United States" in its "na-

62. Hamilton's report included several of the provisions found in a report written by James Madison, Oliver Ellsworth, and Alexander Hamilton in 1783 called "Report on Address to the States by Congress," 25 Apr. 1783, *PJM* 6:487–498. In light of this report, perhaps it was reasonable for Hamilton to have expected Madison's support for his economic plans.

63. JM to Henry Lee, 13 Apr. 1790, *PJM* 13:147.

64. Editor's note, JM speech of 11 Feb. 1790, *PJM* 13:34.

65. JM speech, 11 Feb. 1790, *PJM* 13:34–35.

tional capacity," the "government was nothing more than an agent . . . by which the whole body of the people acted." Reiterating arguments taken from Locke, Madison argued that although "the government has been changed, the nation remains the same. There is no change in our political duty, nor in the moral or political obligation." In other words, the change in government did not destroy civil society; it did not return the United States to a state of nature where, in Hobbes's view, all contracts are void. Rather, the public merely replaced its agent. Moreover, the public expressly reaffirmed its debt obligation when it ratified the Constitution. With equal dispatch, Madison dismissed the idea that a change of agent permitted a renegotiation of the terms of the original debt. "The United States owe the value they received, which they acknowledge, and which they have promised to pay." And that amounted to "a certain sum in principal, bearing an interest of six percent. No logic, no magic, in my opinion, can diminish the force of the obligation." Up to this point, as should be expected, Madison argued that legitimate contracts made by a people do not dissolve with a change of government.[66]

Turning to the thorny question of "to whom the payment is really due," Madison rejected any notion of the simple rules of *caveat emptor* economics. On this point he attempted to substitute "the only principles that can govern" in this "extraordinary" case: "1. Public justice; 2. public faith; 3. public credit; 4. public opinion." Madison divided into four classes the individuals to whom these criteria were to be applied: first, the original creditors who still held their securities; second, the original creditors who had sold or traded their securities; third, the present (but not original) holders of the securities; and fourth, intermediate holders, "through whose hands securities have circulated" but were no longer in their possession.

The first and last classes presented no problem. All four "principles" of justice, faith, credit, and opinion were easily resolved in favor of the former and against the latter. Relative to the intermediate (but not original) holders, Madison introduced the additional, pragmatic consideration that satisfying this group would force Congress "into a labyrinth, for which it is impossible to find a clue." Madison's real reason for rejecting this group's claim, however, addressed

---

66. Ibid.

the principles of justice, faith, credit, and opinion. He stated that since "this class were perfectly free, both in becoming, and ceasing to be creditors; and because, in general, they must have gained by their speculations," the notion of economic justice had not been violated.[67] While Madison could only guess that these intermediate security holders benefited by their speculations, the fact that their choices to purchase and sell were "perfectly free," namely there was no governmental coercion, separated them from the two classes of original creditors.

Concerning the original creditors, who had assigned their titles away, Madison argued that on principles of justice, faith, credit, and opinion they still possessed valid claims against the nation. This argument constituted a notion Madison had rejected in 1783. Nevertheless, by the end of the decade he had changed his mind.[68] The coercive element of the contract provided the linchpin of Madison's position. "The certificates put into the hands of the creditors, on closing their settlements with the public, were of less real value than was acknowledged to be due; they may be considered as having been forced, in fact, on the receivers. They cannot, therefore, be fairly adjudged an extinguishment of the debt."[69] A week later Madison spoke again on this specific issue of coercion. From the perspective of the original creditor, Madison argued that

a debt was fairly contracted: according to justice and good faith, it ought to have been paid in gold or silver: a piece of paper only was substituted. Was this paper equal in value to gold or silver? No: it was worth in the market, which the argument for the purchasing holders makes the criterion, no more than one-eighth or one-seventh of that value. Was this depreciated paper freely accepted? No: the government offered that or nothing. The rela-

67. Ibid., 13:35–36.
68. See "Address to the States," 25 Apr. 1783, *PJM* 6:493, where Madison, as chair of the committee that drafted the report, argued: "To discriminate the merits of these several descriptions of creditors would be a task equally unnecessary & invidious. If the voice of humanity plead more loudly in favor of some than of others; the voice of policy, no less than of justice pleads in favor of all. A wise nation will never permit those who relieve the wants of their Country, or who rely most on its faith, its firmness and its resources, when either of them is distrusted, to suffer by the event."
69. JM speech, 11 Feb. 1790, *PJM* 13:36.

tion of the individual to the government, and circumstances of
the offer, rendered the acceptance a forced, not a free one.

Madison refused to stop. In this specific context, he pushed his argument to its logical limit. Not only was coercion unacceptable between the government and individuals in economic transactions, it
was unacceptable between humans in civil society. He specifically
stated that "the same degree of constraint would viciate a transac-
tion between man and man, before any court of equity on the face of
the earth." While this sentence contained the seeds of a radical notion of economic freedom and property ownership that Madison
refused to draw, it nonetheless demonstrated his appreciation of the
necessity of equity in a fair contract.

After this single sentence on the theoretically noncoercive nature
of legitimate contracts between humans, Madison returned to the
concrete issue at hand: "There are even cases where consent cannot
be pretended; where the property of the planter or farmer had been
taken at the point of the bayonet, and a certificate presented in the
same manner."[70] Then, in one of the most extraordinary of any passages attributed to Madison, he specifically attacked the cold calculus of the market, as he begged his colleagues "not to yield too readily to the artificial niceties of forensic reasoning." In one of his
finest public moments, he asked them to "consider not the form,
but the substance—not the letter, but the equity—not the bark, but
the pith of the business. It was a great and an extraordinary case. It
ought to be decided on the great and fundamental principles of justice. He had been animadverted upon, for appealing to the heart as
well as the head: he would be bold, nevertheless, to repeat, that, in
great and unusual questions of morality, the heart is the best casu-
ist."[71]

Madison conceived of three possible resolutions to the specific issue: "pay both, reject wholly one or the other, or make a *composition* between them on some principle of equity." While the first option had a certain appeal to Madison, he recognized that it would
violate the governmental trust since it would repay more than the
public had received. Nor could he accept the second solution of rejecting altogether one set of claims since that would punish those

70. JM speech, 18 Feb. 1790, *PJM* 13:48–49.
71. Ibid., 13:49.

who had helped the public. Madison's compromise solution he called a "composition": arguing for a "liberal" policy that gave preferential treatment to the current holders, he proposed awarding them "the highest price which has prevailed in the market; and let the residue belong to the original sufferers." Madison's logic remained practical, political, and destined to persuade few legislators.

> This will not do perfect justice; but it will do more real justice, and perform more of the public faith, than any other expedient proposed. The present holders, where they have purchased at the lowest price of the securities, will have a profit that cannot reasonably be complained of; where they have purchased at a higher price, the profit will be considerable; and even the few who have purchased at the highest price cannot well be losers, with a well funded interest of 6 per cent. The original sufferers will not be fully indemnified; but they will receive, from their country, a tribute due to their merits, which, if it does not entirely heal their wounds, will assuage the pain of them.[72]

After listening to his argument rigorously assaulted for several legislative days, Madison did not change his position. He knew "perfect justice would not be done" but had hoped that "a grievous injustice would be lessened."[73] In a private letter to his friend Edmund Pendleton, Madison lamented the fate of his heroic struggle in the name of justice. "I have not been able to persuade myself," he told Pendleton, "that the transactions between the U.S. and those whose services were most instrumental in saving their country, did in fact extinguish the claims of the latter on the justice of the former." To Madison's thinking—or perhaps in this context, his moral sense of justice—there had to be "something radically wrong in suffering those who rendered a bona fide consideration to lose 7/8 of their dues, and those who have no particular merit towards their Country, to gain 7 or 8 times as much as they advanced."[74] To Edward Carrington he stated his position even more forcefully: "There must be something wrong, radically & morally & politically wrong, in a system which transfers the reward from those who paid the most valu-

72. JM speech, 11 Feb. 1790, *PJM* 13:37.
73. JM speech, 18 Feb. 1790, *PJM* 13:55.
74. JM to Edmund Pendleton, 4 Mar. 1790, *PJM* 13:85.

able of all considerations, to those who scarcely paid any consideration at all."[75]

Even though this repayment situation appeared hopeless enough, Madison also believed that his home state of Virginia would be treated unfairly on the issue of "a final settlement and payment of balances among the States." He assumed, incorrectly it turned out, that Virginia had paid off most of its internal debt while other states had behaved in a less judicious manner; he concluded, therefore, that this "project will neither be just nor palatable."[76] Nevertheless, based on Madison's words, the two issues appeared to be on different levels of justice. For a state to cheat another state was one level of injustice; for a state to treat unfairly a citizen who had tried to help it was qualitatively different. Somewhat more successful on the question of assumption, Madison pragmatically brokered his influence on the issue in exchange for a favorable location for the new capital; he thereby satisfied his constituents' need for power even though he could not satisfy his own need for justice.[77]

Madison's essay on "Fashion," his advocacy of state protection from foreign economics, and his reaction to the injustice of the debt issue all accurately capture his less than total acceptance of the norms of modern market economics. While he celebrated the theoretical notion that the whole of society benefited from the unbridled and selfish individual pursuit of self-interest and appreciated the domestic and international advantages of a division of labor, he could not accept the cold, disinterested, and dispassionate mechanism of the market creating human hardship over issues of taste or questions of *caveat emptor*. Madison believed that civil society should pursue justice. And to secure this, he tried to bring politics back into economics. This must be considered ironic: subsequent chapters will show how hard Madison worked to banish politics and passion from his mechanical government. Yet when confronted with an economic system that made choices on a rational calculus of supply and de-

75. JM to Edward Carrington, 14 Mar. 1790, *PJM* 13:104. This specific point on distributive justice Madison would not consider when it came to wage-laborers or slaves.

76. JM to Edmund Pendleton, 4 Mar. 1790, *PJM* 13:86; see also JM to Edward Carrington, 14 Mar. 1790, *PJM* 13:105.

77. Jack Rakove, *James Madison and the Creation of the American Republic* (Glenview, Ill.: Scott, Foresman, 1990), pp. 88–91.

mand, or costs and benefits, Madison's conscience recoiled and forced him to try to modify the market mechanism. This betrays a nostalgic dimension to Madison's political economy. The death of the concept of economic justice had been proclaimed by Hobbes in 1651, setting the tone for all subsequent liberal theories to the point where the category itself virtually disappeared from political and economic theory.[78] Madison's longing for economic justice therefore betrays, on his part, a degree of idealism that for him can only be considered unusual.

78. C. B. Macpherson, *The Rise and Fall of Economic Justice* (Oxford: Oxford University Press, 1985), p. 9.

5 / Property: Rights and Possessions, Democracy and Despair

> In a word, as a man is said to have a right to his property, he may be
> equally said to have a property in his rights.[1]
>
> —*Madison*

While *Federalist* 10 on the control of factions and *Federalist* 54 on slavery contain some of the basic propositions of Madison's theory of property, his 1792 *National Gazette* essay "Property" presents his fullest and most far-reaching insights into this institution. In its dynamic logic and internal tension, "Property" represents the quintessential Madison.[2] The essay demonstrates the richness of Madison's concept of property as well as the temporal, and ultimately destructive, dimensions of the institution. These aspects Madison comprehended. He hoped to forestall their consequences through political and social institutions, even though he knew that on this problem time stood against him.

Madison opened this essay differentiating between the "particular" and the "larger and juster" meanings of property. Undoubtedly referring to Blackstone, Madison explained that "in its particular application [property] means 'that dominion which one man claims and exercises over the external things of the world, in exclusion of every other individual.'" When he explained property's juster meaning, Madison affixed a significant qualification to it: property "embraces every thing to which a man may attach a value and have a

1. "Property," *National Gazette*, 27 Mar. 1792, *The Papers of James Madison*, ed. William T. Hutchinson et al., 17 vols. (Chicago and Charlottesville: University of Chicago Press and University of Virginia Press, 1962–), 14:266 (hereafter cited as *PJM*).
2. See Jennifer Nedelsky, *Private Property and the American Constitution* (Chicago: University Press of Chicago, 1990), chapter 2, where she calls this essay "uncharacteristic" and "atypical" of Madison.

right and *which leaves to every one else the like advantage.*"³ Madison's "particular" definition, linked with his latter qualification, resembled that of John Locke, who had explained how, through the rational use of labor, individuals developed the prepolitical, natural right to appropriate and exclude others from the common earth. Wrote Locke:

> Though the Earth, and all inferior Creatures be common to all Men, yet every Man has a *Property* in his own *Person*. This no Body has any Right to but himself. The *Labour* of his Body, and the *Work* of his Hands, we may say, are properly his. Whatsoever then he removes out of the State that Nature hath provided and left it in, he hath mixed his *Labour* with, and joyned to it something that is his own, and thereby makes it his *Property*. It being by him removed from the common state Nature placed it in, hath by this *labour* something annexed to it, that excludes the common right of other Men. For this *Labour* being the unquestionable Property of the Labourer, no Man but he can have a right to what that is once joyned to, at least where there is enough, and as good left in common for others.⁴

Locke's explicit qualification of "at least where there is enough, and as good left in common for others" Madison repeated at least three additional times in his "Property" chapter. The limitation remains absolutely critical. It attached a notion of fairness to the emerging conceptions of market property by inserting the natural right guarantee of equal opportunity for all rational men.⁵ While Locke's seventeenth-century readers had vast expanses of the globe yet to conquer and subdue, by the second quarter of the nineteenth century Madison already projected the closing of the frontier, the collapse of equal opportunity, and the beginning of the end. The promise of leaving to everyone else the like advantage could not withstand the achievements of *Homo oeconomicus* inside market concepts of morality and property. Nevertheless, these apparently innocent-looking limitations on human appropriation in Locke and

---

3. "Property," *PJM* 14:266; JM's emphasis. See William Blackstone, *Commentaries on the Laws of England*, 4 vols. (Oxford: Clarendon Press, 1765), bk. 2, p. 2.
4. John Locke, *Second Treatise of Government*, ed. C. B. Macpherson (Indianapolis: Hackett, 1980), p. 19; Locke's emphasis.
5. Ibid., pp. 21, 23.

Madison contain the potential of a radical critique of the very institution of property that they originally helped to justify. Locke would not live to see the necessity of this. Madison lived in dread of it.

Madison continued cataloging his bifurcated conception of rights, placing "land, or merchandize, or money" in the first category. In the "juster" category, he listed "his opinions and the free communication of them"; "his religious opinions, and in the profession and practice dictated by them"; "the safety and liberty of his person"; and last, recalling *Federalist* 10, he noted an individual property right "in the free use of his faculties and free choice of the objects on which to employ them." The inventory completed, Madison reunited the hierarchy inside property with a single, striking sentence: "In a word, as a man is said to have a right to his property, he may be equally said to have a property in his rights."[6] Property, at least at some moments, comprised both "things" and "rights." Although both concepts involved the ideal of justice, the latter category—at least in rhetoric—rested on a higher, "juster," plane than the former. Madison, therefore, continued his search for justice in matters of political economy, an exercise that would eventually cause him deep concern given the inevitable development of the market.

Before completing the discussion of his "Property" essay it makes sense to build on Madison's distinction between property as "things" and as "rights" by first retracing his thoughts on this dichotomy. The historic path reflected the classic Madison. He started by protecting religious rights. Forced by political circumstances he moved to protect property as things; and then he shifted back again to property as rights when the issue of a free press and an enlightened citizenry became crucial to balancing the Federalist administration.

Claiming in his *Autobiography* that he held "very early and strong impressions in favor of Liberty both Civil and Religious," Madison vigorously protested the "persecution" of several local dissenting Baptist preachers; he "spared no exertion to save them from imprisonment and to promote their release." His brief, autobiographic account of this episode collapsed years and events to reach Madison's

6. "Property," *PJM* 14:266.

ultimate, but never achieved, goal of "a complete establishment of the Rights of Conscience, without any distinction of sects or individuals."[7]

Three additional letters to his friend William Bradford confirm the impact of these acts of religious intolerance on Madison. Late in 1773 he told Bradford he wanted to know about Pennsylvania's "Origin & fundamental principals of Legislation; particularly the extent of your religious Toleration."[8] He continued the discussion a month later with a note of militancy in his voice as he linked property with liberty in comments on the Boston Tea Party: "Political Contests are necessary sometimes as well as military to afford exercise and practise and to instruct in the Art of defending Liberty and property." Noting the inherent advantages in the culture of Pennsylvania's religious diversity, Madison argued that religious uniformity in Virginia established the preconditions where "slavery and Subjection might and would have been gradually insinuated among us." A lack of pluralism "begets a surprizing confidence and Ecclesiastical Establishments tend to great ignorance and Corruption all of which facilitate the Execution of mischievous Projects."

Try as he might to change the subject in his letter, Madison returned to the intolerance of Virginia, complaining,

I want again to breathe your free Air. I expect it will mend my Constitution & confirm my principles. I have indeed as good an Atmosphere at home as the Climate will allow: but have nothing to brag of as to the State and Liberty of my Country. Poverty and Luxury prevail among all sorts: Pride ignorance and Knavery among the Priesthood and Vice and Wickedness among the Laity. This is bad enough But It is not the worst I have to tell you. That diabolical Hell conceived principle of persecution rages among some and to their eternal Infamy the Clergy can furnish their Quota of Imps for such business. This vexes me the most

7. Douglass Adair, "James Madison's 'Autobiography,'" *William and Mary Quarterly* 3d ser., 2 (Apr. 1945): 198–199; Jack Rakove, *James Madison and the Creation of the American Republic* (Glenview, Ill.: Scott, Foresman, 1990), p. 6.

8. JM to William Bradford, 1 Dec. 1773, *PJM* 1:105–106. Just how far Americans would need to travel before they conceived of the United States itself as a political entity can be seen in Madison's casual reference to "your Country" without mentioning Pennsylvania; see also JM's subsequent letter to Bradford, *PJM* 1:106.

of any thing whatever. There are at this [time?] in the adjacent County not less than 5 or 6 well meaning men in close Goal for publishing their religious Sentiments which in the main are very orthodox.[9]

He closed this letter imploring Bradford "to pity me and pray for Liberty of Conscience."[10] Confronted with the harsh reality of a uniformity of religious thought aggravated by a climate of intolerance, Madison consistently advocated a more radical notion of freedom of conscience, rather than simple religious freedom.

A political culture of toleration had wide-ranging implications for civil society. "You are happy in dwelling in a Land where those inestimable privileges are fully enjoyed and [the] public has long felt the good effects of their religious as well as Civil Liberty," he told Bradford. Consequently, he continued, "foreigners have been encouraged to settle amg. you. Industry and Virtue have been promoted by mutual emulation and mutual Inspection, Commerce and the Arts have flourished and I can not help attributing those continual exertions of Gen[i]us which appear among you to the inspiration of Liberty and that love of Fame and Knowledge which always accompany it." Madison closed this passage demonstrating complete acceptance of liberalism's commitment to Enlightenment reasoning: "Religious bondage shackles and debilitates the mind and unfits it for every noble enterprize every expanded prospect."[11]

Madison's first opportunity to institutionalize his plea for toleration occurred when he was a 1776 delegate to Virginia's Revolutionary convention. As a member of the committee charged with preparing a Declaration of Rights, Madison followed the lead of George Mason except on the issue of religious toleration, where he tried to amend Mason's phrase "fullest Toleration in the Exercise of Reli-

9. JM to William Bradford, 24 Jan. 1774, *PJM* 1:105–106. See also JM to William Bradford, 1 Apr. 1774, *PJM* 1:112, where he contrasted Virginia to Pennsylvania: "The Sentiments of our people of Fortune & fashion on this subject are vastly different from what you have been used to. That liberal catholic and equitable way of thinking as to the rights of Conscience, which is one of the Characteristics of a free people and so strongly marks the People of your province is but little known among the Zealous adherents to our Hierarchy. We have it is true some persons in the Legislature of generous Principles both in Religion & Politicks but number not merit you know is necessary to carry points there."
10. JM to William Bradford, 24 Jan. 1774, *PJM* 1:106.
11. JM to William Bradford, 1 Apr. 1774, *PJM* 1:112–113.

gion" with his more sweeping "free exercise of Religion."[12] When his initial amendment to Mason's version failed, he qualified the universal nature of the unlimited grant with the provision "unless the preservation of equal liberty and the existence of the State are manifestly endangered."[13] In its final form, this language was dropped by the convention and, for the most part, they accepted Madison's earlier wording. However, not until 1785, after he had failed in attempts to implement the religious freedom clauses of the Declaration of Rights in 1776 and to pass Thomas Jefferson's religious freedom legislation in 1779, did Madison gain passage of a bill guaranteeing religious freedom.

In 1785, with a new legislature in place, Madison moved to kill the General Assessment Bill through his anonymous authorship of the famous "Memorial and Remonstrance."[14] This petition, distributed by Madison's ally George Mason, had been designed to secure public support against "A Bill establishing a provision for Teachers of the Christian Religion." With church attendance on the decline and the establishment of religion an idea no longer supported by most Virginians, that Madison maintained secrecy surrounding his authorship of the document until 1826 remains something of a puzzle. Perhaps it can be explained by his preference to stay out of the public eye and work quietly and effectively behind the scenes. Whatever his reasons, "Memorial and Remonstrance" presented Madison's early views of social contact theory, his already mature views on religious toleration, and his encouragement of the practical value of diversity.

In explaining the grounds for the remonstrance, Madison claimed

12. Declaration of Rights and Form of Government of Virginia, 16 May–29 June 1776, Ed. note, *PJM* 1:170–175.
13. JM's Amendments to the Declaration of Rights, 29 May–12 June 1776, *PJM* 1:175. The full wording of the amendment read: "That religion, or the duty which we owe to our Creator, and the manner of discharging it, can be directed only by reason and conviction, not by force or violence; and therefore, that all men are equally entitled to enjoy the free exercise of religion, according to the dictates of conscience, unpunished and unrestrained by the magistrate, Unless the preservation of equal liberty and the existence of the State are manifestly endangered; And that it is the mutual duty of all to practice Christian forbearance, love, and charity towards each other."
14. See Marvin Meyers, ed., *The Mind of the Founder*, rev. ed. (Hanover, Mass.: Brandeis University Press, 1981), p. 6, who notes how the previous year Madison had voted for an act to incorporate the Episcopal church in order to "play for time," until postponement would kill it. For JM's own view, see JM to James Madison Sr., 6 Jan. 1785, *PJM* 8:217.

as "a fundamental and undeniable truth," Article 16 of the Virginia Declaration of Rights: "that Religion or the duty which we owe to our Creator and the manner of discharging it, can be directed only by reason and conviction, not by force or violence." He proceeded to declare this right natural and "unalienable." Madison explained his reasoning based on his conception of the social contract. Man's "duty" to the creator, "is precedent, both in order of time and in degree of obligation, to the claims of Civil Society. Before any man can be considered as a member of Civil Society, he must be considered as a subject of the Governour of the Universe." Given this conception of civil society, Madison explicitly claimed "that in matters of Religion, no mans right is abridged by the institution of Civil Society and that Religion is wholly exempt from its cognizance."[15]

Having established his first postulate, Madison proceeded to deduce fourteen additional propositions. "Exempt from the authority of the Society at large," he argued, meant religion "still less can . . . be subject to that of the Legislative Body." "Free Government" required both a separation of power and that no governmental department "overleap the great Barrier which defends the rights of the people."[16] Foreshadowing themes he would resuscitate in his *National Gazette* essays, where he once more became alarmed at threats posed by an overly powerful administration, Madison instructed his petitioners that "it is proper to take alarm at the first experiment on our liberties." In fact, he declared "this prudent jealousy to be the first duty of Citizens."[17] The establishment bill not only violated the natural right of religious freedom, but also "violates that equality which ought to be the basis of every law." According to the Virginia Declaration of Rights, "men are by nature equally free and independent." Since humans enter "into Society on equal conditions" and relinquish and retain the same natural rights, the

15. To the Honorable the General Assembly of the Commonwealth of Virginia A Memorial and Remonstrance, ca. 20 June 1785, *PJM* 8:298–299. "Property," 27 Mar. 1792, *National Gazette, PJM* 14:266–267, where JM acknowledges "conscience" as "a natural and unalienable right," yet implies that a government that violated religious rights would not automatically be considered completely unjust.

16. "Memorial and Remonstrance," *PJM* 8:299.

17. Ibid., 8:300; cf. "Consolidation," 3 Dec. 1791, *National Gazette, PJM* 14:137–139; "Government," 31 Dec. 1791, *PJM* 14:178–179; "Charters," 18 Jan. 1792, *PJM* 14:191–192; "Government of the United States," 4 Feb. 1792, *PJM* 14:217–219; "A Candid State of Parties," 22 Sept. 1792, *PJM* 14:370–372.

bill violated natural "equality by subjecting some to peculiar burdens" and "granting to others peculiar exemptions."[18]

Wanting to cover every conceivable counterargument, Madison first claimed that neither Christianity nor civil society needed the support of the other to survive; in fact, both flourished best in the air of freedom. He then speculated on the negative impact of attracting people to Virginia, and of forcing Virginians to flee, if the government failed to protect "every Citizen in the enjoyment of his Religion with the same equal hand which protects his person and property."[19] Madison openly worried about the consequences for general order if citizens were forced, for reasons of conscience, to ignore the law.

He brought the petition to closure with all the forensic skill of a twentieth-century lawyer. He started his summation by asserting that "a measure of such singular magnitude and delicacy ought not be imposed, without the clearest evidence that it is called for by a majority of citizens"; and then he proceeded to demonstrate how difficult that would be to determine. In his final proposition, however, it appears evident that even if the majority position could be determined by equating it with the "voice either of the Representatives or of the Counties," Madison would still reject this governmental decision because it could not be considered the genuine will of the citizens. Although he does not explicitly say so, his logic appeared to dictate, nevertheless, that a majority of citizens did have the legitimate power to alienate others' religious rights, at least in 1785. By the time of the Constitutional Convention, Madison would specifically reject this idea as well. But in his "Memorial and Remonstrance" he denied the notion of state power tampering with "the equal right of every citizen to the free exercise of Religion." A "gift of nature," religious freedom cannot be given up without the expressed, direct consent of the people, nor through any legislative voice:

> Either then, we must say, that the Will of the Legislature is the only measure of their authority; and that in the plentitude of this authority, they may sweep away all our fundamental rights; or, that they are bound to leave this particular right untouched and sacred: Either we must say, that they may controul the free-

18. "Memorial and Remonstrance," *PJM* 8:300.
19. Ibid., 8:302.

dom of the press, may abolish the Trial by Jury, may swallow up the Executive and Judiciary Powers of the State; nay that they may despoil us of our very right of suffrage, and erect themselves into an independent and hereditary Assembly or, we must say, that they have no authority to enact into law the Bill under consideration. We the Subscribers say, that the General Assembly of this Commonwealth have no such authority: And that no effort may be omitted on our part against so dangerous an usurpation, we oppose to it, this remonstrance.[20]

Madison's memorial was not the only petition to circulate around the state, nor did it secure the most signatures. Altogether, more than ten thousand signatures were attached to the various petitions.[21] Still, Madison's memorial remains historically significant: it presented a clear expression of the political climate of Virginia and indicated Madison's full development as an Enlightenment thinker. Perhaps more significantly, the memorial signaled Madison's early appreciation of the emerging and ultimate political power of public opinion, a tactic he would employ successfully against the opponents of the Constitution in the late 1780s and against the Federalist-controlled executive branch throughout much of the 1790s.

Having contributed to the defeat of the act to support all teachers of Christianity in the mid-1780s, Madison seized the moment to pass Thomas Jefferson's Act for Establishing Religious Freedom. With Jefferson in France serving as the American minister, Madison skillfully negotiated the political currents of the Virginia legislature and the act passed with minor changes. When Madison informed Jefferson of the bill's passage, he pridefully noted how he "flattered himself" that as a result "this Country [had] extinguished for ever the ambitious hope of making laws for the human mind."[22] This collaborative effort may be one of Jefferson and Madison's finest achievements. A testimonial to the liberal ideals of free discourse, reason, and toleration, it contained language of civil, natural, and irrevocable rights.

The final section of the act specified that the present assembly had "no power to restrain the acts of succeeding assemblies" and that it could not legally declare any "act to be irrevocable" for all

20. Ibid., 8:303–304.
21. Rakove, *Madison*, p. 34.
22. JM to Thomas Jefferson, 22 Jan. 1786, *PJM* 8:474.

time. Nevertheless, this notion of equal sovereignty across time could not restrain them from declaring that any future legislative act that repealed religious freedom would always "be an infringement of natural right."[23] This last point has significance: while Jefferson always accepted both ideas of the fundamental equality of legislative bodies and the risks associated with future government's violating natural right, part of Madison's emerging legacy was that he constructed a national political system specifically designed to impede any simple, democratic repeal, or amendment, of the founding constitutional document.

Religious freedom secured in Virginia, Madison directed his attention to other matters, especially the problems facing the Confederation government. Because the Madison seesaw at this moment appeared to have too much weight on the side of rights and liberty, he shelved his concern with religious freedom and concentrated on strengthening the central government and controlling the state governments. In time, and for pragmatic reasons that had little to do with religion, Madison returned to push for specific legislation to protect religious freedom. In the second half of the 1780s, however, he thought geographic and sociological circumstances alone could protect religious freedom. In fact, freedom for citizens no longer remained Madison's principal concern: he wanted to control factions as a threat to governmental equilibrium and social balance.

As his political experience grew, Madison became less enchanted by the thought of mere legal protection for rights against hostile majorities. "The greater number of citizens and extent of territory," he explained in *Federalist* 10, constituted the "circumstance principally" responsible for controlling the violence of factions. This, of course, would include religious factions: "A religious sect may degenerate into a political faction in a part of the Confederacy; but the variety of sects dispersed over the entire face of it must secure the national councils against any danger from that source."[24] Madison wanted to protect the government from the destabilizing influence

23. Act of Religious Freedom, 31 Oct. 1785, *PJM* 8:400–401.
24. Isaac Kramnick, ed., *The Federalist Papers* (New York: Viking Penguin, 1987), 10:127, 128. See JM to Thomas Jefferson, 20 Aug. 1785, *PJM* 8:345, where,

of religious sects.[25] In *Federalist* 51, still concerned with excessive liberty in the states and among the people, Madison argued that pluralism and diversity contributed to social stability:

> The society itself will be broken into so many parts, interests and classes of citizens, that the rights of individuals, or of the minority, will be in little danger from interested combinations of the majority. In a free government the security for civil rights must be the same as that for religious rights. It consists in the one case in the multiplicity of interests, and in the other in the multiplicity of sects. The degree of security in both cases will depend on the number of interests and sects; and this may be presumed to depend on the extent of country and number of people comprehended under the same government.

Madison noted how the benefits of balancing sect against sect were further increased in "a proper federal system" since it would enlarge the geographic space of the polity. "It is no less certain than it is important," he concluded, "that the larger the society, provided it lie within a practicable sphere, the more duly capable it will be of self-government."[26] Writing in the *National Gazette* in 1792, Madison reasserted this argument of the virtue of pluralism. This time he clarified it by ridiculing the notion that an increase in "different interests and parties" was inevitably a good thing and ought to be encouraged. From Madison's worldview, everything existed as a matter of balance and proportion: neither space nor interests, good things if

---

partially in code, he wrote: "The presbyterian clergy have at length espoused the side of the opposition, being moved either by *a fear of their laity* or *a jealousy of the episcopalians*. The mutual hatred of these sects has been much inflamed by the late act incorporating the latter. *I am far from* being *sorry for it* as *a coalition between them* could *alone endanger our religious rights* and a tendency to *such an event had been suspected*" (JM's emphasis).

25. *Federalist* 19:168; Madison showed how this concern was reasonable since it was "the controversies on the subject of religion, which in three instances have kindled violent and bloody contests, [which] may be said, in fact, to have severed the league" among the Swiss cantons.

26. *Federalist* 51:321–322. It should be noted as well that the federal system supplies additional governments to check factions.

used wisely by the legislator, were infinitely expandable—both had limits beyond which they too would become counterproductive.[27]

What must be considered among the most striking omissions in the entire debates during the drafting of the Constitution is the virtual absence of any discussion of a bill of rights.[28] This omission became of concern to Madison only when ratification seemed in doubt. When rumors filled the air of a second convention to remedy the failure to include a bill of rights, Madison took action. During the ratification debates in Virginia, Madison tried to persuade his audience that a bill of rights was not necessary: "Is a bill of rights a security for religion? Would the bill of rights, in this state, exempt the people from paying for support of one particular sect . . . ? If there were a majority of one sect, a bill of rights would be a poor protection for liberty." Madison considered bills of rights as "paper" or "parchment barriers" that could do little to restrain a determined majority. In place of paper, Madison believed "freedom arises from that multiplicity of sects which pervades America, and which is the best and only security for religious liberty in any society." While the multiplicity of sects would restrain majorities, Madison maintained that an additional bulwark against violations—although itself a kind of paper barrier—resided in the fact that the central government had no specific power to touch religion: "There is not a shadow of right in the general government to intermeddle with religion. Its least in-

27. See "Parties," 23 Jan. 1792, *National Gazette*, *PJM* 14:198, where he drew a distinction between "natural distinctions" and "artificial distinctions"; the former were based on property holdings, the latter on political distinctions between *"kings, and nobles and plebeians."* Madison explicitly showed he understood the faulty logic of the idea by stating its position in terms of balance: "We shall then have the more checks to oppose to each other: we shall then have the more scales and the more weights to perfect and maintain the equilibrium." Rejecting the idea as not being "the voice of reason" or "republicanism," Madison considered the idea of creating additional and artificial vices "absurd." Besides, given the inequality of human nature and Madison's conception of the nature of politics, an increase in the natural variety is inevitable.

28. See JM speech, 6 June 1787, *The Records of the Federal Convention of 1787*, ed. Max Farrand, 4 vols. (New Haven, Conn.: Yale University Press, 1937) 1:135; at the Constitutional Convention, Madison's concern was with religion's ability to "become a motive to persecution & oppression," not with how to maintain its free practice. As in *Federalist* 10 and 51, Madison reasserted the advantages of an extended republic. See also JM speech, 26 June 1787, *Records of the Federal Convention* 1:421–423.

terference with it would be a most flagrant usurpation."[29] Alexander Hamilton would soon teach Madison (and Jefferson) a hard lesson about the value of this type of parchment barrier when the question of the constitutionality of the bank had finally been resolved.

Madison's commitment to the free exercise of religion never wavered, although it reached its apex in his "Memorial and Remonstrance."[30] Once he felt the proper environment had been secured in Virginia following the passage of an Act for Religious Freedom, he never again expended as much energy on this issue. Madison's next contribution to the issue of rights came with the creation of the Constitution. To this specific end must be linked his shrewd maneuvering to secure ratification and head off a second convention by becoming the reluctant champion of the Bill of Rights.

After Jefferson had had several weeks to reflect on the proposed Constitution, from France he reacted unequivocally to its failure to include an explicit bill of rights:

> But I own it astonishes me to find such a change wrought in the opinions of our countrymen since I left them, as that three-fourths of them should be contented to live under a system which leaves to their governors the power of taking from them the trial by jury in civil cases, freedom of religion, freedom of the press, freedom of commerce, the habeas corpus laws, and the yoking them with a standing army. This is a degeneracy in the principles of liberty to which I had given four centuries instead of four years.[31]

Jefferson wrote to several influential Americans suggesting that he hoped the document would not be ratified in its present form; from

29. See Jonathan Elliott, ed., *The Debates of the Several State Conventions on the Adoption of the Federal Constitution*, 4 vols. (Philadelphia: J. B. Lippincott, 1836), 3:330. See also *PJM* 11:85–86: "The powers of the federal government are enumerated; it can only operate in certain cases: it has legislative powers on defined and limited objects, beyond which it cannot extend its jurisdiction."

30. For minor practical exceptions to JM's theoretical position, see Robert S. Morgan, *James Madison on the Constitution and the Bill of Rights* (New York: Greenwood Press, 1988), pp. 151–152.

31. TJ to William Stephens Smith, 2 Feb. 1788, in Julian P. Boyd, *The Papers of Thomas Jefferson*, 20 vols. (Princeton, N.J.: Princeton University Press, 1950–), 12:558 (hereafter cited as *PTJ*).

Paris, he lobbied for the attachment of a bill of rights; and he even urged Madison to poll the citizens on the proposed Constitution and then try again. "A bill of rights," Jefferson told Madison, "is what the people are entitled to against every government on earth . . . and what no just government should refuse, or rest on influence." He concluded his letter by suggesting two options: adoption and then immediate amendment, or convening a second convention after "canvassing" the people. Not overly optimistic about either the prospects for ratification or the strength of the new government, Madison must have felt chagrined by Jefferson's "hope [that] you will not be discouraged from other trials, if the present one should fail of it's full effect."[32]

Jefferson's call for a second convention arrived from France, where he continued to act as America's minister. The convention never materialized. Madison however, heeded the implicit warning. While he adamantly maintained, and from his perspective appropriately, that a specific bill of rights remained unnecessary because the Constitution itself was a bill of rights, Madison astutely if slowly shifted his position to favor and champion the addition of one. To ensure that this movement for a bill of rights did not get out of hand, he would play the lead role in its drafting and ratification. Having his private doubts about the Constitution's power to control the states, the last thing Madison wanted was to watch the document emasculated by amendments or the convening of a second constitutional convention.

Given Madison's earlier legislative efforts on behalf of a Virginia Declaration of Rights, why in 1787 did he seem, at best, indifferent to the need for a bill of rights in the proposed Constitution? How could Madison have perceived the Constitution itself as a bill of rights? To answer these questions requires a discussion of the condition of property from the Revolution through the creation of the Constitu-

32. TJ to James Madison, 20 Dec. 1787, *PTJ* 12:438–444; see also TJ to Edward Carrington, 21 Dec. 1787, ibid., pp. 445–447; TJ to Uriah Forrest, 31 Dec. 1787, ibid., pp. 475–479; TJ to William Stephens Smith, 2 Feb. 1788, ibid., pp. 557–559; TJ to Alexander Donald, 7 Feb. 1788, ibid., pp. 570–572; TJ to James Madison, 15 Mar. 1789, ibid., 14:659–663; and in a letter to Dr. Joseph Priestley, 19 June 1802, *The Works of Thomas Jefferson*, ed. Paul Leicester Ford, 12 vols. (New York: Knickerbocker Press, 1904), 9:381, Jefferson appears to have gone out of his way to see that history recorded the fact that he had no part to play in either the drafting or the passing of the Constitution of 1787.

tion, a brief retelling of the tale of Shays's rebellion, and a look at Madison's understanding of the Constitution as an instrument of limited power as well as a protector of property rights.

Madison's concrete experiences in state and national assemblies had convinced him that reason often failed to persuade others to act correctly; that short-run economic self-interest was an especially powerful motivating factor, particularly for those in a politically superior, but economically inferior, position. When the spirit of either revolution or democracy filled the air, the institution of property—especially in the form of "things," rather than rights—became vulnerable. And in Madison's mind, this threat ultimately involved more than property: property rested at the heart of justice. Of course, his own land holdings and status in Virginia depended on the continued sanctity of the institution of property, but this could be said of all the founders.

During the Revolutionary War, New York Tories lost their estates while Whig landlords did not. "Natural rights" arguments even in America would go only so far in restraining political desires.[33] Throughout a three-year period, the legislature of every state violated individual property rights, although conditions in Rhode Island and especially Massachusetts were the most offensive.[34] Madison, in particular, seemed alarmed at the economic conditions in the states, where nearly one-third of the white males had incurred debts that they had little realistic prospects of repaying; and with the high turnover rate among representatives who had close ties to the *demos*, the political conditions appeared equally bleak. While taxes, stay laws, and inflation had been used by virtually every legislative body to confiscate property, Madison found them offensive, threatening, and unjust. As Drew McCoy stated it, "By wantonly disregarding the rules of property and justice that raised men from savagery to civilized order, these laws threatened to bring republican

33. See Rowland Berthoff and John Murrin, "Feudalism, Communalism, and the Yeoman Freeholder: The American Revolution Considered as a Social Accident," in *Essays on the American Revolution*, eds. Stephen G. Kurtz and James H. Hutson (Williamsburg: University of North Carolina Press, 1973), p. 273.

34. Forrest McDonald, *Novus Ordo Seclorum: The Intellectual Origins of the Constitution* (Lawrence: University Press of Kansas, 1985), p. 156; Rakove, *Madison*, p. 47.

government in America into profound disrepute."[35] Still, it appears that the specter of popular rebellion raised by Henry Knox frightened some of the founders the most.

The significance of the Massachusetts taxpayers' revolt, which historians have dubbed Shays's Rebellion, "can scarcely be over-rated," writes Forrest McDonald. What Daniel Shays and the citizens of Massachusetts actually did seems unimportant; what matters is what George Washington, James Madison, and others believed were the intentions of the Shaysites. For this information, they relied on Henry Knox's imaginative report to Washington. Acting as superintendent of war under the Confederation, Knox constructed a fabricated but frightening account of the rebellion that circulated throughout the East. Knox claimed that Shays's forces were composed of between twelve and fifteen thousand men whose intentions included capturing Boston, looting the Bank of Massachusetts, gaining additional supporters, and marching south and in the process redistributing property.[36]

The impact of Shays's uprising on Madison can be found in his correspondence from the fall of 1786 through at least the following spring. To Washington, Madison noted that Knox's "gloomy" report was "less so than the colours in which I had it thro' another channel."[37] In February he seemed relieved that "information from Massts. gives hopes that the mutiny or as the Legislature there now style it, the Rebellion is nearly extinct."[38] Even as late as 1821, Madison still vividly described the impact of the rebellion on him: "The necessity of such a Constitution was enforced by the gross and disreputable inequalities which had been prominent in the internal administrations of most of the States. Nor was the recent & alarming

35. Drew McCoy, *The Last of the Fathers: James Madison and the Republican Legacy* (New York: Cambridge University Press, 1989), p. 41; see also Gordon Wood, "Interests and Disinterestedness in the Making of the Constitution," in *Beyond Confederation*, ed. Richard Beeman et al. (Chapel Hill: University of North Carolina Press, 1987), p. 73.

36. McDonald, *Novus Ordo Seclorum*, pp. 177–178.

37. JM to George Washington, 8 Nov. 1786, *PJM* 9:166. See JM to James Madison Sr., 1 Nov. 1786, *PJM* 9:154, "They profess to aim only at a reform of their Consti[tu]tion and of certain abuses in the public administration, but an abolition of debts public & private, and a new division of property are strongly suspected to be in contemplation."

38. JM to George Washington, 21 Feb. 1787, *PJM* 9:286. See also letter to Washington, 18 Mar. 1787, *PJM* 9:315.

insurrection headed by Shays, in Massachusetts without a very sensible effect on the pub[lic] mind."[39]

Throughout the revolutionary years prior to the Philadelphia convention, the colonists had expropriated millions of dollars. The men of real property and standing, therefore, had every reason to fear that the *demos* might rise and assert their illegitimate but nonetheless real power and redistribute property either by force or by law.[40] If the republic hoped to survive, Madison, in concert with other propertied patriots, had to find a way to put a lid on the increasing political pressure exerted by the small and nonpropertied interests.[41]

"The men of Philadelphia were," writes J. R. Pole, "without exception, men of property."[42] United by this overarching interest in protecting the institution of property, these property owners were able to resolve particular conflicts by bargaining. This uniformity of economic thinking helps explain the remarkable harmony among the members of the Constitutional Convention. Although Madison willingly invoked divine intervention to explain the absence of fac-

39. JM to John G. Jackson, 27 Dec. 1821, *The Writings of James Madison*, ed. Gaillard Hunt, 9 vols. (New York: G. P. Putnam's Sons, 1900–1910), 9:72.

40. See McDonald, *Novus Ordo Seclorum*, pp. 154–157. Jefferson's reaction to Shays's rebellion was in stark contrast to Madison's. See TJ to JM, 30 Jan. 1787, *PTJ* 11:93: "I hold it that a little rebellion now and then is a good thing, and as necessary in the political world as storms in the physical. Unsuccessful rebellions indeed generally establish the encroachments on the rights of the people which have produced them. An observation of this truth should render honest republican governors so mild in their punishment of rebellions, as not to discourage them too much. It is a medicine necessary for the sound health of government." And to William Smith, 13 Nov. 1787, *PTJ* 12:356–357, he claimed: "God forbid we would ever be 20. years without such a rebellion. . . . We have had 13. states independent 11. years. There has been one rebellion. That comes to one rebellion in a century and a half for each state. What country before ever existed a century and half without a rebellion? And what country can preserve it's liberties if their rulers are not warned from time to time that their people preserve the spirit of resistance? Let them take arms. The remedy is to set them right as to facts, pardon and pacify them. What signify a few lives lost in a century or two? The tree of liberty must be refreshed from time to time with the blood of patriots and tyrants. It is it's natural manure."

41. See Kramnick, "Introduction" to *The Federalist Papers*, p. 25: "The concern of many who repudiated the Articles at the Constitutional Convention would be not simply the immense power of state legislatures, abstractly considered, but the substantive content of the legislation passed by these all powerful legislatures as it threatened vested economic interests and private rights. It would be the redistributive nature of so much of the legislation coming out of the state legislatures in this period which enraged the critics of the Articles."

42. J. R. Pole, *The American Constitution—For and Against: The Federalist and Anti-Federalist Papers* (New York: Hill and Wang, 1987), p. 11.

tions at Philadelphia, he offered his more enlightened readers a few logical reasons in *Federalist* 37: first, "the convention must have enjoyed, in a very singular degree, an exemption from the pestilential influence of party animosities—the disease most incident to deliberative bodies and most apt to contaminate their proceedings"; and second, "that all the deputations composing the convention were either satisfactorily accommodated by the final act, or were induced to accede to it by a deep conviction of the necessity of sacrificing private opinions and partial interests to the public good."[43] Madison's secular explanations seem crucial: they capture the truth. All men of property, the conventioneers had, for all intents and purposes, "the same opinions, the same passions, and the same interests"— the same ideology—when it came to the ultimate issue concerning the institution of property, *viz.* how to protect it against political redistribution. To a person, they opined that the institution of property must be made invulnerable; they felt passionately about this issue, and they fervently believed that it remained in the objective best interests of the nation as well as each of her citizens.[44]

These men of diverse property holdings and different economic interests would have conflicting, particular property interests; they would disagree with each other and espouse mutually exclusive opinions on the best form and optimum structure for the new government.[45] There would be, however, no disagreement among them on the purpose of, and immediate need for, government to protect the institution of property.[46] For weeks, the delegates in secret debated their interests and hammered out compromises. But these were all intrafraternal squabbles, a debate among merchants, planters, bankers, slave owners, manufacturers, creditors, lawyers,

43. *Federalist* 37:246–247.
44. See Michael Parenti, "The Constitution as an Elitist Document," *How Democratic Is the Constitution?* ed. Robert A. Goldwin and William A. Schombra (Washington: Free Enterprise Institute, 1985), p. 51, who makes an important point about this rationalization of self-interest and national interest. It is a "fallacy," writes Parenti, "to presume there is a dichotomy between the desire to build a strong nation and the desire to protect property and that the delegates could not have been motivated by both." "In fact," Parenti reminds us, "like most people, they believed that what was good for themselves was ultimately good for the entire society."
45. See McDonald, *Novus Ordo Seclorum*, pp. 219–224, for a detailed summary of the economic interests of the delegates.
46. See Martin Diamond, "Democracy and *The Federalist:* A Reconsideration of the Framers' Intent," *American Political Science Review* 53 (Mar. 1959): 52–68.

and others. It was a debate of the haves versus the haves. It premised itself on their overriding need to protect themselves, in the name of the commonwealth and justice, from the have-littles and have-nots.[47]

Long before the thought that a strong central state was essential to liberty occurred to Madison, he placed little confidence in "any possible parchment securities against Usurpation."[48] In *Federalist* 40 he warned that the proposed Constitution would "be of no more consequence than the paper on which it is written," unless ratified by the people; and in *Federalist* 48 he warned "that a mere demarcation on parchment of the constitutional limits of the several departments" was an insufficient guard against tyranny.[49] Madison's point: "parchment barriers" could not stand up against power. Only countervailing power could.

When the Philadelphia convention adjourned, Madison found the plan assailed from many directions and on different grounds. The one recurring criticism, arising from many quarters, was the failure to include a specific declaration of rights. In late September 1787, upon returning to New York to fulfill his congressional obligations, Madison reported to Washington that he "found on my arrival here that certain ideas unfavorable to the Act of the Convention which had created difficulties in that body, had made their way into Congress." As he should have anticipated, one fundamental objection was that the framers exceeded their original instructions and authority.[50] Since this topic had previously arisen in Philadelphia, Madison had no difficulty in responding to the charge.

47. Parenti, "Constitution as an Elitist Document," p. 44. See James Hutson, "Riddles of the Federal Constitutional Convention," *William and Mary Quarterly* 44 (July 1987): 422: "The convention was not an ideological encounter because the delegates agreed on so many principles of government before they entered the Pennsylvania State House." See also Jack Rakove, "The Great Compromise: Ideas, Interests, and the Politics of Constitution Making," *William and Mary Quarterly* 44 (July 1987): 425, where he argues that "concessions were made to every interest that manifest itself at the convention."
48. JM to Thomas Jefferson, 15 Mar. 1800, *PJM* 17:373.
49. *Federalist* 40:263; 48:312.
50. Bruce Ackerman, *We the People* (Cambridge, Mass.: Belknap Press of Harvard University Press, 1991), p. 41, with all the assurance of a lawyer, claims that the conventioneers acted illegally. "Modern lawyers are perfectly prepared to admit that the Constitutional Convention was acting illegally in proposing its new document in the name of We The People."

The second objection that caused Madison more concern came from Richard Henry Lee who attempted "to amend the Act of the Convention before it should go forth from Congress" with a bill of rights. Madison told Washington that some delegates argued that the failure to include a bill of rights imposed a "duty" on them as representatives to exercise their "undoubted right" to amend the document because "the essential guards of liberty had been omitted." Their right to amend went unchallenged. But on practical and prudent political grounds, not philosophic ones, the attempt to amend was thwarted. The Congress passed the Constitution on to the states for ratification. This initial, concrete reaction to the Constitution undoubtedly helped Madison realize he had a considerable battle ahead if the document was to survive unscathed. While rumors about ratification from New York, Boston, and Connecticut seemed positive, Madison must have had Mason, Lee, and Jefferson in mind when he confided to Washington, "I am waiting with anxiety for the eccho from Virginia but with very faint hopes of its corresponding with my wishes."[51]

The politics of the Bill of Rights took on a genuine sense of urgency for Madison once it became linked with holding the Constitution hostage, or even worse, with the idea of a second convention. Early in 1788, Madison tactfully told Edmund Randolph that after reading his letter to the Virginia assembly, he felt relieved to "believe" that "the opponents to the Constitution" would not "find encouragement in it." Madison warmed up to the task of explaining to Randolph why "I differ still more from your opinion, that a prosecution of the experiment of a second Convention will be favorable even in Virginia to the object which I am sure you have at heart." The meaning of this sentence becomes clearer as the argument against a second convention progressed; Madison began to question the motives of other, "designing men," such as Patrick Henry. Madison's reasons for a rejection of a second convention, however, run far deeper than this: they revealed his liberal prejudices concerning self-government.

He began his assault asserting "the inference with me is unavoidable that were a second trial to be made, the friends of a good constitution for the Union would not only find themselves not a little dif-

51. JM to George Washington, 30 Sept. 1787, *PJM* 10:180–181.

fering from each other as to the proper amendments; but perplexed & frustrated by men who had objects totally different." He then moved to the heart of his doubts—the capacity of the people to make sound political choices. Recall that this was voiced in a private letter, not a public essay signed Publius. He wrote, "Whatever respect may be due to the rights of private judgment, and no man feels more of it than I do, there can be no doubt that there are subjects to which the capacities of the bulk of mankind are unequal, and on which they must and will be governed by these with whom they happen to have acquaintance and confidence."

With the necessity of popular ratification to legitimize the Constitution a foregone conclusion, Madison feared that confusion would result if disagreements among the elite began to spill over into the public arena. He reminded Randolph that the Constitution had been drafted by "a body possessing public respect & confidence." After implicitly urging Randolph, whom he linked with Mason, Lee, and Henry, to join the good cause of saving the union, he argued that

> if a Government be ever adopted in America, it must result from a fortunate coincidence of leading opinions, and a general confidence of the people in those who may recommend it. The very attempt at a second Convention strikes at the confidence in the first; and the existence of a second by opposing influence to influence, would in a manner destroy an effectual confidence in either, and give a loose to human opinions; which must be as various and irreconcilable concerning theories of Government, as doctrines of Religion; and give opportunities to designing men which it might be impossible to counteract.[52]

By the spring of 1788, Madison's fears and suspicions had escalated. "Conditional amendments or a second general Convention, will be fatal," he told George Nicholas. In marked contrast to Madison's public description of the Philadelphia convention in *The Federalist*, he confided to Nicholas:

> It is a fact, of which you though probably not a great number may be apprized, that the late Convention were in one stage of the business for several days under the strongest apprehensions

52. JM to Edmund Randolph, 10 Jan. 1788, *PJM* 10:354–356.

of an abortive issue to their deliberations. There were moments during this period at which despair seemed with many to predominate. I can ascribe the final success to nothing but the temper with which the Members assembled, and their ignorance of the opinions & confidence in the liberality of their respective constituents.[53]

Madison doubted that another convention, "composed even of wiser individuals," would be successful, especially since it would "contain men, who secretly aimed at disunion."[54] Two days later, Madison fended off "conditional ratification," a new tactic of the disunited opposition. He wrote to Randolph that neither a second convention nor a conditional acceptance were reconcilable "in the present state of things with the dictates of prudence and safety." As increasingly became his pattern, the normally cool and reasonable Madison sounded almost passionate as he skillfully used the fear of "disunion" and the language of the politics of suspicion to alarm his reader: "extreme facility," "secret" aims of "disunion," "schemes" and "masks," "danger," "justly dreaded," "desperate measures," and "licentiousness of animadversion."[55] Although Madison initially believed the Constitution lacked sufficient power to control the states, thoughts of additional cuts to the central government's power alarmed him even more. Until ratification had been assured, he would not cease in his behind-the-scenes soliciting for unconditional ratification.

To Jefferson, who had at one moment or another supported both the idea of a second convention and conditional ratification, Madison maintained his position that if either occurred, "the Constitution, and the Union will be both endangered."[56] Even after ratification had been secured, Madison continued to worry about a second convention. Once more in a letter to Jefferson, who had a penchant for the notion that constitutional conventions were inherently good,

53. JM to George Nicholas, Apr. 1788, *PJM* 11:12–13. The totally secular nature of Madison's description, along with his increasingly frequent implicit and explicit denigration of "the bulk of mankind," suggests that Madison's theological explanation for the convention's harmony was written for the consumption of the masses.
54. JM to George Nicholas, 8 Apr. 1788, *PJM* 11:13.
55. JM to Edmund Randolph, 10 Apr. 1788, *PJM* 11:19.
56. JM to Thomas Jefferson, 22 Apr. 1788, *PJM* 11:28.

Madison wrote, "The great danger in the present crisis is that if another Convention should be soon assembled, it would terminate in
discord, or in alterations of the federal system which would throw
back *essential* powers into the State Legislatures." Time, in this
context, Madison considered his ally: "The delay of a few years will
assuage the jealousies which have been artificially created by designing men and will at the same time point out the faults which really
call for amendment," at which point, he implied to Jefferson, he
might even consider a second convention.[57]

As national attention shifted to a call for a second though limited
convention with "the avowed and sole purpose of revising the Constitution," Madison's position remained unchanged. In light of his
own specific instructions under the Articles of Confederation and
the fact that he ignored them, it seemed "natural" to him that
should a limited convention to amend the Constitution be called,
"it would naturally consider itself as having a greater latitude than
the Congress appointed to administer and support as well as to
amend the system." However, as Madison knew all too well, more
than nature would drive the second convention:

> It would consequently give greater agitation to the public mind;
> an election into it would be courted by the most violent parti-
> zans on both sides; it wd. probably consist of the most heteroge-
> neous characters; would be the very focus of that flame which
> has already too much heated men of all parties; would no doubt
> contain individuals of insidious views, who under the mask of
> seeking alterations popular in some parts but inadmissible in
> other parts of the Union might have a dangerous opportunity of
> sapping the very foundations of the fabric.[58]

The language of the politics of suspicion and fear is manifest. Nor
does Madison contain his fears to domestic frontiers. It would be dif-

57. JM to Thomas Jefferson, 10 Aug. 1788, *PJM* 11:226. See JM to Edmund
Pendleton, 20 Oct. 1788, *PJM* 11:307: "I am glad to find you concurring in the requisite expedients for preventing antifederal elections, and a premature Convention. . . . An early Convention threatens discord and mischief. It will be composed of the most heterogenious characters—will be actuated by the party spirit
reigning among their constituents—will comprehend men having insidious designs agst. the Union—and can scarcely therefore terminate in harmony or the
public good."
58. JM to George Lee Turberville, 2 Nov. 1788, *PJM* 11:331.

ficult to imagine Jefferson, who was in Europe, agreeing with most of Madison's assertion

> that the prospect of a second Convention would be viewed by all Europe as a dark and threatening Cloud hanging over the Constitution just established, and perhaps over the Union itself; and wd. therefore suspend at least the advantages this great event has promised us on that side. It is a well known fact that this event has filled that quarter of the Globe with equal wonder and veneration, that its influence is already secretly but powerfully working in favor of liberty in France, and it is fairly to be inferred that the final event there may be materially affected by the prospect of things here.

Madison halted his projections just short of the entire universe, claiming, "We are not sufficiently sensible of the importance of the example which this Country may give to the world; nor sufficiently attentive to the advantages we may reap from the late reform, if we avoid bringg. it into danger."[59]

The most complete explanation of Madison's shifting posture on the question of a bill of rights can be found in an October 1788 letter to Jefferson. Closing the sweep of his wide net of suspicion, Madison shrewdly began his attack on the Bill of Rights, granting that "it is true nevertheless that not a few, particularly in Virginia have contended for the proposed alterations from the most honorable & patriotic motives." At that time, Madison predicted that "as far as these may consist of a constitutional declaration of the most essential rights, it is probable they will be added." Expressing his own views on the subject, he noted that "there are many who think such addition unnecessary, and not a few who think it misplaced in such a Constitution."

"My own opinion," he wrote Jefferson, "has always been in favor of a bill of rights. . . . At the same time I have never thought the omission a material defect, nor been anxious to supply it even by *subsequent* amendment." Always the practical politician, Madison was candid, if uninspired, in his support: "I have favored it because I supposed it might be of use, and if properly executed could not be of

59. Ibid., II:331–332.

disservice." Further explaining himself to Jefferson, Madison argued against the amendments on four, somewhat logically inconsistent, grounds: they were already part of the Constitution; they would be too limited; the new federal system would protect the citizens; and bills of rights became ineffective when most needed.[60] Reason four launched Madison into a lengthy explanation of his theory of balancing liberty and power.

Madison's frustrating experiences under the Articles of Confederation, soon to be readjusted by the Washington-Adams-Hamilton regimes, led him to believe that too much liberty, rather than too much power, constituted the fundamental American problem. "In our Governments the real power lies in the majority of the Community, and the invasion of private rights is *chiefly* to be apprehended, not from acts of Government contrary to the sense of its constituents, but from acts in which the Government is the mere instrument of the major number of the constituents." He subtly told Jefferson that, living in France, he lacked Madison's perspective. Betraying his own bias for stability over democracy, Madison argued that "wherever there is an interest and power to do wrong, wrong will generally be done, and not less readily by a powerful & interested party than by a powerful and interested prince." Wherever "political and physical power may be considered as vested in the same hands," Madison asked, "what use . . . can a bill of rights serve?" Madison thoughtfully conceived of two uses:

1. The political truths declared in that solemn manner acquire by degrees the character of fundamental maxims of free Government, and as they become incorporated with the national sentiment, counteract the impulses of interest and passion. 2. Altho'

60. JM to Thomas Jefferson, 17 Oct. 1788, *PJM* 11:297: "The rights in question are reserved by the manner in which the federal powers are granted. 2 because there is great reason to fear that a positive declaration of some of the most essential rights could not be obtained in the requisite latitude. I am sure that the rights of Conscience in particular, if submitted to public definition would be narrowed much more than they are likely ever to be by an assumed power. . . . 3. because the limited powers of the federal Government and the jealousy of the subordinate Governments, afford a security which has not existed in the case of the State Governments, and exists in no other. 4. because experience proves the inefficacy of a bill of rights on those occasions when its controul is most needed. Repeated violations of these parchment barriers have been committed by overbearing majorities in every State."

it be generally true as above stated that the danger of oppression lies in the interested majorities of the people rather than in usurped acts of the Government, yet there may be occasions on which the evil may spring from the latter sources; and on such, a bill of rights will be a good ground for an appeal to the sense of the community.[61]

Ultimately, Madison returned to the notion of balancing government and liberty. With Shays's rebellion still haunting his mind, it seemed understandable how at this time he perceived the disequilibrium.

It has been remarked that there is a tendency in all Governments to an augmentation of power at the expense of liberty. But the remark as usually understood does not appear to me well founded. Power when it has attained a certain degree of energy and independence goes on generally to further degrees. But when below that degree, the direct tendency is to further degrees of relaxation, until the abuses of liberty beget a sudden transition to an undue degree of power. With this explanation the remark may be true; and in the latter sense only is it in my opinion applicable to the Governments in America. It is a melancholy reflection that liberty should be equally exposed to danger whether the Government have too much or too little power, and that the line which divides these extremes should be so inaccurately defined by experience.

After completing the agonizing justifications and presenting one last reiteration of the futility of "written prohibitions," Madison finally constructed an initial list of necessary amendments: habeas corpus, standing armies, and monopolies.[62] Rhetoric aside, Madison still appeared uncommitted to a genuine bill of rights.

Again writing to Jefferson at the close of 1788, Madison reported that "the formidable opposition" to the Constitution had been de-

---

61. JM to Thomas Jefferson, 17 Oct. 1788, *PJM* 11:298–299; JM's emphasis.
62. JM to Thomas Jefferson, 17 Oct. 1788, *PJM* 11:299. Perhaps explaining his view of a future Hamilton regime, Madison briefly, and uncannily, acknowledged that governments can be taken over by "a succession of artful and ambitious rulers, [who] may by gradual & well-timed advances, finally erect an independent Government on the subversion of liberty."

feated on the question of ratification; he told Jefferson that the opponents had switched tactics to placing "its administration in the hands of disaffected men." The public's only questions concerning the Constitution, according to Madison, rested on two points: first, "the extent of the amendments; and second, "the mode in which they ought to be made." It remains difficult to conceive of a genuine public concern over the second issue, though Madison continued to be apprehensive about a second convention; and it is curious that his description of the public's attitude on the first question mirrored his own position. The public "agreed that the System should be revised," he wrote, "but they wish the revisal to be carried no farther than to supply additional guards for liberty, without abridging the sum of power transferred from the States to the general Government." He continued to read his own position into that of the public, asserting that citizens "are fixed in opposition to the risk of another Convention."

Still locked inside the politics of sin, cynicism, and suspicion, Madison warned Jefferson of the "zealous" opponents of the Constitution who "urge a Second Convention with the insidious hope, of throwing all things into Confusion, and of subverting the fabric just established, if not the Union itself."[63] Consequently, though Madison for reasons of propriety would have preferred to stay out of the ratification debates in Virginia, he felt the opposition might succeed if he failed to intervene. Once again, then, the ends of ratification justified Madison overcoming his own doubts about his relationship to the appropriate means.

The reasons for Madison's initial reluctance to participate directly in the Virginia ratifying convention are several. The fact that he was a member of the Congress that proposed the Philadelphia convention and a leader in the drafting of the document, not to mention his public role as Publius, all raised questions of impropriety in his own mind. Perhaps if the resolution of the question had not been in jeopardy, he would have abstained. Yet given the strength of opposition

63. JM to Thomas Jefferson, 8 Dec. 1788, *PJM* 11:381–383. Note how Madison always employs the subtle but undoubtedly effective tactic of linking a threat to the new Constitution with the destruction of the Union and a return to a Hobbesian state of nature, in spite of the twin facts that the Articles of Confederation were strong enough to govern during the war and perhaps loose enough to allow the economy to thrive after the war.

in Virginia, headed by Patrick Henry, George Mason, and William Grayson, Madison decided to enter the battlefield once more. In late February 1788, Madison confided to Washington that he had told "friends in Orange that the County may command my services in the Convention if it pleases." It would require, however, that he "sacrifice every private inclination to considerations not of a selfish nature." Madison accurately predicted that the Virginia convention would require "very laborious and irksome discussions." Lasting twenty-two days, convention politics forced him to oppose directly "several very respectable characters whose esteem and friendship I greatly prize," including Madison's old ally George Mason. So committed was he to Virginia's ratification, Madison even volunteered to make the arduous journey from New York to Orange County if his "presence at the election in the County" seemed indispensable. In short, Madison would willingly sacrifice everything necessary to secure Virginia's support of the Constitution.[64]

The Virginians convened. George Mason made two motions that played perfectly into Madison's hands: the first, that the Constitution should be debated clause by clause, from beginning to end; the second, that no vote should be taken until the first task had been completed. While the opposition forces had the powerful oratorical and bombastic skills of Patrick Henry on their side, the soft-spoken Madison had information and knowledge—"the facts"—on his. And over the long run, Madison always believed that cool and calculated, rational argument would win out over passion and hyperbole. On this occasion, he proved to be correct.

With Henry speaking on all but five days, Madison's arduous role took a toll on his delicate health. By constantly reminding the delegates that failure to ratify the document, unamended, would bring about disunion, Madison successfully secured ratification. In a gesture of conciliation, he ultimately accepted a lengthy list of recommended amendments that had no legally binding impact. They were, nevertheless, part of the rationale behind Madison's now determined efforts to secure a bill of rights once the new state was functioning. What remains of interest in the present context is what

64. JM to George Washington, 20 Feb. 1788, *PJM* 10:526–527. While *de jure* ratification was but one state away, JM knew that Virginia constituted one of the four states whose support was essential for *de facto* ratification.

Madison had to say to his Virginia colleagues about property and the absence of a bill of rights.

Throughout June of 1788, the delegates from Virginia met to discuss and vote on the proposed Constitution. Madison played a crucial role in these debates: he possessed the insights, knowledge, and arguments needed to parry the attacks of the plan's opponents. On June 6, Madison rose to address the question of how nations lose their liberty. On the issue of religious freedom, he argued that there could be no reason to assume that a "uniformity of government will produce that of religion." More to the point, if an attempt to introduce religion was made "it would be ineligible" since "the government has no jurisdiction over it." Madison's reading of the Constitution—an interpretation that in time Alexander Hamilton, then John Marshall, and finally the Supreme Court would make the exception rather than the rule—insisted that where there existed no expressed grant of power, the government could not legislate. Consequently, in mid-June he still believed a bill of rights would be superfluous because the Constitution's silence on religion itself created a right to religious freedom. In the United States, he told his audience, religion was "perfectly free and unshackled."[65] Less than a week later, recalling his telling logic of parchment barriers, he queried: "Is a bill of rights a security for religion?" This question he elected to answer: "If there were a majority of one sect, a bill of rights would be a poor protection for liberty." Freedom, he instructed his audience, resulted from pluralism, not law—from "that multiplicity of sects which pervades America, and which is the best and only security for religious liberty in any society."[66]

In what must have been a particularly painful performance for Madison, on June 12 he found himself forced to discredit Jefferson's suggestion, as shrewdly presented by Patrick Henry, that nine states adopt the Constitution and four refuse to do so, until the document had been suitably amended. Employing the oratorical skills for which he had gained a considerable reputation in his day, Henry sarcastically reminded his audience that Jefferson's amendments "go to that despised thing called *a bill of rights*, and all the rights which are dear to human nature—a trial by jury, the liberty of religion and

---

65. JM speech, 6 June 1788, Elliot, *Debates* 3:93
66. JM speech, 12 June 1788, Elliot, *Debates* 3:330.

press, &c.''[67] Henry argued that of the five states which had yet to adopt the Constitution, only Virginia possessed the political weight necessary to force the amendment issue. No matter how the delegates approached the topic, Henry claimed that all arguments stood on his side: ''The necessity of amendments is universally admitted. It is a word which is reechoed from every part of the continent. A majority of those who hear me think amendments are necessary. Policy tells us they are necessary. Reason, self-preservation, and every idea of propriety, powerfully urge us to secure the dearest rights of human nature.''[68] Henry directly attacked the core of Madison's position that a bill of rights in the proposed Constitution was not essential. ''We are told,'' he argued, ''that all powers not given are reserved. I am sorry to bring forth hackneyed observations. But, sir, important truths lose nothing of their validity or weight, by frequency of repetition.''[69] Madison recognized that these arguments threatened ratification and that he had to derail this train before it gained too much momentum.

Exceptionally soft spoken and not inclined by disposition to enjoy public speaking, Madison answered Henry's wide-ranging assault on the Constitution, demonstrating his willingness and ability to slug it out with all challengers. He began his counteroffensive by asking the chair's ''pardon . . . for making a few remarks on what fell from the honorable gentlemen''; moreover, if need be, he too would ''follow the example of gentlemen in deviating from the rule of the house. But as they have taken the utmost latitude in their objections, it is necessary that those who favor the government should answer them.''[70]

After a point-by-point rebuttal of the issues raised by Henry, Madison turned to Henry's invoking of Jefferson's name to assist the amendment cause. Tactfully, Madison destroyed Henry's argument. In the process, he demonstrated that, at least with an ocean between him and Jefferson, he could be his own person. Opening with a series of rhetorical questions, Madison asked: ''Is it come to this, then,

67. Patrick Henry speech, 12 June 1788, Elliot, *Debates* 3:314; Henry's emphasis.
68. Ibid., 3:315.
69. Ibid., 3:316. Rarely a slow learner, Madison, once unqualified ratification had been secured, would adopt some of Henry's rhetoric to his own advantage when he became the champion for the Bill of Rights in the First Congress.
70. JM speech, 12 June 1788, Elliot, *Debates* 3:328.

that we are not to follow our own reason? Is it proper to introduce the opinions of respectable men not within these walls? If the opinion of an important character were to weigh on this occasion, could we not adduce a character equally great on our side? Are we, who (in the honorable gentleman's opinion) are not to be governed by an erring world, now to submit to the opinion of a citizen beyond the Atlantic?" With forensic skills honed through years of public service, Madison left his questions unanswered but reverberating in his audience's mind; he then boldly asserted that while "I wish his name had never been mentioned," if Jefferson "now" stood "on this floor, he would be *for* the adoption of this constitution."[71]

As the convention drew to a close at the end of June, the issue of amendments still held center stage. On June 24, Madison framed the issue in terms of respect versus insult, if Virginia elected to go her own way on ratification. Reminding his audience of the recent past, he described how

> Virginia has always heretofore spoken the language of respect to the other states, and she has always been attended to. Will it be that language to call on a great majority of the states to acknowledge that they have done wrong? Is it the language of confidence to say that we do not believe that amendments for the preservation of the common liberty, and general interest of the states, will be consented to by them? This is the language neither of confidence nor respect.[72]

Not averse to hyperbole to combat the rhetoric of the opposition, Madison confronted the delegates with the reality that "it is a most awful thing that depends on our decision—no less than whether the thirteen states shall unite freely, peaceably, and unanimously, for security of their common happiness and liberty, or whether every thing is to be put in confusion and disorder." In the same spirit, Madison shared his reasoned opinion with his audience: "If Virginia will agree to ratify this system, I shall look upon it as one of the most fortunate events that ever happened for human nature." Con-

71. Ibid., 3:329.
72. JM speech, 24 June 1788, Elliot, *Debates* 3:617.

versely, rejection of the system gave him "the most excruciating apprehensions" and "infinite pain."[73]

Before giving up the floor, Madison reiterated his fundamental and unwavering interpretative stance on the meaning of the Constitution—a position that made additional protection unnecessary.

> Can the general government exercise any power not delegated? If an enumeration be made of our rights, will it not be implied that every thing omitted is given to the general government? Has not the honorable gentleman himself admitted that an imperfect enumeration is dangerous? Does the Constitution say that they shall not alter the law of descents, or do these things which would subvert the whole system of the state laws? If it did, what was not excepted would be granted. Does it follow, from the omission of such restrictions, that they can exercise powers not delegated? The reverse of the proposition holds. The delegation alone warrants the exercise of any power.[74]

One would search in vain for Madison's admission that the framers erred in not providing a specific declaration of rights. At this point, Madison genuinely believed two things: the Constitution *was* a bill of rights; and any scheme short of an unqualified ratification of the Constitution would be disastrous. Consequently, he let it be known that he would consider himself honor bound, after ratification, to amend the Constitution, provided it could be accomplished without a second convention. Madison once more demonstrated the lengths to which he would travel to secure ratification when he discussed slavery and property rights—perhaps the most twisted dimension to his logic of the Constitution as a bill of rights.

73. Ibid., 3:618, 619.
74. Ibid., 3:620. Madison rose later in the day to repeat his position, while offering the hint of an olive branch to the opposition; see JM speech, 24 June 1788, 3:626–627: "As to a solemn declaration of our essential rights, he thought it unnecessary and dangerous—unnecessary, because it was evident that the general government had no power but what was given it, and that the delegation alone warranted the exercise of power; dangerous, because an enumeration which is not complete is not safe. Such an enumeration could not be made, within any compass of time, as would be equal to a general negation, such as his honorable friend (Mr. Wythe) had proposed. He declared that such amendments as seemed, in his judgment, to be without danger, he would readily admit, and that he would be the last to oppose any such amendment as would give satisfaction to any gentleman, unless it were dangerous."

On June 15, Madison spoke to reassure his fellow slave owners that their property—an important right—rested more secure under the new Constitution than under the Confederation. After acknowledging that the traffic in human flesh would be prohibited in twenty years, he pointed out that in the interim their property remained secure from excess taxation (itself a form of taking) and that their ownership had been secured and guaranteed by other states. "At present," he reminded them, "if any slave elopes to any of those states where slaves are free, he becomes emancipated by their laws; . . . But in this Constitution, 'no person held to service or labor in one state, under the laws thereof, escaping into another, shall, in consequence of any law or regulation therein, be discharged from such service or labor; but shall be delivered up on claim of the party to whom such service or labor shall be due.' " While the words *slave* or *slavery* do not explicitly appear in the Constitution, although alluded to in three sections, Madison wanted his conventioneers not to be mistaken: "This clause was expressly inserted, to enable owners of slaves to reclaim them."[75] When the threat of emancipation again arose nine days later, Madison reassured his audience that "if they should ever attempt it, . . . it will . . . be an usurpation of power." Reaffirming the expressed grant-of-powers theory, he maintained that "there is no power to warrant it, in that paper." Slavery remained safe for two reasons: it was part of the institution of property; and it was understood to be the price extracted by the South for its participation in the new nation.[76]

Even after ratification had been achieved, Madison recognized the necessity of gaining additional public support for the new charter. This, along with time, would give legitimacy to the government and make equilibrium easier to maintain. Successfully frozen out of the Senate by the political maneuvering of Patrick Henry, Madison ran for the House of Representatives. He accepted his elected position cognizant of the need for representatives and administrators sympathetic to the Constitution if it was to have a prayer of success. Having explicitly campaigned on a promise to work for a bill of rights,

75. JM speech, 15 June 1788, Elliot, *Debates* 3:453. Madison also acknowledged slavery to be wrong, but disunion worse (3:454), "Great as the evil is, a dismemberment of the Union would be worse."

76. JM speech, 24 June 1788, Elliot, *Debates* 3:621–622; see also JM speech, 15 June 1788, Elliot, *Debates* 3:458–459.

Madison now perceived the issue not only as the fulfillment of an obligation and a mechanism to gain additional public support for the new government, but also as an opportunity to preempt efforts for a second national convention.

Although he was ready to orchestrate a bill of rights, in early 1789 Madison's genuine views remained steadfast. "I freely own that I have never seen in the Constitution as it now stands those serious dangers which have alarmed many respectable Citizens," he wrote George Eve. Acknowledging his opposition to all "previous alterations," he explained, "Circumstances are now changed." With eleven states having ratified the plan, it seemed safe to consider amendments, "if pursued with a proper moderation and in a proper mode." At that moment, his own list of amendments had expanded to contain

> satisfactory provisions for all essential rights, particularly the rights of Conscience in the fullest latitude, the freedom of the press, trials by jury, security against general warrants &c. I think it will be proper also to provide expressly in the Constitution, for the periodical increase of the number of Representatives until the amount shall be entirely satisfactory; and to put the judiciary department into such a form as will render vexatious appeals impossible. There are sundry other alterations which are either eligible in themselves, or being at least safe, are recommended by the respect due to such a wish for them.

His attention remained focused not so much on the appropriate list or expedient manner of altering the text. Rather, Madison wanted to ensure that there would be no second constitutional convention: it "would at least spread a general alarm, and be but too likely to turn every thing into confusion and uncertainty."[77] While Madison would reluctantly add to what the framers accomplished at Philadelphia, he could not tolerate any diminution of the new state's powers. A second convention continued to be out of the question.

A little more than a year after the opening of Virginia's ratifying convention, after an initial two-week postponement, the first United States Congress finally initiated the process of amending the

77. JM to George Eve, 2 Jan. 1789, *PJM* 11:404–405.

Constitution. The first to speak on the topic, Madison explained that he considered it his "duty" to "unfold his ideas" to the House. He warned that further delay might "occasion suspicions, which, though not well founded, may tend to inflame or prejudice the public mind." Appreciating the power of public perception, he astutely proposed that the House not "enter into a full and minute discussion of every part of the subject, but merely to bring it before the house, that our constituents may see we pay proper attention to a subject they have much at heart."[78]

After the failure of Madison's motion to consider the issue as a Committee of the Whole, he proposed a "select committee be appointed to consider and report such amendments as are proper for Congress to propose." Sensing that the House was not enthusiastic about the amendments, Madison apologized for being an "accessary to the loss of a single moment of time by the house." He told his colegislators that "if I thought I could fulfil the duty which I owe to myself and my constituents, to let the subject pass over in silence, I most certainly should not trespass upon the indulgence of this house." This being impossible, he felt "compelled to beg a patient hearing to what I have to lay before you. And I do most sincerely believe that if congress will devote but one day to this subject, so far as to satisfy the public that we do not disregard their wishes, it will have salutary influence on the public councils, and prepare the way for a favorable reception of our future measures."[79] Hardly an enthusiastic launching of the project, thus began the journey that terminated in the Bill of Rights, perhaps the finest solo performance of Madison's public life.[80] Ironically, this was a perfect example of Madisonian praxis: he did the right thing for the wrong reasons.

As Madison sketched out his ideas, it became evident he did not intend a separate, attached list, or bill of rights. He proposed, in its place, that the amendments "can be ingrafted" into the Constitution. Specifically, he urged that offending passages be struck out and that amendments be added directly to the text of the document. Be-

78. JM speech, 8 June 1789, *PJM* 12:196–197.
79. Ibid., 12:197–198. See JM to Richard Peters, 19 Aug. 1789, *PJM* 12:346–347, "The papers inclosed will shew that the nauseous project of amendments has not yet been either dismissed or dispatched."
80. Cf. Herbert Storing, *What the Anti-Federalists Were For* (Chicago: University of Chicago Press, 1981), p. 64, who persuasively argues that the Bill of Rights is the Anti-Federalists' great contribution to American politics.

fore proceeding to propose specific amendments, Madison wanted to make sure the situation did not get out of hand.

> We have in this way something to gain, and, if we proceed with caution, nothing to lose; and in this case it is necessary to proceed with caution; for while we feel all these inducements to go into a revisal of the constitution, we must feel for the constitution itself, and make that revisal a moderate one. I should be unwilling to see a door opened for a re-consideration of the whole structure of the government, for a re-consideration of the principles and the substance of the powers given; because I doubt, if such a door was opened, if we should be very likely to stop at that point which would be safe to the government itself: But I do wish to see a door opened to consider, so far as to incorporate those provisions for the security of rights, against which I believe no serious objection has been made by any class of our constituents, such as would be likely to meet with the concurrence of two-thirds of both houses, and the approbation of three-fourths of the state legislatures.[81]

If the House proceeded with caution and care, Madison confidently predicted that both goals of reaffirming public rights without weakening the state could be accomplished.

Madison's first suggestion, itself telling, called for a "declaration" to be "prefixed to the constitution" that read:

> That all power is originally vested in, and consequently derived from the people.
> That government is instituted, and ought to be exercised for the benefit of the people; which consists in the enjoyment of life and liberty, with the right of acquiring and using property, and generally of pursuing and obtaining happiness and safety.
> That the people have an indubitable, unalienable, and indefeasible right to reform or change their government, whenever it be found adverse or inadequate to the purposes of its institution.

This section reaffirmed Madison's fundamental perception of the Constitution. First, the people constitute the original and ultimate

81. JM speech, 8 June 1789, *PJM* 12:199.

source of all power. Second, government is a trust, created for specific ends, which in Madison's accounting disjointedly echoed the opening of the Declaration of Independence with at least two significant additions.

Madison wanted citizens to possess the right not only of "pursuing" but also "obtaining happiness and safety." Safety always seemed paramount in Madison's calculations; his words deviated significantly from Jefferson's trilogy by inserting a guarantee of "the right of acquiring and using property." In light of Madison's experiences in government, it may be understandable why he inserted this phrase: if he, and most of his colleagues, had to agree to the protection of individual rights, he wanted to ensure—again and again— that property remained outside control by democratic politics. The third paragraph reflected Madison as well: the right of the people "to reform or change their government." Note, however, that Madison did not claim a right to revolution, just to "reform or change." And, in light of the guarantee clause of Article 4, section 4, it could not be considered self-evident that a nonrepublican government would be appropriate, especially if the alteration produced a government "adverse or inadequate to the purposes of its institution"; that is, if the new government attempted to tamper with property rights. A change in government, moreover, required far more time and energy than approval by a simple majority, given the amendment scheme adopted in the Constitution. All of this, of course, remains somewhat speculative because Madison never felt the need for further, explicit clarification.[82] Nevertheless, the tensions between property and democracy developed into an issue Madison directly addressed later in his life.

There appears to be no need for a detailed analysis of each of Madison's nineteen specific suggested amendments. A few should suffice to understand the logic behind his ideas. His second of nine broad categories of changes urged that "in article 1st, section 2, clause 3, these words be stuck out, to wit, 'The number of representatives shall not exceed one for every thirty thousand, but each state shall have at least one representative, and until such enumeration shall be made.'" Madison, always looking for the "golden mean" of a sufficient number of legislators to represent the people adequately, yet

82. Ibid., 12:200.

not too many that the assembly becomes an irrational mob, sought to open up the House. Concerning the House and the Senate, Madison wanted to restrict their ability to give themselves pay raises and suggested inserting in "article 1st, section 6, clause 1," at the end of the first sentence, "But no law varying the compensation last ascertained shall operate before the next ensuing election of representatives."[83] The defensive logic behind Madison's political system was manifest. The legislators could vote to raise their salaries, but before they received any additional monies, the voters would have to endorse this idea by reelecting their representatives; and, on the other hand, the voters could send a clear, negative message concerning the monetary increases by voting the scoundrels out. After all, their salaries came from taxes; taxes are a form of taking property; and that can be done legitimately only with the citizens' consent.

To this point, Madison's changes look nothing like the first ten amendments to the Constitution. Beginning with his fourth category, Madison articulated the core of what eventually came to be known as the Bill of Rights. It is noteworthy that unlike the Declaration of Independence, the rights in the final Bill of Rights are not "unalienable" and, for all intents and purposes, have nothing to do with equality—a fundamental concern of the declaration.

Still assuming that the amendments would be "ingrafted" into the body of the document, Madison specified where the language should be altered. His first declaration of specific guarantees involved religion. He proceeded to delineate, inside one category, what finally developed into the First through Sixth amendments, and the Eighth and Ninth. So significant are Madison's words, and so rarely do they appear in print, they will be quoted at length.

> Fourthly. That in article 1st, section 9, between clauses 3 and 4, be inserted these clauses, to wit, The civil rights of none shall be abridged on account of religious belief or worship, nor shall any national religion be established, nor shall the full and equal rights of conscience be in any manner, or on any pretext infringed.
>
> The people shall not be deprived or abridged of their right to speak, to write, or to publish their sentiments; and the freedom

83. Ibid., 12:200–201. See Rakove, *Madison*, p. 81, who locates nineteen Madison amendments.

of the press, as one of the great bulwarks of liberty, shall be inviolable.

The people shall not be restrained from peaceably assembling and consulting for their common good; nor from applying to the legislature by petitions, or remonstrances for redress of their grievances.

The right of the people to keep and bear arms shall not be infringed; a well armed, and well regulated militia being the best security of a free country: but no person religiously scrupulous of bearing arms, shall be compelled to render military service in person.

No soldier shall in time of peace be quartered in any house without the consent of the owner; nor at any time, but in a manner warranted by law.

No person shall be subject, except in cases of impeachment, to more than one punishment, or one trial for the same offence; nor shall be compelled to be a witness against himself; nor be deprived of life, liberty, or property without due process of law; nor be obliged to relinquish his property, where it may be necessary for public use, without a just compensation.

Excessive bail shall not be required, nor excessive fines imposed, nor cruel and unusual punishments inflicted.

The rights of the people to be secured in their persons, their houses, their papers, and their other property from all unreasonable searches and seizures, shall not be violated by warrants issued without probable cause, supported by oath or affirmation, or not particularly describing the places to be searched, or the persons or things to be seized.

In all criminal prosecutions, the accused shall enjoy the right to a speedy and public trial, to be informed of the cause and nature of the accusation, to be confronted with his accusers, and the witnesses against him; to have a compulsory process for obtaining witnesses in his favor; and to have the assistance of counsel for his defence.

The exceptions here or elsewhere in the constitution, made in favor of particular rights, shall not be so construed as to diminish the just importance of other rights retained by the people; or as to enlarge the powers delegated by the constitution; but ei-

ther as actual limitations of such powers, or as inserted merely
for greater caution.[84]

Because Madison feared local politics in the separate states, it
seems inevitable that lacking the federal veto over state legislation,
for which he lobbied throughout the Constitutional Convention, he
should try to gain added protection against local government. Consequently, his fifth set of changes occurred in Article 1, section 10, between the first and second clauses. Here he wanted to insert the
clause "No state shall violate the equal rights of conscience, or the
freedom of the press, or the trial by jury in criminal cases."[85] The rest
of the language in this section contained explicit limitations on
power in the state governments, including several protections on
property rights. Madison's additional protections were not accepted
by his colleagues; they would have to await Supreme Court action in
the twentieth century when it *undemocratically*, selectively incorporated Madison's ideas.[86]

Madison's sixth and seventh categories of changes, in part, appear
in the Fifth, Sixth, and Seventh amendments to the Constitution.[87]
Madison's eighth change, which would have created a new Article 7,
reaffirmed the notion of separation of powers and contained the language that would become the Tenth Amendment: "The powers not

84. JM speech, 8 June 1789, *PJM* 12:201–202.
85. Ibid., 12:202.
86. See Henry J. Abraham, *Freedom and the Court: Civil Rights and Liberties
in the U.S.*, 5th ed. (New York: Oxford University Press, 1972), pp. 29–88.
87. JM speech, 8 June 1789, *PJM* 12:202; Madison thus expressed his seventh
point: "That in article 3d, section 2, the third clause be struck out, and in its
place be inserted the clauses following, to wit:
The trial of all crimes (except in cases of impeachments, and cases arising in
the land or naval forces, or the militia when on actual service in time of war or
public danger) shall be by an impartial jury of freeholders of the vicinage, with
the requisite of unanimity for conviction, of the right of challenge, and other ac-
customed requisites; and in all crimes punishable with loss of life or member,
presentment or indictment by a grand jury, shall be an essential preliminary,
provided that in cases of crimes committed within any county which may be in
possession of an enemy, or in which a general insurrection may prevail, the trial
may by law be authorised in some other county of the same state, as near as
may be to the seat of the offence.
In cases of crimes committed not within any county, the trial may by law be
in such county as the laws shall have prescribed. In suits at common law, between man and man, the trial by jury, as one of the best securities to the rights
of the people, ought to remain inviolate."

delegated by this constitution, nor prohibited by it to the states, are reserved to the States respectively."[88]

Having presented his suggestions, Madison proceeded to justify his position. The themes sounded familiar: the omissions were never "so essential" as to make ratification "improper," nor were the changes, "altogether useless." Madison was less than enthusiastic in his advocacy not because he held these rights in low regard—indeed, he called them "great rights," "choicest privileges of the people," "pre-existent rights of nature"—but because he seemed genuinely to fear the people, and the state governments as the agents of the people, more than the new central government. Consequently, "all paper barriers against the power of the community, are too weak to be worthy of attention." Never sanguine about its real ability to check legislative abuses of power, Madison reasoned that if a bill of rights constituted a desirable weapon against the new government, it was also essential in "all the states."[89] He emphasized this point by arguing that when it came to abuses of bill of attainder and *ex post facto* laws, "there is more danger of those being abused by the state governments than by the government of the United States."[90]

"Having done what I conceived was my duty," Madison sat down. Once more, he suggested that a committee be formed to continue the discussion, thereby liberating the House of its responsibility to show the public that it had taken some action about their rights. This would free the House to initiate "the absolute necessity . . . of pursuing the organization of the government."[91] After all, in Madison's view, strong government—not paper barriers—guaranteed rights, liberty, as well as stability. At least, that is, until the Federalists began to run the show.

88. JM speech, 8 June 1789, *PJM* 12:202. Before adoption by the House, the words "or to the people" were added. Finally, his ninth change would have renumbered Article 7 as Article 8.

89. Ibid., 12:203-204. See *PJM* 12:205. JM used "the necessary and proper clause" to argue, against his own earlier position that in spite of the logic behind the notion of "enumerated" powers, perhaps some added protection was wise. But he shifted from a fear of abuse of the national government to his real fear of "improper laws . . . enacted by the state legislatures." Indeed, at moments it appears Madison's prime concern was to further check the powers of the states, rather than the federal power.

90. JM speech, 8 June 1789, *PJM* 12:208: "The state governments are as liable to attack these invaluable privileges as the general government is, and therefore ought to be as cautiously guarded against."

91. Ibid., 12:209.

Madison's fears of the *demos* being the primary threat to rights and stability proved short lived. As control of the Washington-Adams regimes quickly slipped out of Madison's and Jefferson's grasps, both men realized an active, free press would be essential to balance the executive branch; Madison eventually realized just how dangerous the chief executive, rather than the legislature, could be.

Madison's views on the role of a free press in a republican government can be seen in less strident form in several of his *National Gazette* essays in the early 1790s. In "Public Opinion" Madison persuaded his readers that the "real sovereign in every free" government was public opinion. He stood in the forefront in understanding just how powerful a force public opinion could be in popular government. But the relationship between the government and public opinion remained dialectical: in some cases, "public opinion must be obeyed by the government"; and in other cases, public opinion "may be influenced by the government." The significance of public opinion, at this point, convinced Madison of the importance of a "*Constitutional Declaration of Rights*" by its widespread acceptance as a "part of the public opinion." Often concerned with the issue of size, Madison argued that a free press would become especially significant to ascertain the "real opinion" of a public spread over a vast territory: "Whatever facilitates a general intercourse of sentiments, as good roads, domestic commerce, a free press, and particularly a *circulation of newspapers through the entire body of the people*, and *Representatives going from, and returning among every part of them*, is equivalent to a contraction of territorial limits, and is favorable to liberty, where these may be too extensive."[92]

The logic behind Madison's politics required that every actor in the political system have some degree of protective power, "a defensive armour for each," as he described it. Unlike Madison of *The Federalist*, when he was in *de facto* power, the Madison of the *National Gazette*, who was out of power, emphasized the ultimate power of the people. If well-informed by the press, the people could form a defensive protection against tyranny.

92. "Public Opinion," 19 Dec. 1791, *National Gazette*, *PJM* 14:170. See also *PJM* 14:168, where JM noted that "the class of literati . . . are the cultivators of the human mind—the manufacturers of useful knowledge—the agents of the commerce of ideas—the censors of public manners—the teachers of the acts of life and the means of happiness." Cf. John Stuart Mill's *On Liberty*.

In bestowing the eulogies due to the partitions and internal checks of power, it ought not the less to be remembered, that they are neither the sole nor the chief palladium of constitutional liberty. The people who are the authors of this blessing, must also be its guardians. Their eyes must be ever ready to mark, their voice to pronounce, and their arm to repel or repair aggressions on the authority of their constitutions; the highest authority next to their own, because the immediate work of their own, and the most sacred part of their property, as recognising and recording the title to every other.[93]

Again, two things must be noted. First, Madison's position remained simply to have the people exercise their voting power to pick men of wisdom. He did not want the *demos* intimately involved in politics. They were not to set the agenda or discuss policy choices; they were restricted to kicking the bums out of office when they got out of line. Second, Madison linked rights and constitutions as "the most sacred part of" the people's property. This theme of Madison's concept of citizenship will be further explored in the next two chapters. For the present, an examination of Madison's more extreme opposition to the Federalist regime as the 1790s drew to a close is necessary.

Counterpressure and balance contained the keys to freedom. In 1798, Madison noted how one newspaper could "be an effectual antidote" to either the executive or another newspaper; he was "glad to find in general that every thing that good sense & accurate information can supply is abundantly exhibited by the Newspapers to the view of the public." Still, Madison realized that this balancing of the government's position by the press would extend only as far as its circulation. Madison's alarm with the machinations at the capitol had yet to reach its peak, although images of Robespierre came readily to his mind. Yet in the spring of 1798 he "hoped however that any arbitrary attacks on the freedom of the Press will find virtue eno' remaining in the public mind to make them recoil on the wicked authors. No other check to desperate projects seems now to be left."[94]

The Alien and Sedition Acts pushed Madison into direct conflict

93. "Government of the United States," 4 Feb. 1792, *National Gazette, PJM* 14:218.
94. JM to Thomas Jefferson, 5 May 1798, *PJM* 17:126.

with the Adams administration. Upon learning of the preliminary details of the alien bill, he told Jefferson that it represented "a monster that must for ever disgrace its parents." Still, Madison thought the proposal so outrageous that he hoped it might backfire on the Federalists: "These addresses to the feelings of the people from their enemies, may have more effect in opening their eyes, than all the arguments addressed to their understanding by their friends."[95] Of course, given Madison's low opinion of the people, relying upon them to save the republic would be a risky business. Newspapers could help; so too could the state governments. Consequently, he moved on the Virginia legislative front in an effort to spur other state legislatures to check the tyrannical federal government. While the crucial issues for Madison in the Virginia Resolution of 1798 undoubtedly consisted in the proper interpretation of the Constitution and the legitimate power of the federal government, our concern for the present is how it related in its language to threats to individual and states' rights.

In December of 1798, the Virginia General Assembly reaffirmed both its "warm attachment to the Union of the States" and its responsibility "to watch over and oppose every infraction of those principles, which constitute the only basis of that union." To that end, as author of this Virginia resolution, Madison argued that whenever "a deliberate, palpable and dangerous exercise of other powers not granted by the said compact" occurred, "the states who are parties thereto have the right, and are in duty bound, to interpose for arresting the pro[gress] of the evil, and for maintaining within their respective limits, the authorities, rights and liberties appertaining to them."[96] Exactly what interpose meant would not become clear until later in the document, when Virginia asked the other states to join in declaring the "alien and sedition acts" an "unconstitutional" violation of the Constitution and one of its amendments.[97] Moreover, Madison argued that the objectionable acts directly contradicted Virginia's ratification of the Constitution since she did so expressly declaring "that among other essential rights, the liberty of conscience and of the press cannot be cancelled,

---

95. JM to Thomas Jefferson, 20 May 1798, *PJM* 17:133–134.
96. Virginia Resolutions, 21 Dec. 1798, *PJM* 17:189.
97. Ibid., 17:189–190. JM used the term *interpose* in *Federalist* 38 and twice in *Federalist* 43.

abridged, restrained or modified by any authority of the United States.'' The resolution closed with a call to other states, ''that the necessary and proper measures will be taken by each, for cooperating with this State in maintaining unimpaired the authorities, rights, and liberties, reserved to the States respectively, or to the people.''[98] When seven states eventually responded to Virginia's request, the replies were uniformly negative.

While there exists considerable evidence to support the position that Madison may not have been the author of either the ''Virginia Resolution of 10 January 1799'' or the ''Address of the General Assembly to the People of the Commonwealth of Virginia, 23 January 1799,'' ''stylometric'' and other evidence indicates that he did write two essays for the Philadelphia-based *Aurora General Advertiser,* which are germane to the issue of rights.[99] In ''Foreign Influence'' Madison turned the Adams administration's arguments against French influence in the United States back against the regime itself. On the issue of a free press, Madison drew some sophisticated and rather modern conclusions about British influence through financial connections. ''Money in all its shapes is influence,'' observed Madison; and ''our monied institutions consequently form another great engine of British influence.'' Either directly or indirectly, Madison claimed, Britain or her connections control ''Our Bank'' through selection of the ''Directors'' who ''dispense the credits and favours of the Banks.'' This control turned ''every dependent'' on credit into ''a kind of vassal, owing homage to his pecuniary superiors, on pain of bankruptcy and ruin.''[100] Not only did Britain control the bank, it exerted a heavy influence, if not direct control, on the American press.

Madison had assumed that there would be foreign influence in banking, but control of the press, far more subtle, had not always been his concern.[101] Becoming aware of this menace, he found it ''de-

---

98. Virginia Resolutions, 21 Dec. 1798, *PJM* 17:190. Unfortunately for JM, this resolution in time became linked by the states' rights movement with Jefferson's more radical Kentucky resolution, a source of much personal discomfort and concern for JM after Jefferson's death.

99. For a detailed discussion of the issues and evidence surrounding JM's authorship of these four documents, see the editorial notes in *PJM* 17:199–206, 211–214.

100. ''Foreign Influence,'' 23 Jan. 1799, *Aurora General Advertiser, PJM* 17:219.

101. See JM speech, 14 Jan. 1794, *PJM* 15:189.

plorable that this guardian of public rights, this organ of necessary truths, should be tainted with partiality at all. How bitter the reflection, that it should be subject to a foreign taint." Madison traced the chain of influence from the interior countryside to the commercial cities back to the British investors.

> The inland papers it is well known copy from the city papers; this city more particularly, as the centre of politics and news. The city papers are supported by advertisements. The advertisements for the most part, relate to articles of trade, and are furnished by merchants and traders. In this manner British influence steals into our newspapers, and circulates under their passport. Every printer, whether an exception to the remark or not, knows the fact to be as here stated. There are presses whose original independence, subsequent apostacies, occasional conversions, speedy relapses, and final prostration to advertising customers, point them out as conspicuous examples.[102]

Whether subjected to pressure from the Adams administration directly or the British investors indirectly, the press struggled to function independently while under attack in the young republic.

Madison's efforts as legislator and editorialist did not produce the results for which he and Jefferson had hoped: North Carolina had recently rejected the Kentucky resolution, causing Madison to worry about "one of the most daring experiments that has been made on the apathy of the people."[103] On 23 February 1799, Madison's second essay, "Political Reflections," appeared in print. In analyzing the French Revolution and its aftermath, especially in light of Adams's reading of those events, Madison artfully turned the public's attention back to the genuine threats presented by the executive at home, rather than mythical threats in Paris. In words that Madison as Publius had used against the American people, factions, and state legislatures, he subtly but tellingly rebuked the current national regime. He began the assault attacking "the doctrine so ardently propagated by many, that in a republic the people ought to consider the whole of their political duty as discharged when they have chosen their repre-

---

102. "Foreign Influence," 23 Jan. 1799, *Aurora General Advertiser, PJM* 17:219–220.
103. JM to Thomas Jefferson, 25 Jan. 1799, *PJM* 17:221.

sentatives."[104] As he had in the past, Madison argued that the citizens had to be ever vigilant to watch for usurpations of power. When violations occurred, the people must exercise their defensive power and then return to their daily routine. Although this was Madison's notion of the role for the average citizen, it still remains a far cry from Aristotle's conception of *zoon politikon*.

Madison continued his argument. In vivid, instructive prose he decoded for his readers "the true lesson" taught by French politics:

> that in no case ought the eyes of the people to be shut on the conduct of those entrusted with power; nor their tongues tied from a just wholesome censure on it, any more than from merited commendations. If neither gratitude for the honor of the trust, nor responsibility for the use of it, be sufficient to curb the unruly passions of public functionaries, add new bits to the bridle rather than to take it off altogether. This is the precept of common sense illustrated and enforced by experience—uncontrouled power, ever has been, and ever will be administered by the passions more than by reason.[105]

Madison pushed his position directly to Adams's doorstep, where he mocked

> the fashionable doctrine of the present day, that elective and responsible rulers ought never to be deemed capable of abusing their trust, much less does it favor the still more fashionable doctrine, that *executive influence* in a *representative* government is *a mere phantom* created by the imaginations of the credulous, or *the arts of the hypocritical friends of liberty*; and that all true patriots will ever unite their efforts *in strengthening the executive force*, by stifling every jealousy of its hostile misapplication.[106]

He closed his well-reasoned diatribe with two "momentous truths" in the "whole field of political sciences" that should be "engraven

104. "Political Reflections," 23 Feb. 1799, *Aurora General Advertiser, PJM* 17:238.
105. Ibid., 17:239.
106. Ibid., 17:240; JM's emphasis.

on the American mind." "First. That *the fetters imposed on liberty at home have ever been forged out of the weapons provided for defence against real, pretended, or imaginary dangers from abroad. Secondly,* That *there never was a people whose liberties long survived a standing army.*"[107]

With the huge success of the revolution of 1800, Madison's attention again shifted away from freedom of the press to affairs of the state. His consistency on the relationship between diversity, balance, and freedom, be it religion or press, never wavered. This can be seen in an 1828 letter to Nicholas Trist. Commenting on the less than favorable state of newspaper publishing, Madison reminded Trist that "falsehood and slanders must always be controuled in a certain degree by contradictions in rival or hostile papers where the press is free." Then he told Trist,

> It has been said, that any country might be governed at the will of one who had the exclusive privilege of furnishing its popular songs. The result would be far more certain from a monopoly of the politics of the press. Could it be so arranged that every newspaper, when printed on one side, should be handed over to the press of an adversary, to be printed on the other, thus presenting to every reader both sides of every question, truth would always have a fair chance.[108]

With Madison's historic view of the Bill of Rights and his special interest in freedom of the press and religious toleration in mind, it is appropriate to return to his intriguing essay "Property."

Considered among the most remarkable of all his public essays, "Property" comes closest to expressing what might be considered the heart and soul of Madisonian politics. The perfect logic of his words presented the hope of achieving genuine economic justice through the appropriate public understanding of the meanings of the

107. Ibid., 17:242; JM's emphasis. See also "Notes for Essays," 19 Dec. 1791–3 Mar. 1792, *PJM* 14:160–161, where JM wrote, "Fear & hatred of other nations, the greatest cement, always appealed to by rulers when they wish to impose burdens or carry unpopular points."

108. JM to N. P. Trist, 23 Apr. 1828, *Letters and Other Writings of James Madison*, ed. William C. Rives and Philip R. Fendall, 4 vols. (Philadelphia: J. B. Lippincott, 1884), 3:630.

terms *property* and *rights*; however, the reality of a rapidly developing market economy, with its inevitably increasing mass of propertyless humans, would make a mockery of Madison's noble attempt.
He would remain committed implicitly to the market principles of
possessive individualism.[109]

Throughout this 1792 essay, Madison linked himself with the philosophic tradition that as late as Hobbes and Locke continued to
think of property, by contemporary standards, in an extraordinarily
wide sense. Hobbes included a person's "own life and limbs, and in
the next degree (in most men), those things that concern conjugal
affection; and after them riches and means of living." Locke, as is
well known, defined property as a man's life, liberty, and estate.[110]

Historically, then, property comprised much more than material
things. In what Madison called "its larger and juster meaning,"
property "embraces every thing to which a man may attach a value
and have a right; and *which leaves to every one else the like advantage.*"[111] He listed some of the "things" included under property in
its "particular" meaning: land, merchandise, or money. In its
"larger and juster meaning" he enumerated a person's opinions (and
the free communication of them), an individual's religious opinions
(in the profession and practice of them), the safety and liberty of his
person, and "the free use of his faculties and free choice of the objects on which to employ them." Property, in either meaning, was
essential to humanity, yet it remained threatened on two fronts: "an
excess of power" or "an excess of liberty." In the previous decade,
Madison's attention had focused on the latter threat; in the 1790s,
his concern turned to the former. In time, his attention would return
to the problem of too much liberty as his fears of surplus population
began to rematerialize.

Madison reminded his late-eighteenth-century readers of his fundamental premise: "Government is instituted to protect property of
every sort; as well that which lies in the various rights of individ-

109. C. B. Macpherson, *The Political Theory of Possessive Individualism* (Oxford: Clarendon Press, 1962), pp. 263–264. See also McDonald, *Novus Ordo Seclorum*, p. 4, where he reminds scholars that terms like *property, liberty, society,* and *rights* were, "during the eighteenth century, in a state of flux."
110. Quoted in C. B. Macpherson, *The Rise and Fall of Economic Justice: And
Other Essays* (Oxford: Oxford University Press, 1985), pp. 76–85.
111. "Property," 27 Mar. 1792, *National Gazette, PJM* 14:266; JM's emphasis.

uals, as that which the term particularly expresses."[112] At that moment in American history, Madison's worry consisted not of excessive governmental power taking "particular" property through taxes, or inflation, or credit schemes, but the "taking" of individual rights of opinion, of conscience, of the press. Again like Hobbes and Locke, Madison's stated hierarchy of rights implied that material property held lesser import than property rights to nonmaterial, but essential, human rights. Echoing the spirit of *The Federalist*, Madison wrote that the protection of property "being the end of government, that alone is a *just* government, which *impartially* secures to every man, whatever is his *own*."[113] Madison's analysis of justice and the absolute necessity of securing material property compared to the less than absolute necessity to protect nonmaterial property demonstrated, in spite of his words, the genuine primacy of a right to property in the narrow, "particular" sense. His writings on suffrage and property, discussed in the next chapter, further established his actual position.

"The praise of affording a just security to property," he wrote, "should be sparingly bestowed on a government which, however scrupulously guarding the possessions of individuals, does not protect them in the enjoyment and communication of their opinions, in which they have an equal, and in the estimation of some, a more valuable property."[114] Notice how he failed to state that such a government should simply be considered unjust; he preferred, instead, to withhold a degree of praise. Notice also that on speech and press, he does not argue that he personally thinks these rights are superior to "particular" property rights, but that "some" hold that position.

He addressed next the right he always considered first in his personal hierarchy, "conscience . . . the most sacred of all property." Even here, however, the security of material property appeared implicitly more significant than conscience. Madison argued:

112. Ibid. See also "Observations on Jefferson's Draft," 15 Oct. 1788, *PJM* 11:287: "This middle mode reconciles and secures the two cardinal objects of Government, the rights of persons, and the rights of property"; see also JM's "preamble" to the Constitution as part of his ideas on a bill of rights, 8 June 1789, *PJM* 12:200. "That government is instituted, and ought to be exercised for the benefit of the people; which consists in the enjoyment of life and liberty, and the right of acquiring and using property, and generally of pursuing and obtaining happiness and safety."
113. "Property," 27 Mar. 1792, *National Gazette, PJM* 14:266; JM's emphasis.
114. Ibid.

More sparingly should this praise be allowed to a government, where a man's religious rights are violated by penalties, or fettered by tests, or taxed by a hierarchy. Conscience is the most sacred of all property; other property depending in part on positive law, the exercise of that, being a natural and unalienable right. To guard a man's house as his castle, to pay public and enforce private debts with the most exact faith, can give no title to invade a man's conscience which is more sacred than his castle, or to withhold from it that debt of protection, for which the public faith is pledged, by the very nature and original conditions of the social pact.[115]

Where Madison will "spare" praise on a government that intruded on these rights, even though he attributed these rights to natural rather than positive law, he drew a distinct line when the violations touched the body or things of an individual. "That is not a just government, nor is property secure under it," he wrote, "where the property which a man has in his personal safety and personal liberty, is violated by arbitrary seizures of one class of citizens for the service of the rest."[116] He presented a specific example of such an injustice that diverted the reader's attention away from the southern domestic scene: "A magistrate issuing his warrants to a press gang, would be in his proper functions in Turkey or Indostan, under appellations proverbial of the most compleat despotism."[117] Madison remained unequivocal. Where "arbitrary seizures" in any form took place, the government could not be considered just. This particular violation did not involve the question of how "sparingly" a government should be praised or blamed; "arbitrary seizures" made it categorically unjust. That arbitrary actions especially infuriated the rational Madison will be shown later. For a brief moment, a private note by Madison on slavery must be considered.

In preparing his notes for the *National Gazette* essays, Madison indicated he had been explicitly thinking of the questions slavery raised in terms of property and democracy. That he elected not to incorpo-

115. Ibid., 14:266–267.
116. Coming from a slaveholder, this was an interesting statement indeed, though one could argue that it was the "arbitrary" nature of the seizures that made them unjust to Madison.
117. "Property," 27 Mar. 1792, *National Gazette, PJM* 14:267.

rate his thoughts into his public essays can be readily appreciated since he comprehended fully the obvious contradictions. "In proportion as slavery prevails in a State, the Government, however democratic in name, must be aristocratic in fact," he wrote. "The power lies in a part instead of the whole; in the hands of property, not of numbers." After describing "the antient popular governments," he compared them to the South and concluded both were "aristocratic." "In Virginia" he noted that "the aristocratic character is increased by the rule of suffrage, which requiring a freehold in land excludes nearly half the free inhabitants, and must exclude a greater proportion, as the population increases. At present the slaves and non-freeholders amount to nearly 3/4 of the State." It must be pointed out that Madison did not appear critical of this situation. After all, as a liberal concerned with the institution of property, not democratic politics, why should he be? However, with whiffs of democracy in the air, Madison was not about to share these private thoughts with the public. He closed this passage of his notes with an incredible understatement: "Were the slaves freed and the right of suffrage extended to all, the operation of the Government might be very different." Indeed. With slavery institutionalized in the South, Madison knew power flowed "much more into the hands of property, than in the Northern States. Hence the people of property in the former are much more contented with their establishd. Governments, than the people of property in the latter."[118] This would include Madison as well, given his position on the appropriate relationship between stable government, property, and suffrage. None of the above, however, ever saw the light of day during his lifetime, although hints did appear in his "Property" essay.

Returning to that essay, under the category of actions that resulted in an unjust government, Madison presented a few examples: "where arbitrary restrictions, exemptions, and monopolies deny to part of its citizens that free use of their faculties, and free choice of their occupations, which not only constitute their property in the general sense of the word; but are the means of acquiring property strictly so called." With the shadow of slavery blocking the light of justice contained in this sentence, Madison presented specific examples for consideration, lest his ideal notions of justice get out of con-

118. "Notes for Essays," *PJM* 14:163–164.

trol. He continued his recitation of unqualifiedly unjust governmental actions, where the "arbitrary" nature of the behavior remained essential:

A just security to property is not afforded by that government, under which unequal taxes oppress one species of property and reward another species: where arbitrary taxes invade the domestic sanctuaries of the rich, and excessive taxes grind the faces of the poor; where the keenness and competitions of want are deemed an insufficient spur to labor, and taxes are again applied, by an unfeeling policy, as another spur; in violation of that sacred property, which Heaven, in decreeing man to earn his bread by the sweat of his brow, kindly reserved to him, in the small repose that could be spared from the supply of his necessities.[119]

The language and sentiment of Locke (and Madison's "Agricultural Address" of 1818) pervades. Humans labor out of necessity, not choice. Consequently, on occasion even "the keenness and competition of want" prove to be an "insufficient spur to labor" and must be supplanted by additional taxes. Madison labeled this an "unfeeling policy" as he warned that this taxing had divine limits; if it "took" away from the day of rest, which God gave to man in exchange for decreeing that he had "to earn his bread by the sweat of his brow," it constituted a property violation.

This essay on property, its essence captured neatly by Madison in a single sentence—"In a word, as a man is said to have a right to his property, he may be equally said to have a property in his rights"—makes it undeniable that Madison precariously tried to straddle two traditions inside of liberalism. Each tradition contained different, but not necessarily mutually exclusive, concepts of humanity. Madi-

---

119. "Property," 27 Mar. 1792, *National Gazette, PJM* 14:267. JM also wrote: "If there be a government then which prides itself in maintaining the inviolability of property; which provides that none shall be taken *directly* even for public use without indemnification to the owner, and yet *directly* violates the property which individuals have in their opinions, their religion, their persons, and their faculties; nay more, which *indirectly* violates their property, in their actual possessions, in the labor that acquires their daily subsistence, and in the hallowed remnant of time which ought to relieve their fatigues and soothe their cares, the influence will have been anticipated, that such a government is not a pattern for the United States."

son embraced "the society and politics of choice, the society and politics of competition, the society and politics of the market."[120] In short, he viewed the world through liberal eyes. The earlier moment of the liberal tradition, from Hobbes to Locke, viewed the individual as essentially a consumer of goods and utilities, an appropriator of land and capital. This ontological view of man continues to be crucial for the development of the full market society. In Madison's essay, this concept was reflected in the protection of property in "external things," an individual's "right to his property."

More importantly, as if in anticipation of John Stuart Mill and T. H. Greene (or perhaps it may have been his reading of Aristotle), Madison also perceived at least some individuals as more than "a bundle of appetites seeking satisfaction" through ownership of property. He simultaneously viewed man's essence, in the words of C. B. Macpherson, as that of "a doer, a creator, an enjoyer of his human attributes. . . . Whatever the uniquely human attributes are taken to be, in this view of man their exertion and development are seen as ends in themselves, a satisfaction in themselves."[121] This second, later model of humanity found expression in Madison's discussions of freedom of conscience and of opinion and the free use of one's faculties—the individual's "property in his rights." The problem of Madison simultaneously sustaining these two views of humanity becomes insurmountable: he will not give up his market assumptions of capitalist property. While he could balance a man's "right to his property" as well as a man's "property in his rights" in the late eighteenth century, early in the next century—given Madison's economic and political assumptions—one side of his seesaw would swell in mass and crash to the ground.

Recall that Madison published "Property" a week after his essay "Fashion." The implicit subtheme of each article, as well as his heroic defense of the original creditors on the national debt, circled around the ideal of maintaining economic justice in an emerging market economy.[122] Madison's rhetorical arguments for justice in the institution of property are sound, but doomed, because of his Mal-

120. C. B. Macpherson, *The Real World of Democracy* (Toronto: CBC Learning Systems, 1965), p. 6.

121. C. B. Macpherson, *Democratic Theory: Essays in Retrieval* (Oxford: Clarendon Press, 1973), chapters 1–3.

122. See "Fashion," 20 Mar. 1790, *National Gazette, PJM* 14:257–259.

thusian worldview based on scarcity and his unwillingness to redistribute material property democratically. When free land ran out, which was inevitable, it would be impossible in the "larger and juster meaning" of property to claim that those without property are in an economic condition *"which leaves to everyone else the like advantage."*[123] Land provided the equal opportunity that, to Madison, made the protection of unequal property holdings fair and just. It also kept economic exploitation to a minimum. As the population grew and the free land became exhausted, a "monopoly" in the form of a class who owned property would indeed develop and have the power to "deny to part of its citizens the free use of their facilities, and free choice of their occupations." There would be, however, nothing arbitrary about this: it would be the normal, ongoing, systematic exploitation by those with property of those without property, requiring the latter to pay for access to the means of life.

When this finally occurred, not only would the propertyless outnumber the propertied, but in Madison's own terms the relationship could no longer be considered just. In short, in a full market economy, "a property in rights" becomes effectively meaningless without property in external things. All would still be free. Some, however, would be more free than others. When presented with the choice of a democratic politics reestablishing justice or protecting the institution of property and therein social stability, Madison stood for stability.[124] That Madison remained deeply concerned over this dynamic situation will become evident when his views of property joined to suffrage are presented. Trapped inside his Calvinistic-Lockean view of history, humanity, and property, there seemed little beyond education, political manipulation, and hope that could be done on behalf of a system that would finally run out of time. When that occurred, as Rakove describes Madison's vision, "Wage labor and urban life would sap the manly independence of the republic's citizens."[125]

On the other hand, Madison's "Property" essay contained the seeds of a radical notion of property that could have politically solved his economic race against time. All Madison had to do was

---

123. "Property," 27 Mar. 1792, *National Gazette, PJM* 14:266; JM's emphasis.
124. Sheldon Wolin, *The Presence of the Past* (Baltimore: Johns Hopkins University Press, 1989), p. 45.
125. Rakove, *Madison*, p. 135.

logically link his ideas of an individual having ''a right to his property'' as well as ''a property in his rights'' with his assertion that an individual ''has an equal property in the free use of his faculties and free choice of the objects on which to employ them,'' along with his fairness condition that individuals may take from the common so long as it *"leaves to every one else the like advantage."* At the historic moment when it finally became impossible to guarantee the last requirement, a political solution to maintaining justice remained possible provided property as effective ''rights'' to be exercised, rather than ''things'' to be possessed, took priority.[126] This Madison would not do. It would have required faith in politics as well as humanity; it would have required less fear of chaos and instability. It would have required Madison to be Jefferson.

126. See Macpherson, *Rise and Fall*, pp. 76–91.

6 / Madisonian Government:
"The greatest of all reflections . . . ?"

A Government like ours has so many safety-valves, giving vent to over-heated passions, that it carries within itself a relief against the infirmities from which the best of human Institutions cannot be exempt.[1]

—*Madison*

Madison was not inclined to abstract intellectualizing about a theoretically perfect system, and his thoughts were usually grounded in the context of the political reality of space and time. At this point, it should come as no surprise that the Constitution of 1787 did not embrace many of Madison's most basic ideas on government. Since these additional ideas cannot readily be located in *The Federalist*, it becomes obvious that Madison's Publius presented less than his real thoughts on an ideal political system.[2]

A few dimensions of Madison's theory of government did evolve with time, but the bedrock notions of stability, balance, and equilibrium, as the goals of a system designed automatically to balance liberty and rights with power and authority, remained constant. In one of the most cited passages in all of Madison's writings, he described the overarching rationale of his politics: "Ambition must be made to counteract ambition. The interest of the man must be connected with the constitutional rights of the place. It may be a reflection of human nature that such devices should be necessary to control the abuses of government. But what is government itself but the greatest

1. JM to General LaFayette, 25 Nov. 1809, *Letters and Other Writings of James Madison*, ed. William C. Rives and Philip R. Fendall, 4 vols. (Philadelphia: J. B. Lippincott, 1884), 3:190.

2. Forrest McDonald calculated, on the basis of convention records, that "of seventy-one specific proposals that Madison moved, seconded, or spoke unequivocally in regard to, he was on the losing side forty times" (*Novus Ordo Seclorum: The Intellectual Origins of the Constitution* [Lawrence: University Press of Kansas, 1985], pp. 208–209).

of all reflections on human nature? If men were angels, no government would be necessary." Knowing well that humans were far from angelic creatures, Madison designed government—like civil society—to balance itself, except in rare, extraordinary situations. Madison continued to present his position for a specific governmental structure with the advice: "In framing a government which is to be administered by men over men, the great difficulty lies in this: you must first enable the government to control the governed; and in the next place oblige it to control itself. A dependence on the people, is no doubt, the primary control on the government; but experience has taught mankind the necessity of auxiliary precautions."[3]

Madison's words are significant. The framers of the government must "first enable the government to control the governed." Stability remained the leading priority. Instability was perceived primarily as the result of actions by the governed, although sometimes the state governments, acting as the democratic agents of the people, had been directly involved in creating insecurity. The citizens were not to participate in designing the system: their task, as always, would be simply to vote yes or no. After "control" had been achieved and humans had left the state of nature, the creators must "in the next place oblige" the government "to control itself."

A classic liberal, Madison never forgot that the state existed as the Leviathan; it too needed to be feared; it too needed to be controlled. With ratification of the Constitution resting in the hands of the people, Madison tactfully clarified how the government would exert self-control through "a dependence on the people" as "the primary control on the government." Given his rather low regard for the political capacities of the people and his significant apprehension about their rational abilities and potential power in the late 1780s, it seemed inevitable that he should qualify this remark with the warning that "experience has taught mankind the necessity of auxiliary precautions." Note that Madison's theory embraced both of these apparently conflicting notions. The people were "primary" in the sense of the ultimate, most important, control: they constituted the

3. Isaac Kramnick, ed., *The Federalist Papers* (New York: Viking Penguin, 1987), 51:319-320.

court of last resort.[4] Armed with the vote, those who were granted suffrage could exercise their defensive power to check the ambition of the government by voting out of power the members of one of the legislative bodies.[5] This power, severely restricted in the Constitution, Madison would have preferred to limit even more. Nevertheless, once every two years some of the white males could participate in picking their representative to the House of Representatives.

In an 1829 document titled "Outline," Madison discussed his fully matured views on what possibilities might exist once all the normal constitutional and auxiliary checks on the government had failed. He first suggested amending the document. Next he urged that states issue "remonstrances and instructions" as well as employ "recurring elections and impeachments." He then wrote:

Finally should all the constitutional remedies fail, and the usurpations of the Genl. Govt. become so intolerable as absolutely to forbid a longer passive obedience & non-resistance, a resort to the original rights of the parties becomes justifiable; and redress may be sought by shaking off the yoke, as of right, might be done by part of an individual State in a like case; or even by a single citizen, could he effect it, if deprived of rights absolutely essential to his safety & happiness. In the defect of their ability to resist, the individual citizen may seek relief in expatriation or voluntary exile a resort not within the reach of large portions of the community.

The language reflects Madison well: no call for revolution, revolt, or even legitimate violence. Rather, the discussion stayed on the ra-

4. JM to M. L. Hurlbert, May 1830, *The Writings of James Madison*, ed. Gaillard Hunt, 9 vols. (New York: G. P. Putnam's Sons, 1900–1910), 9:375 (hereafter cited as *WJM*). JM acknowledged the absolute right to revolution after all other remedies had been exhausted: "Should all these provisions fail, and a degree of oppression ensue, rendering resistance & revolution a lesser evil than a longer passive obedience, there can remain but the ultima ratio, applicable to extreme cases, whether between nations or the component parts of them." This was not, however, what he meant by primary control in *The Federalist* passage cited above.

5. See McDonald, *Novus Ordo Seclorum*, p. 162, who reports that although suffrage in the United States resulted in "the broadest-based electorate in the world, only one American in six was eligible to participate in the political process, and far fewer were eligible to hold public office."

tional level of "a resort to the original rights of the parties." He asserted that these rights belonged undeniably to "an individual state . . . or even by a single citizen" who could "seek relief in expatriation or voluntary exile."[6] A calm response, Madison's words capture the logic of a Hobbesian natural right to self-preservation. His words, however, created no Jeffersonian images of "the tree of liberty . . . refreshed from time to time with the blood of patriots and tyrants" or "a little rebellion now and then is a good thing."[7] Indeed, if Madison's system functioned as designed, such drastic measures would become necessary only in the long run.

Madison wanted to be sure that this extreme situation never developed, and "auxiliary precautions" remained exceptionally significant to him. Checks and balances, separation of powers, a limited Constitution, federalism, a scheme of representation, and an extended republic, among other precautions, created a self-balancing machine that worked because of its structure, its design, not because humans were either angelic or virtuous. In fact, when the auxiliary precautions functioned as designed, there would be little need for the people to exercise their primary control of voting the representatives out of power; in the late 1780s, furthermore, exercise of this primary control constituted one of the "many safety-valves" in which Madison had little faith. Less than a decade later, however, he would shift his position on the utility of this check, but only after he perceived tyranny to be on the rise.

Before proceeding to a discussion of Madison's ideal government, it must be recalled that government was but one facet of his political theory. Civil society, composed of plural groups with diverse interests and passions that would balance and check each other over a vast expanse of territory, played at least an equally significant role in maintaining the status quo. As long as humans found satisfaction in this arena, they would have little time or energy to expend in the political arena—except, of course, to keep an eye on the rascals.

Depending on how one counts, there may be more than twenty separate components of Madison's grand design, many of which had not

---

6. JM "Outline," Sept. 1829, *WJM* 9:353; see also JM to M. L. Hurlbert, May 1830, *WJM* 9:375.
7. Thomas Jefferson to William Smith, 13 Nov. 1787, *The Papers of Thomas Jefferson*, ed. Julian P. Boyd, 20 vols. (Princeton, N.J.: Princeton University Press, 1950–), 12:356–357 (hereafter cited as *PTJ*); Thomas Jefferson to JM, 30 Jan. 1787, *PTJ* 11:93.

been discussed in *The Federalist*. Some had been rejected at Philadelphia, and several had developed in his mind after the Constitution was functioning. Although initially pessimistic about the probability of success of the new Constitution, Madison understood quickly how with time and political maneuvering by the Federalists, the document he helped draft had been significantly changed into something rather different than what he thought he had created. Experience confirmed a valuable lesson for Madison. No framer, no matter how knowledgeable, could construct a system of government for all time. Change was required. Though to a lesser degree than might be expected, a few of Madison's ideas on government evolved as his views of suffrage and citizenship subtly changed to match the political necessity of the changing circumstances.

What emerges from the discussion that follows is an image of a political construction that was the product of a brilliant liberal mind. From Hobbes (and Locke) Madison borrowed the concepts of the state of nature and an individual's right to self-preservation. Locke supplied the notions of a neutral sovereign, kingly prerogative, and a dual contract theory of society. An extended republic as the cure to the disease of faction he adopted from Hume. And finally, he created a suffrage strategy based on his theory of economic development that directly paralleled the later-day suggestions of James Mill. Part Hobbes, part Locke, part Hume, and heuristically part Mill, Madison's construct—framed for a Malthusian world and a Calvinist universe—uniquely reflected the optimum political barriers required of a worldview based on balance and reason, passion and decay. And like all political constructs, it had been established on certain values and assumptions that generated particular consequences—all of which need to be critically evaluated.

To understand Madisonian government, then, we will begin by looking at his diagnosis of the ills of the Confederation government and his prescription for a cure to its condition. It took several years before Madison became convinced of the necessity to alter radically the Articles of Confederation, but once he reached that conclusion he prepared diligently for the rigorous process of creating a new system of politics. From the spring of 1786 through the spring of 1787, he recorded and refined his thoughts on the problems of the Confederation government and possible solutions to its defects. These preliminary ideas can be found in his "Vices of the Political System of the United States" and three coterminous letters to Thomas Jefferson, Edmund Randolph, and George Washington.

In "Vices" Madison described the "evils" in the political system under twelve separate headings, with the last section, "Impotence of the laws of the States," left uncompleted. Two interrelated problems constituted the core of Madison's assessment: the weakness of the federal government and the ineffectiveness of the state governments in controlling the actions of majorities and therein failing to protect the property rights of individuals. Madison's perception of the democratic nature of the legislative bodies in the various states as a primary defect in the Confederation goes a long way to explain his specific political prescriptions prior to the 1790s.

The first two vices concerned the federal government's impotence: its inability to force "the States to comply with the Constitutional requisitions" and the "Encroachments by the States on the federal authority."[8] In Madison's mature theory, there existed no balanced power relationship between the center and the periphery—and parts of the periphery operated out of control. While these vices might be considered "permanently inherent" in the structure of this type of government, the third vice recalled Madison's fascination with questions of size and his implicit tendency toward class bias. Under "Violations of the law of nations and of treaties" Madison attributed the causes to three factors: "the number of Legislatures, the sphere of life from which most of their members are taken, and the circumstances under which their legislative business is carried on."[9] All three reasons caused Madison to worry about the possibility of a rational relationship between the United States and the rest of the world. The caliber of men who made the state laws, circumstances less than conducive to cool, collected, and independent decision making, as well as the sheer number of thirteen separate governments writing their own legal relationship with foreign nations, all combined to create a dangerous situation. Madison called

8. See Jonathan Elliott, ed., *The Debates of the Several State Conventions on the Adoption of the Federal Constitution*, 4 vols. (Philadelphia: J. B. Lippincott, 1836), 7 June 1788, 3:131, where JM stated: "Governments destitute of energy, will ever produce anarchy."

9. "Vices," Apr. 1787, *The Papers of James Madison*, ed. William T. Hutchinson et al., 17 vols. (Chicago and Charlottesville: University of Chicago Press and University of Virginia Press, 1962–), 9:348–349 (hereafter cited as *PJM*).

it "the greatest of public calamities," since no single "part of the Community" should be able "to bring on the whole" conflicts with other nations.[10]

Lacking a single supreme source of authority and power, the states treated each other as if they were still in Locke's state of nature: they "trespassed" on each others' rights because they acted as judges in their own cases. When Madison detailed this vice, the specific rights being violated were property rights, narrowly conceived. In this set of notes, he thought of the property problem in terms of states violating the property rights of other states, rather than individuals: "Paper money, instalments of debts, occlusion of Courts, making property a legal tender, may likewise be deemed aggressions on the rights of other States."[11] The fifth vice also involved economic considerations, as he worried over arbitrary and inconsistent policies in the nation's "commercial affairs." The nation's "dignity, interest, and revenue" had suffered from the failure of a "uniformity in the laws concerning naturalization & literary property; of provisions for national seminaries, for grants of incorporation for national purposes, for canals and other works of general utility."[12]

With vivid memories of Shays's rebellion still haunting his thoughts, Madison noted in number six the "want of [a] Guaranty to the States of their Constitutions & laws against internal violence." In his discussion of this vice, Madison separated theory from practice. "According to Republican Theory," he wrote, "Right and power being both vested in the majority, are held to be synonimous." He then acknowledged that "according to fact and experience a minority may in an appeal to force, be an overmatch for the majority." Although at that moment Madison remained far more concerned with a majority controlling the minority, he speculated on the power of "one third" to "conquer the remaining two thirds." Another one-third, "those who participate in the choice of the rulers, may be rendered a majority by the accession of those whose poverty excludes them from a right of suffrage, and who for obvious reasons will be

10. Ibid., 9:349.
11. Ibid., 9:349. Madison drew that conclusion based on his observation that "as the Citizens of every State aggregately taken stand more or less in the relation of Creditors or debtors, to the Citizens of every other States, Acts of the debtor State in favor of debtors, affect the Creditor State, in the same manner, as they do its own citizens who are relatively creditors towards other citizens."
12. Ibid., 9:350.

more likely to join the standard of sedition than that of the established Government.''[13] In private, Madison noted for himself that "where slavery exists the republican Theory becomes still more fallacious.''[14] Madison's point: Theory and right do not automatically align themselves with power. Minorities can trample on the majority, and, what may be more likely, minorities can manipulate others and become a majority that will tyrannize minorities and individuals. In short, the practice of republicanism, not the theory, was what ultimately mattered to those who wished to act as The Legislator.

The seventh vice, the federal government's lack of coercive power, made the Confederation "in fact nothing more than a treaty of amity of commerce and of alliance, between so many independent and Sovereign States." This error in governing was so fundamental that Madison assumed it must have been the result of "a mistaken confidence that the justice, the good faith, the honor, the sound policy, of the several legislative assemblies would render superfluous any appeal to the ordinary motives by which the laws secure the obedience of individuals." Madison's conception of humanity assumed states, like citizens, subjected themselves to similar controls. He rhetorically asked: "If the laws of the States, were merely recommendatory to their citizens, or if they were to be rejudged by County authorities, what security, what probability would exist, that they would be carried into execution?''[15] Since this question appeared in his private memorandum, he felt no need to answer the obvious.

"Want of ratification by the people of the articles of Confederation" was the eighth vice, among the most basic flaws in this early

13. What was obvious for Madison may be less so today. One of two (or perhaps both) explanations are likely: Propertyless, these men, who had no stake in society, had little to lose and the hope of much to gain in overthrowing the government; Propertyless, these men were not rational enough to earn the right to suffrage or to play the economic game on an equal footing with men of property. Furthermore, not being fully rational they would not understand how government was preferable to sedition for all members of society since it protected not only everyone's property but their lives (which Madison thought of as property) as well.

14. "Vices," *PJM* 9:350–351; he repeated this argument at the Constitutional Convention in reply to the New Jersey Plan, on 19 June 1787 (*The Records of the Federal Convention of 1787*, ed. Max Farrand, 4 vols. [New Haven, Conn.: Yale University Press, 1937], 1:318); see also "Notes for Essays," 19 Dec. 1791–3 Mar. 1792, *PJM* 14:163–164.

15. "Vices," Apr. 1787, *PJM* 9:351–352.

attempt at popular government. Its cure became one of the fundamental concerns of Madison. The new central government would have to be superior to any state government, would have to be able to act on the citizens directly, and would have to have the consent of the governed. Lacking any one of these, the chaos in the state governments, delineated in the ninth, tenth, and eleventh vices, would continue unabated.[16]

The final trilogy of evils concerned the shortcomings of the individual state governments, producing a "multiplicity," "mutability," and "injustice" of state laws. When discussing the problem of "the multiplicity of laws from which no State is exempt," he observed that the governments have produced far too much legislation: "The short period of independency has filled as many pages as the century which preceded it. Every year, almost every session, adds a new volume." Madison suggested that the number of laws in the "least voluminous" of the state codes could still be reduced into "one tenth" of its present form.[17] Madison recognized the necessity for both laws and governmental coercion but believed they should be kept to a minimum if society hoped to function rationally.

As laws multiplied, it would become increasingly difficult for citizens to know the law and behave accordingly. Vice number ten, the "mutability of the laws of the States," was connected to the "multiplicity of the laws" but "deserves a distinct notice as it emphatically denotes a vicious legislation." Madison explained briefly that state laws were "repealed or superseded, before any trial can have been made of their merits." In general, this constituted bad public policy, though Madison specifically stated that "in the regulations of trade this instability becomes a snare not only to our citizens but to foreigners also."[18] Again, constant change in the laws, by either addition or alteration, made rational behavior in civil society problematic since no one could be sure what constituted legal behavior from one day to the next. A rational and energetic government could create an environment in which citizens could pursue their own self-interest with little interference from others, where balance and

16. Ibid. Vice twelve, "Impotence of the laws of the States," was never spelled out, suggesting that Madison had yet to finish his criticism of the state governments.

17. Ibid., 9:353.

18. Ibid., 9:353–354.

equilibrium would characterize the social milieu. A possessive market society needed the liberal state to ensure rational norms of behavior.

Vices number nine and ten lead up to the longest discussion in his notes—vice number eleven, a presentation of the "Injustice of the laws of States." Madison began this section demonstrating just how deep his doubts about republicanism ran: "The multiplicity and mutability of laws prove a want of wisdom, their injustice betrays a defect still more alarming . . . because it is a greater evil in itself, but because it brings into question the fundamental principle of republican Government, that the majority who rule in such Governments, are the safest Guardians both of public Good and of private rights." Looking for the cause of this "greater evil," Madison naturally turned to the human dimension of state governments: "the Representative bodies" and "the people themselves."

Madison believed that representatives sought office "from 3 motives. 1. ambition. 2. personal interest. 3. public good." Unfortunately for humanity, "the two first are proved by experience to be most prevalent." Looking into these motives, Madison asserted that those individuals driven by personal interest were the "most industrious, and most successful in pursuing their object." These individuals possessed clever talents permitting them to "mask" their "base and selfish measures" with the "pretexts of public good and apparent expediency." Along with Madison's lack of confidence in the people, he thought it probable that such artful and industrious individuals could fool "the unwary to misplace their confidence." Not only were the people easily deceived, so "too will the honest but unenligh[t]ened representative be the dupe of a favorite leader, veiling his selfish views under the professions of public good, and varnishing his sophistical arguments with the glowing colours of popular eloquence."[19]

As deeply troubling as he perceived the condition of the state governments, "a still more fatal if not more frequent cause" for this great evil existed "among the people themselves." After acknowledging the pluralist nature of civil society and the majoritarian essence of republican government, Madison wanted to know what could possibly restrain a majority "from unjust violations of the

19. Ibid., 9:354.

rights and interests of the minority, or of individuals?" The discussion in chapter 3 of Madison's arguments for rejecting "prudence," "respect for character," or "religion" as restraints on majorities set the stage for an analysis here of Madison's thoughts on the significance of, and possible restraint by, public opinion.

Group behavior, Madison observed, existed "in proportion to the number which is to share the praise or the blame." What constituted praiseworthy or blameworthy behavior, moreover, would be determined with "reference to public opinion, which within a particular Society, is the opinion of the majority." Never overestimating the limited nature of parochial public opinion, he assumed that "the public opinion without the Society, will be little respected by the people at large of any Country." Even though "individuals of extended views, and of national pride, may bring the public proceedings to this standard," he wrote, "the example will never be followed by the multitude." To emphasize his point, Madison raised his doubts about the capacities of "the multitude" to have "extended views" one small rung on his hierarchical ladder of human capacities as he questioned the ability of "even an assemblyman of R. Island" to think about his state's actions relative to foreign nations. Finding this evil in the system a direct, albeit natural, result of human nature, Madison had to discover as many nonhuman cures for the governmental condition as possible.[20]

In the final three paragraphs of "Vices," Madison noted three solutions to the human factor of government: "an enlargement of the sphere"; a "sufficiently neutral" sovereign; and "a process of elections as most certainly will extract from the mass of the Society the purest and noblest characters." Space, the first part of the cure, remained a perfect corrective measure since it functioned independent of human will; the vast size of the country would make "a common interest or passion . . . less apt to be felt and the requisite combinations less easy to be formed." In an age where the communication revolution still remained decades away, majorities could not readily form because individuals had "less opportunity of communication and concert." The specific characteristics of a "sufficiently neutral" sovereign remained undeveloped in "Vices." Instead, the gen-

---

20. Ibid., 9:355–356; in a few years, however, Madison would alter his views on public opinion as he sought to rally the citizens to stop the unconstitutional actions of the high Federalists. See also *Federalist* 10:122–128, 49:312–316.

eral theme consisted of the government's responsibility to control the governed and then being appropriately structured to control itself. Again, Madison believed the extensive size of the republic would contribute to an appropriately constructed government's ability to meet its twin responsibilities.

Representation, his final thought, did necessitate a reliance on humans. Still, if the correct electoral process could be constructed, the right kind of humans could be selected: those who "at once feel most strongly the proper motives to pursue the end of their appointment, and be most capable to devise the proper means of attaining it."[21] Although merely hinted at in "Vices," the Madisonian voting logic was constructed on the premise that through each successive level of selecting individuals to represent larger districts, the more pure and noble the representatives would, ideally, be.[22]

Madison offered several additional cures to these ills he perceived to be destroying the United States in 1787. Detailing his diagnosis of, and grim prognosis for, the Confederation in "Vices," Madison sketched out his preliminary thoughts on the measures necessary to save the republic in sequential letters to Jefferson, Randolph, and Washington. In the first letter, to Jefferson, Madison adopted the style of a physician. He discussed the prospects of the ensuing "political experiment," the "mortal diseases" of the existing system, and "symptoms which are truly alarming, which have tainted the faith of the most orthodox republicans, and which challenge from the votaries of liberty every concession in favor of stable Government not infringing fundamental principles." Madison presented six creative palliatives, "leading ideas which have occurred to me, but which may appear to others as improper, as they appear to me necessary."[23]

The initial requirement constituted "ratification by the people themselves of the several States as will render it clearly paramount to their Legislative authorities." The second change called for "the positive power of regulating trade and sundry other matters in which

21. "Vices," Apr. 1787, *PJM* 9:356–357.
22. See JM speech, 6 June 1787, Farrand, *Records* 1:143–144; King's notes: "The election may safely be made by the People if you enlarge the Sphere of Election—Experience proves it—if bad elections have taken place from the people, it will generally be found to have happened in small Distracts."
23. JM to Thomas Jefferson, 19 Mar. 1787, *PJM* 9:318–319. JM's count listed four changes even though he discussed six.

uniformity is proper." A "positive power" by itself, however, would be an insufficient check on local government, Madison feared. So his third change insisted that the "federal head" be armed with a "defensive power" of "a negative *in all cases whatsoever* on the local Legislatures."[24] Madison offered a fourfold rationale for this "negative prerogative": (1) "paper" boundaries between federal and state powers were ineffective; (2) the veto would "guard the national rights and interests against invasion"; (3) the veto would also "restrain the States from thwarting and molesting each other"; and (4) the veto would restrain the states from "oppressing the minority within themselves by paper money and other unrighteous measures which favor the interests of the majority." Clearly, Madison viewed the state governments as far too powerful, arbitrary, and responsive to majority influence, which threatened not only property owners but, from Madison's perspective, the entire republic as well.

Madison's fourth alteration, which he misjudged as being readily acceptable to all the states, required a change in "the principle of Representation in the federal system" so that it would be based on population, not equality of state sovereignty. His fifth suggestion created a sharper separation of powers than under the articles: to "organise the federal powers in such a manner as not to blend together those which ought to be exercised by separate departments." Finally, Madison repeated his plea for "an enlargement not only of the powers, but the number, of the federal Representatives."[25]

After bringing Jefferson up to date on domestic politics, Madison closed his letter showing how deep a hold Shays's rebellion continued to have over his conceptual thinking. In fact, Madison mentioned the rebellion in two of these three critical letters in which he conveyed his ideas on necessary changes in the government. To Jefferson, he explained that while "the insurgents" had been dispersed, he had not been at all reassured that "the calm" would last. Madison appeared appalled that some of these "offenders," who he believed committed "treason," "not only appeared openly on public

24. JM to Thomas Jefferson, 19 Mar. 1787, *PJM* 9:318; JM's emphasis. Jefferson unequivocally rejected this idea in his 20 June 1787 letter to JM, *PTJ* 11:480–481: "Prima Facie I do not like it. . . . It fails in an essential character, that the hole and patch should be commensurate. But this proposes to mend a small hole by covering the whole garment."
25. JM to Thomas Jefferson, 19 Mar. 1787, *PJM* 9:318–319.

occasions but distinguished themselves by badges of their character''; a few had even been elected "to local offices of trust & authority."[26] This anarchic image clouding his consciousness, it seems a small wonder Madison wanted a new, national government with unchallenged supremacy and a mechanism by which it could control directly the state governments. Anything less spelled unrelenting episodes of chaos, if not outright anarchy, and eventually a return to the state of nature.

Madison's subsequent letter to Edmund Randolph offered three additional changes and helped clarify the logic behind his earlier six proposals. As often reflected his style, Madison started his case appearing to agree with his correspondent: "I think with you that it will be well to retain as much as possible of the old Confederation," only to close the paragraph candidly arguing the contrary, that "In truth my ideas of a reform strike so deeply at the old Confederation, and lead to such a systematic change, that they scarcely admit of the expedient" of permitting a partial adoption of specific changes.

While in his letter to Jefferson, Madison's comments on the necessity of controlling the state governments were relatively terse, to Randolph he forthcomingly wrote:

> I hold it for a fundamental point that an individual independence of the States, is utterly irreconcilable with the idea of an aggregate sovereignty. I think at the same time that a consolidation of the States into one simple republic is not less unattainable than it would be inexpedient. Let it be tried then whether any middle ground can be taken which will at once support a due supremacy of the national authority, and leave in force the local authorities so far as they can be subordinately useful.[27]

About a decade after writing this letter, Madison would come to appreciate more fully just how "subordinately useful" the states could be in checking a central government that seemed out of control. But in the late 1780s, Madison's fear focused on state governments that behaved irresponsibly and needed to be checked by some superior power. He further clarified his call for a legislative veto by comparing it to the power exercised by the king over "the Legislative

26. Ibid., 9:321.
27. JM to Edmund Randolph, 8 Apr. 1787, *PJM* 9:369.

Acts of the States" in colonial America, an analogy he probably could not have employed in public. Concerning the supremacy of the national government, he specifically extended it to the judiciary as well and clarified the separation of powers by explicitly bifurcating the legislature. Madison appeared unconcerned with the representatives being chosen by the people, though the upper house would "consist of a more select number, holding their appointments for a longer term." Because its members were fewer and more select, Madison proposed placing the national veto power over state legislation in this branch.

Madison then presented three more changes he had thought about since his letter to Jefferson: the first consisted of "A Council of Revision"; the second, "A National Executive"; and the third, "An article . . . expressly guarantying the tranquility of the States agst. internal as well as external dangers." Yet another indication of Shays's clouding of Madison's vision, he closed his letter to Randolph without further clarifying his suggested alterations while predicting "that unless the Union be organized efficiently & on Republican Principles . . . the partition of the Empire into rival & hostile confederacies, will ensue."[28]

The final letter, to George Washington, clarified still further the themes of the prior two letters. One of two new notions, implied though not made explicit in the Randolph and Jefferson letters, was Madison's insistence that "the right of coercion should be expressly declared." The ability of the central government to coerce the state governments Madison believed to be among the foremost alterations required in the new system. He repeated his desire to find a "middle ground" where "the local authorities" could be made "subordinately useful." And again, he suggested a national veto on terms similar to that "exercised by the kingly prerogative." This time, when Madison explained his thinking, he asserted that the prerogative might help make up "the great desideratum which has not yet been found for Republican Governments," that is, "some disinterested & dispassionate umpire in disputes between different passions & interests in the State." While this veto would have no impact on directly controlling national policy, Madison believed it would allow the federal government to function as "sufficiently disinterested for

28. Ibid., 9:370–371.

the decision of local questions of policy."[29] Given his near fatal absorption with the immediate problem of controlling state governments, at that moment he seemed little concerned with the question of a "disinterested and dispassionate umpire" for the nation-state, a question he could never solve with the same degree of theoretical tidiness. Still, he now possessed a model of how the national government should function—*sine ira et studio*.

While Madison's suggestion for representation based on population would not be accepted at the convention, his failure to secure the national veto, at least initially, constituted what he felt would be a fatal flaw to the proposed government. Early in September of 1787 he confided to Jefferson: "I hazard an opinion nevertheless that the plan should it be adopted will neither effectually answer its national object nor prevent the local mischiefs which every where excite disgusts agst. the state governments."[30] The single fullest expression of his disappointment over the defeat of the national veto occurred in a follow-up letter to Jefferson. When Madison initially proposed the veto, Jefferson first tried to spare Madison's pride by subtly appearing to misunderstand the full implications of it; still he made it evident that he did not think much of the idea. No doubt remembering Jefferson's rebuff, Madison offered a "modest digression" of several pages to justify his advocacy of the veto. He expressed substantial alarm at its omission. Noting that the measure "was finally rejected by a bare majority," Madison argued that the newly constructed system, lacking "a compleat supremacy some where," remained vulnerable to "the evil of imperia in imperio." The proposed Constitution replaced a "Confederacy of independent States" with a "feudal system of republics" leaving the greatest threat to the general republic still in the states themselves. While Madison admitted "it may be said that the Judicial authority under our new system will keep the States within their proper limits, and supply the place of a negative on their laws," it nevertheless seemed more reasonable "to prevent the passage of a law, than to declare it void after it is passed."[31]

29. JM to George Washington, 16 Apr. 1787, *PJM* 9:383–385.
30. JM to Thomas Jefferson, 6 Sept. 1787, *PJM* 10:163–164. See also Charles F. Hobson, "The Negative on State Laws: James Madison, the Constitution, and the Crisis of Republican Government," *William and Mary Quarterly* 36 (Apr. 1979): 215–235.
31. JM to Thomas Jefferson, 24 Oct. 1787, *PJM* 10:209–211.

In light of Madison's essentially defensive view of sound politics, this remark seemed perfectly understandable.

The veto's ultimate purpose had been to protect "individuals agst. encroachments on their rights." But what rights, what encroachments, concerned Madison? In the rest of this paragraph Madison demonstrated that, as always, he worried about property violations by the *demos*. He wrote that "the restraints agst. paper emissions, and violations of contracts are not sufficient" protection in themselves. He repeated for Jefferson his economic analysis of "Vices" and *Federalist* 10 concerning distinctions of property being derived from the different faculties of individuals, thereby creating antagonistic interests. He called these interests "natural" because they develop from human faculties. He noted as well distinctions based on political and religious beliefs; these distinctions he typed "artificial," even though they too had to come from human faculties. Obviously, the implicit distinction he drew centered on rational and nonrational faculties, with the enlightened Madison as the neutral arbiter of the two categories.[32]

Confronted with the multiplicity of factions, Madison urged the creative adoption of "the reprobated axiom of tyranny"—"divide et imperia." Even this stabilizing mechanism needed to be supplemented by a "neutral" sovereign designed "to controul one part from invading the rights of another."[33] Without the veto, Madison believed the new government lacked the energy necessary to control the state governments and protect individuals. Madison's apprehension faded but slowly: it helps explain not only his shift of position on the Bill of Rights, which could now attempt to function as a weak substitute for the veto, but also his rigorous advocacy of a specific amendment applying portions of the Bill of Rights against the state governments. Be that as it may, Madison remained profoundly disappointed with the limited power lodged in the new central government.

---

32. Ibid., 10:212–213: "In addition to these natural distinctions, artificial ones will be founded, on accidental differences in political, religious or other opinions, or an attachment to the persons of leading individuals. However erroneous or ridiculous these grounds of dissention and faction, may appear to the enlightened Statesman, or the benevolent philosopher, the bulk of mankind who are neither Statesmen nor Philosophers, will continue to view them in a different light."

33. JM to Thomas Jefferson, 24 Oct. 1787, *PJM* 10:214.

To summarize, Madison conceived of fourteen distinct features necessary for a good constitutional system: (1) an extended republic; (2) a "sufficiently neutral," "dispassionate and disinterested" national government to arbitrate disputes among factions within individual states; (3) an appropriate scheme of representation; (4) popular ratification to ensure national supremacy; (5) regulation of trade and other issues requiring uniform policy; (6) a national veto of state laws; (7) representation in both houses based on population; (8) greater separation of powers; (9) enlargement of both the power and number of representatives; (10) national supremacy of the judiciary; (11) a council of revision to check the efforts of the legislature; (12) a national executive; (13) a national guaranty of state tranquillity; and (14) the expressed power of the national government to coerce state governments. Of these many points, Madison's three fundamental reforms were popular ratification of a supreme national government that acted directly on the people, proportional representation of both branches of the national legislature, and the power to veto *"in all cases whatsoever* on the legislative acts of the States."[34] Only the first radical change was adopted by the convention; the other two, on successive days in mid-July, failed. Their defeat, however, cannot be attributed to a lack of effort, extending to intimidation, by Madison. Even as late as September, Madison continued to try to revive the negative on local legislatures. Consequently, while there remains a reasonable argument for still perceiving of Madison as the father of the Constitution, that cannot be taken to mean that the Constitution of 1787 ever represented his notion of ideal government.

At this juncture, it may be as significant to examine what Madison failed to conceive of as necessary to a republican government as what he did think about. The most impressive omission may have been that of a single mention of citizenship, including his limited discussion of suffrage.[35] Or perhaps his silence on the necessity of a bill of rights deserves preeminent status. Because of Madison's liberal tendencies, the first oversight might seem quite understandable, but the second does not.

34. See editorial note, "Madison at the Federal Convention 27 May–17 September 1787," *PJM* 10:3.
35. Those who see Madison as a civic humanist fail to explain this signal omission.

As an advocate of popular ratification who embraced a notion of republicanism that required "the scheme of representation takes place" and that government "derives all its powers directly or indirectly from the great body of the people," Madison would eventually have to address both of these issues.[36] As Isaac Kramnick points out with regard to the term *republicanism*, "Madison's brilliant achievement was the appropriation of a word with unmistakable populist connotations for a governmental structure which, while ultimately based on popular consent, involved a serious diminution of popular participation."[37] Indeed, by Madison's minimalist definition of a republic, it becomes problematic to think of any modern government that could not be considered republican.[38] While Madison spent virtually no energy on the issues of citizenship or a bill of rights before the debates on ratification, in time he addressed these issues. In a moment it will be logical to turn to his postconvention ideas of government as they developed in response to concrete political issues; for the present, a discussion of his views on the democratic issue of suffrage appears necessary.

Although he never claimed authorship of the Virginia Plan, which had successfully set the initial agenda for the Constitutional Convention, Madison undoubtedly played a leading role in drafting these resolutions. Formally introduced to the convention by Edmund Randolph, then governor, the fifteen points embody much of the spirit of Madison, although the precise letter of the resolutions occasionally differed, as in the wording on the national veto and the method of selecting "inferior tribunals."[39] Since he spoke more than two hundred times at Philadelphia, and in spite of the significant doubts surrounding the accuracy of the convention notes as well as the political maneuvering that may have been the real cause behind some of his speeches, the notes are a reliable source of information on Madison's ideas about government.

36. *Federalist* 10:126, 39:255.
37. Kramnick, "Introduction" to *Federalist*, p. 41.
38. See McDonald, *Novus Ordo Seclorum*, p. 287: "That government defied categorization by any existing nomenclature: it was not a monarchy, nor an aristocracy, nor a democracy, neither yet was it a mixed form of government, nor yet a confederated republic. It was what it was, and if Madison was presumptuous in appropriating the word republic to describe it, he was also a prophet, for thenceforth republic would mean precisely what Madison said it meant."
39. The Virginia Plan, 29 May 1787, *PJM* 10:16.

Although suffrage had never been a major concern in Madison's letters and writings immediately preceding the convention, his initial thoughts on the issue can be found in an August 1785 letter to Caleb Wallace in which he presented his ideas on an appropriate constitution for Kentucky. When Madison got to the issue of suffrage, he warned that "I think the extent which ought to be given to this right a matter of great delicacy and of critical Importance." Here Madison first framed his unchanging perception of the fundamental dilemma confronting republics on this issue: "To restrain it to the landholders will in time exclude too great a proportion of citizens; to extend it to all citizens without regard to property, or even to all who possess a pittance may throw too much power into hands which will either abuse it themselves or sell it to the rich who will abuse it."

In a typical Madison compromise, he suggested that "it might be a good middle course to narrow this right in the choice of the least popular, & to enlarge it in that of the more popular branch." While Madison noted that he assumed this idea might "offend the sense of equallity which re[i]gns in a free Country," he nevertheless perceived "no reason why the rights of property which chiefly bears the burden of Government & is so much an object of Legislation should not be respected as well as personal rights in the choice of Rulers."[40] His solution, like his perception of the issue, would remain essentially the same throughout his life: extend suffrage only as required and as slowly as politically possible. Given the laws of economic development, the wise legislator must recognize that in the long run suffrage may well have to be extended to all white males. Consequently as many auxiliary precautions and "safety-valves" as possible should be built into the sociopolitical system to accommodate the newly enfranchised.

Two years later, during the debates over suffrage at the convention, Madison's position came into sharper focus. On 7 June 1787 he reiterated the spirit of the Wallace letter when he argued that "the Senate ought to come from, & represent, the Wealth of the nation."[41] A week later, Madison felt no logical inconsistency with his earlier claim about whom the Senate should represent, although his position appeared, at best, politically naive. When the question of re-

40. JM to Caleb Wallace, 23 Aug. 1785, *PJM* 8:353.
41. JM speech, 7 June 1787, Farrand, *Records* 1:158; King's notes.

stricting the origination of money bills to the House arose, Madison observed:

> The Senate would be the representatives of the people as well as the 1st. branch. If they sh. have any dangerous influence over it, they would easily prevail on some member of the latter to originate the bill they wished to be passed. As the Senate would be generally a more capable sett of men, it wd. be wrong to disable them from any preparation of the business, especially of that which was most important and in our republics, worse prepared than any other.[42]

This passage reflects well both his class bias and his scheme of representation: senators had the capacity to represent "wealth" as well as "the people." As he put it differently on other occasions, senators could represent property as well as persons, while the House—run by men of lesser vision—could best reflect only the interest of persons. Moreover, since money bills involved the "taking" of property, who better than those specifically charged with its protection should be involved directly.

In the last days of June, still discussing the Senate, Madison argued that "the people" and the House "were liable to temporary errors" where they lose sight of "their true interests." The solution to this problem? The creation of a second legislative branch the members of which would have a term of office long enough to acquire "a competent knowledge of the public interests" and thereby the capacity to "interpose" themselves against "impetuous counsels" based on "fickleness and passion."[43] Madison's next comments moved to the core of his system—property. Since he foresaw economic change as inevitable, he urged his associates that "we shd. not lose sight of the changes which ages will produce." The change he most feared remained the proportionate increase "of those who will labour under all the hardships of life, & secretly sigh for a more equal distribution of its blessings." After raising the frightful image of "agrarian attempts . . . of a leveling spirit," Madison supported further his assertion that the Senate would be the "body in the Govt. sufficiently respectable for its wisdom & virtue" and therein

42. JM speech, 13 June 1787, Farrand, *Records* 1:233.
43. JM speech, 26 June 1787, Farrand, *Records* 1:421–422.

concerned with "justice." Again, Madison implicitly demonstrated that his own conception of justice chiefly involved the protection of material property. He could not yet fathom a theory of justice that held a property right to human development to be more important than property in things.[44]

The specific details of Yates's version of Madison's speech of June 26 differed significantly from Madison's own account; yet each rendition sounded like Madison, illustrating just one of the difficulties surrounding the myth of original intent.[45] According to Yates, Madison first pointed out the "unsteady" nature of "Democratic communities" that are subject "to action by the impulse of the moment" and "the turbulency and weakness of unruly passions." In his notes, Yates recorded Madison stating "the man who is possessed of wealth, who lolls on his sofa or rolls in his carriage, cannot judge of the wants or feelings of the day laborer." Madison coolly recognized that the rich, in Rousseau's more colorful image, "have feelings in each of their possessions."[46] But note, Madison's electoral system had been designed to keep the idle and unfeeling wealthy out of office. He next reiterated his theory of economic development in which the number of citizens who failed to own property would eventually constitute an overwhelming majority, threatening property and justice. Consequently, he maintained that "our government ought to secure the permanent interests of the country against innovation. Landholders ought to have a share in the government, to support these invaluable interests and to balance and check the other. They ought to be so constituted as to protect the minority of the opulent against the majority. The Senate, therefore, ought to be this body."[47] It never was the wealthy, those who "cannot judge of the wants or feelings of the day laborer," that Madison wanted to

44. Ibid., 1:422–423.

45. James Hutson, "The Creation of the Constitution: The Integrity of the Documentary Record," in *Interpreting the Constitution: The Debate over Original Intent*, ed. Jack Rakove (Boston: Northeastern University Press, 1990), pp. 151–178.

46. Quoted in Sheldon Wolin, *Politics and Vision: Continuity and Innovation in Western Political Thought* (Boston: Little, Brown & Company, 1960), p. 251: The truth of Rousseau's observation can be fully appreciated after visiting Montpelier.

47. JM speech, 26 June 1787, Farrand, *Records* 1:430–431; Yates's notes.

protect or, for that matter, to govern; rather, he sought to protect the institution of property and therein the security of the republic.

When the questions of qualifications for holding legislative office were debated, Madison moved to strike out the word "landed," before the word "qualifications." Because of his repeated movements to protect property, this may appear perplexing; however, Madison's rationale untangles even the slightest appearance of inconsistency. "Landed possessions," he argued, "were no certain evidence of real wealth. Many enjoyed them to a great extent who were more in debt than they were worth." Madison, who detested credit and believed that debt caused many of the unjust measures taken by the state governments, lectured the convention: "The unjust laws of the States had proceeded more from this class of men, than any others. It had often happened that men who had acquired landed property on credit, got into the Legislatures with a view of promoting an unjust protection agst. their Creditors."

Madison next claimed that "it was politic as well as just that the interests & rights of every class should be duly represented & understood." Madison's own class analysis listed "the landed, the commercial, & the manufacturing" as the "principle classes into which our citizens were divisible."[48] Madison always acknowledged, nevertheless, that the most basic property distinction was between those who possessed it and those who did not.[49] His sophisticated appreciation of class can be seen in that he understood the effects of class compared to space: "These classes understand much less of each others interests & affairs, than men of the same class inhabiting different districts." Absolutely silent on the possible need for representation of those without property, with tunnel vision and class logic Madison argued that it remained "particularly requisite therefore that the interests of one or two of them [the propertied classes] should not be left entirely to the care, or the impartiality of the third. This must be the case if landed qualifications should be required." Madison concluded his speech with two specific proposals. First "he wished if it were possible that some other criterion than the mere possession of land should be devised." Second, he agreed

48. JM speech, 26 July 1787, Farrand, *Records* 2:123–124.
49. See Martin Diamond, "Democracy and *The Federalist:* A Reconsideration of the Framers' Intent," *American Political Science Review* 53 (Mar. 1959): passim.

with Gouverneur Morris "in thinking that qualifications in the Electors would be much more effectual than in the elected."[50]

When the framers finally got around to the question of qualifications for voting, Madison defended the position that "viewing the subject in its merits alone, the freeholders of the Country would be the safest depositories of Republican liberty." Merits alone, however, would not provide the political solution to the suffrage issue. In time, "a great majority of the people will not only be without landed, but any other sort of, property." He predicted that "these will either combine under the influence of their common situation; . . . or which is more probable, they will become the tools of opulence and ambition."[51] Many years later, Madison amended his convention notes of this day, adding a specific design that he would never abandon: "Persons and property being both essential objects of Government, the most that either can claim, is such a structure of it as will leave a reasonable security for the other. And the most obvious provision of this double character, seems to be that of confining to the holders of property, the object deemed least secure in popular Governments, the right of suffrage for one of the two Legislative branches." Madison's addendum unequivocally demonstrated that in his view the "conflicting feelings of the Class with, and the Class without property" was "the most difficult of all political arrangements"; it required the "adjusting of the claims of the two Classes as to give security to each, and to promote the welfare of all."[52]

The convention failed to reach agreement on voting qualifications. It left the issue up to the individual states to resolve. Still, it must not be forgotten that voting was a question relevant to the House of Representatives only, since the other three governing bodies—the Senate, the executive, and the Supreme Court—were placed well beyond direct popular control. The Constitution fixed the voting qualifications for the House: "The House of Representatives shall be composed of members chosen every second year by the people of the several states, and the electors in each state shall have the qualifica-

50. JM speech, 26 July 1787, Farrand, *Records* 2:124.
51. JM speech, 7 Aug. 1787, Farrand, *Records* 2:203–204.
52. N. 17 to JM speech of 7 Aug. 1787, *Records of the Federal Convention* 2:204; the exact date of this note is unknown, although it appears to have been added after JM's retirement.

tions requisite for electors of the most numerous branch of the state legislature."[53]

In light of this standard, Madison in *Federalist* 57 wrote:

Who are to be the electors of the federal representatives? Not the rich, more than the poor; nor the learned, more than the ignorant; not the haughty heirs of distinguished names, more than the humble sons of obscurity and unpropitious fortune. The electors are to be the great body of the people of the United States. They are to be the same who exercise the right in every State of electing the corresponding branch of the legislature of the State.[54]

And with regard to the qualifications necessary for running for office in the House, Madison wrote in *Federalist* 52:

A representative of the United States must be of the age of twenty-five years; must have been seven years a citizen of the United States; must . . . be an inhabitant of the State he is to represent; and, during the time of his service, must be in no office under the United States. Under these reasonable limitations, the door of this part of the federal government is open to merit of every description, whether native or adoptive, whether young or old, and without regard to poverty or wealth, or to any particular profession of religious faith.[55]

What, from these passages, appeared to be a set of relatively egalitarian voting measures, devoid of property qualifications, was anything but that. Madison, furthermore, knew it. In *Federalist* 54 he stated: "The qualifications on which the right of suffrage depend are not, perhaps, the same in any two States. In some of the States the difference is very material. In every State, a certain proportion of inhabitants are deprived of this right by the constitution of the State."[56] Exactly what this meant in actual figures of disenfranchisement remains difficult to tell, even though all states had property-

53. United States Constitution, Article 1, section 2, paragraph 1.
54. *Federalist* 57:343.
55. Ibid., 52:323.
56. Ibid., 54:333.

owning or tax-paying qualifications. As a result of the resolution of
suffrage in the Constitution "only about one American in six was eligible to participate in the political process, and far fewer were eligible to hold public office."[57] Madison understood and willingly accepted the restrictiveness of this position: the *demos* were to be
feared; their participation had to be limited as far as politically feasible; and they were to be granted full membership in the political system when there appeared to be no other option available.[58]

Sometime during 1821, Madison returned to his convention notes
to make a significant addition. He wanted to now record his "more
full & matured view" on the right of suffrage. He recognized it as "a
fundamental Article in Republican Constitutions" that must be
handled with "peculiar delicacy" because it can be so restricted as
to lead to the oppression of "the rights of persons" or so enlarged as
to infringe on the "rights of property." However, Madison still faced
considerable difficulty balancing political stability and liberty with
his dreaded rise of the masses. This note makes it evident that Madison's extended discussion was not abstract theorizing about the simple virtues and risks entailed in suffrage. He grounded his perspective, rather, in the political context of "civilized communities,"
that is, market societies based on land, commerce, and manufacturing. "In civilized communities," wrote Madison, "property as well
as personal rights is an essential object of the laws, which encourage
industry by securing the enjoyment of its fruits: that industry from
which property results, & that enjoyment which consists not merely
in its immediate use, but in its posthumous destination to objects of
choice and of kindred affection."[59]

As he had maintained throughout his life, perhaps most notably in
his *National Gazette* essay "Property," Madison perceived government to be the protector of justice, rights, property, and persons. He
wrote, "In a just & a free, Government, therefore, the rights both of
property & of persons ought to be effectually guarded." While tension in civil society was inevitable, Madison believed "the holders of

57. McDonald, *Novus Ordo Seclorum*, p. 162.
58. See Gordon S. Wood, *The Creation of the American Republic*, 1776-1787
(Chapel Hill: University of North Carolina Press, 1969), p. 327.
59. JM, Note to his speech on the Right of Suffrage, ca. 1821, *Records of the
Federal Convention* 3:450; cf. Richard K. Matthews, *The Radical Politics of
Thomas Jefferson* (Lawrence: University Press of Kansas, 1986), pp. 19-29.

property have at stake all the other rights common to those without property'' and, consequently, ''may be the more restrained from infringing, as well as the less tempted to infringe the rights of the latter.'' Moreover, they too had no right to sleep under the bridges of Paris. Madison, nevertheless, believed men, even those with property, were neither angels nor philosophers. It remained therefore ''necessary that the poor should have a defence against'' the ''various ways in which the rich may oppress the poor.''[60]

That most Americans in the early decades of the republic either possessed property or were content with the realistic and ''universal hope of acquiring'' it presented a ''precious advantage.'' Still, the laws of economic development were foreboding to Madison:

> The U. States have a precious advantage also in the actual distribution of property particularly the landed property; and in the universal hope of acquiring property. This latter peculiarity is among the happiest contrasts in their situation to that of the old world, where no anticipated change in this respect, can generally inspire a like sympathy with the rights of property. There may be at present, a Majority of the Nation, who are even freeholders, or the heirs, or aspirants to Freeholds. And the day may not be very near when such will cease to make up a Majority of the community. But they cannot always so continue.[61]

Extending the analysis to the inevitable future in which ''the Majority shall be without landed or other equivalent property and without the means or hope of acquiring it,'' Madison asked, ''What is to secure the rights of property agst. the danger from an equality & universality of suffrage, vesting complete power over property in hands without a share in it: not to speak of a danger in the mean time from a dependence of an increasing number on the wealth of a few?'' Aware of the dangers from both the rich and the poor, Madison could conceive of no permanent, transhistoric solution—political or economic—to the impasse. In feudal and commercial societies, the latter dependence was inherent in ''the relations between Landlords & Tenants'' or ''from the relations between wealthy capitalists and in-

60. JM, Note, Farrand, *Records* 3:450–451.
61. Ibid., 3:451.

digent labourers.'' Making clear that he understood America's present and future economic situation, Madison stated:

> In other Countries this dependence results in some from the relations between Landlords & Tenants in other both from that source, & from the relations between wealthy capitalists & indigent labourers. In the U.S. the occurrence must happen from the last source; from the connection between the great Capitalists in Manufactures & Commerce and the members employed by them. Nor will accumulations of Capital for a certain time be precluded by our laws of descent & of distribution; such being the enterprize inspired by free Institutions, that great wealth in the hands of individuals and associations, may not be unfrequent. But it may be observed, that the opportunities, may be diminished, and the permanency defeated by the equalizing tendency of the laws.

Those who hold property and those who do not face genuine danger from each other—especially when a theorist has Hobbes's atomistic view of society in contrast to an organic vision of society as a natural community, as found in the writing of Edmund Burke and Thomas Jefferson. "An obvious and permanent division of every people is into the owners of the Soil, and the other inhabitants."[62] But Madison, adopting the prejudice of the possessive individualist wing of the liberal tradition, believed that the propertied were more restrained and less tempted to infringe the rights of the latter."[63] Indeed, Madison even argued that "in a certain sense the Country may be said to belong" to "the owners of the Soil."[64] In a return to the language of *Federalist* 10 he reasoned that "bodies of men are not less swayed by interest than individuals, and are less controlled by the dread of reproach and the other motives felt by individuals." "Agrarian laws, and other leveling schemes," like "cancelling or evading of debts," or "other violations of contract" remained Madison's primary concern. Employing the rhetoric of "Vices," *Federalist* 51, and his favorite example of the impossibility of three individuals finding justice by their own efforts, he warned: "We must not shut our eyes

62. Ibid., 3:452.
63. Ibid., 3:452–453.
64. Ibid., 3:452.

to the nature of man, nor to the light of experience. Who would rely on a fair decision from three individuals if two had an interest in the case opposed to the rights of the third?''[65]

Madison's liberal argument concluded that it ''would seem unreasonable to extend the right'' of suffrage so far as to give the property-less, when they become ''the majority, a power of Legislation over the landed property without the consent of the proprietors.'' The propertied need ''a defensive right'' to protect what they owned; Madison proceeded to evaluate five voting schemes, three of which would afford adequate protection to the men of property, those ''having the most at stake.''[66]

The first restricted suffrage to ''freeholders, & to such as hold an equivalent property.'' While not altogether content with this option at the Constitutional Convention, Madison now rejected it on two grounds: first, it violated ''the vital principle of free Government that those who are to be bound by laws, ought to have a voice in making them''; and second, it seemed ''unpropitious'' since it would require a standing army to keep the majority in line.[67] Obviously Madison appreciated the fact that stability could be achieved with the appropriate suffrage scheme. But note that the goal was stability, not the virtue of citizen participation. The second option restricted ''suffrage for one Branch to the holders of property, and for the other Branch to those without property.'' The logic of this plan consisted of the fact that it gave each class ''a mutual defence'' against the other. The problem with the design, according to Madison, was that it only appeared to be equal and fair: ''It wd. not be in fact either equal or fair, because the rights to be defended would be unequal, being on one side those of property as well as those of persons, and on the other those of persons only.'' Given Madison's vision of things, it becomes all too clear why ''slaves'' dream that freedom consists of being the master.

---

65. Ibid., 3:451. Compare the response of the Shawnee chief Tecumseh to the land sales of 1805: ''The only way to stop this evil is for red men to unite in claiming a common and equal right in the land, as it was at first, and should be now—for it was never divided, but belongs to all. . . . *Sell a country! Why not sell the air, the great sea, as well as the earth.*'' In Virginia Irving Armstrong, ed., *I Have Spoken: American History through Voices of Indians* (New York: Pocket Books, 1972), pp. 50–51; Tecumseh's emphasis.

66. JM, Note, Farrand, *Records* 3:452–453.

67. Ibid., 3:453.

Madison then endorsed a plan that met his two earlier objections:

> Confining the right of electing one Branch of the Legislature to
> freeholders, and admitting all others to a common right with
> holders of property, in electing the other Branch. This wd. give a
> defensive power to holders of property, and to the class also
> without property when becoming a majority of electors, with-
> out depriving them in the mean time of a participation in the
> public Councils. If the holders of property wd. thus have a two-
> fold share of representation, they would have at the same time a
> twofold stake in it, the rights of property as well as of persons
> the twofold object of political Institutions. And if no exact &
> safe equilibrium can be introduced, it is more reasonable that a
> preponderating weight shd. be allowed to the greater interest
> then to the lesser.[68]

Madison's final two voting schemes, which he did not endorse,
dealt with a distant future when "experience or public opinion require an equal & universal suffrage for each branch." Time and
space, the old checks from "Vices" and *The Federalist* were prof-
fered as helpful restraints on the majority. Referring to the House of
Representatives, he argued that "a resource favorable to the rights of
landed & other property, when its possessors become the Minority,
may be found in an enlargement of the Election Districts . . . and an
extension of its period of service." The "virtue" of these devices
was that they did not rely on the virtue of the voters. In fact, it could
be argued that these mechanisms were designed to make an extended suffrage feasible because it would be rather ineffectual. The
call for a longer term of office employed one of Madison's favorite
tactics of playing for time: he assumed that passion would cool over
time and permit "reason & justice" to "regain their ascendancy."
"Large districts," noted Madison, "are manifestly favorable to the
election of persons of general respectability, and of probable attachment to the rights of property, over competitors depending on the
personal solicitations practicable on a contracted theatre. And altho'
an ambitious candidate, of personal distinction, might occasionally
recommend himself to popular choice by espousing a popular

68. Ibid., 3:453–454.

though unjust object it might rarely happen to many districts at the same time."[69]

Finally, Madison turned to the ultimate, worst case scenario: "Universal suffrage and very short periods of elections within contracted spheres . . . for each branch." But notice that Madison never even considered the issue of direct suffrage for the executive or judiciary; he assumed that these already filtered political bodies would still function as checks to modify the legislature.[70] Although he withheld his endorsement of this plan, should this hypothetical situation ever develop "security for the holders of property . . . can only be derived from the ordinary influence possessed by property, & the superior information incident to its holders; from the popular sense of justice enlightened & enlarged by a diffusive education; and from the difficulty of combining & effectuating unjust purposes throughout an extensive country."[71] He concluded this addition to his convention notes with a rhetorical choice that, in light of the rest of the essay, initially appears contradictory: "If the only alternative be between an equal & universal right of suffrage for each branch of the Govt. and a confinement of the *entire* right to a part of the Citizens, it is better that those having the greater interest at stake namely that of property & persons both, should be deprived of half their share in the Gov.; than, that those having the lesser interest, that of personal rights only, should be deprived of the whole."[72]

Madison hoped that this choice would never have to be made. He thought that only *if* the above context developed should the propertyless be favored. This, however, was exactly the political situation a wise legislator would try to ensure never developed. Therefore, the best that can be said about Madison's "democratic" yearnings is that—with extreme reluctance—he *theoretically* accepted a democratic franchise when forestalling it could no longer be accomplished and its impact had been diminished. Yet even then, the role of the voter remained absolutely minimal: it was simply to vote for representatives who both represented larger constituencies and

69. Ibid., 3:454. See JM speech, 11 June 1788, Elliot, *Debates* 3:257; see also JM to Caleb Wallace, 23 Aug. 1785, *PJM* 8:350–358.

70. Martin Diamond, "The Federalist," in Leo Strauss and Joseph Cropsey, eds., *The History of Political Philosophy* (Chicago: Rand McNally, 1963), p. 645.

71. JM, Note, Farrand, *Records* 3:454.

72. Ibid., 3:454–455; JM's emphasis.

served for longer terms, thereby continuing to serve as a filtering device to manage the interests of local factions and minimize the influence of the *demos*.[73] Put another way, Madison would extend the vote only when forced to and only after he had altered the scheme of representation so as to make the vote even less responsive to the people. These additions to his convention notes identify another facet of Madison's idea of good government—the need for education and an enlightened citizenry since they could not be kept out of politics forever.

If Madison had not been such a complete liberal, if he had had so much as a touch of the Tory or civic humanist in him, he might have been capable of holding an organic notion of society.[74] Such a notion would have permitted him an avenue to cope with the rise of the masses through a model of representation that was articulated best by Edmund Burke when he explained his theory of representation to his own Bristol constituents:

> Your representative owes you, not his industry only, but his judgement; and he betrays, instead of serving you, if he sacrifices it to your opinion. . . . Parliament is not a *congress* of ambassadors from different and hostile interests; which interests each must maintain, as an agent and advocate, against other agents and advocates; but parliament is a *deliberative* assembly of *one* nation, with *one* interest, that of the whole; . . . You chose a member indeed; but when you have chosen him, he is not a member of Bristol, but he is a member of *parliament*.[75]

While Madison would concur with Burke's first observation, he would have difficulty imagining the rest of the speech. Ambition counteracting ambition was the cornerstone of Madison's politics.

73. David Epstein, *The Political Theory of The Federalist* (Chicago: University of Chicago Press, 1984), p. 145. He correctly claims that Publius's intention was "*the total exclusion of the people in their collective capacity*"; and individuals were to have "a very rare participation." See also Neal Riemer, *James Madison: Creating the American Constitution* (Washington, D.C.: Congressional Quarterly, 1986), p. 126: "This does not mean that Madison in 1787 or 1828 was, practically speaking, a modern democrat on the question of suffrage. He was not in his lifetime even an advocate of universal white male suffrage."

74. Louis Hartz, *The Liberal Tradition in America* (New York: Harcourt, Brace, & Company, 1955).

75. Edmund Burke, *Works*, Rivington ed., 16 vols. (London: F. C. & J. Rivington, 1803–1827), 3:19–20.

English Parliaments are but potential Athenian mobs. That a representative from Virginia could "virtually represent" a district in Maine he would consider a chimera; and the idea that any legislature over the course of its existence could be anything but "a congress of . . . different and hostile interests" would constitute nonsense to him. Madison's atomistic vision, then, left him with little hope in terms of the never-ending rise of the *demos*.

The constant liberal Prince, Madison never abandoned his commitment to protecting individuals: both their rights of person and of property. That the latter were more vulnerable and venerable to Madison appears manifest. That Madison shifted his position from advocate of a strong national government to control the *demos* in the 1780s to supporter of a more active centinel-citizenry to check the encroachments of the central government in the 1790s is consistent with his liberal politics: power must be adjusted and readjusted to maintain the balance between authority and liberty. The rare elements of virtue in Madison remain those negative liberal measures intended to protect the individual from others. As for the *demos*, they had to be held at arms length, slowly brought into the political arena as necessity dictated, but only after they had been appropriately enlightened and the political machinery had been adjusted to accommodate their entrance. In the process, liberalism would be democratized.[76]

In late 1829, performing his last act as a public servant, Madison again found himself delegate to a Constitutional Convention, this time held in Richmond. Unlike in his younger days, he played a far from active role in the proceedings. Although he made several motions, he delivered but one address, which he later supported with a memorandum to the delegates. The speech itself focused indirectly on suffrage; directly, it dealt with how to protect property—property in men—from a majority of voters who had no interest in this peculiar form of the institution.

This grand finale to a distinguished career is intriguing. First, it demonstrated the consistency and linkage of Madison's thoughts on both property and suffrage for half a century. Second, it made evident that although he always abhorred the institution of slavery—in fact

76. C. B. Macpherson, *The Real World of Democracy* (Toronto: CBC Learning Systems, 1965), p. 11.

he had advocated a plan for the just ending of slavery by paying off the owners from revenues generated from the Louisiana Purchase and returning the slaves to Africa—legislative manumission without just compensation for the property loss would constitute injustice. He would allow nothing to threaten property, even in the form of human property. Consequently, he claimed "that persons now and property are the two great subjects on which Governments are to act; and that the rights of persons, and the rights of property, are the objects, for the protection of which Government was instituted." In Madison's hierarchy property still came first.[77] It may have been not that he loved humanity less, but that he trusted (inhuman) property more.

Once the suffrage issue had been framed in his persons-versus-property trade-off, Madison sounded the familiar warning that "in Republics, the great danger is, that the majority may not sufficiently respect the rights of the minority."[78] In light of the specific context of this speech—slavery, among the grossest instances of majority tyranny over a minority—all of Madison's words can take on multiple meanings, depending upon where the listener stands in the master/slave relationship. What remains particularly intriguing, in closely examining Madison's words, are the hints that Madison may have been aware, on some "unconscious" level, of the larger hypocrisy hiding behind his defense of property in humans. Still addressing the question of how to protect the minority of property holders of slaves, Madison drew on themes from "Vices" and *The Federalist*. (The words in brackets below are mine, to suggest an alternative reading of this passage.) He wrote:

> Some gentlemen, consulting the purity and generosity of their own minds, without adverting to the lessons of experience, would find a security against that danger [*slavery or majority tyranny?*], in our social feelings; in a respect for character [*against slavery? or for property?*]; in the dictates of the monitor within [*who ought to rebel against property in human flesh?*]; in the interests of individuals [*to run their own lives?*]; in the aggregate interests of the community [*in showing how humans*

77. JM, "Speech in the Virginia Constitutional Convention," 2 Dec. 1829, *WJM* 9:360.
78. Ibid., 9:361.

matter more than things?]. But man is known to be a selfish, as well as a social being.

Slavery, and Madison's defense of it, certainly verified the truth of the final sentence. He continued his argument, still rejecting "respect for character" and "conscience" as adequate protection for minorities. "We all know," he asserted, "that conscience is not a sufficient safe-guard; and besides, that conscience itself may be deluded; may be misled, by *an unconscious bias*, into acts which an enlightened conscience would forbid.'"[79] Physician, heal thyself.

The constant Prince, Madison rejected every "auxiliary" protection: "They will not serve as a substitute for the coercive provision belonging to Government and Law. . . . The only effectual safe-guard to the rights of the minority must be laid in such a basis and structure of the Government itself, as may afford, in a certain degree, directly or indirectly, a defensive authority in behalf of a minority having right on its side." The virtue of the machine, not its operators, would guarantee the rights of the masters and the justice of the system. From the perspective of the nonmasters, however, the machine brilliantly albeit demonically supported the status quo of exploitation, stopped the possibility of democratic politics redefining both property and justice along more egalitarian lines, and maintained the illusion that the political system, being legal, must also have been fair and just. No wonder other famous Virginians had nightmares of brutal slave revolts when God would have no choice but to side with the slave.[80]

After this extended introduction to Madison's direct comments on "that peculiar feature in our community, which calls for a peculiar division in the basis of our government, I mean the coloured part of our population," he admitted his concern was that once "the power

79. Ibid.; my emphasis.
80. See, for example, Thomas Jefferson, *Notes on the State of Virginia*, ed. William Peden (New York: W. W. Norton, 1972), p. 163; and his letter to Jean Nicolas Demeonier, 26 June 1786, *PTJ* 10:63, where he wrote: "But we must await with patience the workings of an overruling providence, and hope that that is preparing the deliverance of these our suffering brethren. When the measure of their tears shall be full, when their groans shall have involved heaven itself in darkness, doubtless a god of justice will awaken to their distress, and by diffusing light and liberality among their oppressors, or at length by his exterminating thunder, manifest his attention to the things of this world, and that they are not left to the guidance of a blind fatality."

of the Commonwealth shall be in the hands of a majority, who have no interest in this species of property," that through "excessive taxation, injustice may be done to its owners." Madison pleaded for a mechanism that would "incorporate that interest" of the owner into the system.

His stream of logic—which once more takes on different meanings for the slave than for the master—on the justice of his position ran thus: "Such an arrangement is recommended to me by many very important considerations. It is due to justice; due to humanity; due to truth; to the sympathies of our nature; in fine, to our character as a people, both abroad and at home, that they should be considered, as much as possible, in the light of human beings, and not as mere property." In quite an understatement, Madison next observed that "if they were of our own complexion, much of the difficulty would be removed. But the mere circumstance of complexion cannot deprive them of the character of men."[81] Admitting that "the Federal ratio is a favourite resource with me," he urged its adoption; he thought of it in "a spirit of compromise" to accommodate both the property holders who owned slaves and property holders who did not. What the slaves actually thought of the notion remains conjecture.

Madison did not fail, however, to consider the welfare of the slave in this discussion. Indeed, he specifically argued that those who were not slave owners "are apt to sympathize with the slaves, more than may be the case with their masters; and would, therefore, be disposed, when they had the ascendancy, to protect them from laws of an oppressive character, whilst the masters, who have a common interest with the slaves, against undue taxation, which must be paid out of their labour, will be their protectors when they have the ascendancy."[82] This twisted logic represented what in time would become a nonanomalous flaw in classic Madison theory: out of the clash of interests, compromise will work to the advantage of all, even the victim.

A few additional words on Madison and slavery permit a more complete view of his attitude to surface. Like Jefferson, Madison never faltered in his condemnation of the institution of slavery as

81. JM, "Speech in Va. Con.," 2 Dec. 1829, *WJM* 9:362.
82. Ibid., 9:363–364.

morally wrong. Moreover, he too thought all the rights of the Declaration of Independence applied to slaves. While Madison's prose on this injustice, as on almost any other topic, never approached the sublime language of Jefferson, neither did his private letters—as far as they have been published—betray the level of racism contained in Jefferson's. In his impressive study of Madison, Drew McCoy captures the significant differences between Madison and Jefferson.

> Unlike his friend Jefferson, he did not advance the tentative suspicion that blacks were by nature inferior to whites in their physical and mental endowments. Nor did Madison identify the danger of proliferating sexual relations between the two races as an important reason for separating them; again unlike Jefferson, he never voiced any personal concern about "amalgamation," which would allegedly debase whites by mixing their blood with that of a primitive race. Madison simply accepted white prejudice against blacks as a part of American culture that was, for the time being at least, impervious to change or reform. And under these circumstances, emancipating the blacks without removing them was a formula not for progress, but for disaster.[83]

Most astutely, McCoy employs Edward Coles, neither Jefferson nor Madison, as the appropriate model of public action on slave ownership. In 1819, Coles, Madison's former secretary, left Virginia and took his family to Illinois; along the way he emancipated ten slaves and in the process gave each family 160 acres of land. While both Jefferson and Madison hoped to follow George Washington's example of freeing his slaves upon his death, neither did. This short voyage into

83. Drew McCoy, *The Last of the Fathers: James Madison and the Republican Legacy* (New York: Cambridge University Press, 1989), pp. 278–279. See also p. 286, where McCoy details JM's description of "a free negro" he observed in upstate New York while on a 1791 trip with Jefferson. It is difficult to think of Jefferson writing these words: "He possesses a good farm of about 250 Acres which he cultivates with 6 white hirelings for which he is said to have paid about 2-1/2 dollars per Acre and by his industry & good management turns to good account. He is intelligent; reads writes & understands accounts, and is dextrous in his affairs. During the late war he was employed in the Commissary department. He has no wife, and is said to be disinclined to marriage; nor any woman on his farm." See also *Radical Politics*, pp. 57, 66–74.

what Madison called America's original sin completed, it is appropriate to return to his speech on suffrage and slavery.[84]

Madison added a memorandum to this 1829 speech. In a few hundred words, he briefly summarized his lifelong views of property, economic development, and the probable future of the United States. His note advocated extension of the vote "to House keepers & heads of families" and recorded his perspective on a future he could easily predict but not live to see. Always thinking in terms of dynamic economic change, Madison began by agreeing that "an unlimited extension of the right w[ould] probably vary little the character of our public councils or measures." That, however, would be appropriate for the present moment only, since "time is rapidly producing" changes that required this set of framers "to prepare a system of Govt. for a period which is hoped will be a long one." Through Malthusian glasses, Madison darkly predicted, due to propagation rates combined with science and technological development, a "surplus of consumers," the lot of which, for "a large proportion is necessarily reduced by a competition for employment to wages which afford them the bare necessities of life." Madison keenly sensed that this ever-increasing surplus mass, who were denied the liberal dream of equal opportunity through free land, would become dangerous to his rational empire of property: "That proportion being without property, or the hope of acquiring it, cannot be expected to sympathize sufficiently with its rights, to be safe depositories of power over them."[85]

Madison rhetorically asked the obvious: "What is to be done with this unfavored class of the community?" Still searching for balance and equilibrium, he wrote that while it was "unsafe to admit them to a full share of political power, it must be recollected, on the other, that it cannot be expedient to rest a Republican Govt. on a portion of the society having a numerical & physical force excluded from, and liable to be turned against it." Confronted with a vision of economic development that spelled for many Americans relative misery and

84. See JM to General La Fayette, 25 Nov. 1820, *Letters and Other Writings* 3:190, where he writes, "All these perplexities develope more and more the dreadful fruitfulness of the original sin of the African trade."

85. JM, "Note during the Convention for Amending the Constitution of Virginia," 22 Dec. 1829, *WJM* 9:358–359.

little hope for change and embracing a theory of economic justice designed to protect the past against the instability of the future, Madison was willing to extend the vote only to "every description of citizens having a sufficient stake in the public order . . . and particularly the House keepers & Heads of families; most of whom 'having given hostages to fortune,' will have given them to their Country also." Madison appreciated fully the advantages of cooption—especially when the role of the voter remained merely to pick "men of wisdom" and continued to be restricted to one legislative house. He still believed, moreover, that "the territorial proprietors . . . in a certain sense may be regarded as the owners of the Country itself, [and] form the safest basis of free Government."

Some "sufficient stake in the public order" remained the *sine qua non* to voting. Madison considered universal suffrage "to every individual bound to obey" the laws "a Theory, which like most Theories, confessedly requires limitations & modifications" if it hoped to work "in practice."[86] Of course, it continued to be the future, not the present, that concerned Madison most. He calculated that if current population rates were maintained, "in a century or a little more"—which would mean 1929—the United States would be as crowded as Great Britain or France.

Placing minimum faith in "the Republican laws of descent and distribution, in equalizing the property of citizens," Madison's vision of the future could have been lifted from the future pages of Marx:

> One result would seem to be a deficiency of the capital for the expensive establishments which facilitate labour and cheapen its products on one hand, and, on the other, of the capacity to purchase the costly and ornamental articles consumed by the wealthy alone, who must cease to be idlers and become labourers. Another the increased mass of labourers added to the production of necessaries by the withdrawal for this object, or a part of those now employed in producing luxuries, and the addition to the labourers from the class of present consumers of luxuries.

86. Ibid., 9:359.

Seeing the inevitable class tensions that would produce, Madison feared a democratic franchise and called upon "all the wisdom of the wisest patriots" to "adapt" the "institutions and laws of the Country," "to handle the effect of these changes, intellectual, moral, and social."[87] Madison believed, given the size of the nation and the rate of population growth, it had approximately a century before the rot set in. Democracy had to be liberalized before it could be employed safely.[88]

This extended digression into Madison's ideas on suffrage acknowledges his basic philosophic distrust of democracy and yet his begrudging acceptance of its inevitability. It may now be time to return to his remaining notions on good government found primarily in *The Federalist*, "The Virginia Resolution and Virginia Report," and a few *National Gazette* essays. Never prone to Platonic speculations on abstract ideals, Madison accepted the Constitution, once it had surfaced from the debates and compromises of Philadelphia, as a *fait accompli* and worked to ensure its success. Virtually all speculation on what could or should have been part of the grand design ceased; ratification and implementation required all his energies.

    The Federalist contains extended discussions of many of the themes Madison endorsed prior to the convention: the virtue of an extended republic, the details of his scheme of representation, and the completion of his ideas on separation of powers. The two fundamental additions were his acceptance of a stronger view of federalism and his then-novel view of the precise power granted by the Constitution itself. Given the unambiguous thrust of his preconvention thoughts on the absolute necessity to tame the state governments, making them "subordinately useful" through the national veto, many of his comments on the positive dimensions of federalism in *The Federalist* should be viewed as Madison's realistic perspective on politics. Remember, moreover, that at this historic moment Madison believed liberty had gotten out of control; restoring balance required added energy in a national authority. Yet once the Washington

87. Ibid., 9:360. Cf. Karl Marx, "Wage Labor and Capital," in *Mark-Engels Reader*, ed. Robert Tucker (New York: W. W. Norton, 1978), p. 216: "Thus the forest of uplifted arms demanding work becomes ever thicker, while the arms themselves become ever thinner."
88. Macpherson, *Real World*, p. 5.

regime was ensconced and Hamilton had isolated the president from Madison and Jefferson, the latter two slowly began to see tyranny arise. At that point, Madison had to readjust his seesaw. The institution of federalism, ironically, helped him do it. He rediscovered the power of public opinion through an awakened citizenry; and he appreciated how the state(s) government(s) could serve as an agency to "interpose" itself against the encroachments of a national Leviathan that had lost the ability to control itself.[89]

Madison's renewed interest in the states and their citizens as checks on government can be found in his *National Gazette* essays. Philip Freneau published eighteen unsigned Madison essays, but four additional essays never appeared in print. Looking at these essays as a whole, it would not be too far off the mark to call at least a section of them "Lectures on Citizenship."[90] But do not be misled: this citizenship was that of a dedicated liberal who believed in defensive, negative power and the role of fear and mutual distrust in the creation of a protective state.[91] The term *citizenship* does not even appear in the original Constitution but does get added to it with the Fourteenth Amendment; but then why should it, since silence, at least in Madison's theory of constitutional interpretation, always spoke as loudly as words?[92] That was the late 1780s. Then again, the citizenship models of neither Aristotle nor Jefferson will be found in Madison's essays of the 1790s because these philosophers held a notion of humanity as the *zoon politikon.*

In "Consolidation" Madison argued that there existed a distinct advantage "in proportion as uniformity is found to prevail in the interests and sentiments of the several states, will be the practicability of accommodating *Legislative* regulations to them, and thereby of withholding new and dangerous prerogatives from the executive." In what appeared to be in direct contrast to the sentiment of the theory of counterpoise in *The Federalist*, Madison asserted that "the

89. See *Federalist* 45 and *Federalist* 51.

90. See Collen Sheen, "The Politics of Public Opinion: James Madison's 'Notes on Government,' " *William and Mary Quarterly* 49 (Oct. 1992): 609–627, for an exercise in wish fulfillment as she discovers a civic humanist Madison through an imaginative reading of these essays.

91. See "Notes for Essays," 19 Dec. 1791–3 Mar. 1792, *PJM* 14:161, 165, 167.

92. Judith N. Shklar, *American Citizenship* (Cambridge, Mass.: Harvard University Press, 1991), p. 15. The Constitution does define the conditions under which an individual can be considered a citizen and how this pertains to office holding, but it does not discuss the concept of citizenship.

less the supposed difference of interests, and the greater the concord and confidence throughout the great body of people, the more readily must they sympathize with each other" and "the more certainly will they take the alarm at usurpation or oppression, and the more effectually will they *consolidate* their defence of the public liberty." Madison closed this essay calling for "the patriotic study of all, to maintain the various authorities established by our complicated system, each in its respective constitutional sphere; and erect over the whole, one paramount Empire of reason, benevolence and brotherly affection."[93] This did not signal a change of heart.[94] Rather, it reflected Madison's acute understanding that his balancing machine required shifting emphasis to meet the demands of the time. Indeed, once the "Jeffersonian Revolution" of 1800 had succeeded, in part because of the efforts of Madison to awaken the citizens, never again did Madison feel the need to address the people as directly. This is not to imply that the *demos*, having fulfilled its immediate function of unmaking the federalist-controlled government, could now be discarded; rather, Madison believed that the seesaw had been rebalanced and that the role of the *demos* had shifted to one of never-ending vigilance, thereby diminishing the possibilities of future tyranny.

In an essay published in late 1791, Madison astutely identified "Public Opinion" as "the real sovereign in every free" government. He observed that while "there are cases where the public opinion must be obeyed by the government; so there are cases, where not being fixed, it may be influenced by the government."[95] With public opinion playing an increasingly active role in setting the bounds of government, the political system would not have to wait for an election to send an unmistakable message to those in power. His final essay of this year, "Government" clarified further his views of a limited citizenship. Since "a republic involves the idea of popular rights," which Madison assumed individuals would be interested in protecting, he advocated that "every good citizen will be at once a

93. "Consolidation," *National Gazette*, 3 Dec. 1791, *PJM* 14:138–139; JM's emphasis.
94. Cf. Marvin Meyers, ed., *The Mind of the Founder*, rev. ed. (Hanover, Mass.: Brandeis University Press, 1981), pp. xl–xliii.
95. "Public Opinion," *National Gazette*, ca. 19 Dec. 1791, *PJM* 14:170. JM believed the government's power to influence opinion was particularly acute in foreign affairs.

centinel over the rights of the people; over the authorities of the confederal government; and over both the rights and the authorities of the intermediate governments." While a sense of civic virtue could not be counted on to produce this resolve, a keen sense of self-interest could.[96]

"Charters," one of the finest of Madison's *National Gazette* essays, published three weeks later, continued his call for an active citizen-centinel to watch over the rights of the nation. The opening lines convey Madison's sense of the fundamental difference between European and American politics: "In Europe, charters of liberty have been granted by power. America has set the example and France has followed it, of charters of power granted by liberty." Power and liberty were not an either/or choice; good government always involved a balancing of the two. Madison reinforced his notion of guardianship, extending it to both the private and public arenas. He reiterated as well his assertion that public opinion played a critical role in questions of power, rights, and stability. Here he openly linked the factors of public opinion, a citizenry on guard, and the need for the citizens to be enlightened. "How devoutly is it to be wished," wrote Madison, "that the public opinion of the United States should be enlightened." He closed his essay with this admonition: "Liberty and order will never be *perfectly* safe, until a trespass on the constitutional provisions for either, shall be felt with the same keenness that resents an invasion of the dearest rights; until every citizen shall be an Argus to espy, and an Aegeon to avenge, the unhallowed deed."[97]

Madison's essay "Government of the United States" reinforced the above arguments. This time Madison urged "those who love their country, its repose, and its republicanism" to "study" their government so as to "avoid the alternative" of "schism, or consoli-

---

96. "Government," *National Gazette*, 31 Dec. 1791, *PJM* 14:179. Cf. *Federalist* 57:343. See JM to Caleb Wallace, 23 Aug. 1785, *PJM* 8:352, where he argues that judges' salaries must "be liberal" or "the bar will be superior to the bench which destroys all security for a Systematick administration of Justice." Justice could be secured through money, not civic virtue.

97. "Charters," *National Gazette*, 18 Jan. 1792, *PJM* 14:191–192. In *Federalist* 51:320, JM wrote: "We see it particularly displayed in all the subordinate distributions of power, where the constant aim is to divide and arrange the several offices in such a manner as that each check on the other—that private interest of every individual may be a sentinel over the public rights." Notice that Madison was relying on public officials, not the *demos*, to function as the centinel.

dation." In words consistent with the letter if not the spirit of *The Federalist*, Madison unequivocally wrote that "the partitions and internal checks of power . . . are neither the sole nor the chief palladium of constitutional liberty. The people who are the authors of this blessing, must also be its guardians. Their eyes must be ever ready to mark, their voice to pronounce, and their arm to repel or repair aggressions on the authority of their constitutions." Then in typical Madison logic, he concluded that under the circumstances, state constitutions were of supreme importance because they constituted "the highest authority next to their own, because the immediate work of their own, and the most sacred part of their property, as recognising and recording the title to every other."[98]

Although he had already published one article on parties in January of 1792, in late September he published an additional essay called "A Candid State of Parties." In it, he extended the scope of topics a citizen should study to include "the duty of the citizen at all times to understand the actual state" of parties. If citizens failed to do so, the ever-suspicious Madison warned that "an opportunity is given to designing men, by the use of artificial or nominal distinctions, to oppose and balance against each other those who never differed as to the end to be pursued, and may no longer differ as to the means of attaining it." So that such "artificial" distinctions do not gain validity in the United States, Madison lectured his audience on the three distinct party periods in American history: parties in favor and opposed to independence; parties in favor and opposed to the Constitution of 1787; and parties in favor and opposed to "the doctrine that mankind is capable of governing themselves." This last epoch continued to be a battle, fought out over how the new state should be administered. Recalling the distinct advantages inherent in labeling opponents "Anti," Madison labeled the group who "are more partial to the opulent" and who doubted the capacities of mankind to self-government "Anti-republicans." People like himself (and Jefferson) he called "Republicans."[99] This distinction between "Anti-republican" and "Republican" in the most polemical of all the *National Gazette* essays, "Who are the Best Keepers of the People's

98. "Government of the United States," *National Gazette*, 4 Feb. 1792, *PJM* 14:218.

99. "A Candid State of Parties," *National Gazette*, 22 Sept. 1792, *PJM* 14:370–372.

Liberties,'' Madison seemed uniquely prepared to delineate since, at different times in his political career, he advocated the spirit of each side.[100]

The *National Gazette* essays present Madison appreciating the defensive power inherent in public opinion combined with an informed citizenry and periodic elections. The citizen's task, however, remained simply vigilant guardianship, not the active citizen-participation model of Aristotle requiring citizens to fulfill the functions of ruling and being ruled. Madisonian citizens were to let the government know that they were watching its performance and, if need be, willing to change rulers. Beyond that, their political function remained solely to participate in a process of selection designed ''to obtain for rulers men who possess most wisdom to discern, and most virtue to pursue, the common good of the society.''[101]

At the Virginia ratifying convention, in what may be the single favorite passage among Madison scholars who want to view him as a civic humanist, he argued:

> But I go on this great republican principle, that the people will have virtue and intelligence to select men of virtue and wisdom. Is there no virtue among us? If there be not, we are in a wretched situation. No theoretical checks, no form of government, can render us secure. To suppose that any form of government will secure liberty or happiness without any virtue in the people, is a chimerical idea. If there be sufficient virtue and intelligence in the community, it will be exercised in the selection of these men; so that we do not depend on their virtue, or put confidence in our rulers, but in the people who are to choose them.[102]

Of course, Madison was right. In fact, there is nothing particularly difficult in meeting this minimum level of virtue. The role of the citizens in 1787 remained exclusively ''to select men of virtue and wisdom.'' In a few years he would expand that role to include being a

100. Who Are the Best Keepers of the People's Liberties,'' *National Gazette,* 20 Dec. 1792, *PJM* 14:426–427.

101. *Federalist* 57:343. Note how JM does not even trust the virtue of the men of ''most wisdom . . . and most virtue'' since the next line of the paper stated ''and in the next place, to take the most effectual precautions for keeping them virtuous whilst they continue to hold their public trust.''

102. Elliot, *Debates* 3:536–537.

self-interested watchdog over their own rights. Beyond that, however, they were to find meaning and dignity in the pursuit of self-interest in civil society. Consequently, education and mechanisms to facilitate political communication, such as newspapers, would become crucial to keeping the citizens informed and enlightened.

In his private notes for the *National Gazette* essays, Madison recorded an interesting addendum to his earlier thoughts on the virtue of an extended republic found in *The Federalist*. As if suffering a momentary spell of amnesia, in 1791–1792 he wrote: "Whatever facilitates a general intercommunication of sentiments & ideas among the body of the people, as a free press, compact situation, good roads, interior commerce &c. is equivalent to a contraction of the orbit within wch. the Govt. is to act: and may favor liberty in a nation too large for free Govt. or hasten its violent death in one too small & so vice versa."[103] Not exactly a repudiation of his *Federalist* argument of the virtue of space to control democracy, this passage demonstrated that the wise liberal Prince understood how to use almost any political situation to the appropriate end. Nevertheless, education and information remained absolutely essential if the people were to play even their minimal part. In an 1822 letter, Madison noted that "the liberal appropriations made by the Legislature of Kentucky for a general system of Education cannot be too much applauded." In a rather eloquent statement of the rationale for this position, he concluded: "A popular Government, without popular information, or the means of acquiring it, is but a Prologue to a Farce or a Tragedy; or, perhaps both. Knowledge will forever govern ignorance: And a people who mean to be their own Governors, must arm themselves with the power which knowledge gives."[104]

Perhaps the ultimate dimension of Madison's system of government resided in his interpretation of the Constitution, which he first began to delineate in *The Federalist*. Initially, he believed the Constitution would itself serve as a check on abuses of power; after his retirement from the presidency and years of watching first Hamilton and then the Marshall Court undemocratically change the meaning of the document, Madison became, as Robert Morgan described it,

103. "Notes to Essays," 19 Dec. 1791–3 Mar. 1792, *PJM* 14:159. Cf. *Federalist* 10:127–128, 51:322.
104. JM to W. T. Barry, 4 Aug. 1822, *WJM* 9:103.

"almost obsessed during the last ten years of his life with maintaining a pure interpretation of the Constitution."[105] And "pure," of course, meant the way Madison thought the document should be interpreted. If Madison had succeeded in establishing his theory of interpreting the Constitution, it would have further enhanced his ability to have the past control the future, to maintain his influence from beyond the grave.

As early as *The Federalist* and the Virginia ratification debates, Madison found himself advocating a strict, limited interpretation of the Constitution. As discussed previously, Madison argued repeatedly that a bill of rights was unnecessary since the national government could only exercise those powers explicitly given to it.

From the first consideration of the question of "original intent," Madison—the single person who possessed the most complete notes and therein the potential to exercise the most influence, if "original intent" meant what the Philadelphia framers intended—usually rejected this particular interpretative approach. In a 1796 speech on the Jay Treaty, he expressed the essence of his position on the question of the significance of the original framers.

> But, after all, whatever veneration might be entertained for the body of men who formed our Constitution, the sense of that body could never be regarded as the oracular guide in expounding the Constitution. As the instrument came from them it was nothing more than the draft of a plan, nothing but a dead letter, until life and validity were breathed into it by the voice of the people, speaking through the several State Conventions. If we were to look, therefore, for the meaning of the instrument beyond the face of the instrument, we must look for it, not in the General Convention, which proposed, but in the State Conventions, which accepted and ratified the Constitution.[106]

The political difficulty, from Madison's perspective, however, was that lacking some agreed upon theory of interpretation, combined

105. Robert S. Morgan, *James Madison on the Constitution and the Bill of Rights* (New York: Greenwood Press, 1988), p. 192.
106. "The Jay Treaty. Speech in the 4th Congress," 6 Apr. 1796, *WJM* 6:272. See "The Bank Bill," 2 Feb. 1791, *PJM* 13:372–388. See also JM to Andrew Stevenson, 25 Mar. 1826, *Letters and Other Writings* 3:521–522: "I cannot but highly approve the industry with which you have searched for a key to the sense of the

with the changing meaning of words and the inevitable attempt to influence, by passion and politics, the method of interpreting the document, the Constitution would lose all rational meaning with time and circumstances. Consequently, in the 1820s and 1830s Madison returned to the themes of *Federalist* 37, the imprecision of language and the changing meaning of words.

The epitome of the rational actor, Madison begrudgingly accepted the inevitable change in the meaning of words and language. Consequently, he enthusiastically endorsed Webster's prospectus for a dictionary. Knowing that the days were limited in which he could serve as a check on distorted or perverse interpretations of the meaning of the words and phrases in the Constitution, Madison in an 1826 letter wrote:

> Whilst few things are more difficult, few are more desirable than a standard work, explaining, and as far as possible fixing, the meaning of words and phrases. All languages, written as well as oral, though much less than oral, are liable to changes, from causes, some of them inseparable from the nature of man and the progress of society. A perfect remedy for the evil must, therefore, be unattainable. But as far as it may be attainable, the attempt is laudable; and next to compleat success, is that of recording with admitted fidelity the state of a language at the epoch of the record. In the exposition of laws, and even of Constitutions, how many important errors may be produced by mere innovations in the use of words and phrases, if not controulable by a recurrence to the original and authentic meaning attached to them![107]

Constitution, where alone the true one can be found, in the proceedings of the Convention, the contemporary expositions, and, above all, in the ratifying conventions of the States. If the instrument be interpreted by criticisms which lose sight of the intention of the parties to it, in the fascinating pursuit of objects of public advantage or convenience, the purest motives can be no security against innovations materially changing the features of the government."

107. JM to Converse Sherman, 10 Mar. 1826, *Letters and Other Writings* 3:519. See also JM to N. P. Trist, 2 Mar. 1827, *Letters and Other Writings* 3:565: "The imperfection of language, especially when terms are to be used the precise import of which has not been settled by a long course of application, is one cause. The change which the meaning of words inadvertently undergoes, examples of

Even the overtones of sin and corruption, reminiscent of the 1780s, returned as Madison considered the mere mutability of words an "evil." A pragmatist, he realized the ideal of a transhistorical, fixed definition of words could not be achieved; nevertheless, at least the meaning of the words—at a specific time in history—could be recorded and thus help establish the meaning of legal documents enacted during that time. Madison, then, did indeed have an interpretative theory of "original intent"—one not based on the intent of the Philadelphia framers, but on the meaning of the document as understood by the parties who agreed to it, that is, the people in the state ratifying conventions.

The fact that the meaning of some words changes over time was but one of the interpretative difficulties of the Constitution. A related problem was the *sui generis* nature of the government constructed in 1787. Because the framers had created a "political system . . . without a model," to avoid "error and confusion" it remained essential "in debating constitutional questions" to "define the terms used in argument." Madison's logic was flawless: "Known words express known ideas; and new ideas, such as are presented by our novel and unique political system, must be expressed either by new words, or by old words with new definitions. Without attention to this circumstance, volumes may be written, which can only be answered by a call for definitions, and which answer themselves as soon as the call is complied with."[108]

If the record of the debates of the framers did not constitute *the* source for understanding what the Constitution meant, how was its meaning to be determined? In an 1830 letter to M. L. Hurlbert, Madison repeated his prior position: "But whatever respect may be thought due to the intention of the Convention, which prepared & proposed the Constitution, as presumptive evidence of the general understanding at the time of the language used, it must be kept in

---

which are already furnished by the Constitution of the U. States, is another. And more frequent and formidable than either cause is the spirit of party or the temptations of interest. Nor is the public good, real or supposed, without occasional effect in betraying honest minds into misconstructions of the Constitutional test. These are evils which cannot be altogether avoided, but they are not to be compared with those inherent in arbitrary and undefined forms of Government."

108. JM to Edward Livingston, 17 Apr. 1824, *Letters and Other Writings* 3:436.

mind that the only authoritative intentions were those of the people of the States, as expressed thro' the Conventions which ratified the Constitution.'' Madison offered further guidelines for interpreting the Constitution:

> As there are legal rules for interpreting laws, there must be analogous rules for interpreting const[itutions] and among the obvious and just guides applicable to the Const[itution] of the U.S. may be mentioned—
>
> 1. The evils & defects for curing which the Constitution was called for & introduced.
>
> 2. The comments prevailing at the time it was adopted.
>
> 3. The early, deliberate & continued practice under the Constitution, as preferable to constructions adapted on the spur of occasions, and subject to the vicissitudes of party or personal ascendencies.[109]

Madison began by drawing a distinction between interpreting ''laws'' and interpreting ''constitutions,'' tipping his hand on part of what separated his interpretative theory from many others.[110] It remains intriguing to note that Madison did not appear to give special credibility to *The Federalist* as an extra appropriate guide to understanding the meaning of the Constitution. As if holding the memory of Publius in mind, he warned Edward Livingston that ''it cannot be denied, without forgetting what belongs to human nature, that, in consulting the contemporary writings which vindicated and recommended the Constitution, it is fair to keep in mind that the authors might be sometimes influenced by the zeal of advocates.''[111] Months later, in response to Jefferson's suggestion that *The Federalist* be part

---

109. JM to M. L. Hurlbert, May 1830, *WJM* 9:372. See also JM's will, 1835, *WJM* 9:548–551, where he makes arrangements to publish posthumously his convention notes.

110. See McCoy, *Last of the Fathers*, p. 64: ''Madison would insist throughout his retirement that the Constitution be elevated to a separate plane of discourse and debate, as far removed from the frenzied excitement of partisan furor and popular controversy as republican principle allowed.''

111. JM to Edward Livingston, 17 Apr. 1824, *Letters and Other Writings* 3:436. See JM to Thomas Jefferson, 8 Feb. 1799, *PJM* 17:229: ''The idea of publishing the Debates of the Convention ought to be well weighed before the expediency of it, in a public as well as personal view be decided on. Besides the intimate connec-

of the reading list at the Virginia law school, Madison appeared somewhat reluctant to include it as he reminded Jefferson that

> the "Federalist" may fairly enough be regarded as the most authentic exposition of the text of the Federal Constitution, as understood by the Body which prepared and the authority which accepted it. Yet it did not foresee all the misconstructions which have occurred, nor prevent some that it did foresee. And what equally deserves remark, neither of the great rival parties have acquiesced in all its comments. It may, nevertheless, be admissible as a school book, if any will be that goes so much into detail.[112]

Since Hamilton's liberal reading of the Constitution, with his notion of implied powers, won the day, it is understandable that Madison would not want to give too much attention to the other Publius.

The first crucial confrontation over how the Constitution should be interpreted resulted from the creation of the national bank. While Alexander Hamilton and Thomas Jefferson squared off against each other in the cabinet, Madison played a vocal and by no means insignificant role in the House debates where he argued a position he felt required to justify in later years. Jefferson and Madison believed the creation of the bank to be a power neither explicitly nor implicitly granted by the Constitution. The Congress acted, therefore, unconstitutionally. Though Madison and Jefferson were ideologically predisposed to dislike credit and banks, it was not the soundness of the policy that concerned them but that Congress lacked the "authority . . . to pass it." Not inhibited in 1791 from claiming "he well recollected that a power to grant charters of incorporation had been pro-

---

tion between them, the whole volume ought to be examined with an eye to the use of which every part is susceptible. In the Despotism at present exercised over the rules of construction, and the Counter reports of the proceedings that would perhaps be made out & mustered for the occasion, it is a problem what turn might be given to the impression on the public mind."

112. JM to Thomas Jefferson, 8 Feb. 1825, *Letters and Other Writings* 3:481. See also JM to N. P. Trist, 1 Mar. 1829, *Letters and Other Writings* 4:16–17. In 1829, he told N. P. Trist that "the best aids in investigating the true scope of 'contracts,' a violation of which is prohibited by the Constitution, will be found where you intend to look for them. I wish I could abridge your researches. *The Federalist* touches on the origin of the prohibition; but my copy not being at home, I cannot refer to the passage."

posed in the general convention and rejected," Madison would momentarily, albeit subtly, move away from a position granting added authority to what had been recorded as being said at Philadelphia.[113]

His position on the power authorized in the new government remained consistent. Regarding "the peculiar manner in which the federal government is limited," Madison maintained its power was "not a general grant, out of which particular powers are excepted—it is a grant of particular powers only, leaving the general mass in other hands. So it had been understood by its friends and its foes, and so it was to be interpreted." Then Madison presented to the House, "as preliminaries to a right interpretation," certain rules to be followed:

> An interpretation that destroys the very characteristic of the government cannot be just.
> Where a meaning is clear, the consequences, whatever they may be, are to be admitted—where doubtful, it is fairly triable by its consequences.
> In controverted cases, the meaning of the parties to the instrument, if to be collected by reasonable evidence, is a proper guide.
> Cotemporary and concurrent expositions are a reasonable evidence of the meaning of the parties.
> In admitting or rejecting a constructive authority, not only the degree of its incidentality to an express authority, is to be regarded, but the degree of its importance also; since on this will depend the probability or improbability of its being left to construction.[114]

Having determined the appropriate manner in which the Constitution should be read, Madison found "it was not possible to discover in it the power to incorporate a Bank." Neither the "common defence," the "general welfare," the "power to borrow money," nor "the power to pass all laws necessary and proper to carry into execution those powers" could justify the attempt to establish a national bank. The last clause caused the deepest concern, for if Hamilton's position carried the day, Madison feared the fundamentally limited

113. JM appeared willing on this occasion to claim that the deliberations of the Philadelphia convention were authoritative.
114. JM speech, "The Bank Bill," 2 Feb. 1791, *PJM* 13:374.

nature of legislative power in the new state would be altered into a grant of virtually unrestricted power.

The *third* clause is that which gives the power to pass all laws necessary and proper to execute the specified powers.

Whatever meaning this clause may have, none can be admitted, that would give an unlimited discretion to Congress.

Its meaning must, according to the natural and obvious force of the terms and the context, be limited to means *necessary* to the *end*, and *incident* to the *nature* of the specified powers.

The clause is in fact merely declaratory of what would have resulted by unavoidable implication, as the appropriate, and as it were, technical means of executing those powers. In this sense it had been explained by the friends of the constitution, and ratified by the state conventions.

The essential characteristic of the government, as composed of limited and enumerated powers, would be destroyed: If instead of direct and incidental means, any means could be used, which in the language of the preamble to the bill, ''might be conceived to be conducive to the successful conducting of the finances; or might be *conceived* to *tend* to give *facility* to the obtaining of loans.''[115]

Madison openly worried that if creative, non-Madisonian interpretations of the Constitution based on a notion of implied powers gained acceptance, ''implications, thus remote and thus multiplied, can be linked together, a chain may be formed that will reach every object of legislation, every object within the whole compass of political economy.'' He concluded his speech, initially relying on his interpretative position that constitutional ''silence'' constituted the functional equivalent of a prohibition against a grant of power. Still, on every conceivable ground, Madison thought the bill a violation of the Constitution:

It appeared on the whole, he concluded, that the power exercised by the bill was condemned by the silence of the constitution; was condemned by the rule of interpretation arising out of the constitution; was condemned by its tendency to destroy the

115. Ibid., 13:375–376; JM's emphasis. See *Federalist* 44:287–289.

main characteristic of the constitution; was condemned by the expositions of the friends of the constitution, whilst depending before the public; was condemned by the apparent intention of the parties which ratified the constitution; was condemned by the explanatory amendments proposed by Congress themselves to the Constitution; and he hoped it would receive its final condemnation, by the vote of this house.[116]

This episode, rich in irony, disappeared along with the high Federalist. It remained dormant throughout the reign of the Virginia dynasty, only to haunt Madison in retirement when he strove to explain his eventual acceptance, years later, of the bank as constitutionally legitimate based on his unique view of constitutional legitimacy bestowed over time. The fundamental irony may well be how Hamilton, who understood and enjoyed politics, appreciated from the start that the issue of interpretation constituted perhaps *the* political question—not, like Madison, that it was a matter of rational argument upon which all rational individuals would agree. Moreover, Hamilton's theory of interpretation appears to constitute the historically legitimate one. It was Madison, the nonlawyer, who presented the radical interpretative positions, all of which must be briefly explained.

When the question of the constitutionality of a national bank originated, President Washington requested both the secretary of the treasury and the secretary of state to prepare written opinions on the issue. Jefferson viewed the question in terms almost identical to Madison; he even attached a copy of Madison's 2 February speech in the House to his opinion. However, at no point did Jefferson raise the idea of determining the intention of the Constitution based on the legislative history of the drafting and ratifying of the document.

Jefferson instead argued for a restricted meaning of the necessary and proper clause, where mere "convenience" would be insufficient grounds for legislative action. Echoing the logic of Madison, Jefferson argued that "the Constitution allows only the means which are '*necessary*,' not those which are merely 'convenient' for effecting the enumerated powers. If such a latitude of construction be allowed

116. JM speech, "The Bank Bill," 2 Feb. 1791, *PJM* 13:378, 381; see also his speech of 8 Feb. 1791, *PJM* 13:383–388. It is appropriate to wonder if this rule of interpreting silence applied to citizenship as well.

to this phrase as to give any non-enumerated power, it will go to every one, for there is not one which ingenuity may not torture into a *convenience* in some instance *or other*, to *some one* of so long a list of enumerated powers." On at least one significant point, however, Jefferson differed from Madison.

After he reminded Washington that the power "to protect the invasions of the legislature" resided with not only the executive but the judiciary, the states, and the state legislatures, Jefferson also told the president that in his view, "unless the President's mind on a view of everything which is urged for and against this bill, is tolerably clear that it is unauthorized by the Constitution; if the pro and con hang so even as to balance his judgment, a just respect for the wisdom of the legislature would naturally decide the balance in favor of their opinion."[117] As a democrat, Jefferson could assert no less a standard. A liberal who always looked for cool and rational decisions rather than democratic ones, Madison cared for the ends rather than the means. Ultimately Madison amended and adopted this notion of settling constitutional questions through the legislature, provided successive legislatures endorsed specific policies over an extended period of time.

Before turning to Madison's novel idea for resolution of questions concerning constitutionality, Hamilton's theory of interpretation should be briefly presented. Madison's hermeneutics demanded attention be given to the intent of the Constitution as found in the discussion of the parties to it, located primarily in the state ratification debates and secondarily in the people and to the slightest degree among the Philadelphia framers. Hamilton, in contrast, followed the long-standing (and continuing) practice of English jurisprudence in which law is interpreted on the basis of the words of the document itself, paying virtually no attention to the actions of any legislative actors. Words stand by themselves, their meaning fixed by the common understanding of the terms. Furthermore, the English tradition never distinguished between a law and a constitution, as Madison attempted to do. Consequently, since the question of how the Con-

---

117. Thomas Jefferson, "Opinion on the Constitutionality of a National Bank," 15 Feb. 1791, *Thomas Jefferson: Writings*, ed. Merrill D. Peterson (New York: Library of America, 1984): 416–421; TJ's emphasis. See also H. Jefferson Powell's "The Original Understanding of Original Intent," in Rakove, *Interpreting the Constitution*, pp. 53–116.

stitution ought to be interpreted never arose at Philadelphia, Hamilton had legal history on his side. More importantly, when he won the political battle over the issue, the Constitution would be read through his lens.

To Hamilton, the narrow question on the bank concerned incorporation. He wrote,

> that this *general principle* is *inherent* in the very *definition* of *Government* and *essential* to every step of the progress to be made by that of the United States; namely—that every power vested in a Government is in its nature *sovereign*, and includes by *force* of the *term*, a right to employ all the *means* requisite, and fairly *applicable* to the attainment of the *ends* of such power; and which are not precluded by restrictions & exceptions specified in the constitution; or not immoral, or not contrary to the essential ends of political society.

The larger issue involved implied versus expressly enumerated and resulting powers. "It is not denied, that there are *implied*, as well as *express* powers, and that the former are as effectually delegated as the latter. And for the sake of accuracy it shall be mentioned, that there is another class of powers, which may be properly denominated *resulting* powers." Having established the notion of implied power, Hamilton (like Madison) asserted that "the only question must be, in this as in every other case, whether the mean to be employed . . . has a natural relation to any of the acknowledged objects or lawful ends of government." Hamilton's brilliant argument claimed that the intent of the framers, based on the actual words of the Constitution—ignoring any other grounds—supported his interpretation:

> The whole turn of the clause containing it, indicates that it was the intent of the convention, by that clause to give a liberal latitude to the exercise of the specified powers. The expressions have peculiar comprehensiveness. they are—"to make *all laws*, necessary & proper for *carrying into execution* the foregoing powers & all *other powers* vested by the constitution in the *government* of the United States, or in any *department* or *officer* thereof." To understand the word as the Secretary of State does,

would be to depart from its obvious & popular sense, and to give it a *restrictive* operation; an idea never before entertained. It would be to give it the same force as if the word *absolutely* or *indispensably* had been prefixed to it.

Hamilton presented a criterion of what established constitutionality and what did not:

> This criterion is the *end* to which the measure relates as a *mean*. If the end be clearly comprehended within any of the specified powers, & if the measure have an obvious relation to that end, and is not forbidden by any particular provision of the constitution—it may safely be deemed to come within the compass of the national authority. There is also this further criterion which may materially assist the decision. Does the proposed measure abridge a preexisting right of any State, or of any individual? If it does not, there is a strong presumption in favour of its constitutionality; & slighter relations to any declared object of the constitution may be permitted to turn the scale.

Finally, Hamilton again reminded Washington of the long-established rules of interpretation.

> But whatever may have been the nature of the proposition or the reasons for rejecting it concludes nothing in respect to the real merits of the question. The Secretary of State will not deny, that whatever may have been the intention of the framers of a constitution, or of a law, that intention is to be sought for in the instrument itself, according to the usual & established rules of construction. Nothing is more common than for laws to *express* and *effect*, more or less than was intended. If then a power to erect a corporation, in any case, be deducible by fair inference from the whole or any part of the numerous provisions of the constitution of the United States, arguments drawn from extrinsic circumstances, regarding the intention of the convention, must be rejected.[118]

118. Alexander Hamilton, "Final Version of an Opinion on the Constitutionality of an Act to Establish a Bank," 23 Feb. 1791, *The Papers of Alexander Hamilton*, ed. Harold C. Syrett et al. (New York: Columbia University Press, 1961–1979), 8:97–134; Hamilton's emphasis.

That Madison lost this initial skirmish with Hamilton in large measure explains how the new state moved beyond the defensive structure Madison designed it to be and how it became, over time, a more positive, interventionist state. That Madison's theory of interpretation eventually gained some acceptance may also explain why, even as a positive, interventionist state, America remained less so than European counterparts. For the present, it seems appropriate to present Madison's intriguing ideas for resolving constitutional controversy over time.

At least as early as his 1815 veto message of the bank bill, Madison argued that constitutional legitimacy may be bestowed on legislation over the course of time. While he opposed, on constitutional grounds, the bank in the 1790s, he now thought it legitimate, "waiving the question of the constitutional authority of the Legislature to establish an incorporated bank as being precluded in my judgment by repeated recognitions under varied circumstances of the validity of such an institution in acts of the legislative, executive, and judicial branches of the Government, accompanied by indications, in different modes, of a concurrence of the general will of the nation."[119] This notion can be found repeated as late as 1828, when Madison presented his views on the constitutionality of a bill to protect manufacturing. He explained that

> A further evidence in support of the Cons[titution's], power to protect & foster manufactures by regulations of trade, an evidence that ought of itself to settle the question, is the uniform & practical sanction given to the power, by the Genl. Govt. for nearly 40 years with a concurrence or acquiescence of every State Govt. throughout the same period; and it may be added thro all the vicissitudes of Party, which marked the period. No novel construction however ingeniously devised, or however respectable and patriotic its Patrons, can withstand the weight of such authorities, or the unbroken current of so prolonged & universal a practice.[120]

Naturally, stability remained the ultimate rationale for Madison's theory of constitutional legitimacy: if successive governmental

119. "Veto Message," 30 Jan. 1815, *WJM* 8:327.
120. JM to Joseph C. Cabell, 18 Sept. 1828, *WJM* 9:333; see also p. 334: "And may it not be fairly left to the unbiased judgment of all men of experience & of

bodies combined with the "general will" of the population determined a course of action should be taken where the Constitution did not explicitly prohibit it, then the legislation, through time, achieved constitutional status.

In summary, Madison always viewed the Constitution as a further stabilizing force in society. He had a fairly strict constructionist view of the Constitution and how to interpret it. He did not embrace either nullification or secession by single states, but he did believe in reasonable protests and the ultimate right to revolution.[121]

What, then, are the consequences of Madisonian government? The greatest of all reflections on human nature, Madison's governmental system was designed to control nonangelic men; he designed it to regulate itself as well. The first part of the plan he based on a civil society where Hobbes's war of all against all could continue, so long as individual behavior complied with certain rules of the economic game. An enormous receptacle that could absorb the energies of these power-hungry individuals, the expanded territory helped create and maintain the balance and equilibrium Madison desired. As the population increased, therefore, so too would the need for ever more space to absorb the pressure of competing individuals and factions. Manifest destiny, signaling ruin for the Native Americans and international difficulties for England, Spain, Mexico, and Canada, helped maintain the equilibrium and hope of equal opportunity Madison believed essential to American harmony.

Control of the governed was but part of the task; the machine must also control itself. Government must be structured to maintain homeostasis. Since the legislative branch, closest to the people, was perceived to be the least stable and most risky, it had to be di-

---

intelligence, to decide which is most to be relied on for a sound and safe test of the meaning of a Constitution, a uniform interpretation by all the successive authorities under it, commencing with its birth, and continued for a long period, thro' the varied state of political contests, or the opinion of every new Legislature heated as it may be by the strife of parties, or warped as often happens by the eager pursuit of some favourite object; or carried away possibly by the powerful eloquence, or captivating address of a few popular Statesmen, themselves influenced, perhaps by the same misleading causes. If the latter test is to prevail, every new Legislative opinion might make a new Constitution; as the foot of every new Chancellor would make a new standard of measure."

121. Riemer, *Madison*, p. 97.

vided in two. The entire design of the governmental edifice pitted power against power, ambition counteracting ambition. It gave the advantage to those who wanted to keep the status quo, to stop change: if any one of the four political bodies responded negatively, political change would not occur. Those who wanted to pass legislation, consequently, would have to sustain political pressure over an extended period and must be ready to compromise if they hoped for legislative success. To Madison, inefficiency in the speed of legislative action was in itself a political good: time allowed the passions to cool and reason to control the process. For Madison, the system should always play for time, believing it would allow cooler heads to prevail. Legislative change, then, should occur in a slow and not necessarily steady manner; after all, the fundamental governmental concern remained the protection of property first and persons second.

Those who desired more than passing a law and wanted fundamental change of the Constitution itself had an even more difficult task before them as the amending procedure in Article 5 required a superdemocratic effort, over an extended period, against a system specifically structured to privilege those who wanted no change. Moreover, if the property laws were what one wanted to change, that would be virtually impossible to accomplish—except through a new constitutional convention—since, as Madison pointed out, property laws were established in each of the states and were guaranteed by the Constitution itself. Both civil society and government—established on the principle of placing power against power, faction against faction, individual against individual—achieved stability. Even then, by at least 1819 Madison could see how his system of counterpoise, designed to handle multiple factions, could not adjust to a situation where only two factions developed and, in spite of the normal cooling effects of time, remained committed in their intentions. On the Missouri question Madison queried:

> Parties under some denominations or other must always be expected in a Govt. as free as ours. When the individuals belonging to them are intermingled in every part of the whole Country, they strengthen the Union of the Whole, while they divide every part. Should a State of parties arise, founded on geographical boundaries and other Physical & permanent distinctions which

happen to coincide with them, what is to controul those great repulsive Masses from awful shocks agst. each other?[122]

The Civil War and Lincoln, not Madison and his balancing machine, would ultimately resolve this question: it created a problem Madison's system could not defuse.

In a system designed to minimize citizen participation to a public arena reduced to the tiny area required for an individual act of voting—now done in a closet—once every two years, what were the real human costs of accepting Madison's ingenious machine? While a complete answer to this vital question can be appreciated only in contrast to an alternative vision of what might have been, for the present it should be evident that Madisonian politics produced a fragmented society with no hope of fraternity, equality, or community. And though it may be based on reason and function in a rational manner, the system as a whole remains irrational nonetheless. That he banished human passion and compassion from the political arena and eventually restricted them to limited portions of the civil society as well only begins to scratch the surface of the iron cage of modern humanity. The genuine tragedy of America's choice of the rational liberal model of Madison can be appreciated more completely when his polity stands in contrast to the alternative vision America never embraced, that of the radical democracy of Thomas Jefferson.

122. JM to Robert Walsh, 27 Nov. 1819, *WJM* 9:12.

7 / Jefferson's Madison: "Frigid Speculations" or "Generous Spasms of the Heart"

In all very numerous assemblies, of whatever characters composed, passion never fails to wrest the scepter from reason. Had every Athenian citizen been a Socrates, every Athenian assembly would still have been a mob.[1]

—*Madison*

He who made us would have been a pitiful bungler if he had made the rules of our moral conduct a matter of science. For one man of science, there are thousands who are not. What would have become of them? Man was destined for society. His morality therefore was to be formed to this object. He was endowed with a sense of right and wrong merely relative to this. The sense is as much a part of his nature as the sense of hearing, seeing, feeling; it is the true foundation of morality and not the το χαλον truth, &c., as fanciful writers have imagined. The moral sense, or conscience, is as much a part of man as his leg or arm.[2]

—*Jefferson*

Of this much, there can be no dispute. Madison and Jefferson were lifelong, intimate friends who, upon Jefferson's return from France in 1789 and Madison's rupture with Alexander Hamilton in the early 1790s, renewed one of the great political alliances in American history. Perhaps no clearer testimony of Jefferson's inestimable regard for Madison can be found than that contained in his final request of him.

In failing health and languishing spirits during the winter of 1826, Jefferson wrote Madison to report on difficulties surrounding the appointment of faculty to their university. Concerned about the power-

---

1. Isaac Kramnick, ed., *The Federalist Papers* (New York: Viking Penguin, 1987), 55:336.
2. TJ to Peter Carr, 10 Aug. 1787, *The Papers of Thomas Jefferson*, ed. Julian P. Boyd, 20 vols. (Princeton, N.J.: Princeton University Press, 1950–), 12:14–15 (hereafter cited as *PTJ*).

ful influence exercised by judges and lawyers in the United States who had "slid into toryism" though they deceived themselves "to be whigs, because they no longer know what whigism or republicanism means," Jefferson hoped that the "vestal flame" of republicanism could be kept alive at the university and from there "spread anew over our own and the sister States." This letter, in fact, represented Jefferson's own passing of the vestal flame to Madison, not only on this critical issue of political education and the training of lawyers, but on the memory and reputation of Jefferson himself.

Jefferson spelled out for Madison the serious and embarrassing financial situation that currently overwhelmed him. Seeing no resolution to it, he ultimately feared the possibility of having "to sell everything" at Monticello and move "with my family, where I have not even a log hut to put my head into, and whether ground for burial, will depend on the depredations which, under the form of sales, shall have been committed on my property." Candidly, he lamented to Madison, "the question then with me was *ultrum horum*. But why afflict you with these details?" Why indeed? Although there undoubtedly existed no need for an explicit answer to the question between such close friends, Jefferson responded in language reminiscent of a letter he had written more than four decades earlier to another intimate, Maria Cosway. To Madison, he explained that he was sharing his dismal state of affairs with him because "pains are lessened by communication with a friend."[3] Jefferson fondly reflected on "the friendship which has subsisted between us, now half a century, and the harmony of our political principles and pursuits, have long been sources of constant happiness to me through that long period."[4] Jefferson closed his epistle to Madison, foretelling his own death while recalling the comfort their friendship continued to

3. Cf. TJ to Maria Cosway, 12 Oct. 1786, *PTJ* 10:445, 449.
4. The editors of the *Papers of James Madison* correctly point out that the period from about 1786 until Jefferson's return in 1789 contained some sharp exchanges and serious disagreements between the two. As the editors described in 11:282: "In their long and close relationship the differences between JM and Jefferson on fundamental political and constitutional questions were perhaps never more sharply defined than during the latter half of the 1780s. The preceding year [1787] they had disagreed over JM's proposal for a negative on state laws; during the present one they would express differing views on the necessity and efficacy of a bill of rights' and they soon would have a memorable exchange on Jefferson's proposition that 'the earth belongs to the living' " (Jefferson to JM, 20 June 1787, and JM to Jefferson, 24 Oct. 1787 [*Papers of James Madison*, ed. Wil-

provide for him in his final, less than triumphant days. In classic Jefferson prose, he wrote,

> And if I remove beyond the reach of attentions to the University, or beyond the bourne of life itself, as I soon must, it is a comfort to leave that institution under your care, and an assurance that it will not be wanting. It has also been a great solace to me, to believe that you are engaged in vindicating to posterity the course we have pursued for preserving to them, in all their purity, the blessings of self-government, which we had assisted too in acquiring for them. If ever the earth has beheld a system of administration conducted with a single and steadfast eye to the general interest and happiness of those committed to it, one which, protected by truth, can never know reproach, it is that to which our lives have been devoted. To myself you have been a pillar of support through life. Take care of me when dead, and be assured that I shall leave with you my last affections.[5]

Their personal friendship and political alliance acknowledged, it remains the major argument of this chapter that as political theorists—individuals with relatively consistent and coherent views of humanity, history, politics, and the meaning of life—Madison and Jefferson were, from an ideological perspective, worlds apart. The chapter contains as well a minor, albeit often implicit, argument. Although potent political allies during their earliest days in Virginia politics and throughout the Second Republic of the United States— once, that is, Jefferson had returned to America—the "great collaboration" in American history was not theirs, except in length of time, but the collaboration between Madison and Hamilton. Although Madison and Hamilton's alliance lasted less than a decade, what

---

liam T. Hutchinson et al., 17 vols. (Chicago and Charlottesville: University of Chicago Press and University of Virginia Press, 1962–), 10:64, 209–214 (hereafter cited as *PJM*)]; JM to Jefferson, 17 Oct. 1788; Jefferson to JM, 15 Mar., 6 Sept. 1789, and JM to Jefferson, 4 Feb. 1790 [*PTJ* 14: 659–661; 15:392–397; 16: 147–150]).

Nevertheless, when an individual is contemplating his own demise with an exceptionally close friend, such divisive recollections do not surface to add additional pain, especially when asking the friend to take care of one's reputation in the future.

5. TJ to JM, 17 Feb. 1826, *Thomas Jefferson: Writings*, ed. Merrill Peterson (New York: Library of America, 1984), pp. 1513–1514.

they accomplished together—the destruction of a constitution and a government, and the creation, ratification, and implementation of a new constitution and state—was *the* fundamental political act of founding. This act, moreover, left Jefferson and succeeding generations in such a disadvantageous political position that all they could do was tinker with the structures bequeathed to them by their fathers. Quite keenly and very personally, Jefferson felt the injustice of this loss of his rights. Consequently he left his finest legacy to his country not simply in the ideals contained in the Declaration of Independence but in the democratic ideas contained in his notion that "the earth belongs to the living."

Given the enormity of correspondence between Madison and Jefferson, it would take more than another book to present the abundant scholarly evidence to prove these claims. This book, however, is part of a project that seeks to reopen a dormant dialogue on what America might have become—and may yet achieve—if it had not been channeled into the pathways constructed by Madison, Hamilton, Marshall, and others. Consequently, I hope to persuade open-minded readers by the use of a simple model of political ideologies and two of the most extraordinary of all Jefferson letters: his 1786 "Head and Heart" letter to Maria Cosway and his 1789 "The Earth Belongs to the Living Letter" to James Madison. It would certainly not be incorrect to view this chapter as an attempt at persuasion by metaphor.[6] These metaphors are meant to suggest, to excite, to provoke, but ultimately to illuminate the categorical differences between a political theory constructed on instrumental reason and fear, where equilibrium was the *telos*, to a political theory constructed on moral sense and faith, where the ultimate goal of politics may have been less important than the process used in attempting to define and reach it.

Presenting, discussing, and examining political ideologies can all too easily become an activity where, as Madison understood well, crucial words such as republicanism, liberalism, radicalism, and democracy are used as if everyone agreed on what these complex concepts represent.[7] Indeed, humans, particularly contemporary Ameri-

---

6. See Norman O. Brown, *Love's Body* (New York: Vintage, 1966), p. 266: "Everything is only a metaphor; there is only poetry."
7. See *Federalist* 37.

cans, may be no closer to understanding these specific notions than they were in the late eighteenth and early nineteenth centuries. In an attempt to bring a higher degree of clarity to the present discussion, at least in terms of what this author means by Madisonian politics and Jeffersonian politics, paradigms of each are presented.[8] Undoubtedly, neither Madison nor Jefferson ever held anything remotely resembling this sharp and analytic a model of their own ideas: individuals who are building empires or dreaming of revolutions have little time for such armchair intellectualizing. In a certain sense, we probably know these thinkers better than they knew themselves. The paradigms are intended to be metaphoric and heuristic devices that will assist in the sweeping discussion that follows by more clearly demarcating the philosophic gulf that separated Madison from Jefferson.

Madisonian Liberalism	*Jeffersonian Democracy*
reason (the head)	moral sense (the heart)
equality (of opportunity)	equality (of moral sense)
individualism (A-partness)	individualism (social individuality)
rights (property teleological)	rights (property instrumental)
politics (minimum participation)	politics (maximum participation)
liberty (secondary to authority)	liberty (more important than authority)
future (decay and fear)	future (development and faith)

Once the discussion proceeds beyond the obvious observations that both thinkers believed in reason, both knew politics was inevitable, both fought for rights and valued liberty, it will become evident that on each of these seven points of comparison, Madison and Jefferson held rather divergent viewpoints. What each saw as the role of reason, the scope and value of politics, the nature and hierarchy of rights, the essence of humanity, and the promise of the future remained altogether different: they operated from inside two rather distinct philosophic universes where Madisonian pragmatism supplied the theoretical complement to Jeffersonian idealism.

8. For this approach I am, in general, indebted to C. B. Macpherson's pioneering work in *The Political Theory of Possessive Individualism: Hobbes to Locke* (Oxford: Clarendon Press, 1962), and *The Life and Times of Liberal Democracy* (Oxford: Oxford University Press, 1977); and, in particular, I am indebted to Asher and Gad Horowitz, *"Everywhere They Are in Chains": Political Theory from Rousseau to Marx* (Nelson, Canada: Scarborough House, 1988), pp. 1-14.

It makes sense to begin by summarizing Madison's politics as detailed throughout the book and as presented in the paradigm. Reason can be seen as the thread that connects and intertwines the other six characteristics. Modern, narrow, instrumental reason—not the global Reason of a Plato or a Hegel—was the species-specific faculty that permitted humans to build political systems that, in spite of their nonangelic and nonphilosophic disposition, allowed them to live together. Of course, while the political life they shared avoided anarchy neither did it permit humans to enjoy genuine peace. Reason and merit, moreover, were to determine an individual's place in civil society in contrast to the older Tory view in which hierarchy and place were determined by birth, or tradition. Jefferson, in contrast, also believed reason constituted a uniquely human attribute, though he never believed that all humans possessed this capacity in anything approaching equal terms. What remains significant, however, is that Jefferson believed reason should play a secondary role in politics. Moral sense (the heart), not reason (the head), was what made politics and community possible. Furthermore, although Jefferson believed some individuals lacked the capacity to reason on a fully human level, all people were nevertheless equal in that they possessed a moral sense and therefore must be allowed to participate in politics.[9]

The issue of equality of opportunity in a developing commercial society concerned Madison from his earliest legislative days. With a world he perceived to be designed to close around them, few modern nations would continue to have rich opportunities and most would witness their chances for advancement diminish to the point where even hope would disappear.[10] Madison consistently maintained that humans were equally nonangelic. Unlike some who thought politics

9. See Richard K. Matthews, *The Radical Politics of Thomas Jefferson* (Lawrence: University Press of Kansas, 1986), 53–75; TJ to Peter Carr, 10 Aug. 1787, *PTJ* 12:14–15; TJ to Maria Cosway, 12 Oct. 1786, *PTJ* 10:443–452; TJ to John Adams, 14 Oct. 1816, *Adams-Jefferson Letters*, ed. Lester Cappon (New York: Simon & Schuster, 1971), p. 492; *Notes on the State of Virginia*, ed. William Peden (New York: W. W. Norton, 1792), pp. 138, 142–143, passim; TJ to the Marquis de Condorcet, 30 Aug. 1791, *The Works of Thomas Jefferson*, ed. Paul Leicester Ford, 12 vols. (New York: Knickerbocker Press, 1904), 6:311; TJ to Benjamin Banneker, 30 Aug. 1791, *Works of TJ* 6:309–310; TJ to Henri Grégoire, 25 Feb. 1809, *Works of TJ* 11:100; TJ to David Rittenhouse, 19 July 1778, *Works of TJ* 2:345.

10. For both Madison and Jefferson, education provided a support not only to creating an enlightened citizenry, but to assist in providing those with better

a simple matter of getting the right sort of people into office, Madison knew that even the noblest aristocracy, one composed totally of Socrateses, would have to be checked: humans are not gentle creatures. Even as few as three would find it impossible to live justly together in a state of nature. For Jefferson, in contrast, equality resulted from humanity's moral sense. Since all humans had this capacity, although like any human sense it could remain underdeveloped, alienated, or on rare occasion absent, they were equally capable of making moral and political decisions. All humans, then, had to be free. Slavery constituted an abomination. Equality of opportunity, which for Jefferson meant the chance for individuals and generations to make the world anew, remained so critical to leading a meaningful life that he would willingly risk past success to maintain future freedom. In the following discussion of Jefferson's design for institutionalized revolution it will become self-evident why Madison's obsessive fear of the future was simply nonexistent for Jefferson.

Madison thought that individuals were timid and cautious creatures. Their psychological disposition and the sociological realities of commercial society always forced individuals to join groups either out of a desire to pursue their own interests, to protect their interests, or often both. Madison's liberalism accepted, because it could only see, the atomization, the *a-partness*, of the human condition in civil society. He conceived of people as separate beings with no natural connection to each other; yet he could not—in fact, he never felt the need to—explain why a group of good individuals like Socrates, if not restrained, would inevitably turn into a mob. Thus, one of the principal premises of Madison's entire theoretical edifice rests on an unchallenged philosophic assumption not grounded in reason.[11]

---

minds, regardless of economic circumstances, an equal opportunity to be educated. However, it would take many decades before this idea would fully mature in the United States.

11. Cf. TJ to JM, 28 Aug. 1789, *Works of TJ* 5:492, where Jefferson wrote: "I know but one code of morality for men whether acting singly or collectively. He who says I will be a rogue when I act in company with a hundred others but an honest man when I act alone, will be believed in the former assertion, but not in the latter. I would say with the poet, '*hic niger est, hunc tu Romane cavato*. If the morality of one man produces a just line of conduct in him, acting individually, why should not the morality of 100 men produce a just line of conduct in them, acting together?''

Given the centrality of this concept of individual *a-partness* to Madison's thinking, it needs further elucidation. In premodern societies, humans conceived of themselves as part of some greater, organic community where all members of the community, from the king to the pauper, were linked in meaningful social and political ways. For a member of the community to perceive himself or herself as separate or autonomous from the whole was considered an aberration to be treated and healed.[12] Born into a universe of self-made Lockean Virginians, Madison never experienced this world of Tory values and norms. He viewed individuals as separate parts of a state, not members of a human family or community. Though it might be difficult to conceive of Madison explicitly celebrating human "a-partness"—human autonomy—he accepted this radical individualist view of the universe as natural. Viewing himself in the Cartesian absolutism of *Je pense, donc je suis*, Madison had no choice but to view others as limitations of, and threats to, self.

Beginning from a fundamentally different premise, Jefferson conceived of humans as inherently social beings. Humans needed others not merely to make existence possible, but to make life meaningful.[13] The Indian communities supplied him with empirical evidence to support his position that, under the appropriate conditions, there would be no need for a state. In fact, these value-coordinated, harmonious communities functioned as a kind of Platonic ideal in Jefferson's political theory. While Americans, because of population and advancement, could never achieve the level of harmony enjoyed by the Native Americans, the attempt at the absolute minimization of government remained the utopian goal toward which the philo-

12. See Horowitz and Horowitz, *Chains*, pp. 1–14; on p. 2 they use the following example: "Autonomy of the parts is identified with some sort of disease of the entire body. Society makes a systematic effort to not see it, or to deny experiencing it; all manifestations of it are condemned and suppressed. In the language of political theory, this can be put in terms of authority and obedience: your arm, a subordinate part, cannot consult with your brain, offer suggestions, or rebel; it does what your brain tells it—it obeys."

13. TJ to John Adams, 14 Oct. 1816, *Adams-Jefferson Letters*, p. 492; TJ to Francis W. Gilmer, 7 June 1816, *The Writings of Thomas Jefferson*, ed. Albert Ellery Bergh, 20 vols.(Washington: Thomas Jefferson Memorial Association, 1903–1904), 15:24–25; TJ to Thomas Law, 13 June 1814, *Writings of TJ* (Bergh) 14:142; TJ to James Fishback, 27 Sept. 1809, *Writings of TJ* (Bergh) 12:315.

sophic Jefferson always aimed.[14] This end, however, must not be confused with a diminution of politics because both the scope and arenas of politics would expand in the Jeffersonian ideal.

Rights, natural as well as civil, were central to both thinkers. From Madison's perspective, property was the nucleus around which all other rights and goals revolved. At different moments he championed religious freedom and freedom of the press. Once the immediate threat to their autonomy had been vanquished, he moved on to other concerns. The protection of the institution of property never left his mind, because in his worldview it would always and inevitably be under attack. In spite of the rhetoric in his "Property" essay, in which he momentarily argued that an individual had "a property in his rights" that was more equal than his "right to his property," he failed to develop this notion knowing that doing so would require alteration of his bourgeois notion of property.[15] To Jefferson, property also possessed critical import; and yet, as the discussion of his "Earth Belongs to the Living" letter will manifest, his view of it became radically democratic. For the moment, suffice it to say that Jefferson, contra Locke and Madison, never believed in an individual, natural property right while he did argue for a *natural, generational right* constructed around a notion of property as a right for all humans to be the moral agents of their own political and economic lives.

As an Enlightenment liberal whose god was reason, Madison viewed politics as a necessary evil that had to be accepted as part of the mechanism by which humans made collective decisions. Nevertheless, he viewed politics as a dangerous exercise since it always stirred the unpredictable human passions. Only under the appropriate conditions could politics be counted on to reach rational conclusions. If an immortal philosopher-king had been a possible alternative, Madison would have had no philosophic objections to the idea; rather, he would have merely appreciated the political impossibility of its acceptance.[16] More importantly, it seems entirely appropriate to view Madison's complete socio-economic-political system as pre-

14. *Notes on the State of Virginia*, ed. William Peden (New York: W. W. Norton, 1972), p. 93, passim; TJ to Edward Carrington, 16 Jan. 1787, *PTJ* 11:49; TJ to James Madison, 30 Jan. 1787, *PTJ* 11:92–93.

15. JM, "Property," *National Gazette*, 27 Mar. 1792, *PJM* 14:266–268.

16. *Federalist* 49:314.

cisely that: the closest human construct for a philosopher-*machine*, designed to produce rational solutions to human problems across time. Politics, then, remained an evil necessity humans had to engage in to protect themselves, since people would try to use politics to their own, selfish advantage. However, by forcing citizens to work their way through a political system that had been structurally designed to favor the status quo and to play for time, Madison believed the chances for rational solutions would be increased while the opportunities for hasty and disastrous actions would be minimized.

Jefferson, on the other hand, conceived of citizenship as an ennobling activity. Humans had both a right and a duty to participate in politics. Since every person had a moral sense, every person should be capable of not only governing his or her own life, but also of participating in the public arena. Along these lines, Jefferson viewed the local ward-republics as the specific arena in which humans could, in part, achieve their humanity. As expressed to Joseph C. Cabell in a February of 1816 letter, Jefferson stated:

> The elementary republics of the wards, the county republics, the State republics, and the republic of the Union, would form a graduation of authorities, standing each on the basis of law, holding every one its delegated share of powers, and constituting truly a system of fundamental balances and checks for the government. Where every man is a sharer in the direction of his ward-republic, or of some of the higher ones, and feels that he is a participator in the government of affairs, not merely at an election one day in the year, but every day; when there shall not be a man in the State who will not be a member of some one of its councils, great or small, he will let the heart be torn out of his body sooner than his power be wrested from him by a Caesar or a Bonaparte.[17]

Where Jefferson wanted citizens involved in politics as a matter of their daily affairs, Madison designed a system that asked them, once every two years, to pick men of superior ability. Then they were to return to their private lives.[18]

Like the other postulates in the ideology paradigm, there is no dis-

17. TJ to Joseph C. Cabell, 2 Feb. 1816, *Writings of TJ* (Bergh), 6:543–544.
18. *Federalist*, passim; and *National Gazette Essays*, passim.

puting the fact that liberty was a cardinal value for each thinker. Be that as it may, where Madison always thought in terms of balance—adjusting authority and liberty so that his seesaw rested in stasis—Jefferson always thought in terms of liberty being so vital to life, to humanity, that he was willing to risk life and liberty itself to enjoy and maintain it. He put it most forcefully in a 1793 letter to William Short discussing the excesses of the French Revolution and the price of liberty: "The liberty of the whole earth was depending on the issue of the contest, and was ever such a prize won with so little innocent blood? My own affections have been deeply wounded by some of the martyrs to this cause, but rather than it should have failed, I would have seen half the earth desolated." To further dramatize his position Jefferson wrote, "Were there but an Adam & an Eve left in every country, & left free, it would be better than it now is."[19] This view of the primacy of liberty remains closely linked with Jefferson's hopes for the future, as well as Madison's fear of it. It explains furthermore how the latter desired an empire of reason, the former an empire of liberty.

A Malthusian before Malthus, Madison perceived a Calvinist universe that, in the long run, would fail. Accepting that failure as a given, he constructed a political system that would postpone the inevitable decay for as long as reason would allow. His legacy, however, would someday be unable to control the natural forces of change. In the short run, Madison could look west from the porch at Montpelier and revel in the time that the free land would buy his brilliant self-balancing machine; yet in the long run, he knew his dream had been founded on sands of time that would eventually bury all his best efforts. Such was the human condition. Even after living a life adorned with incredible achievements but also scarred deeply by human tragedy, Jefferson looked on the future as an opportunity to be embraced, a chance to begin the world anew.[20] Characteristically he expressed this view in a letter to John Adams in 1816, "I like the dreams of the future better than the history of the past."[21] Given his

19. TJ to William Short, 3 Jan. 1793, *Jefferson: Writings* (Peterson), p. 1004.
20. The final letter to Madison indicates that Jefferson was less than optimistic about his future. Nevertheless, he had been aware of his disastrous financial situation for years, and it failed to distort his views of the future.
21. TJ to John Adams, 1 Aug. 1816, *Adams-Jefferson Letters*, p. 485.

glorious role in the past, and his diminishing influence on the present and future, these words were remarkable indeed.

This modest defense and brief explanation of the ideological models will be supported by an extended interpretative discussion of two of Jefferson's most extraordinary letters.[22] Their impact on American politics has been virtually nil; and given their potential meaning, their insignificance itself explains a large part of our history and the role of scholars in keeping the myth of the great collaboration of Jefferson and Madison alive. Still, as one student of American political thought has noted well, "To restore the past is, perhaps, to recover the future."[23]

In October of 1786 Jefferson bid farewell to Maria Cosway, a young artist with whom, to put it mildly, he seemed smitten. He had just spent several glorious days showing her (and her husband) the sights of Paris. Jefferson's wife had perished four years earlier, and by all accounts, he missed her sorely. In love with Cosway, Jefferson sat down to record for her his innermost thoughts and feelings about her after performing "the last sad office of handing you into your carriage at the pavilion de St. Denis" for her return voyage to England. Although it is clearly a letter of seduction intended to convince Cosway to visit Jefferson again, preferably in the United States, its political insights remain highly significant.

This exceptional letter, constructed in the form of a dialogue between Jefferson's Head and his Heart, offers a rare glimpse into this private man's soul. Written at a moment of human frailty and vulnerability, it permits the reader a unique vantage point into Jefferson's thoughts on politics and life. In the context of this discussion it serves as a symbolic representation of much of what separated Jeffersonian from Madisonian politics. Although Jefferson wrote both parts of the dialogue, the Head symbolized science, reason, the avoidance of pain—and Madisonian politics; the Heart represented politics, the moral sense, the pursuit of happiness—and Jeffersonian politics. Furthermore, the Heart represented not only an essential dimension of Jef-

22. Although the interpretation is significantly expanded here, readers familiar with the discussion of the Cosway Head/Heart letter in my *Radical Politics of Thomas Jefferson* may prefer to move directly to the analysis of the second Jefferson letter on "The Earth Belongs to the Living."

23. Wilson Carey McWilliams, *The Idea of Fraternity in America* (Berkeley: University of California Press, 1973), p. x.

ferson's politics, it presented—to borrow a phrase and an ideal from Carol Gilligan's powerful book—the possibility of a politics "in a different voice."[24] Perhaps more significantly, textual evidence indicates that, at some level of his unguarded soul, Jefferson directly equated Madison with the Head. In the final sentence of the dialogue, the Heart promised to keep the Head informed on appropriate material from "Condorcet, Rittenhouse, Madison, La Crettelle, or any other of those worthy *sons of science* whom you so justly prize."[25]

Setting the emotional stage for the dialogue that followed, Jefferson described his actions after watching his love depart. "I turned on my heel & walked, more dead than alive," to the carriage into which he, along with a Mr. Danquerville, "were crammed . . . like recruits for the Bastile, & not having soul enough to give orders to the coachman, he presumed Paris our destination." After depositing Danquerville at his residence, Jefferson proceeded to his. There, "seated by my fireside, solitary & sad, the following dialogue took place between my Head & my Heart."

Speaking first and attempting to exert his authority, the Head admonished the Heart: "Well, friend, you seem to be in a pretty trim." The Heart, capable of feeling the gravity of the situation, articulated more fully the depth of her despair. "I am indeed the most wretched of all earthly beings," she exclaimed. "Overwhelmed with grief," she continued, "every fibre of my frame distended beyond its natural powers to bear, I would willingly meet whatever catastrophe should leave me no more to feel or to fear."

The Head, thinking he had the upper hand because of the emotional distress of the Heart, again lectured her that "these are the eternal consequences of your warmth & precipitation. This is one of the scrapes into which you are ever leading us." The Heart, not wanting an "I told you so" lesson, interrupted the Head, suggesting "this is no moment

24. Carol Gilligan, *In a Different Voice* (Cambridge, Mass.: Harvard University Press, 1982), p. 2; she notes that "the different voice . . . is characterized not by gender but theme." On p. 73 she writes: "Women's construction of the moral problem as a problem of care and responsibility in relationships rather than as one of rights and rules ties the development of their moral thinking to changes in their understanding of responsibility and relationships, just as the conception of morality as justice ties development to the logic of equality and reciprocity. Thus the logic underlying an ethic of care is a psychological logic of relationships, which contrasts with the formal logic of fairness that informs the justice approach."
25. TJ to Maria Cosway, 12 Oct. 1786, *PTJ* 10:452; emphasis added.

to upbraid my foibles. I am rent into fragments by the force of my grief! If you have any balm, pour it into my wounds; if none, do not harrow them by new torments.'' Without the capacity to feel what might constitute an appropriate oil for the Heart's scars, the instrumentally rational Head pressed on to seize the moment to make his logical point. Refusing to listen to the Heart (who wanted a ''discussion'' with the Head, while the Head wanted to ''lecture'' the Heart), the Head responded that ''on the contrary I never found that the moment of triumph with you was the moment of attention to my admonition. While suffering under your follies, you may perhaps be made sensible of them, but, the paradoxysm over, you fancy it can never return.'' The Head, showing how politics was never far from Jefferson's mind, explained that ''harsh therefore as the medicine may be, it is my office to administer it.'' The Head returned to the lecture style, reminding the Heart that he had warned her of the inherent danger in all friendships because of ''the regret at parting.''

Demonstrating that in spite of the emotional distress she was fully capable of both remembering the past and rational discourse, the Heart corrected the Head on the precise history by which they had arrived at their present emotional situation. According to her memory, it had been the Head that ''desired the meeting at Legrand & Molinois. I never trouble myself with domes nor arches. The *Halle aux bleds* might have rotted down before I should have gone to see it.'' The Heart, caught up in the reverie of that moment, subtly switched the objects of her attention from ''this wonderful piece of architecture'' to ''the lady''—whom, once he had seen her, Jefferson considered ''the most superb thing on earth!'' Returning to the real concerns of the Head, the Heart corrected his version of history: ''You then, Sir, & not I, have been the cause of the present distress.'' As Jefferson made explicitly clear, the Head, in addition to rational thought, possessed the capacities for falsification and rationalization.

On public utility grounds, the Head justified the visit as an information-gathering expedition since ''a market is to be built in Richmond'' and ''a bridge as they shewed us can be thrown across the Schuylkill in Philadelphia,'' not to mention the trickle-down benefits of such civic activities in terms of providing ''wood & provisions, to warm & feed the poor of that city.'' This demonstrated that just as the Heart could think, so too could the Head have a sense of compassion—although it developed as the last thought that crossed its frontier. The Head then counterattacked. It challenged the Heart's recollection of the day by again reminding her that while the Head was fulfilling his public obligations, "you were dilating with your new acquaintances, & contriving how to prevent a separation from them." In a telling passage, the Head upbraided the Heart for dispatching "lying messengers . . . into every quarter of the city" so that Jefferson could spend more time with Cosway. Perhaps more revealingly still, the Head acted insulted: the Heart "wanted me to invent a more ingenious excuse; but I knew you were getting into a scrape, & I would have nothing to do with it."[26] Note well: the Head admitted he possessed the ability to invent a better lie, but since his primary function was to protect self-interest narrowly defined, he refused to do so. The critical significance of the automatic functioning of the Head in terms of protection of the self and its minor position in politics will be made evident when Jefferson turns to the relationship between morality and politics.

Patiently listening to, and reveling in, the Head's history sermon, the Heart responded: "Oh! my dear friend, how you have revived me by recalling to my mind the transactions of that day! How well I remember them all, & that when I came home at night & looked back to the morning, it seemed to have been a month agone. Go on then, like a kind comforter & paint to me the day we went to St. Germains. How beautiful was every object!" Jefferson's Heart refused to listen to the Head's reason. While the Head provided him with words containing sound, prudential, rational advice, his Heart heard in these words comforting memory traces and a *raison d'être*.

At this juncture in the dialogue, the Head demonstrated his exasperation, complaining:

Thou art the most incorrigible of all the beings that ever sinned! I reminded you of the follies of the first day, intending to deduce from thence some useful lessons for you, but instead of listening to these, you kindle at the recollection, you retrace the whole series with a fondness which shews you want nothing but the opportunity to act it over again. I often told you during its course that you were imprudently engaging your affections under circumstances that must have cost you a great deal of pain:

26. Ibid., 10:444-445.

that the persons indeed were of the greatest merit, possessing good sense, good humour, honest hearts, honest manners, & eminence in a lovely art; that the lady had moreover qualities & accomplishments, belonging to her sex, which might form a chapter apart for her: such as music, modesty, beauty, & that softness of disposition which is the ornament of her sex & charm of ours, but that all these considerations would increase the pang of separation: that their stay here was to be short: that you rack our whole system when you are parted from those you love, complaining that such a separation is worse than death, inasmuch as this ends our sufferings, whereas that only begins them: & that the separation would in this instance be the more severe as you would probably never see them again.[27]

Implicitly here, explicitly later, the avoidance of pain constituted the Head's idea of happiness; moreover, the avoidance of others— since they could not be controlled by the self—was the basis for a rational life plan constructed on the premise of minimizing costs. Note also that while the Head has some minor conception of sin, it seems to be of little concern to the Heart. Indeed, the politics of sin and corruption constitutes the soul of Madison's system. It appears to have had virtually no place in Jefferson's.

After a brief, sharp exchange on the probability of Jefferson ever seeing Maria again, the Heart constructed a fantasy, inside of which was a thinly veiled plea for Maria to leave her husband and join Jefferson in Virginia. Imagining alternatives to the Cosways returning to France, Jefferson reflected on all the beautiful sights for a young artist in the United States. From the "Cascade of Niagara" to "the Natural bridge" and "our own dear Monticello," Jefferson assured her "it is worth a voyage across the Atlantic to see these objects; much more to paint, and make them, & thereby ourselves, known to all ages." If aesthetic considerations proved insufficient by themselves to move Maria, the Heart then boldly wrote:

I hope in God no circumstance may ever make either seek an asylum from grief! With what sincere sympathy I would open every cell of my composition to receive the effusion of their

27. Ibid., 10:446.

woes! I would pour my tears into their wounds: & if a drop of balm could be found on the top of the Cordilleras, or at the remotest sources of the Missouri, I would go thither myself to seek & to bring it. Deeply practised in the school of affliction, the human heart knows no joy which I have not lost, no sorrow of which I have not drunk! Fortune can present no grief of unknown form to me! Who then can so softly bind up the wound of another as he who has felt the same wound himself?[28]

Unfortunately for Jefferson, Maria never took him up on his offer; fortunately for him, neither did her husband. This passage, nevertheless, provided a crucial Jeffersonian insight that he explicitly built upon in his "Earth Belongs to the Living" letter. Jefferson's Heart, touched by tragedy on several occasions, knew well that perhaps the sole virtue of an individual's personal hell was that humans need not be lonely there: tragedy is part of the human condition, and sharing the experience can help begin the healing. His subsequent reveries also indicated that perhaps a flaw in liberal paradise was that the individual may indeed be lonely there: so few can even envision it, and fewer still—thanks to the domineering logic of the Head— seem willing to take the risks required to taste it.

After another brief and heated exchange over the false image Europeans had of a barbaric America, the Head tried to reassert control of the "lecture": "Let us return then to our point. I wish to make you sensible how imprudent it is to place your affections, without reserve, on objects you must so soon lose." At this point, the Head lectured the Heart on the correct behavioral norms for living a rational life.

In fine, my friend, you must mend your manners. This is not a world to live at random in as you do. To avoid those eternal distresses, to which you are forever exposing us, you must learn to look forward before you take a step which may interest our peace. Everything in this world is a matter of calculation. Advance then with caution, the balance in your hand. Put into one scale the pleasures which any object may offer; but put fairly

28. Ibid., 10:447.

into the other the pains which are to follow, & see which preponderates.[29]

A master of rational-choice calculation, this accountant mentality continued. He advised the Heart that when "making an acquaintance" never forget to examine the "advantages" as well as to what "inconveniences it may expose you. Do not bite at the bait of pleasure till you know there is no hook beneath it." Then, in words that could have been lifted directly from Sigmund Freud's *Civilization and Its Discontents*, the Head told the Heart the secret of living a successful life: "The art of life is the art of avoiding pain: & he is the best pilot who steers clearest of the rocks & shoals with which he is beset. Pleasure is always before us; but misfortune is at our side: while running after that, this arrests us." The Head equated avoiding pain with the pursuit of happiness. And, in a narrow sense, that's true. This still did not capture the Heart's conception of happiness. Consequently, the Head did not let up on his sermonizing:

> The most effectual means of being secure against pain is to retire within ourselves, & to suffice for our own happiness. Those, which depend on ourselves, are the only pleasures a wise man will count on: for nothing is ours which another may deprive us of. Hence the inestimable value of intellectual pleasures. Even in our power, always leading us to something new, never cloying, we ride serene & sublime above the concerns of this mortal world, contemplating truth & nature, matter & motion, the laws which bind up their existence, & that eternal being who made & bound them up by those laws. Let this be our employ. Leave the bustle & tumult of society to those who have not talents to occupy themselves without them.[30]

This expresses the liberal's dream, life without others—except those the individual can control—and preference for concrete things (like property) and abstract ideas since neither have a will of their own. The Head, concluding its part of the entire dialogue, returned to its original diatribe against "friendship"—"another name for an alliance with the follies & the misfortunes of others." Given the na-

29. Ibid., 10:448
30. Ibid., 10:449.

ture of the Head's reality, it appeared to urge the avoidance of friend-ship: "Our own share of miseries is sufficient: why enter then as volunteers into those of another." Then clearly recalling Jefferson's own personal hell, the Head's last line tortured the Heart by recol-lecting the deep torment of losing "a child, a parent, or a partner: we must mourn the loss as if it were our own."

Intuitively knowing that the personal and the political were criti-cally intertwined, the Heart tenderly corrected the Head on its dis-torted view of human relationships. Then the Heart moved on to an extended discussion of her domain of expertise. "What more sub-lime delight than to mingle tears with one whom the hand of heaven hath smitten!" Although the Heart appreciated the reality princi-ple—"this world abounds indeed with misery"—its solution was not withdrawal into self but "to lighten" misery's "burden" by shar-ing it with others. Demonstrating her ability to play the Head's ra-tional-calculus game, the Heart argued:

> But let us now try the virtues of your mathematical balance, & as you have put into one scale the burthen of friendship, let me put it's comforts into the other. When languishing then under disease, how grateful is the solace of our friends! how are we penetrated with their assiduities & attentions! how much are we supported by their encouragements & kind offices! When heaven has taken from us some object of our love, how sweet is it to have a bosom whereon to recline our heads, & into which we may pour the torrent of our tears! Grief, with such a com-fort, is almost a luxury![31]

Not only did the Heart make it plain that she was addressing "your mathematical balance," she demonstrated that by its own logic, if the Head could conceive of anything beyond the protection of the self from pain, it would realize that it too would come down in favor of friendship.

The Heart, continuing to correct the Head's worldview, showed how by the Head's own utilitarian logic its arguments failed. "In a life where we are perpetually exposed to want & accident, yours is a wonderful proposition, to insulate ourselves, to retire from all aid, &

31. Ibid.

to wrap ourselves in the mantle of self-sufficiency! For assuredly nobody will care for him who cares for nobody. But friendship is precious, not only in the shade but in the sunshine of life; & thanks to a benevolent arrangement of things, the greater part of life is sunshine."[32] If the Head followed its own logic to its extreme conclusion, when he most needed help he would be alone. Fortunately for the Head and a wise, benevolent arrangement of the universe, the Heart could be his friend if he would but listen.

The Heart then painted for the Head a pitiful picture of what the Head mistook for paradise. "Let the gloomy monk, sequestered from the world, seek unsocial pleasures in the bottom of his cell! Let the sublimated philosopher grasp visionary happiness while pursuing phantoms dressed in the garb of truth! Their supreme wisdom is supreme folly; & they mistake for happiness the mere absence of pain."[33] Cutting to the heart of their differences, she told the Head that if either the monk or the philosopher had "ever felt the solid pleasure of one generous spasm of the heart, they would exchange for it all the frigid speculations of their lives." Indeed, mistaking the mere absence of pain for happiness, the Head's paradise would be as lonely as it was frigid. Yet in the world of the Heart, her hell would be neither lonely nor cold.

Not content to rest after exposing the absurdity of the Head's logic, the Heart rejected the Head's view as well as his claim to have any authority whatsoever in the domain of politics. It "is a miserable arithmetic," she responded, "which could estimate friendship at nothing, or at less than nothing." Having said this, she then separated herself from his universe: "Respect for you has induced me to enter into this discussion, & to hear principles uttered which I detest & abjure." Pushed to the limits of her patience, the Heart now proceeded to banish the Head to his appropriate kingdom—science.

"Respect for myself now obliges me to recall you into the proper limits of your office," admonished the Heart. Explaining the nature of the universe from her perspective, she told the Head:

When nature assigned us the same habitation, she gave us over it a divided empire. To you she allotted the field of science; to me that of morals. When the circle is to be squared, or the orbit

32. Ibid., 10:449–450.
33. Ibid., 10:450.

of a comet to be traced; when the arch of greatest strength, or the solid of least resistance is to be investigated, take up the problem; it is yours; nature has given me no cognizance of it. In like manner, in denying to you the feelings of sympathy, of benevolence, of gratitude, of justice, of love, of friendship, she has excluded you from their controul. To these she has adapted the mechanism of the heart. Morals were too essential to the happiness of man to be risked on the incertain combinations of the head.[34]

A radical democrat who nevertheless held his own prejudices on the intellectual differences among humans, Jefferson believed that in their ability to make correct moral choices, all humans had been created equal.[35] As the Heart stated it, since morality remained so "essential to the happiness of man . . . she laid their foundation therefore in sentiment, not in science. That she gave to all, as necessary to all: this to a few only, as sufficing with a few."

In one of the most telling passages of the entire dialogue, the Heart demonstrated just how insightful and strong she could be: "I know indeed that you pretend authority to the sovereign control of our conduct in all its parts." The Heart, echoing the pattern of the Head in using memory to assist in her argument, recalled "a few facts" that "will suffice to prove to you that nature has not organized you for our moral direction." The Heart retrieved two specific episodes from the past when Jefferson behaved immorally. The first involved a soldier who had "begged" Jefferson for a ride in his "chariot"; naturally, the Head instantly "began to calculate that the road was full of soldiers, & that if all should be taken up our horses would fail in their journey." Jefferson left the individual stranded and continued on his way. "But soon becoming sensible you had made me do wrong," he turned around in hopes of providing a ride for the man. Failing to locate him, Jefferson lamented his inability "to ask his forgiveness." The second incident involved a "poor woman" who, when she asked "a charity in Philadelphia, you whispered that she looked like a drunkard, & that half a dollar was enough to give her for the ale-house." When Jefferson regained his moral sense, this time he found his victim and rectified the injustice. The Heart

34. Ibid.
35. See Matthews, *Radical Politics*, pp. 71–75.

moreover reminded the Head of its council prior to the Revolutionary War.

> If our country, when pressed with wrongs at the point of the bayonet, had been governed by it's heads instead of it's hearts, where should we have been now? Hanging on a gallows as high as Haman's. You began to calculate & to compare wealth and numbers: we threw up a few pulsations of our warmest blood; we supplied enthusiasm against wealth and numbers; we put our existence to the hazard when the hazard seemed against us, and we saved our country: justifying at the same time the ways of Providence, whose precept is to do always what is right, and leave the issue to him.[36]

As well she should, Jefferson's Heart understood that the Head, by design, automatically calculated what would protect the self, save it from pain, and then, perhaps more importantly, attempt to rationalize its behavior in the name of either justice or morality. Still, the Heart would have none of it: she could peer through the mental gymnastics. "In short, my friend, as far as my recollection serves me, I do not know that I ever did a good thing on your suggestion, or a dirty one without it." Having said this, the Heart banished the Head from politics: "I do forever then disclaim your interference in my province."[37]

In this extraordinary letter can be seen the beginning of Jefferson's unique view of politics as well as his own implicit view of Madison. To Jefferson, humans were social, moral, political creatures who, possessing the moral sense of "The Heart," were all equally capable of self-government. Politics should not be built on an empire of reason, on "frigid speculations"; rather it had to be constructed on moral sentiment, on "generous spasms of the heart." As far apart as Jefferson and Madison were on their conceptions of the universe and the nature of humanity as implicit in the Cosway letter, the ultimate division can be explicitly seen in their direct exchange of letters on Jefferson's idea that "the earth belongs to the living."

The critical, explicit differences between Madison's and Jefferson's political theories never presented themselves more sharply than in

36. TJ to Maria Cosway, 12 Oct. 1786, *PTJ* 10:450–451.
37. Ibid., 10:451.

an exchange of letters in late 1789 and early 1790. Written in Paris, but carried by Jefferson back to the United States to assure its safe passage, Jefferson's letter presented for Madison's keen intellect "a question of such consequences as not only to merit decision, but place also, among the fundamental principles of every government." While Jefferson suggested the ingenious question arose as the inevitable result of "the course of reflection in which we are immersed here on the elementary principles of society," there can be little doubt that he simultaneously recalled the fact that his attendance had not been requested at the Philadelphia convention and that the new government in the United States was enjoying its genesis.

Like other momentous questions in political theory, Jefferson's imaginative query appeared deceptively simple: "whether one generation of men has a right to bind another." Claiming this particular issue seemed "never to have been started either on this or our side of the water," Jefferson preceded the specifics of his argument by stating the conclusion: "No such obligation can be so transmitted. . . . I set out on this ground which I suppose, to be self-evident, '*that the earth belongs in usufruct to the living;*' that the dead have neither powers nor rights over it."[38] That Jefferson thought his truth, like the other natural-right truths contained in the Declaration of Independence, was self-evident and that Madison did not indicates the vast differences in their fundamental political ideas. The full expression of this difference, perhaps Jefferson's most radical notion, must be fully described.

Starting with an individual's right to inherit property from others, Jefferson explained that "the child, the legatee or creditor takes it, not by any natural right, but by a law of the society." Conversely, he asserted, "no man can by *natural right* oblige the lands he occupied, or the persons who succeeded him in that occupation, to the paiment of debts contracted by him." Jefferson's logic centered around the term *usufruct*. It emphasizes the essence of the relationship between humans and the earth as being that of a trust, a guardianship, where the future takes priority over the present or past. The doctrine of usufruct deprived the dead of legitimate power over the living. Thus, implicitly, it requires the existence of ancestors and a notion of inheritance without material encumbrance from the past as well

38. TJ to JM, 6 Sept. 1789, *PTJ* 15:392.

as a duty to pass the inheritance along to the next generation in at least as good a condition.

In light of Jefferson's extensive knowledge of Native Americans, it may be no small coincidence that at this time only Native Americans would have held a similar view of the earth and its fruits, although this potentially radical notion can also be found in Locke.[39] If an individual had complete and ongoing control over his property, "he might during his own life, eat up the usufruct of the lands for several generations to come, and then the lands would belong to the dead, and not to the living." As implicit in the silence of the Declaration of Independence, Jefferson never believed in an individual, natural property right. Property was a civil and instrumental right; while it remained significant to economic and political freedom and therein to the pursuit of happiness, property still existed as a means, not an end.

Shifting from the right of an individual to the rights of a generation, Jefferson's heart led him to conclusions of radical proportion. Using an intellectual fiction not unlike that of the prior state-of-nature theorists Hobbes, Locke, and Rousseau, Jefferson imaginatively reframed his question with the words "let us suppose a whole generation of men to be born on the same day, to attain mature age on the same day, and to die on the same day, leaving a succeeding generation in the moment of attaining their mature age all together." Obviously, Jefferson knew this situation never could happen; rather, he suggested to Madison, in order "to keep our ideas clear," that he conceive of Jefferson's ideas as if this could be the case. He originally calculated the life of a generation to be thirty-four years (and then amended it to nineteen years), and the age for full citizenship rights to be twenty-one years: "Each successive generation would, in this way, come on and go off the stage at a fixed moment, as individuals do now. Then I say the earth belongs to each of these generations during it's course, fully, and in their own right." The crippling impact of debt never far from Jefferson's consciousness, the first implication of this idea insisted to him that "no generation can contract debts greater than may be paid during the course of it's own existence. At 21. years of age they may bind themselves and their lands

39. I am indebted to J. G. A. Pocock for these insights presented at the Library of Congress, 13 May 1993. See John Locke, *Second Treatise of Government*, ed. C. B. Macpherson (Indianapolis: Hackett, 1980), "Property" chapter.

for 34. years to come: at 22. for 33: at 23 for 32. and at 54 for one year.''[40]

To ensure that Madison comprehended fully the implication of his notion of debt, Jefferson presented a specific hypothetical example for illustration. If "Louis XIV. and XV. had contracted debts in the name of the French nation to the amount of 10.000 milliards of livres,'' could the creditors demand that failing to repay the debt that they should be "ceded" the territory? "No,'' replied Jefferson. His logic, based on the natural right of generations, claimed that the present generation of Frenchmen "have the same rights over the soil on which they were produced, as the preceding generations had. They derive these right not from their predecessors, but from nature. They then and their soil are by nature clear of the debts of their predecessors.''[41] That public debts could not "devolve" from one generation to the next Jefferson thought would serve as a "bridle to the spirit of war.'' This specific implication, however, was just the start of Jefferson's daring logic.

From inheritance and a natural right to begin the world free and clear of debt, Jefferson argued explicitly:

> On similar ground it may be proved that no society can make a perpetual constitution, or even a perpetual law. The earth belongs always to the living generation. They may manage it then, and what proceeds from it, as they please, during their usufruct. They are masters too of their own persons, and consequently may govern them as they please. But persons and property make the sum of the objects of government. The constitution and the laws of their predecessors extinguished them, in their natural course, with those who gave them being. This could preserve that being till it ceased to be itself, and no longer. Every constitution, then, and every law, naturally expires at the end of 19. years. If it be enforced longer, it is an act of force and not of right.[42]

40. TJ to JM, 6 Sept. 1789, *PTJ* 15:393. At another point in the letter, *PTJ* 15:394, Jefferson suggested, ''19. years is the term beyond which neither the representatives of a nation, nor even the whole nation itself assembled, can validly extend a debt.'' The exact time frame remains trivial; it is what Jefferson's idea represents that is significant.
41. TJ to JM, 6 Sept. 1789, *PTJ* 15:394–395.
42. Ibid., 15:395–396.

To conceive of the complete consequences of these words remains staggering. Where he began with an assumption he held in common with Madison, that "persons and property make the sum of the objects of government," Jefferson reached conclusions of an altogether different nature. He sought to institutionalize the spirit of revolution behind the Declaration of Independence: robbed of his chance to participate in the drafting of the Constitution, Jefferson felt cheated; moreover, he did not want succeeding generations, upon whom the future of the republic rested, to feel the same sense of having had their natural rights taken from them.

Anticipating Madison's specific reaction to his idea, Jefferson raised the point that "it may be said that the succeeding generation exercising in fact the power of repeal, this leaves them as free as if the constitution or law had been expressly limited to 19. years only." Jefferson grasped the inherent imbalance of this objection—even before he had a chance to see exactly how Madison's new machine would make the suggestion of either repeal or amendment as the functional equivalent to Jefferson's idea of temporal legislative limits an even greater absurdity.

> But the power of repeal is not an equivalent. It might be indeed if every form of government were so perfectly contrived that the will of the majority could always be obtained fairly and without impediment. But this is true of no form. The people cannot assemble themselves; their representation is unequal and vicious. Various checks are opposed to every legislative proposition. Factions get possession of the public councils. Bribery corrupts them. Personal interests lead them astray from the general interests of their constituents; and other impediments arise so as to prove to every practical man that a law of limited duration is much more manageable than one which needs a repeal.[43]

Jefferson started to draw his argument to conclusion admitting, "This principle that the earth belongs to the living and not the dead is of very extensive application and consequences." He closed his letter, as if talking to his Head, asking Madison to "turn this subject

---

43. Ibid., 15:396. Notice how the description—"factions," "bribery," "personal interests"—sounds Madisonian, but the solutions proposed are profoundly different.

in your mind, my Dear Sir, and particularly as to the power of contracting debts, and develope it with that perspicuity and cogent logic which is so peculiarly yours.'' Madison took Jefferson at his word. He replied with a devastating, instrumental critique. It could not have helped Jefferson's chances for a fair hearing that he had reminded Madison of Madison's elite status in the nation and hinted that he should consider the idea as ''a fine preamble to our first law for appropriating the public revenue.''[44] Having spent many months trying to tame democracy, the last thing Madison wanted was to let the *demos* escape again.

Madison waited nearly a month to respond. Using his considerable skills of persuasion, Madison began by flattering Jefferson: ''The idea . . . is a great one, and suggests many interesting reflections to Legislators, particularly when contracting and providing for public debt.'' Although Madison quickly dismissed every aspect of Jefferson's radical notion, in time he eventually embraced the idea of limiting the public debt—what he had perceived as being of possible value in the fanciful idea from his initial reading of the letter.[45]

Preparing Jefferson for the barrage that would follow, Madison opened the door for doubt and polite disagreement by confiding that ''whether it can be received in the extent your reasonings give it, is a question which I ought to turn more in my thoughts than I have yet been able to do, before I should be justified in making a full opinion on it.''[46] Admitting the possibility that his evaluation might be either hasty or simply wrong, Madison turned to basic philosophic premises to destroy the keystone of Jefferson's radical notion of politics. ''My first thoughts,'' he wrote, ''lead me to view the doctrine as not in *all* respects compatible with the course of human affairs. I will endeavour to sketch the grounds of my skepticism.'' Madison was a political thinker who believed not only that humans were not angels, but that even a roomful of philosophers would break down into a state of war; to characterize his position as ''skeptical'' would be an understatement, to say the least.

44. Ibid., 15:396–397.
45. Hamilton's report of 16 Jan. 1795 (*The Papers of Alexander Hamilton*, 27 vols., ed. Harold C. Syrett et al. [New York: Columbia University Press] 18:46–148), also suggested that whenever the government borrowed money it provide for the means to retire the debt.
46. JM to Thomas Jefferson, 4 Feb. 1790, *PJM* 13:19.

After collapsing Jefferson's complex idea down to less than one hundred words, Madison, with the skill of a pathologist, began to dissect and evaluate the pieces of the argument. He reminded Jefferson that, in Madison's unique view of political development, the acts of a political society can be divided into three classes:

1. The fundamental Constitution of the Government.
2. Laws involving stipulations which render them irrevocable at the will of the Legislature
3. Laws involving no such irrevocable quality.

By simply framing his response in this manner, Madison demonstrated he had subtly altered Jefferson's idea since Jefferson never embraced the concept that any constitution would be superior to any other law. To Jefferson a constitution was simply the founding law, but as such it held no structurally extrasignificant position. Still, Madison's argument revealed much else that separated the two theorists.

Dealing with the first act, that of the fundamental constitution, Madison employed his theory-versus-practice tactic to dismiss Jefferson: it "seems liable in practice to some very powerful objections." Showing a Hobbesian predisposition and reminiscent of his position in "Vices of the Political System of the United States" as well as *Federalist* 10, Madison asked Jefferson:

Would not a Government so often revised become too mutable to retain those prejudices in its favor which antiquity inspires, and which are perhaps a salutary aid to the most rational Government in the most enlightened age? Would not such a periodical revision engender pernicious factions that might not otherwise come into existence? Would not, in fine, a Government depending for its existence beyond a fixed date, on some positive and authentic intervention of the Society itself, be too subject to the casualty and consequences of an actual interregnum?

Moving to "the 2d. class, exceptions at least to the doctrine seem to be requisite both in Theory and practice." Here, Madison began to raise questions implicitly related to the institution of property. He reasoned that "if the earth be the gift of nature to the living their title can extend to the earth in its natural State only. The *improvements* made by the dead form a charge against the living who take the benefit of them. This charge can no otherwise be satisfyed than by executing the will of the dead accompanying the improvements.''[47] Madison then argued a less abstract position, claiming that ''debts may be incurred for purposes which interest the unborn, as well as the living: such are debts for repelling a conquest, the evils of which descend through many generations.'' Ironically, it would be this specific dimension of Jefferson's notion on which Madison eventually changed his position.

With regard to the ''3d. class of acts'' Madison conceded his objections ''may perhaps be merely practical.'' Yet this being Madison, a ''merely practical'' objection remained as lethal as any other. Moreover, he saved his final arguments to protect the heart of his politics, the institution of property.

> Unless such laws should be kept in force by new acts regularly anticipating the end of the term, all the rights depending on positive laws, that is, most of the rights of property would become absolutely defunct; and the most violent struggles be generated between those interested in reviving and those interested in new-modelling the former State of property. Nor would events of this kind be improbable. The obstacles to the passage of laws which render a power to repeal inferior to an opportunity of rejecting, as a security agst. oppression, would here render an opportunity of rejecting, an insecure provision agst. anarchy.

Of course, Jefferson held a fundamentally different view of property and its place in the human condition; he had no difficulty seeing all the advantages of having an opportunity to begin the world anew, to redivide the earth. Madison could see only the potential problems of such a system. In fact, Madison predicted that anarchy would be the result of Jefferson's notion. He suggested that Jefferson needed to consider the negative impact his very idea would have on the value of property—it ''could not fail to depreciate its value.'' He detailed his fears thus:

> that the approach of the crisis would increase this effect; that the frequent return of periods superseding all the obligations de-

47. Ibid; JM's emphasis.

pending on antecedent laws & usages, must by weak[en]ing the reverence for those obligations, co-operate with motives to licentiousness already too powerful; and that the uncertainty incident to such a state of things would on one side discourage the steady exertions of industry produced by permanent laws, and on the other, give a disproportionate advantage to the more, over the less, sagacious and interprizing part of the Society.[48]

Madison rejected virtually every facet of Jefferson's idea. What Jefferson presented as an opportunity for humans to reassert their citizenship, Madison viewed as a crisis. Before concluding, Madison extended an olive branch to his friend. He tried to revive the notion of "tacit assent" to meet the same needs as Jefferson's call for periodic revolution. Madison added a final utilitarian, pragmatic objection concerning the apparent need for unanimity if the new society wanted to be legitimate.

In characteristic style, Madison stroked Jefferson's ego by reaffirming his earlier claims that his objections "are not meant however to impeach either the utility or the principle in some particular cases; or the general importance of it in the eye of the philosophical Legislator." Madison's cynicism, however, could not be restrained. In the closing of this letter to Jefferson, he wrote:

On the contrary it would give me singular pleasure to see it first announced in the proceedings of the U. States, and always kept in their view, as a salutary curb on the living generation from imposing unjust or unnecessary burdens on their successors. But this is a pleasure which I have little hope of enjoying. The spirit of philosophical legislation has never reached some parts of the Union, and is by no means the fashion here, either within or without Congress. The evils suffered & feared from weakness in Government, and licentiousness in the people, have turned the attention more towards the means of strengthening the former, than of narrowing its extent in the minds of the latter. Besides this, it is so much easier to espy the little difficulties immediately incident to every great plan, than to comprehend its general and remote benefits, that our hemisphere must be

48. Ibid., 13:19–20.

still more enlightened before many of the sublime truths which are seen thro' the medium of Philosophy, become visible to the naked eye of the ordinary Politician.[49]

Having played the role of "philosophic Legislator" at Philadelphia and understanding fully that Jefferson's idea would make many of his accomplishments vulnerable and eventually void, Madison himself had metamorphosed into an "ordinary Politician" who self-interestedly wanted to protect his own work, his own property, his own fame.

Like most other scholarly critics of Jefferson's "earth belongs to the living" letter, Madison—focusing on its feasibility—missed its meaning.[50] It *was* and *is* its *meaning* that remains significant and holds the promise of a renewed democracy.[51] What, then, was one of the meanings of Jefferson's radical notion? A parable taken from Montesquieu's *Persian Letters* may help make Jefferson's idea more intelligible.[52]

Usbeck, the main character of the *Persian Letters*, recounts the parable of the Troglodytes in a series of letters to his friend. In the story Montesquieu asked metaphorically, Can virtue withstand the ravages of time? The political lessons derived from the tale are complicated, invoking the complex relationships among virtue and responsibility, memory and amnesia. In addition, it demonstrated Montesquieu's understanding of the vital importance that "with truths of a certain kind, it is not enough to make them appear convincing: one must also make them felt." The Troglodyte parable goes like this.

49. Ibid., 13:21.
50. For example, see Judith Shklar, "Redeeming American Political Theory," *American Political Science Review* 85:1 (Mar. 1991): 7, where she calls Jefferson's idea a "daft proposal."
51. See Benjamin Barber, *Strong Democracy: Participatory Politics for a New Age* (Berkeley: University of California Press, 1984); and C. B. Macpherson, *Democratic Theory: Essays in Retrieval* (Oxford: Clarendon Press, 1973) and *The Life and Times of Liberal Democracy* (Oxford: Oxford University Press, 1977). Ironically, Macpherson (a Canadian) sees more clearly Jefferson's democratic spirit than does Barber.
52. This section follows the argument in my essay "The Presidency and the Public Philosophy: Jefferson's Permanent Revolution," in *The Virginia Papers on the Presidency, vol. 26*, ed. Kenneth Thompson (Lanham, Md.: University Press of America, 1991), pp. 137–147.

"More like animals than men," the first Troglodytes were ruled by a foreign king.[53] Even before they killed him and eliminated the royal bloodline, the Troglodytes resembled Hobbesian humans prior to the installation of a Leviathan. With the regicide completed, the Troglodytes descended rapidly into a state of war, where their condition remained "poor, nasty, brutish, and short."[54] God, perceiving their "wickedness," sent upon them a plague as punishment. As a direct consequence of their own selfishness, the Troglodytes were reduced to all but two families who had to begin the arduous task of building a virtuous nation. These two families were spared because they "understood what justice was . . . [and] loved virtue." They formed the core of the new nation.

From the start, they realized the significance of "bringing up their children to be virtuous." Part of the children's education consisted of the constant retelling of the history of the recent past, letting the "wretchedness" of their former countrymen serve as a vivid reminder of the futility of politics without civic virtue. The children were taught, by parental example, what the relationship between their social and individual selves ought to be, if virtue was to be sustained: "Above all they made them realize that the individual's self-interest is always to be found in the common interest; that wanting to cut oneself off from it is the same as wanting to ruin oneself; that virtue is not such as to cost us anything, and should not be considered as a wearisome exercise; and that justice to others is charity to ourselves." The social ethos of the Troglodyte community remained such that all its members were permitted the chance to experience the above truth. So long as these principles were *felt*, the Troglodytes had no need of government, yet they lived together in joy, virtue, and freedom. Time passed. Generations changed. The population grew, prospered, and spread throughout the nation. This was not all: memory faded and amnesia settled in. Civic virtue disappeared.

Eventually, perhaps inevitably, the Troglodytes decided they needed a king. Foolishly believing that with their wealth they could afford a monarch, they unanimously offered the crown to an elder Troglodyte whom they perceived as being the most just and wise

53. Charles-Louis de Secondat Montesquieu, *Persian Letters*, trans. C. J. Betts (New York: Penguin Books, 1973), p. 53.

54. Thomas Hobbes, *Leviathan*, ed. C. B. Macpherson (New York: Penguin Books, 1968), p. 186.

among them. Comprehending fully the tragic implications of this collective decision, the old man initially declined: ''God forbid . . . I should do such a wrong to the Troglodytes.'' He ultimately resigned himself to fate but lamented to his ''subjects'': ''I see . . . quite well . . . your virtue has begun to be a burden to you.''[55] Obedience to a king—rather than to their individual, social selves—became a luxury the new generation of prosperous Troglodytes believed they could not do without. But social decay had already manifested itself, as the mere thought of attempting to transfer responsibility for their own virtue to a monarch made clear. In spite of their education, the new generations of Troglodytes had forgotten their brutal, tragic past because, in a sense, it was not genuinely *their* past. Prosperity and amnesia permitted them to no longer *feel* historic truth. Montesquieu concluded the parable before returning the Troglodytes to their original Hobbesian state of war. Nevertheless, in forgetting their past, degeneration became their future.

Why did the virtuous Troglodyte republic fail? Montesquieu may have simply believed, as Plato, Aristotle, Machiavelli, and Calvin before him, that every political regime would invariably deteriorate: degeneration and decay constitute the natural order of things, political and otherwise. After all, if the forgetting of *felt* historic truths by successive generations created the preconditions of decay for the Troglodytes, what is to be done? Given human mortality, how can experience transcend generations? If this defines the human condition, it becomes imperative to discover a type of educational experience that provides more than the intellectual passing on of names, dates, places, and explanations of history. The initial, postfall Troglodytes *felt* and vividly remembered the past: it was theirs. The experiences, emotions, and felt truths could perhaps be passed along to the immediately succeeding generation. But what of the third and fourth generations?[56] In time, historic events become, at best, vicariously remembered. At that point, history as a felt truth dies.

This generational problem of maintaining a virtuous citizenry across time became a, perhaps *the*, central concern of Thomas Jefferson's political theory. His ideas and ideals contained in his notion

---

55. Montesquieu, *Persian Letters*, pp. 53–61.
56. Cf. Louis Hartz, *The Liberal Tradition in America* (New York: Harcourt, Brace, & Company, 1955), and *The Founding of New Societies* (New York: Harcourt, Brace, & World, 1964), passim.

that the earth belongs to the living, furthermore, supplied the rudimentary outlines of a possible solution to this political problem. But Jefferson's fiction of the complete passing of a generation remains unique and difficult to appreciate, especially for those who fixate on the seemingly impossible, practical logistics of the ideal.

Jefferson's argument insisted that every generation has the *natural right* to create—*de novo*—all of its laws and constitutions. "No society," he claimed, "can make a perpetual Constitution, or even a perpetual law. . . . The Constitution and the laws of their predecessors [are] extinguished then in their natural course with those that give them being." He explicitly rejected Locke's and Madison's argument that every generation's power to repeal or amend legislation already in existence gave that generation's "tacit consent" to the present laws. For Jefferson, "the power to repeal is not an equivalent." To the contrary, he believed that every generation had a natural right to start the world anew. Perhaps more important, he already understood, on some rudimentary level, that this right involved the positive act of creative politics. Through constructing the rules by which individuals would run their own lives, they would experience—*feel*—the joys of being founding mothers and fathers. The revolution would be their revolution; the laws, their laws. Creative, Jeffersonian politics was critical to both the virtue of the citizenry and its ability to remain free. Radical as this idea appeared, Jefferson continued to spell out explicitly for Madison its implications. Given this generational, natural right of humans to make their own constitution and laws, all existing constitutions and laws "naturally expire" at the end of a generation. "If [a law] be enforced longer, it is an act of force, and not of right."[57] Jefferson's desire to keep the republic virtuous by creating a state of *permanent revolution*, for that phrase captures what he wanted, represents a radical notion of politics. The relationship remains genuinely dialectical: revolution created and sustained civic virtue, and civic virtue permitted progressive revolution. Revolution and civic virtue were inseparable. Jefferson's idea of permanent revolution, when tied with his unorthodox views of property and his politics of the heart, places his political theory beyond the boundaries of even bourgeois radicalism. It presents a radi-

---

57. TJ to JM, 6 Sept. 1789, *Jefferson: Writings* (Peterson), 959–964.

cal alternative to the rest of mainstream American political thought.[58]

Had Jefferson written just this single letter on the theme of permanent revolution, it could perhaps be explained away as a byproduct of the heady revolutionary air of 1789 Paris. It was not, however, an isolated moment in his life. Almost twenty years later, the passing of a Jeffersonian generation, he sent a similar letter to Samuel Kercheval. The now elder statesman told Kercheval that Virginia's Constitution could not be considered republican, and by implication, neither could the United States Constitution. For Virginia he recommended the following political alterations: general suffrage, equal representation in the legislature, direct election to all offices, periodic amendments of the constitution, and the creation of ward-republics. The last of these changes, the establishment of the ward-republics, was the base upon which good government could be constructed.[59]

If each generation must experience the founding function for itself, its members needed a political space where they could be citizens and create political measures. Jefferson envisioned the wards fulfilling this purpose. The astute historian of political theory Hannah Arendt compared Jefferson's ward-republics to the Paris communes and the Moscow soviets. She noted as well the failure of most scholars to appreciate the significance of the wards as "an entirely new form of government, with a space for freedom."[60] The omission of ward-republics from the Constitution most assuredly cannot be considered an oversight on the part of either Madison or the other

58. Consider Jefferson relative to Thomas Paine, the person most often associated with American radicalism. While Paine railed against the irrationality of a hereditary monarch in *The Rights of Man*, he failed to push the logic of his own argument to the idea of a perpetual law or a hereditary constitution. Ironically, in his earlier *Common Sense*, he unknowingly made this connection when he contrasted absolute governments, where "the King is law," and America, where "THE LAW IS KING" (Michael Foot and Isaac Kramnick, eds., *The Thomas Paine Reader* [New York: Viking Penguin, 1987], p. 92). When Paine originally wrote these words during the revolutionary era, they had yet to take on the validity that Madison's Constitution and time would grant them. But to Jefferson the connection was self-evident: neither kings nor constitutions could perpetuate themselves, for that would violate natural right.

59. Jeffersonian wards fulfilled four functions: (1) to check petty tyrants at home; (2) to maintain the revolutionary spirit of 1776; (3) to provide general education; and (4) to ensure a space in which every citizen could experience and become proficient in the art of politics.

60. Hannah Arendt, *On Revolution* (New York: Viking Press, 1963), pp. 252–253.

original framers. It seems telling that the word *citizenship* does not even appear in the unamended Constitution. In the collective view of the framers, state politics in the 1780s verged on anarchy—the direct result of the excesses of democracy associated with local rule by the *demos*. The last thing the framers wanted to create in 1787, then, was an arena for freedom in the state legislatures. The Constitution, after all, was about redirecting power from the periphery back to the center, where it could be more rationally controlled.

Jefferson argued vigorously for his ward-republics. Here existed the space in which humans could be political, where "the whole is cemented by giving to every citizen personally, a part in the administration of public affairs." Here was the arena from where succeeding constitutional conventions could be called and in which the political issues deliberated upon. Jefferson believed that these political experiences would create the "strongest feelings" of attachment among the citizens to their independence and their republican government. Experience in politics remained essential: "Forty years of experience in government is worth a century of book-reading." But experience provided something more. It permitted the citizen to feel—rather than merely intellectually know—what a founding genuinely meant. Jefferson concluded his letter to Kercheval with an explicit reiteration of "the earth belongs to the living" theme. At a minimum of every nineteen years, he instructed Kercheval, each generation has "a right to choose for itself the form of government it believes most promotive of its own happiness." If Jefferson's advice had been followed, he predicted that civic virtue and freedom might have been "handed on . . . from generation to generation, to the end of time."[61] Even though this Jeffersonian dream never materialized, it still constitutes a Jeffersonian inheritance to which both individuals and generations have a natural right.

Jefferson believed humans capable of self-government because he held a fundamentally different view of humanity from that of his in-

61. TJ to Samuel Kercheval, 12 July 1816, *Jefferson: Writings* (Peterson), 1395–1403. Jefferson wrote: "But I know also, that laws and institutions must go hand in hand with the progress of the human mind. As that becomes more developed, more enlightened, as new discoveries are made, new truths disclosed, and manners and opinions change with the change of circumstances, institutions must advance also, and keep pace with the times. We might as well require a man to wear still the coat which fitted him when a boy, as civilized society to remain ever under the regimen of their barbarous ancestors."

timate, Madison. Where the latter began with a market, liberal concept of the atomized individual, Jefferson began with a moral and social concept of humanity. Order and harmony characterized Jefferson's universe. His cosmology and concept of humanity help explain, in part, his lack of concern with the potential problem of political continuity in a society that has institutionalized revolution. Furthermore, he viewed these ongoing constitutional conventions as an "invented tradition," to borrow a term from the historian Eric Hobsbawm. As Hobsbawm explains his term, the very nature of an invented tradition "automatically implies continuity with the past" even though "it does not preclude innovation and change."[62]

These rituals of renewal, reaffirmation, and revolution are classic Jefferson. They demonstrate his faith in humanity as well as his desire to return to a condition of innocence where humans, as far as possible, could begin their lives anew. The mere fact that these constitutional conventions were to become part of the political culture would help ensure a decent regard for the past without becoming enslaved by it. They could remind humans that they make their own history, even if they do not make it just as they please and under circumstances directly found in, given by, and transmitted from the past. They could remind us that the tradition of all the dead generations need not weigh like a nightmare on the brain of the living. They would reconcile freedom inside of the realm of necessity.

In ways that have yet to be fully explored by scholars, Jefferson's politics at crucial points parallels, in an uncanny manner, dimensions of the political theory of Rousseau. Perhaps by ultimately comparing Jefferson to Rousseau, rather than to any American thinker, Jefferson's uniqueness can be appreciated. Both men understood the necessity of humans—to be fully human—to participate in politics according to the Aristotelian notion of citizenship, of ruling and being ruled. Like Rousseau, Jefferson's implicit notion of moral freedom required "obedience to a law one proscribes for oneself." Even stronger than Rousseau's position that humans instinctively do not like to see other creatures suffer, Jefferson argued that "Nature hath implanted in our breasts a love of others, a sense of duty to them, a

---

62. Eric Hobsbawm and Terrence Ranger, eds., *The Invention of Tradition* (Cambridge: Cambridge University Press, 1983), pp. 1–2.

moral instinct," which made humans political and social creatures. In his celebrated image: "The Creator would indeed have been a bungling artist, had he intended man for a social animal, without planting in him social dispositions."[63] To be a moral creature required the presence of others. The moral sense, not merely the rational intellect, permitted humans to be just, political creatures. It required that they govern themselves. And finally, once again as if echoing Rousseau, Jefferson embraced the concept of human "perfectibility": like Rousseau, he understood fully that while humans were ontological creatures endowed with the capacity to govern themselves morally, they were equally capable—given reason's ability to deceive—of self-destructive and dominating measures. Self-government, therefore, always entailed risk.

Finally, and this may well be the ultimate point in Jefferson's radicalism, he recognized the necessity of providing citizens with the opportunity for failure in order for them to achieve freedom. A natural right to fail remained part of Jefferson's politics. No society could be considered democratic, virtuous, or free if it did not allow its citizens, on a daily basis, to govern themselves. Neither Platonic philosopher-kings, Rousseauean legislators, nor Madisonian self-balancing machines could sit in final judgment, permitting only those citizen actions of which they approved. Citizens must be permitted to run the risks of freedom and failure.[64] As Jefferson explained to a friend: "We both consider the people as our children and love them with parental affection. But you love them as infants whom you are afraid to trust without nurses; and I as adults whom I freely leave to self-government."[65]

At the risk of being accused of presenting a reductionist interpretation, the concept of a "defining moment" may be instructive. Both Madison and Jefferson appear to have had defining moments in their lives. For Madison, the moment consisted of the drafting, ratifying, and implementing of the Constitution; for Jefferson, the moment was the writing and signing of the Declaration of Indepen-

---

63. TJ to Thomas Law, 13 June 1814, *Jefferson: Writings* (Peterson), p. 1337.

64. As the German philosopher G. W. F. Hegel put it: "It is solely by risking life that freedom is obtained; . . . the individual who has not staked his life may, no doubt, be recognized as a Person; but he has not attained the truth of this recognition as an independent self-consciousness" (*The Phenomenology of Mind* [New York: Harper & Row, 1967], p. 233).

65. TJ to P. S. Dupont de Nemours, 24 Apr. 1816, *Works of TJ* II:522.

dence. Each man's moment shaped his life markedly. Madison devoted his energies to protecting the Constitution (and his association with it); Jefferson continued to espouse revolution and protect his association with the Declaration of Independence. These distinct political events continued to have far-reaching influence on the thoughts and actions of these political theorists. These documents represent, as well, the vast differences between the two conceptions of political theory.

Yet make no mistake. Jefferson's dream of a democratic and virtuous republic currently lives only in the realm of utopian fantasy. Madisonian reality continues to dominate the political and cultural wasteland. Perhaps the question of a contemporary social critic captures best the essence of this dichotomy: "Is a dream a lie if it don't come true, or is it something worse?" In the context of American history, the answer can only be "something worse." Madison's dream of reasonable, self-controlled citizens, further restrained by a self-balancing, sociopolitical machine, turned out to be a nightmare—for increasing numbers of Americans—as he knew it would. And that Jefferson's dream remains untried, places it in the realm of tragedy. Americans do not know if the Jeffersonian dream represented a lie: they never gave it a chance.

Americans continue to be either unaware of or unwilling to risk a democratic present. The Jeffersonian ideal still haunts a future that looks increasing bleak, while it simultaneously represents the opportunity for Americans to regain their natural rights to life, liberty, and the pursuit of happiness. This ideal continues to be a matter of courage and will; it remains standing in the face of the closing of the horizon of history. Americans must remember, and this is crucial, that the point remains not to recapture a Jeffersonian past that never materialized, but to transcend it. And in that very process of self- and social-transcendence, to make it felt—to make it our own.

8 / *The Madisonian Dream: The Illusion of a Future*

> Having outlived so many of my contemporaries, I ought not to forget
> that I may be thought to have outlived myself.[1]
>
> —*Madison*

In the midst of the Eisenhower years, the poet Robert Frost presented
a commencement address simply called "A Talk for Students." Like
most graduation speeches, Frost's began by proclaiming his admira-
tion for the students' accomplishments, especially that of completing "a four year plan." This was a task he assured the students he
could not accomplish: "I lose my interest." He then proceeded to
lecture the assembly on his "expectations" of them as they entered
into the real world. By that, he told his listeners, he "expected a
good deal": they were not to continue "to go on thinking that learning was all—piling up knowledge is as bad as piling up money, indefinitely." He insisted that "at some point" they "begin to kick
around what you know."

Deftly, Frost moved on to think, to talk, and to speculate about
freedom, a word, he claimed, that currently could be heard "on
everybody's lips." Subtly, he told his listeners that "I never have valued any liberty conferred on me in particular. I value myself on the
liberties I take, and I have learned to appreciate the word 'unscrupu-
lous.' " Frost encouraged the graduates to think, write, and speak
freely. He further suggested they take up "knitting." By knitting, he
explained, he meant for them to think deeply about an idea, put it
down for a while, and take it up once again to think, to knit some

---

1. JM to Jared Sparks, 1 June 1831, *The Writings of James Madison*, ed. Gaillard
Hunt, 9 vols. (New York: G. P. Putnam's Sons, 1790–1802), 9:460 (hereafter cited
as *WJM*).

more about it; and when they assumed they had "finished" with their project, to pick it up and continue the knitting process.

Frost shared with his audience one of the ideas about which he personally had been knitting. It consisted of an idea in common with a theme of this book—the notion of "the dream." By this Frost explicitly meant the American dream. What caused him to knit about this particular notion appears to have been several unsolved and troubling issues surrounding it: "I wonder what the dream is, or why. And the next time I pick it up, I wonder who dreamed it. Did Tom Paine dream it, did Thomas Jefferson dream it, did George Washington dream it? Gouverneur Morris?" Then Frost explained that after all his knitting he had lately "decided the best dreamer of it was Madison." Notice that Frost does not say that Madison had the best dream; he simply asserted that he was "the best dreamer" of it.

That a poet of Frost's talent should knit his way to this particular conclusion and feel the need publicly to knit some more about it becomes understandable when he revealed that the source for this particular illumination resulted from his recently having spent time "reading the *Federalist Papers*." Ultimately, Frost seemed to want to knit a bit more on a few of the crucial questions contained in his interpretation of the dream: Has the dream come true? Or, has it failed to become so? Perhaps, Frost suggested, over the passage of time something even more troubling than these two options occurred. Frost shared his poet's sense of Madison's dream and the question of its wish fulfillment, as he "knitted" and encouraged his audience to knit along with him.

Now I know—I think I know, as of today—what Madison's dream was. It was just a dream of a new land to fulfill with people in self-control. In self-control. That is all through his thinking. And let me say that again to you. To fulfill this land— a new land—with people in self-control.

"In Self-control." This certainly expresses the essence of Madison. It represents as well the dominant theme of Madison's dream. Make no mistake, Frost (at least in part), admired this dream. Frost was, furthermore, apparently troubled by dimensions to it as well. If the latent meanings of dreams were that easy to unravel, interpret, and understand, Frost would not have had to have spent so much time and energy knitting about Madison's. Frost candidly presented his own serious ambiguity over this dream. Once again penetrating to the heart of the matter, he asked, "And do I think that dream has failed? Has come to nothing, or has materialized too much? It is always the fear. We live in constant fear, of course. To cross the road, we live in fear of cars. But we can live in fear, if we want to, of too much education, too little education, too much of this, too little of that. But the thing is, the measure." "Fear . . . constant fear" recalls but one of the inevitable consequences of Madisonian politics. Given Madison's concept of humanity, a Malthusian nature trapped inside a Calvinist universe, fear can never be vanquished, only channeled and controlled. While Madison's ingenious balancing seesaw has maintained equilibrium for more than two centuries (excluding the War Between the States), it cannot halt the internalized civil war of all against all and the constant individualized fear of a life that threatens to be brutish if not necessarily short.

In the course of his knitting, this poet asked the fundamental question concerning the Madisonian dream: "Has the dream, instead of having come true, has it done something that the witches talk about? Has it simply materialized? . . . Has the ethereal idealism of the founders materialized into something too material?" To conceive of Madison in terms of "ethereal idealism" may initially appear to require enormous imagination, until we remember that his heavenly vision remained one founded somewhere between Hobbes and Calvin, Smith and Malthus. Once the inherent limits to the beauty of his dream are accepted, the other dimension to Frost's query—has it materialized too much?—can be readily answered— yes. However, and this remains the point: this materialization was inevitable in the grand Madisonian design. Madison, moreover, always knew it.

Madison's incredible sociopolitical edifice of checks and balances, pitting faction against faction, with a neutral and neutralized government looking for rational solutions, had been constructed to function like the ideal Leviathan—to constantly perpetuate itself. It sought to banish emotion and passion from the decision-making process and base politics exclusively on rational calculations. Its heart, moreover, concerned itself primarily with maintaining the institution of property in material things, not in the faculties of individual, human development.

In Madison's design, the very notion of a future is an illusion. Once the new state had been founded and was governing, succeeding generations had little to do but play around the margins of power, given its rules and procedures. His system successfully functions to protect the status quo, to maintain equilibrium, and to ensure that change continues to be minor and incremental, never radical. Finally, it is not by coincidence that before he died, Madison arranged for his copy of the notes of the Philadelphia convention to be published: even from beyond the grave he could continue to exert his Princely influence over the future of the system he created.[2]

Madison lacked any realistic faith in the *demos*. He believed, instead, in the virtue of rational political systems that would have filtered the lifeblood out of even a roomful of Socrateses. That humans are far from angelic few will deny. Still, is there truly no room between angels and beasts? Could three humans not get along without a government? Would every Athenian assembly really have been a mob? How could Jefferson have lived through similar experiences and hold such starkly contrasting pictures of humanity, politics, and the world?

In ways reminiscent of Plato's warning about the poets, whom he charged with speaking the truth without knowing exactly when or why, Frost seems to have sensed this troubling dimension to Madison in a brief poem he offered to his audience. Also recited at the inauguration of John F. Kennedy, the poem, known as "The Gift Outright," Frost described as a "poem about what Madison may have thought."

2. See JM's will, *WJM* 9:549: "Considering the peculiarity and magnitude of the occasion which produced the convention at Philadelphia in 1787, the Characters who composed it, the Constitution which resulted from their deliberation, it's effects during a trial of so many years on the posterity of the people living under it, and the interest it has inspired among friends of free government, it is not an unreasonable inference that a careful and extended report of the proceedings and discussions of that body, which were with closed doors, by a member who was constant in his attendance, will be particularly gratifying to the people of the United States, and to all who take an interest in the progress of political science and the cause of true liberty. It is my desire that the report as made by me should be published."

The land was ours before we were the land's.
She was our land more than a hundred years
Before we were her people. She was ours
In Massachusetts, in Virginia,
But we were England's, still colonials,
Possessing what we still were unpossessed by,
Possessed by what we now no more possessed.
Something we were withholding made us weak
Until we found out that it was ourselves
We were withholding from our land of living,
And forthwith found salvation in surrender
Such as we were we gave ourselves outright
(The deed of gift was many deeds of war)
To the land vaguely realizing westward,
But still unstoried, artless, unenhanced,
Such as she was, such as she would become.

This fascinating poem elegantly expresses the wonderful albeit twisted ambiguity of Madison. Could Madison even imagine an "outright gift?" Indeed, the words themselves imply that Americans gave with expectations of returns on their investment. What is genuinely striking about the poem may be how well it captures the possessive quality of Madison, the United States, and their shared dream.[3]

In the middle of the twentieth century, after a horrible war over ideals and land, that Frost should do some serious knitting about the American dream, worry that it may have materialized too much, yet conclude that it has not, may be understandable. At the same time, he implicitly urged his listeners to do their part to minimize the materialistic dimension of the dream and optimize the "ethereal idealism" of the founding. Nevertheless, more than a century earlier, Alexis de Tocqueville—having the advantages of a contrasting class and culture, as well as the virtue of not having his vision clouded by internalization of the materialized Madisonian dream—grasped better the possessive individualistic core of the American dream. Com-

---

3. Robert Frost, "A Talk for Students," Sarah Lawrence College, 7 June 1956, distributed by The Fund for the Republic, 60 East 42nd Street, New York, New York.

menting on the Americans he met on his journey into the American frontier, where pioneers actively pursued the dream, Tocqueville seemed most struck by their simple-minded motivation "when it's a question of gaining a dollar" and their extreme "avidity for gain." He noted critically the ambiguity of both the Americans and their dream: "A people which, like all great people, has but one thought, and which is advancing toward the acquisition of riches, sole goal of its efforts, with a perseverance and a scorn for life that one might call heroic, if that name fitted other than virtuous things."[4]

Then again, what else could be expected of a cultural system designed to limit citizens to the single political activity of voting, once every two years; where both *eros* and *thanatos* had to be channeled into activities of the market; where the *vita activa* can be expressed by the many solely through *vita oeconomicus*. In such an environment, there can be reason and stability, but no community. Ironically, Madison built so well that his political machine, in the age of democracy, has outlived itself. As Jefferson stated it, Americans continue to be ruled from the grave. Or as Madison suggested in the opening quote, he has "outlived" himself indeed.

More than a century and half after Tocqueville, and several decades after Frost, the gifted writer and talented historian Gordon Wood lamented this materialistic nature of the American experience. As if in direct response to Frost's query—"Has the ethereal idealism of the founders materialized into something too material?"—Wood convincingly writes that "the founding fathers were unsettled and fearful not because the American Revolution had failed but because it had succeeded, and succeeded too well." Showing the ongoing ideological power of Jefferson implicit in the automatic association of certain ideals with his very name, Wood concludes his monumental book describing the "disillusionment felt by Jefferson and others of the founding fathers" over America's future. The postfounding generation, Wood maintains, "would discover its greatness by creating a prosperous free society belonging to obscure people with their workaday concerns and their pecuniary pursuits of happiness—common people with their common interests in making money and getting ahead. No doubt the cost that

4. Alexis de Tocqueville, "Fortnight in the Wilderness," in *Beaumont and Tocqueville in America*, trans. and ed. George Wilson Pierson (Oxford: Oxford University Press, 1938), pp. 239, 244.

Americans paid for this democracy was high—with its vulgarity, its materialism, its rootlessness, its anti-intellectualism."[5] With the public arena closed to all but a few, where else but in the pursuit of money could the next generations look for meaning? It was Madison, not Jefferson, who designed the system.

Madison's liberal dream has, as he knew it would, turned into a nightmare for increasing numbers of marginalized Americans. Instead of the chance to pursue happiness, they have neither the opportunity, the hope, nor even the illusion of either. Perhaps it may be appropriate that while there exists no genuine Madison Memorial for pilgrims to flock to at Montpelier (or for that matter in the nation's political capital), the avenue in civil society where the myth of America continues to be invented, generated, and recreated to fit the needs of the times was named after him. On Madison Avenue, appearance may not be everything, but it is the only thing. America no longer reflects Locke's dream. Rather, it has metamorphosed into an intriguing Orwellian-Kafkaesque labyrinth, where a few Ks still search for the reality behind the ideological myth, while the rich find meaning in each of their possessions.[6] And those systematically cut out of the Madison vision *cum* nightmare neither dream nor revolt. They simply wait. So it goes.

Meanwhile, patriotic Americans flock to the Jefferson Memorial and Monticello, paying tribute to what they authentically wish to believe their country represents. They long to touch the democratic idealism of an America that never was, but might have been. So long as the alternative dream of Jefferson lives, if only in speech, so too does the hope that someday Americans will no longer merely quote the Declaration of Independence while they live *The Federalist*. Instead, Americans may reclaim their natural birthright to live the ideals of the Declaration of Independence, to enjoy all the fruits of an earth that belongs in *usufruct* to the living, to turn the world into a holiday.

5. Gordon Wood, *The Radicalism of the American Revolution* (Dekalb: Northern Illinois University Press, 1976), pp. 368–369. Observe how it seems almost always Jefferson who is trotted out for idealistic purposes. Then again, who better to articulate the American dream of a democratic way of life.

6. See Paul N. Goldstene, *The Collapse of Liberal Empire* (Novato, Calif.: Chandler & Sharp, 1977), p. 53.

Selected Bibliography

Abernethy, Thomas P. *The South in the New Nation, 1789–1819.* Baton Rouge: Louisiana State University Press, 1961.

Abraham, Henry J. *Freedom and the Court: Civil Rights and Liberties in the U.S.* 5th ed. New York: Oxford University Press, 1972.

Ackerman, Bruce. *We the People.* Cambridge, Mass.: Belknap Press of Harvard University Press, 1991.

Adair, Douglass Greybill. *Fame and the Founding Fathers: Essays by Douglass Adair.* Edited by Trevor Colbourn. New York: Published for the Institute of Early American History and Culture, Williamsburg, Virginia, by W. W. Norton & Company, 1974.

————. "James Madison's 'Autobiography,' " *William and Mary Quarterly* 3d ser., 2 (Apr. 1945): 191–209.

Adams, Henry. *Henry Adams: The Education of Henry Adams, and Other Selected Writings.* Abridged and edited by Edward N. Saveth. New York: Washington Square Press, 1963.

————. *History of the United States during the Administrations of Jefferson and Madison.* 9 vols. New York: Scribner's, 1889–1891.

Adams, John Q. *The Lives of James Madison and James Monroe.* Boston: Phillips, Sampson & Company, 1850.

Appleby, Joyce Oldham. "America as a Model for the Radical French Reformers of 1789." *William and Mary Quarterly* 28 (Apr. 1971): 267–286.

————. *Capitalism and a New Social Order: The Republican Vision of the 1790s.* New York and London: New York University Press, 1983.

————. *Economic Thought and Ideology in Seventeenth-Century England.* Princeton, N.J.: Princeton University Press, 1978.

————. "Republicanism in Old and New Contexts." *William and Mary Quarterly* 43 (Jan. 1986): 20–34.

————. "Republicanism in the History and Historiography of the United States." *American Quarterly* 37 (Fall 1985): 461–598.

————. "The Social Origins of American Revolutionary Ideology." *Journal of American History* 64 (Mar. 1978): 935–958.

Arendt, Hannah. *The Human Condition.* Chicago: University of Chicago Press, 1974.

————. *On Revolution.* New York: Viking Press, 1963.

Armstrong, Virginia I., ed. *I Have Spoken: American History through Voices of Indians.* New York: Pocket Books, 1972.

Bailyn, Bernard. "The Central Themes of the American Revolution: An Interpretation." In *Essays on the American Revolution,* edited by Stephen G.

Kurtz and James H. Hutson, pp. 3–31. Chapel Hill and New York: Published for the Institute of Early American History and Culture, Williamsburg, Virginia, by the University of North Carolina Press and W. W. Norton & Company, 1973.

_____. *The Ideological Origins of the American Revolution.* Cambridge, Mass.: Belknap Press of Harvard University Press, 1967.

_____. *The Origins of American Politics.* New York: Alfred A. Knopf, 1970.

Bailyn, Bernard, ed. *Pamphlets of the American Revolution, 1750–1776.* Cambridge, Mass.: Belknap Press of Harvard University Press, 1965.

Banning, Lance. "The Jeffersonian Ideology Revisited: Liberal and Classical Ideas in the New American Republic." *William and Mary Quarterly* 43 (Jan. 1986): 3–19.

_____. *The Jeffersonian Persuasion: Evolution of a Party Ideology.* Ithaca, N.Y.: Published for the Institute of Early American History and Culture, Williamsburg, Virginia, by Cornell University Press, 1978.

_____. "Republican Ideology and the Triumph of the Constitution, 1789 to 1798." *William and Mary Quarterly* 3d ser., 31:2 (Apr. 1974): 167–188.

Barber, Benjamin. *Strong Democracy: Participatory Politics for a New Age.* Berkeley: University of California Press, 1984.

Beard, Charles A. *American Government and Politics.* 8th ed. New York: Macmillan, 1939.

_____. *An Economic Interpretation of the Constitution of the United States.* New York: Macmillan, 1913 and 1935.

_____. *Economic Origins of Jeffersonian Democracy.* New York: Macmillan, 1915.

Beeman, Richard R. "Deference, Republicanism, and the Emergence of Popular Politics in Eighteenth-Century America." *William and Mary Quarterly* 49:3 (July 1992): 401–430.

Beitzinger, Alfons J. *A History of American Political Thought.* New York: Dodd, Mead & Company, 1972.

Bell, Daniel. *The End of Ideology: On the Exhaustion of Political Ideas in the Fifties.* Glencoe, Ill.: Free Press, 1960.

Berman, Marshall. *The Politics of Authenticity.* New York: Basic Books, 1976.

Blackstone, William. *Commentaries on the Laws of England.* 4 vols. Oxford: Clarendon Press, 1765.

Boorstin, Daniel. *The Americans: The Colonial Experience.* New York: Random House, 1958.

_____. *The Genius of American Politics.* Chicago: University of Chicago Press, 1953.

_____. *The Lost World of Thomas Jefferson.* New York: Henry Holt & Company, 1948.

Boyd, Julian P., ed. *The Declaration of Independence: The Evolution of the Text.* Princeton, N.J.: Princeton University Press, 1945.

Boyd, Julian P., et al., eds. *The Papers of Thomas Jefferson.* 19 vols. to date. Princeton, N.J.: Princeton University Press, 1950–.

Brant, Irving. *James Madison.* 6 vols. Indianapolis: Bobbs-Merrill, 1941–1961.

Brown, Norman O. *Love's Body.* New York: Vintage, 1966.

Brown, Robert E. *Charles Beard and the Constitution.* Princeton, N.J.: Princeton University Press, 1956.

Buel, Richard, Jr. *Securing the Revolution: Ideology in American Politics, 1789–1815.* Ithaca, N.Y.: Cornell University Press, 1972.

Burns, Edward McNall. *James Madison, Philosopher of the Constitution.* New Brunswick, N.J.: Rutgers University Press, 1938.

Cappon, Lester J., ed. *The Adams-Jefferson Letters.* New York: Simon & Schuster, 1971.

Carpenter, William Seal. *The Development of American Political Thought.* Princeton, N.J.: Princeton University Press, 1930.

Coleman, Frank M. "The Hobbesian Basis of American Constitutionalism." *Polity* 7:1 (Fall 1974): 57–89.

Coles, Harry L. *The War of 1812.* Chicago: University of Chicago Press, 1965.

Conklin, Paul K. *Self-Evident Truths: Being a Discourse on the Origins & Development of the First Principles of American Government.* Bloomington: Indiana University Press, 1974.

Crosskey, William W. *Politics and the Constitution.* 2 vols. Chicago: University of Chicago Press, 1953.

Cunningham, Noble E. *The Jeffersonian Republicans: The Formation of Party Organization, 1789–1801.* Chapel Hill: University of North Carolina Press, 1957.

———. *The Jeffersonian Republicans in Power: Party Operations, 1801–1809.* Chapel Hill: University of North Carolina Press, 1963.

Dahl, Robert A. *A Preface to Democratic Theory.* Chicago: University of Chicago Press, 1956.

Davis, Richard Beale. *Intellectual Life in Jefferson's Virginia.* Chapel Hill: University of North Carolina Press, 1965.

Diamond, Martin. *As Far as Republican Principles Will Admit.* Edited by William A. Schambra. Washington, D.C.: American Enterprise Institute Press, 1992.

———. "The Declaration and the Constitution: Liberty, Democracy, and the Founders." *Public Interest* 41 (Fall 1973): 39–55.

———. "Democracy and *The Federalist:* A Reconsideration of the Framers' Intent." *American Political Science Review* 53 (Mar. 1959): 52–68.

———. "*The Federalist.*" In *The History of Political Philosophy,* edited by Leo Strauss and Joseph Cropsey. Chicago: Rand McNally, 1974.

———. "What the Framers Meant by Federalism." In *A Nation of States,* edited by Robert A. Goldwin. Chicago: Rand McNally, 1963.

Dietze, Gottfried. *The Federalist.* Baltimore: Johns Hopkins University Press, 1960.

Diggins, John Patrick. "Comrades and Citizens: New Mythologies in American Historiography." *American Historical Review* 90 (June 1985): 614–638.

———. *The Lost Soul of American Politics.* New York: Basic Books, 1984.

Dunn, John. *The Political Thought of John Locke.* Cambridge: Cambridge University Press, 1982.

Eidelberg, Paul. *The Philosophy of the Constitution.* New York: Free Press, 1968.

———. *On the Silence of the Declaration of Independence.* Amherst: University of Massachusetts Press, 1976.

Elliot, Jonathan, ed. *The Debates of the Several State Conventions on the*

Adoption of the Federal Constitution. 5 vols. Philadelphia: J. B. Lippincott, 1830–1836.

Ellis, Richard E. *The Jeffersonian Crisis: Courts and Politics in the Young Republic.* New York: Oxford University Press, 1971.

Epstein, David. *The Political Theory of The Federalist.* Chicago: University of Chicago Press, 1984.

Fallon, Richard H., Jr. "What Is Republicanism and Is It Worth Reviving?" *Harvard Law Review* 102 (May 1989): 1695–1735.

Farrand, Max, ed. *The Records of the Federal Convention of 1787.* Revised edition. 4 vols. New Haven, Conn.: Yale University Press, 1937.

Ferguson, Adam. *An Essay on the History of Civil Society, 1767.* Edited by Duncan Forbes. Edinburgh: Edinburgh University Press, 1966.

Freud, Sigmund. *Civilization and Its Discontents.* New York: W. W. Norton & Company, 1961.

Frost, Robert. "A Talk for Students." New York: Fund for the Republic, 1956.

Furtwangler, Albert. *The Authority of Publius: A Reading of the Federalist Papers.* Ithaca, N.Y.: Cornell University Press, 1984.

Gilligan, Carol. *In a Different Voice: Psychological Theory and Women's Development.* Cambridge, Mass.: Harvard University Press, 1982.

Goldstene, Paul N. *The Collapse of Liberal Empire.* Novato, Calif.: Chandler & Sharp, 1977.

Hamilton, Alexander. *The Papers of Alexander Hamilton.* Edited by Harold C. Syrett et al. 27 vols. New York: Columbia University Press, 1961–1979.

———. *The Reports of Alexander Hamilton.* Edited by Jacob E. Cooke. New York: Harper & Row, 1964.

———. *The Works of Alexander Hamilton.* Edited by Henry Cabot Lodge. 12 vols. New York: G. P. Putnam's Sons, 1903.

Hamilton, Alexander, John Jay, and James Madison. *The Federalist Papers.* Edited by Isaac Kramnick. New York: Viking Penguin, 1987.

Hartz, Louis. *The Founding of New Societies: Studies in the History of the United States, Latin America, South Africa, Canada and Australia.* New York: Harcourt, Brace, & World, 1964.

———. *The Liberal Tradition in America: An Interpretation of American Political Thought since the Revolution.* New York: Harcourt, Brace, & Company, 1955.

———. "The Rise of the Democratic Idea." In *Paths of American Thought,* edited by Arthur M. Schlesinger, Jr., and Morton White, pp. 37–51. London: Chatto & Windus, 1964.

Hegel, G. W. F. *The Phenomenology of Mind.* New York: Harper & Row, 1967.

Higham, John. "Beyond Consensus: The Historian as Moral Critic." *American Historical Review* 67:3 (Apr. 1962): 609–625.

———. "The Cult of the 'American Consensus': Homogenizing Our History." *Commentary* 27 (Feb. 1959): 93–100.

Hobbes, Thomas. *Leviathan.* Edited by C. B. Macpherson. New York: Penguin Books, 1968.

Hobson, Charles F. "The Negative on State Laws: James Madison, the Constitution and the Crisis of Republican Government." *William and Mary Quarterly* 36 (Apr. 1979): 215–235.

Hofstadter, Richard. *The Age of Reform: From Bryan to D.D.R.* New York: Alfred A. Knopf, l955.
————. *America at 1750: A Social Portrait.* New York: Random House, 1973.
————. *The American Political Tradition and the Men Who Made It.* New York: Random House, 1973.
Horkheimer, Max. *Eclipse of Reason.* New York: Continuum, 1974.
Horowitz, Asher, and Gad Horowitz. *"Everywhere They Are in Chains": Political Theory from Rousseau to Marx.* Nelson, Canada: Scarborough House, 1988.
Horwitz, Robert H., ed. *The Moral Foundations of the American Republic.* Charlottesville: University Press of Virginia, 1977.
Hobsbawm, Eric, and Terence Ranger, eds. *The Invention of Tradition.* Cambridge: Cambridge University Press, 1983.
Howe, Daniel Walker. "European Sources of Political Ideas in Jeffersonian America." *Reviews in American History* (Dec. 1982): 28–44.
Hume, David. *A Treatise of Human Nature.* In *Hume's Moral and Political Philosophy,* edited by Henry Aiken. New York: Hafner Publishing Company, 1972.
Hutson, James. "Riddles of the Federal Constitutional Convention." *William and Mary Quarterly* 44 (July 1987): 411–423.
Ignatieff, Michael. *A Just Measure of Pain: The Penitentiary in the Industrial Revolution, 1750–1850.* New York: Pantheon Books, 1978.
Ingersoll, David. "The Constant Prince: Private Interests and Public Goals in Machiavelli." *Western Political Quarterly* 21 (Dec. 1968): 588–596.
————. "Machiavelli and Madison: Perspectives on Political Stability." *Political Science Quarterly* 85:2 (June 1970): 259–280.
Jacobson, Norman. "Political Science and Political Education." *American Political Science Review* 57:3 (Sept. 1963): 561–569.
Jaenicke, Douglas W. "Madison v. Madison: The Party Essays v. The Federalist Papers." In *Reflections on the Constitution: The American Constitution after Two Hundred Years,* edited by Richard Maidment and John Zvesper, pp. 116–147. New York: Manchester University Press, 1989.
Jaffa, Harry V. "Conflicts within the Idea of the Liberal Tradition." *Comparative Studies in Society and History* 5:3 (Apr. 1963): 274–278.
Jefferson, Thomas. *The Complete Anas of Thomas Jefferson.* Edited by Franklin B. Sawvel. New York: Round Table Press, 1903.
————. *Notes on the State of Virginia.* Edited by William Peden. New York: W. W. Norton, 1972.
————. *The Papers of Thomas Jefferson.* Edited by Julian P. Boyd. 20 vols. Princeton, N.J.: Princeton University Press, 1950–.
————. *The Works of Thomas Jefferson.* Edited by Paul Leicester Ford. 12 vols. New York: Knickerbocker Press, 1904.
————. *The Writings of Thomas Jefferson.* Edited by Albert Ellery Bergh. 20 vols. Washington, D.C.: Thomas Jefferson Memorial Association, 1903–1904.
————. *The Writings of Thomas Jefferson.* Edited by H. A. Washington. 9 vols. Washington, D.C.: Washington, Taylor & Maury, 1853–1854.
Jensen, Merrill. *Articles of Confederation: An Interpretation of the Social Constitutional History of the American Revolution.* Madison: University of Wisconsin Press, 1948.

Jordan, Winthrop D. *White over Black: American Attitudes toward the Negro,* 1550–1812. New York: W. W. Norton, 1977.

Kammen, Michael. *A Machine That Would Go of Itself: The Constitution in American Culture.* New York: A. A. Knopf, 1986.

Kariel, Henry. *Beyond Liberalism.* New York: Harper & Row, 1977.

Kenyon, Cecilia M. "Alexander Hamilton: Rousseau of the Right." *Political Science Quarterly* 73:2 (June 1958): 161–178.

Ketcham, Ralph L. *James Madison: A Biography.* New York: Macmillan, 1971.

————. "James Madison and the Nature of Man." *Journal of the History of Ideas* 19:1 (Jan. 1958): 62–76.

————. "Notes on James Madison's Sources for the Tenth Federalist Paper." *Midwest Journal of Political Science* 1:1 (May 1957): 20–25.

Kloppenberg, James T. "The Virtues of Liberalism: Christianity, Republicanism, and Ethics in Early American Political Discourse." *Journal of American History* 74 (June 1987): 9–33.

Koch, Adrienne. *Jefferson and Madison: The Great Collaboration.* New York: Oxford University Press, 1976.

————. *Madison's "Advice to My Country."* Princeton, N.J.: Princeton University Press, 1966.

————. *The Philosophy of Thomas Jefferson.* Chicago: Quadrangle Books, 1964.

————. *Power, Morals, and the Founding Fathers: Essays in the Interpretation of the American Enlightenment.* Ithaca, N.Y.: Cornell University Press, 1961.

Kramnick, Isaac. *Bolingbroke and His Circle: The Politics of Nostalgia in the Age of Walpole.* Cambridge, Mass.: Harvard University Press, 1968.

————. "Republican Revisionism Revisited." *American Historical Review* 87:3 (June 1982): 629–664.

————. *Republicanism and Bourgeois Radicalism: Political Ideology in Late Eighteenth-Century England and America.* Ithaca, N.Y.: Cornell University Press, 1990.

Kurtz, Stephen G., and James H. Hutson, eds. *Essays on the American Revolution.* Chapel Hill: Published for the Institute of Early American History and Culture, Williamsburg, Virginia, by the University of North Carolina Press, 1973.

LaCapra, Dominick. *Rethinking Intellectual History: Texts, Contexts, Language.* Ithaca, N.Y.: Cornell University Press, 1983.

Laski, Harold. *Introduction to Politics.* New York: Barnes and Noble, 1963.

Lea, James F. *Political Consciousness and American Democracy.* Jackson: University Press of Mississippi, 1982.

Lerner, Ralph. "Commerce and Character: The Anglo-American as New-Model Man." *William and Mary Quarterly* 3d ser., 36 (Jan. 1979): 3–26.

Lienesch, Michael. *New Order of the Ages: Time, the Constitution, and the Making of Modern American Political Thought.* Princeton, N.J.: Princeton University Press, 1988.

Locke, John. *An Essay Concerning Human Understanding.* Edited by A. D. Woozley. London: William Collins Sons & Company, 1964.

————. *Second Treatise of Government.* Edited by C. B. Macpherson. Indianapolis: Hackett, 1980.

Lovejoy, Arthur O. *The Great Chain of Being: A Study of the History of an Idea.* Cambridge, Mass.: Harvard University Press, 1976.

_____. *Reflections on Human Nature.* Baltimore: Johns Hopkins University Press, 1961.

Lutz, Donald S. *A Preface to American Political Theory.* Lawrence: University Press of Kansas, 1992.

McColley, Robert. *Slavery and Jeffersonian Virginia.* Urbana: University of Illinois Press, 1973.

_____. *The Elusive Republic: Political Economy in Jeffersonian America.* Chapel Hill: Published for the Institute for Early American History and Culture, Williamsburg, Virginia, by the University of North Carolina Press, 1980.

_____. *The Last of the Fathers: James Madison and the Republican Legacy.* New York: Cambridge University Press, 1989.

McDonald, Forrest. *Alexander Hamilton: A Biography.* New York: W. W. Norton & Company, 1979.

_____. *Novus Ordo Seclorum: The Intellectual Origins of the Constitution.* Lawrence: University Press of Kansas, 1985.

_____. *The Presidency of George Washington.* Lawrence: University Press of Kansas, 1974.

_____. *The Presidency of Thomas Jefferson.* Lawrence: University Press of Kansas, 1976.

_____. *We the People: The Economic Origins of the Constitution.* Chicago: University of Chicago Press, 1958.

Mace, George. *Locke, Hobbes, and the Federalist Papers: An Essay on the Genesis of the American Political Heritage.* Carbondale: Southern Illinois University Press, 1979.

Macpherson, C. B. *Democratic Theory: Essays in Retrieval.* Oxford: Clarendon Press, 1973.

_____. *The Life and Times of Liberal Democracy.* New York: Oxford University Press, 1977.

_____. *The Political Theory of Possessive Individualism: Hobbes to Locke.* Oxford: Clarendon Press, 1962.

_____. *The Real World of Democracy.* Toronto: CBC Learning Systems, 1965.

_____. *The Rise and Fall of Economic Justice: And Other Essays.* Oxford: Oxford University Press, 1985.

McWilliams, Wilson Carey. *The Idea of Fraternity in America.* Berkeley: University of California Press, 1973.

Madison, James. *Letters and Other Writings of James Madison.* Edited by William C. Rives and Philip R. Fendall. 4 vols. Philadelphia: J. B. Lippincott, 1884.

_____. *The Mind of the Founder: Sources of the Political Thought of James Madison.* Edited by Marvin Meyers. Indianapolis and New York: Bobbs-Merrill, 1973.

_____. *The Papers of James Madison.* Edited by William T. Hutchinson et al. 17 vols. Chicago and Charlottesville: University of Chicago Press and University of Virginia Press, 1962–.

_____. *The Writings of James Madison.* Edited by Gaillard Hunt. 9 vols. New York: G. P. Putnam's Sons, 1900–1910.

Maidment, Richard, and John Zvesper, eds. *Reflections on the Constitution: The American Constitution after Two Hundred Years*. New York: Manchester University Press, 1989.

Marcuse, Herbert. *Eros and Civilization: A Philosophical Inquiry into Freud*. Boston: Beacon Press, 1955.

Marx, Leo. *The Machine in the Garden: Technology and the Pastoral Ideal in America*. New York: Oxford University Press, 1964.

Matthews, Richard K. "Liberalism, Civic Humanism, and the American Political Tradition: Understanding Genesis." *Journal of Politics* 49 (Nov. 1987): 1121–1153.

———. *The Radical Politics of Thomas Jefferson*. Lawrence: University Press of Kansas, 1986.

Matthews, Richard K., ed. *Virtue, Corruption, and Self-Interest*. Bethlehem, Pa.: Lehigh University Press, 1994.

May, Henry F. *The End of American Innocence: A Study of the First Years of Our Own Time, 1912–1917*. Oxford and New York: Oxford University Press, 1979.

———. *The Enlightenment in America*. New York: Oxford University Press, 1976.

Meyer, Donald H. *The Democratic Enlightenment*. New York: G. P. Putnam's Sons, 1976.

Meyers, Marvin. "Founding and Revolution: A Commentary on Publius-Madison." In *The Hofstadter Aegis*, edited by Stanley Elkins and Eric McKitrick. New York: Alfred A. Knopf, 1974.

———. "The Least Imperfect Government: On Martin Diamond's 'Ethics and Politics'," *Interpretation* 8 (May 1980): 5–15.

———. "Revolution and Founding: On Publius-Madison and the American Genesis." *Quarterly Journal of the Library of Congress* 37 (Spring 1980): 192–200.

Mill, John Stuart. "Considerations on Representative Government." In *"Utilitarianism," "On Liberty," and "Considerations on Representative Government,"* edited by H. B. Acton, chap. 8. London: J. M. Dent & Sons, 1972.

Miller, John C. *The Federalist Era, 1789–1801*. New York: Harper & Row, 1960.

Miller, John Chester. *The Wolf by the Ears: Thomas Jefferson and Slavery*. New York: Free Press, 1977.

Miller, Perry. *Errand into the Wilderness*. Cambridge, Mass.: Belknap Press of Harvard University Press, 1956.

Montesquieu, Charles-Louis de Secondat. *Persian Letters*. Translated by C. J. Betts. New York: Penguin Books, 1973.

Morgan, Edmund Sears. *The Challenge of the American Revolution*. New York: W. W. Norton, 1976.

———. *Virginians at Home: Family Life in the Eighteenth Century*. Williamsburg, Va.: Colonial Williamsburg, 1952.

Morgan, Robert S. *James Madison on the Constitution and the Bill of Rights*. New York: Greenwood Press, 1988.

Morris, Richard. *Witnesses at the Creation*. New York: Holt, Rinehart and Winston, 1985.

Mosteller, Frederick, and David L. Wallace. *Inference and Disputed Authorship: The Federalist*. Reading, Mass.: Addison Wesley, 1964.

Murrin, John M. "Feudalism, Communalism and the Yeoman Freeholder." In *Essays on the American Revolution*, edited by Stephen G. Kurtz and James H. Hutson, pp. 256–288. Williamsburg: University of North Carolina Press, 1973.

———. "The Great Inversion, or Court versus Country: A Comparison of the Revolution Settlements in England (1688–1721) and America (1776–1816)." In *Three British Revolutions: 1641, 1688, 1776*, edited by J. G. A. Pocock, pp. 368–453. Princeton, N.J.: Princeton University Press, 1980.

Nedelsky, Jennifer. *Private Property and the Limits of American Constitutionalism*. Chicago: University of Chicago Press, 1990.

Onuf, Peter S. "Reflections on the Founding." *William and Mary Quarterly* 66:2 (Apr. 1989): 341–375.

Paine, Thomas. *The Life and Works of Thomas Paine*. Edited by William M. van der Weyde. 10 vols. Patriots' ed. New Rochelle, N.Y.: Thomas Paine National Historical Association, 1925.

Pangle, Thomas L. *The Spirit of Modern Republicanism*. Chicago: University of Chicago Press, 1988.

Parenti, Michael. "The Constitution as an Elitist Document." In *How Democratic Is the Constitution?* edited by Robert A. Goldwin and William A. Schambra. Washington, D.C.: Free Enterprise Institute, 1985.

Parrington, Vernon Louis. *Main Currents in American Thought: An Interpretation of American Literature from the Beginning to 1920*. 3 vols. New York: Harcourt, Brace & Company, 1927–1930.

Perkins, Bradford. *Prologue to War: England and the United States, 1805–1812*. Berkeley: University of California Press, 1961.

Peterson, Merrill. *Jefferson and Madison and the Making of Constitutions*. Charlottesville: University Press of Virginia, 1987.

———. *The Jefferson Image in the American Mind*. New York: Oxford University Press, 1960.

———. *Thomas Jefferson: A Profile*. New York: Hill & Wang, 1967.

———. *Thomas Jefferson and the New Nation: A Biography*. New York: Oxford University Press, 1970.

Peterson, Merrill, ed. *Thomas Jefferson: Writings*. New York: Library of America, 1984.

Pocock, J. G. A. *The Ancient Constitution and the Feudal Law: A Study of English Historical Thought in the Seventeenth Century*. Cambridge: Cambridge University Press, 1957.

———. "Cambridge Paradigms and Scotch Philosophers: A Study of the Relations between the Civic Humanist and the Jurisprudential Interpretation of Eighteenth-Century Social Thought." In *Wealth and Virtue*, edited by Istvan Hont and Michael Ignatieff. Cambridge: Cambridge University Press, 1985.

———. *The Machiavellian Moment: Florentine Political Thought and the Atlantic Republican Tradition*. Princeton, N.J.: Princeton University Press, 1975.

———. *Politics, Language and Time: Essays on Political Thought and History*. New York: Atheneum, 1971.

———. *Virtue, Commerce, and History: Essays on Political Thought and History, Chiefly in the Eighteenth Century*. Cambridge: Cambridge University Press, 1985.

Pocock, J. G. A., ed. *Three British Revolutions:* 1641, 1688, 1776. Princeton, N.J.: Princeton University Press, 1980.

Pole, J. R. *The American Constitution—For and Against: The Federalist and Anti-Federalist Papers*. New York: Hill and Wang, 1987.

_____. *Political Representation in England and the Origins of the American Republic*. New York: St. Martin's Press, 1966.

Pope, James Gray. "Republican Moments: The Role of Direct Popular Power in the American Constitutional Order." *University of Pennsylvania Law Review* 139:2 (Dec. 1990): 287–368.

Rakove, Jack. "The Great Compromise: Ideas, Interests, and the Politics of Constitution Making." *William and Mary Quarterly* 44 (July 1987): 424–457.

_____. *James Madison and the Creation of the American Republic*. Glenview, Ill.: Scott, Foresman, 1990.

Rakove, Jack, ed. *Interpreting the Constitution: The Debate over Original Intent*. Boston: Northeastern University Press, 1990.

Richardson, James D., ed. *A Compilation of the Messages and Papers of the Presidents*, 1789–1897. Vol. 1. Washington, D.C.: Government Printing Office, 1897.

Riemer, Neal. *The Democratic Experiment*. Princeton, N.J.: Van Nostrand, 1967.

_____. *James Madison: Creating the American Constitution*. Washington, D.C.: Congressional Quarterly, 1986.

_____. "James Madison's Theory of the Self-Destructive Features of Republican Government." *Ethics* 65 (Oct. 1954): 34–43.

_____. "The Republicanism of James Madison." *Political Science Quarterly* 69 (Mar. 1954): 45–64.

Rives, William C. *History of the Life and Times of James Madison*. 3 vols. Boston: Little, Brown, 1859–1868.

Robinson, William A. *Jeffersonian Democracy in New England*. New Haven, Conn.: Yale University Press, 1916.

Rodgers, Daniel T. "Republicanism: The Career of a Concept." *Journal of American History* 79 (June 1992): 11–13, 37.

Roelofs, H. Mark. "The American Polity: A Systematic Ambiguity." *Review of Politics* 48:3 (Summer 1986): 323–348.

_____. *Ideology and Myth in American Politics: A Critique of a National Political Mind*. Boston and Toronto: Little, Brown & Company, 1876.

Rossiter, Clinton, ed. *Alexander Hamilton and the Constitution*. New York: Harcourt, Brace & World, 1964.

Rousseau, Jean-Jacques. *The First and Second Discourses*. Edited by Roger Masters and translated by Roger D. Masters and Judith R. Masters. New York: St. Martin's Press, 1964.

_____. *The Social Contract: Or, Principles of Political Right*. Edited by Charles M. Sherover. Rev. trans., New York: New American Library, 1974.

Rutland, Robert A. *The Birth of the Bill of Rights*, 1776–1791. New York: Collier Books, 1962.

_____. *James Madison: The Founding Father*. New York: Macmillan, 1987.

_____. *The Presidency of James Madison*. Lawrence: University Press of Kansas, 1990.

Schachner, Nathan. *Thomas Jefferson: A Biography.* 2 vols. New York: Appleton-Century-Crofts, 1951.

Schlesinger, Arthur M. "The Lost Meaning of 'The Pursuit of Happiness.'" *William and Mary Quarterly* 21:3 (July 1964): 325–327.

Scott, William B. *In Pursuit of Happiness: American Conceptions of Property from the Seventeenth to the Twentieth Century.* Bloomington: Indiana University Press, 1977.

Shalhope, Robert E. "Republicanism and Early American Historiography." *William and Mary Quarterly* 39:2 (Apr. 1982): 334–356.

———. "Toward a Republican Synthesis: The Emergence of an Understanding of Republicanism in American Historiography." *William and Mary Quarterly* 29:1 (Jan. 1972): 49–80.

Sherry, Suzanna. "Civic Virtue and the Feminine Voice in Constitutional Adjudication." *Virginia Law Review* 72 (Apr. 1986): 543–616.

Shklar, Judith N. *American Citizenship.* Cambridge, Mass.: Harvard University Press, 1991.

———. "Redeeming American Political Theory." *American Political Science Review* 85:1 (Mar. 1991): 3–15.

Skidmore, Max J. *American Political Thought.* New York: St. Martin's Press, 1978.

Skinner, Quentin. *The Foundations of Modern Political Thought.* 2 vols. Cambridge: Cambridge University Press, 1978.

Smelser, Marshall. *The Democratic Republic, 1801–1815.* New York: Harper & Row, 1968.

Smith, Henry Nash. *Virgin Land: The American West as Symbol and Myth.* Cambridge, Mass.: Harvard University Press, 1950.

Smith, Maynard. "Reason, Passion and Political Freedom in *The Federalist.*" *Journal of Politics* 22 (Feb. 1960): 525–544.

Spurlin, Paul Merrill. *Rousseau in America: 1760–1809.* University: University of Alabama Press, 1969.

Storing, Herbert. *What the Anti-Federalists Were For.* Chicago: University of Chicago Press, 1981.

Stourzh, Gerald. *Alexander Hamilton and the Idea of Republican Government.* Stanford, Calif.: Stanford University Press, 1970.

Strout, Cushing. "Liberalism, Conservatism and the Babel of Tongues." *Partisan Review* 25:1 (Winter 1958): 101–109.

Sunstein, Cass R. "Interest Groups in American Public Law." *Stanford Law Review* 38 (Nov. 1985): 29–87.

Takaki, Ronald T. *Iron Cages: Race and Culture in Nineteenth-Century America.* New York: Alfred A. Knopf, 1979.

Tawney, R. H. *Religion and the Rise of Capitalism.* New York: Harcourt, Brace & World, 1926.

Tocqueville, Alexis de. *Democracy in America.* 2 vols. New York: Schocken Books, 1961.

Turner, Frederick Jackson. *The Significance of the Frontier in American History.* New York: H. Holt & Company, 1920.

Tushnet, Mark. *Red, White, and Blue: A Critical Analysis of Constitutional Law.* Cambridge, Mass.: Harvard University Press, 1988.

Weber, Max. *Economy and Society.* Edited by Guenther Roth and Claus Wittich. 2 vols. Berkeley: University of California Press, 1978.

_____. *The Protestant Ethic and the Spirit of Capitalism.* Translated by Talcott Parsons. New York: Oxford University Press, 1958.

White, Morton. *The Philosophy of the American Revolution.* New York: Oxford University Press, 1978.

_____. *Philosophy, The Federalist, and the Constitution.* New York: Oxford University Press, 1987.

_____. *Pragmatism and the American Mind: Essays and Reviews in Philosophy and Intellectual History.* New York: Oxford University Press, 1973.

Williamson, Chilton. *American Suffrage: From Property to Democracy,* 1760–1860. Princeton, N.J.: Princeton University Press, 1960.

Wills, Garry. *Explaining America: The Federalist.* Garden City, N.Y.: Doubleday & Company, 1981.

_____. *Inventing America: Jefferson's Declaration of Independence.* Garden City, N.Y.: Doubleday & Company, 1978.

Wolin, Sheldon. "Political Ideology of the Founders." In *Toward a More Perfect Union: Six Essays on the Constitution,* edited by Neil L. Young. Salt Lake City: Brigham Young University Press, 1988.

_____. *Politics and Vision: Continuity and Innovation in Western Political Thought.* Boston: Little, Brown & Company, 1960.

_____. *The Presence of the Past: Essays on the State and the Constitution.* Baltimore: Johns Hopkins University Press, 1989.

Wood, Gordon. *The Creation of the American Republic,* 1776–1787. Chapel Hill: Published for the Institute of Early American History and Culture at Williamsburg, Virginia, by the University of North Carolina Press, 1969.

_____. "Democracy and the Constitution." In *How Democratic Is the Constitution?* edited by R. A. Goldwin and W. A. Schambra. Washington, D.C.: American Enterprise Institute Press, 1980.

_____. "The Fundamentalists and the Constitution." *New York Review of Books* 35:2 (18 Feb. 1988): 33–40.

_____. *The Radicalism of the American Revolution.* New York: Alfred A. Knopf, 1992.

Young, Alfred F., ed. *The American Revolution: Explorations in the History of American Radicalism.* Dekalb: Northern Illinois University Press, 1976.

Zvesper, John. "The Madisonian Systems." *Western Political Quarterly* 37 (June 1984): 236–256.

Index